SAT

FOR

DUMMIES

A Wiley Brand

9th Edition
with Online Practice Tests

by Geraldine Woods and
Ron Woldoff

SAT For Dummies®, 9th Edition with Online Practice Tests

Published by:
John Wiley & Sons, Inc.,
111 River Street,
Hoboken, NJ 07030-5774,
www.wiley.com

For general information on our other products and services, please contact our Customer Care Department within the U.S. at 877-762-2974, outside the U.S. at 317-572-3993, or fax 317-572-4002. For technical support, please visit www.wiley.com/techsupport.

Wiley publishes in a variety of print and electronic formats and by print-on-demand. Some material included with standard print versions of this book may not be included in e-books or in print-on-demand. If this book refers to media such as a CD or DVD that is not included in the version you purchased, you may download this material at http://booksupport.wiley.com. For more information about Wiley products, visit www.wiley.com.

Library of Congress Control Number: 2015937644

ISBN 978-1-118-91149-5 (pbk); ISBN 978-1-118-91152-5 (ebk); ISBN 978-1-118-91175-4 (ebk)

Manufactured in the United States of America

10 9 8 7 6 5 4 3 2

Contents at a Glance

Table of Contents

Introduction

Change is good, right? So why do so many people hop on the nervous-breakdown train when they hear that the SAT is changing? Perhaps because the SAT is an important step on your journey to college, and anything to do with the admissions process is enough to give applicants an instant panic attack. Nervous or not, you have to take the SAT when you apply to most colleges or universities in the United States and to some English-speaking institutions abroad. The "old" SAT existed between 2005 and January 2016. That version was actually a redesign of a still older exam. The "new" SAT appears in March 2016. Because it's new, that version of the SAT may seem extra scary.

You have nothing to worry about, though, because you've been preparing for this version of the SAT for many years. What? You say you haven't been memorizing vocabulary words and drilling key math concepts since you were in your crib? How neglectful of you! Actually, you *have* been getting ready for the redesigned SAT, because you've been studying the necessary material during every single minute you devote to schoolwork, not counting lunch and the time you spend texting your friends from the phone hidden behind your science book. But those small lapses don't count for much when you consider the amount of time you've been analyzing and uncovering meaning when you read, organizing your ideas and writing papers, and solving math problems (more than 10,000 hours between kindergarten and tenth grade, according to a recent survey). All those skills come in handy on the new SAT. The final step in preparing for the exam is the one you're taking now. You're reading this book and therefore becoming acquainted with the format of the test. By the time you're finished with *SAT For Dummies,* 9th Edition with Online Practice Tests, you'll have every possible tool for conquering the "new" SAT.

Why change at all? The old SAT was loudly criticized for several reasons. It was long, hard, and tricky. Most important, it didn't accurately predict college success, its stated purpose. The College Board, which creates and administers the SAT, heard the complaints and hit the drawing board. What it came up with is still long and relatively hard, but the test more closely resembles the stuff you actually do in school. The reading and writing passages come from history, science, literary, and career-oriented sources. Some math questions draw on real-world situations. The 2016 SAT also tests your ability to understand information presented visually, often in graphs or charts, and to recognize and evaluate evidence. The 2016 SAT eliminates some of its old tricks, such as the penalty for guessing, and lets you decide whether you want to write the essay. Add everything up, and you arrive at a test that concentrates on the skills you need to succeed in college and the workplace. (For details on the changes, check out Chapter 1.)

About This Book

SAT For Dummies, 9th Edition with Online Practice Tests, is a whirlwind tour of the redesigned SAT. (If you expect to take the old SAT at some point before the spring of 2016, turn to *SAT For Dummies,* 8th Edition, also published by Wiley.) This book takes you through each section of the redesigned SAT, explaining what the test-makers are looking for and how you can deliver it. For example, this version of the SAT makes a point of testing vocabulary in context, and that's how vocabulary shows up in *SAT For Dummies,* 9th Edition with Online Practice Tests with Online Practice. As you read, keep an eye out for words and definitions, including in paragraphs that have nothing to do with vocabulary *per se.* (By the way, ***per se*** means "as such" or "for itself.")

To help you step up your game on the SAT, this book includes in-depth analysis and samples of each type of question that the SAT dumps on you — reading comprehension, math grid-ins, and so forth. To kill still more of your free time (and help you improve your SAT-tested skills), you get a detailed explanation with each answer so you know what you answered correctly, what you got wrong, and why. To give you a feel for how ready you are to take the new SAT, try your hand at the practice tests. No, they're not real versions of the SAT because the company that produces the actual test is sitting on those rights. The test you get on test day may not have exactly the same number of questions in exactly the same order as the ones here, because the test-makers continue to tinker with the format. But the tests in this book are as close as anyone can come without invoking lawyerly attention, and they'll prepare you well for the real thing. As a bonus, you may find that preparing for the SAT improves your schoolwork, too, as you sharpen your reading skills, polish your grammar, and solve math problems more efficiently.

This book also utilizes a few special conventions to help different bits of info better stand out.

✔ *Italics* have three different duties:

- To introduce new terms, particularly those that apply to math, analytical reading, and writing

- To refer to portions of a question or answer choice

- To emphasize a particular word or point

✔ **This font** highlights words that may be useful when you take the SAT. Check out the definitions that follow these words, and notice the context. (Mastering words in context can really improve your score on the SAT.)

✔ **Boldface** indicates the action part of numbered steps and the main items in bulleted lists.

Foolish Assumptions

In writing this book, we assume several things about you, the reader, including the following:

✔ You probably hate standardized tests (nearly everybody does!) but want to achieve a high score on the SAT with minimum effort and maximum efficiency.

✔ You've taken the usual math and language arts courses through, say, algebra, geometry, and sophomore English. If you haven't taken one of those classes or if you did and still feel puzzled by the subject, you may want to read some other *For Dummies* books that teach you what you missed. Take a look at *English Grammar For Dummies,* 2nd Edition, for basic information or go for grammar practice with the *English Grammar Workbook For Dummies,* 2nd Edition, and *1,001 Grammar Practice Questions For Dummies*. Those of you who struggle with the math will find these books helpful: *Algebra I For Dummies,* 2nd Edition, and *Algebra II For Dummies,* by Mary Jane Sterling, and *Geometry For Dummies,* 2nd Edition, by Mark Ryan. Wiley publishes all these titles.

One assumption we haven't made is age. True, most people who take the SAT are teenagers, but not everyone follows the same life path. If you're hitting college after living a little, good for you. This book can help you remember the schoolwork you need for the SAT, no matter how many years have passed since you sat in a classroom.

Icons Used in This Book

Icons are those cute little pictures that appear in the margins of this book. They indicate why you should pay special attention to the accompanying text. Here's how to decode them:

This icon points out helpful hints about strategy — what the all-star test-takers know and the rookies want to find out.

This icon identifies the sand traps that the SAT-writers are hoping you fall into as you take the test. Take note of these warnings so you know what to do (and what not to do) as you move from question to question on the real SAT.

When you see this icon, be sure to file away the information that accompanies it. The material will come in handy as you prepare for (and take) the 2016 SAT.

This icon identifies questions that resemble those on the actual SAT. Be sure to read the answer explanations that always follow the questions.

Beyond the Book

After you've struggled through two practice exams in this book, you can go online for two more. (Oh, joy! Seven more hours of testing, plus time to check the answers!) You also find articles explaining how to build stamina for an exam that lasts more than three hours, how to insert evidence into the SAT essay, how to interpret graphic elements, and get through the math. Plus, the Cheat Sheet tells you what you should look for when you correct writing and language mistakes, answer reading questions, and tackle the math problems.

What you'll find online

The online practice that comes free with the book contains two complete SAT practice tests, complete with the optional essay. You can customize your online practice to focus on specific areas (only Reading, for example, or just Math), or you can opt to take an entire timed practice test to prepare yourself for the big day. Articles help you answer questions based on graphic elements, explain how to insert evidence into an essay, build up your test-taking muscles gradually, and become a pro at the math.

This product also comes with an online Cheat Sheet (www.dummies.com/cheatsheet/SAT) and bonus articles (www.dummies.com/extras/SAT) that help you increase your SAT knowledge even further. (No PIN required. You can access this info before you even register.)

How to register

To gain access to additional tests and practice online, all you have to do is register. Just follow these simple steps:

1. **Find your PIN access code:**

   - **Print-book users:** If you purchased a print copy of this book, turn to the inside front cover of the book to find your access code.

   - **E-book users:** If you purchased this book as an e-book, you can get your access code by registering your e-book at www.dummies.com/go/getaccess. Go to this website, find your book and click it, and answer the security questions to verify your purchase. You'll receive an email with your access code.

2. **Go to** Dummies.com **and click** Activate Now.

3. **Find your product (*SAT For Dummies*) and then follow the on-screen prompts to activate your PIN.**

Now you're ready to go! You can come back to the program as often as you want — simply log on with the username and password you created during your initial login. No need to enter the access code a second time.

For Technical Support, please visit http://wiley.custhelp.com or call Wiley at 1-800-762-2974 (U.S.), +1-317-572-3994 (international).

Where to Go from Here

Okay, now that you know what's what and where to find it, you have a choice. You can read every single word of the first four parts and then take the practice exams, or you can check out only the parts of the book that address your "issues," as they say on daytime talk shows, concentrating on the kinds of questions you struggle with. Another good way to start is to take one sample test in Part V, score it using the appendix, and then focus on your weak spots. Feel free to check out www.dummies.com, where you'll find up-to-the-minute information on any changes the College Board has made to the test.

No matter what you do next, start by doing something simple: Calm down, stay loose, and score big on the SAT.

Part I
Getting Started with the SAT

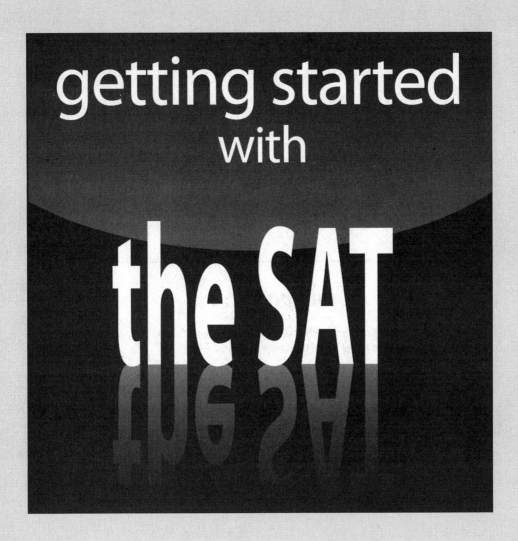

In this part . . .

✔ Get to know your **adversary** (opponent) by finding out all you need to know about the newly designed SAT.

✔ Discover and practice great strategies to help you prepare for test day.

Chapter 1

Erasing the Worry: Getting to Know the SAT

In ancient Greek mythology — and in the Harry Potter series — a three-headed monster guards a magical place. In the real world, a different sort of three-headed monster — the SAT — protects another magical place: the college of your dreams. The SAT's three heads are tests of your skills in reading, writing, and math. Instead of chomping its victims like an imaginary monster, the SAT chops you up into a series of numbers — scores that play a *crucial* (extremely important) role in determining whether you receive a *please come to our school* or a *sorry to disappoint you* response at decision time.

In this chapter, you find the ABCs of the SAT: how it's changing as well as when, where, and how often you should take the test. This chapter also tells you what sort of scores you receive, explains how to deal with special needs, and gives you a peek into the structure of the exam itself.

Not an ACT: Getting Real with the SAT

Most college applicants take one of two giant exams on their way into U.S. colleges and some foreign schools. One is the ACT, and the other is the SAT. Most colleges accept scores from either test; check with the admissions office of the colleges on your list to be sure you're taking the test(s) they prescribe. (A good general rule for college admissions is to give them what they want, when they want it.) The SAT and the ACT are roughly the same in terms of difficulty, but each exam is of a different nature. As of this writing, you can access free PDFs from www.collegeboard.org and www.actstudent.org (homes of the SAT and ACT, respectively). If you're so inclined, you can download and review each exam and see which one you like more (or rather, which one you *dislike* less). Because you're reading *SAT For Dummies,* 9th Edition with Online Practice Tests, presumably you're taking the SAT. But if you're also taking the ACT, don't forget to check out *ACT For Dummies,* 6th Edition, by Lisa Zimmer Hatch, MA, and Scott A. Hatch, JD (Wiley).

Don't confuse the SAT with the SAT Subject Tests, which used to be called the SAT II, a name that is now officially *obsolete* (outdated, so yesterday). The SAT Subject Tests cover biology, history, math, and a ton of other stuff. Depending on the schools you apply to, you may have to take one or more Subject Tests or none at all.

All colleges have websites, where you can find out exactly which exam(s) your favorite schools require. Many libraries and nearly all bookstores also carry college guides — 20-pound paperbacks describing each and every institution of higher learning you may apply to. If you're relying on printed material, be sure to check the copyright date. With the *advent* (arrival) of the new SAT, some colleges may change their requirements, and earlier books may not be accurate. The official website of the College Board (www.collegeboard.org) also lists popular colleges and the tests they want to *inflict* (impose) on you. The College Board creates the exams, so its website is *replete* (well supplied) with helpful information.

If college isn't in your immediate future, you may want to take the SAT just to see how you do. If your plans include a stint in the armed forces or climbing Mount Everest before hitting higher education, you can keep your options open by taking the SAT before you go. Your score on the SAT may be higher while formal "book learning" is still fresh in your mind. Then when you're ready to return to an actual classroom education, you have some scores to send to the college of your choice, though if a long period of time has passed, the college may ask for a retest. How long is *a long period of time?* It depends on the college you're applying to. Some may ask for an updated score after only a couple of years; others are more *lenient* (easygoing). Obviously, whether you took three years off to relax on the beach or five to create a gazillion-dollar Internet company also influences the admissions office's decision on SAT scores. Check with the college(s) you're interested in and explain your situation.

A Whole New Ballgame: Comparing the Old and New SAT

What a difference a couple of months make! If you take the SAT in January 2016 and then again in March 2016, the exams you face will *not* be identical twins. Like any family members, they may share the arch of an eyebrow or the shape of the nose, but otherwise they're quite different. Check out Table 1-1 for a side-by-side comparison of the old and new exams.

For more information on the changes to the SAT, see the section "Examining Your Mind: What the New SAT Tests," later in this chapter.

Table 1-1	Old SAT versus New SAT
Old SAT	*New SAT*
Critical Reading: 67 questions, 70 minutes	Reading: 52 questions, 65 minutes
Essay: Mandatory, 25 minutes, respond to a prompt with your own point of view and evidence	Essay: Optional, 50 minutes, analyze writing techniques in a passage
Multiple-Choice Writing: 49 questions, 60 minutes	Multiple-Choice Writing and Language: 44 questions, 35 minutes
Mathematics: 54 questions, 70 minutes, divided into 3 sections	Mathematics: 58 questions, 80 minutes, divided into 2 sections
Calculators allowed for all 3 sections.	Calculators allowed for 1 section and not for the other.

Old SAT	New SAT
Multiple-Choice and Grid-In Scoring: 1 point for each correct answer, 1/4-point deduction for each wrong multiple-choice answer (no penalty for incorrect grid-in answers)	Multiple-Choice and Grid-In Scoring: 1 point for each correct answer (and two questions worth 2 points each), no deduction for wrong answers
Multiple-Choice Format: 5 possible answers	Multiple-Choice Format: 4 possible answers
Score Types: 200–800 points each for Critical Reading, Writing, and Mathematics (total: 600–2400 points)	Score Types: 200–800 points for a combination of the Reading and Writing and Language sections; another 200–800 points for Mathematics, for a total of 400–1600 for the entire exam, separate essay score, cross-test subscores for analysis in history and science, section subscores for various skills

Signing Up Before Sitting Down: Registering for the SAT

The SAT is given at multiple times at select high schools throughout the United States and in English-speaking schools in many other countries. Home-schoolers can also take the SAT, though not in their own living rooms. This section explains how and when to register for an exam and acceptable methods of payment. *Note:* The SAT *waives* (drops) fees for low-income test-takers. Check out the section "Meeting Special Needs" in this chapter for more information.

How to register

You can register for the SAT online, by mail, or, if you've taken the SAT before, by phone.

Online registration is simple: Go to www.sat.collegeboard.org/register to sign up and to choose a test center and date. You need a credit card or a PayPal account and a digital photo of yourself ready to upload. Be sure the photo meets the College Board's *criteria* (standards). The College Board wants what Hollywood agents call "a head shot" — a photo featuring everything above shoulder level. You should be the only one in the picture, and your whole face must be visible. Head coverings are okay only if they're religious in nature. The College Board accepts JPEG, GIF, and PNG formats.

You can also register by mail. In fact, you have to do so if you're younger than 13 or older than 21 or if you need to take the exam on a Sunday for religious reasons. Ask the college or guidance counselor at your school for a registration form. If you're home-schooled, call the nearest public or private high school. Older test-takers (over 21 years of age): Call the College Board Customer Service Center for help (within the U.S.: 866-756-7346; outside the U.S.: 212-713-7789). You have to attach a photo (no smaller than 2 x 2 inches and no larger than 2.5 x 3 inches) to the paper registration. Follow the same guidelines for the online photo, and make sure it shows your face clearly. Tape the photo to the designated area of the application. With the application, enclose payment (credit card number, a check from a United States bank, or a bank draft).

If you're suffering through the SAT for a second time, you can register by phone, though you pay an extra $15 to do so. Call the College Board's Customer Service center (within the U.S.: 866-756-7346; outside the U.S.: 212-713-7789). Hearing-impaired test-takers can call the TTY Customer Service number (within the U.S.: 888-857-2477; outside the U.S.: 609-882-4118).

However you register, you'll be asked whether you want to sign up for the Student Search Service. Answer yes, and fill out the questionnaire. Colleges, universities, and some scholarship-granting organizations receive information about you from this service. Expect lots of emails and letters — a little annoying, perhaps, but you may discover a school or scholarship that meets your needs perfectly.

Neither the Student Search Service nor any other part of the College Board markets products to you via email or regular mail, but some scam artists do. Don't send personal or financial information to any organization unless you know it's legitimate. Not sure? Call the College Board to check (within the U.S.: 866-756-7346; outside the U.S.: 212-713-7789).

When you register for the SAT, you also choose the type of score reports you want to receive. See the section "Scoring on the New SAT," later in this chapter, to explore your options.

When to take the test

The last "old" SAT is scheduled through January 2016; the first "new" SAT debuts in March 2016. Keep those dates in mind as you make your own personal test schedule.

The SAT pops up on the calendar seven times a year. You can take the exam as often as you want. If you're a *masochist* — that is, you enjoy pain — you can take all seven tests, but most people stick to this schedule:

✔ **Autumn of junior year** (about 1¾ years before college entrance): Time to take the PSAT/NMSQT, the exam that serves as a preview of the real thing. Even if you don't believe you need a preview, take the PSAT/NMSQT anyway; this test serves as a sorting tool for several scholarship opportunities and special programs. The first redesigned PSAT/NMSQT was given in October 2015.

✔ **Spring of junior year** (about 1¼ years before college entrance): Take the SAT strictly for practice, though you can send in your scores if you're pleased with them.

✔ **Autumn of senior year** (a bit less than a year before entrance): The SAT strikes again. Early-decision candidates should take the test in October or November; regular applicants may choose from any of the three autumn dates, including December.

✔ **Winter of senior year** (half-year before entrance): Some SAT-lovers take the exam in autumn and again in winter, hoping that practice will make them perfect, at least in the eyes of the colleges. The high scores won't hurt (and you probably will improve, just because the whole routine will be familiar), but don't put a lot of energy into repeated bouts of SAT fever. Your grades and extracurriculars may suffer if you're too *fixated on* (obsessed with) the SAT, and you may end up hurting your overall application.

If you're transferring or starting your college career midyear, you may sit for the SAT in January, March, May, or June. Check with your counselor or with the college of your choice and go with that recommendation.

Everyone takes the SAT on Saturday except for those students who can't for religious reasons. If you fall into that category, your SAT may be on a Sunday or a Wednesday following a Saturday SAT day. Get a letter from your *cleric* (religious leader) on letterhead and mail it in with your registration form.

In terms of test sites, the early bird gets the worm. (Do you ever wonder why no one talks about the worm? He got up early, too, and look what happened to him.) When you register, you may request a test site, but if it's filled, you get an alternate. So don't delay; send in the form or register online as soon as you know when and where you want to take the exam.

Meeting Special Needs

In a speech introducing the redesigned SAT, the president of the College Board stressed fairness and equal access for all students, including those with special needs. Even if you don't think you belong in that category, skim this section. You may discover an option that will help you "show what you know" when it matters most.

Learning disabilities

If you have a learning disability, you may be allowed to take the SAT under special conditions. The first step is to get an Eligibility Form from your school counselor. (Home-schoolers, call the local high school.) You may also want to ask your college counseling or guidance office for a copy of the *College Board Services for Students with Disabilities Brochure* (pamphlet). If your school doesn't have one, contact the College Board directly (212-713-8333, TTY 609-882-4118) or check the testing agency's website (www.collegeboard.org/students-with-disabilities). You can also contact the College Board by mail at this address: College Board SSD Program, P.O. Box 8060, Mount Vernon, IL 62864-0060.

After you've been certified for accommodations on one College Board test (an AP, a SAT Subject Test, or the PSAT/NMSQT), you're certified for all, unless your need arises from a temporary medical condition. If you fall into that category, see the next section for more information.

File the form well in advance of the time you expect to take the test. Generally, if you're entitled to extra test time in your high school, you'll be eligible for extra time on the SAT. What does *extra time* really mean? Extra time equals 1½ the usual amount for each section. So if regular test-takers have 50 minutes to write the essay, for example, extended-timers get 75 minutes.

¡Atención! What every foreign student needs to know about the new SAT

First, welcome to the U.S.'s worst invention, the Seriously Annoying Test (SAT), which you're taking so that you can attend an American institution. Getting ready for this exam may make you consider another American institution, one with padded rooms and bars on the windows. But a high score on the new exam is certainly within reach for individuals who have studied English as a second language. Because the new SAT tests vocabulary in context, you can usually figure out the answer, even if you don't know the formal definition, by plugging in a *plausible* (reasonable) alternative word. As a foreign student, pay special attention to the vocabulary words in this book, which, like *plausible,* are defined in context. You may want to keep a notebook or a computer file of new words you come across as you work through the sample questions. Also, a number of questions on the new SAT involve visual data in the form of graphs, charts, and diagrams. These require little knowledge of English.

Be sure to turn your concentration up to "totally intense" in the math section of this chapter and Chapter 3 because arithmetic doesn't change from language to language. Neither does geometry or algebra. If you can crack the basic language used to put forth the problem, you should be able to score a ton of points.

Physical issues

At no additional charge, the SAT also provides wheelchair accessibility, large-print tests, and other accommodations for students who need them. The key is to submit the Eligibility Form early so that the College Board can ask for suitable documentation and set up appropriate test conditions for you. You can send paper documentation or file an Eligibility Form via the Internet. Check out www.collegeboard.com/students-with-disabilities for details.

If a physical problem (a broken arm, perhaps) occurs shortly before your scheduled SAT and you can't easily take the exam at a later date, call the College Board (212-713-8333, TTY 609-882-4118), explain the situation, and have your physician fill out the forms requesting whatever accommodation you need.

Questions about special needs? Your high school's counselor or principal can help, or you can email the College Board (ssd@info.collegeboard.org).

Financial help

If your special need resides in your wallet, you can apply for a fee waiver, which is available to low-income high-school juniors and seniors who live in the United States, Puerto Rico, and other American territories. (United States citizens living in other countries may also be eligible for fee waivers.) Not only does the College Board waive its fee for the exam, but it also gives you four extra score reports for free. And, as they say on television infomercials, "Wait! There's more!" When you apply to college, you usually have to pay an application fee. If the College Board has waived its fee, you receive four request forms for college application fee-waivers. Not a bad deal!

For any financial issues, check with your school counselor for fee-waiver applications. (As with everything to do with the SAT, if you're a home-schooler, call the local high school for a form.) And be careful to avoid additional fees when you can. You run into extra charges for late or changed registration and for some extras — super-speedy scores, an analysis of your performance, and the like. (See the section "Scoring on the SAT" later in this chapter for more information on score-reporting options.)

Examining Your Mind: What the New SAT Tests

Reality isn't just material for television shows anymore. It takes a starring role in the redesigned SAT. Nearly all the changes on the exam attempt to measure the skills you need to succeed in school and in the workplace. Gone are questions that fall into the "guessing game" category — sentence completions and recognition of grammar mistakes in random sentences, for instance. Questions on the new SAT tend to be longer and to rely more closely on the most common elements of the average school's curriculum.

That said, the SAT is still just a snapshot of your mental *prowess* (ability) on one weekend morning. College admissions offices are well aware of this fact. No matter how *rigorous* (tough, demanding) your high school is, other factors may influence your score, such as whether you deal easily with multiple-choice questions and how you feel physically and mentally on SAT day (fight with Mom? bad romance? week-old sushi?). Bottom line: Stop obsessing about the SAT's unfairness (and it is unfair) and prepare.

The college admission essay is a great place to put your scores in perspective. If you face some special circumstances, such as a learning disability, a school that doesn't value academics, a family tragedy, and so on, you may want to explain your situation in an essay. No essay wipes out the bad impression created by an extremely low SAT score, but a good essay gives the college a way to interpret your achievement and to see you, the applicant, in more detail. For help with the college admission essay, check out *College Admission Essays For Dummies* by Geraldine Woods (published by Wiley).

The SAT doesn't test facts you studied in school; you don't need to know when Columbus sailed across the Atlantic or how to calculate the molecular weight of magnesium to answer an SAT question. Instead, the SAT takes aim at your ability to follow a logical sequence, to comprehend what you've read, and to write clearly in Standard English. The math portion checks whether you were paying attention or snoring when little details like algebra were taught. Check out the following sections for a bird's-eye view of the three SAT topics.

Reading

This portion of the exam used to be called Critical Reading, but for some reason the test-writers dropped half of the name. However, reading-comprehension passages still play a *critical* (vital, essential) role in your SAT score. Besides dropping sentence completions — statements with blanks and five possible ways to fill them — reading-comprehension questions now ask you to choose among four, not five, possible answers. Here's what you see on the new SAT Reading section:

- ✔ **Quantity:** A total of four single passages plus one set of paired passages, each from 500 to 750 words long, with each passage or pair accompanied by 10 to 11 questions, for a total of 52 questions.

- ✔ **Content:** Two passages, or one passage and one pair, in science; one literary passage, either narrative fiction or nonfiction; and two passages, or one passage and one pair, in history/social studies. One of the history/social studies passages or pair deals with what the College Board calls the "Great Global Conversation" — a historical document, such as a presidential speech or a modern discussion of an issue relating to democracy and human rights.

- ✔ **Reading level:** Some passages on the 9th and 10th grade level, some on the college-entry level (12th grade and beyond).

- ✔ **Graphics:** Charts, tables, graphs, diagrams: one to two in science, and one to two in history/social studies.

Reading-comprehension questions are a mixture of literal (just the facts, ma'am) and interpretive/analytical. You'll be asked to choose the meaning of a word in context and to understand information presented graphically (though you don't need to know math to answer these questions). You may also have to assess the author's tone or point of view. At least two questions per passage or pair ask you to recognize supporting evidence for your answer. Take a look at this pair of questions.

Tim was frantic to learn that the first GC-MP8 handheld was already in circulation. And here he was wasting his time in college! The degree that he had pursued so doggedly for the past three years now seemed nothing more than a gigantic waste of time. The business world, that's where he belonged, marketing someone else's technology with just enough of a twist to allow him to patent "his" idea. Yes, Tim now knew what he must do: Spend time with YouTube until he found an inventor unlikely to sue Tim for intellectual property theft.

In this passage, the word *his* is in quotation marks

(A) because it's a pronoun

(B) because the reader is supposed to hiss at Tim, whom everyone hates

(C) to show that the idea is really someone else's

(D) because the typesetter had some extra quotation marks

The best evidence for the answer to the preceding question is

(A) "Tim was frantic . . . circulation."

(B) "The degree . . . years now"

(C) "The business world . . . belonged"

(D) "marketing someone else's . . . twist"

Note: In the real exam, the lines will be numbered and the questions will include the line they're interested in.

The answer to the first question is Choice (C). These quotation marks refer to Tim's claim to "someone else's technology." Although he isn't quoted directly, the quotation marks around *his* imply that Tim says that a particular invention is his, when in fact it isn't.

The answer to the second question is Choice (D). As you see in the explanation to the first question, these words reveal that the technology isn't Tim's invention and support the correct answer, *to show that the idea is really someone else's.*

Writing and language

To the *chagrin* (disappointment or embarrassment) of English teachers everywhere, the new SAT Writing and Language section contains even less actual writing: one optional 50-minute essay analyzing the writing style of a passage you've never seen before plus 35 minutes' worth of short answers. Why so little writing? As those of us who sit with four-foot-high piles of essays on our laps know, it takes a long time to read student prose. The SAT test-makers must pay people to read and score essays — a much more expensive and time-consuming proposition than running a bubble sheet through a scanner. Here are the details.

The essay

The prompt, or question, never changes, but the passage does. You have to figure out the author's point of view, what he or she is arguing for or against. Then you must pick apart the passage, discussing *how* the author attempts to persuade the reader to accept this point of view. Finally, you get 50 minutes to write your own essay, describing what you've discovered. Your own ideas on the subject, by the way, are *irrelevant* (beside the point). The College Board doesn't care what you think; graders simply want to know whether you can identify the relationship between style and content in someone else's work.

Many standardized tests may now be taken on a computer. The College Board has begun to move toward a computer-based SAT, too, at the speed of an elderly turtle. As of this writing, the computer-based SAT will be available at only a few sites. The College Board promises that at some point it will be everywhere. When? Don't hold your breath! No date has been given, and the College Board has never been famous for its speed in technical innovation. Currently, only those who have been certified as *dysgraphic* (having a learning disability that affects handwriting) may type the essay. For everyone else, handwriting is your only option. Start practicing your penmanship.

Multiple-choice questions

You get four passages, each from 400 to 450 words long, accompanied by 11 questions per passage. The passages represent fairly good student writing, but they all have room for improvement in grammar, punctuation, organization, logic, and style. The multiple-choice questions address those areas. In terms of content, you see one passage in each of these areas: careers, history/social studies, humanities, and science. One or two passages will make an argument for a particular idea, one or two may be informative or explanatory, and one will be a narrative. At least one passage (and probably more) includes a graphic element — a chart, table, diagram or graph relating to the subject matter. One question checks that the passage accurately represents the information in the graphic element. The questions may focus on a single word (to check your vocabulary-in-context skill) or on the passage as a whole (to determine your ability to organize information).

Take a look at this example, which, on the real exam, would be part of a longer passage. Your job is to decide which answer best changes the underlined portion of the sentence.

Having been turned down by 15 major league baseball teams, Milton changed to basketball, and he succeeded <u>in his goal where he was aiming to be a professional athlete</u>.

(A) NO CHANGE

(B) in that he reached his goal of aiming to be a professional athlete

(C) where he became a professional athlete

(D) in his goal of becoming a professional athlete

The answer is Choice (D), because that version conveys the information smoothly and correctly. Did you notice that Choice (A) keeps the wording of the original passage? That's the design in most multiple-choice Writing and Language questions.

Mathematics

SAT math questions rely on Algebra II and some advanced topics in geometry, statistics, probability, and trigonometry. The new SAT Mathematics section contains one 55-minute section when you can use a calculator and one 25-minute section when you can't. Of the 57 questions, 45 are multiple-choice, in which you choose an answer from four possibilities, and 12 are *grid-ins,* in which you supply an answer and bubble in the actual number, not a multiple-choice letter. Whether calculator or no calculator, multiple-choice or grid-in answer, each question is worth the same except for one grid-in question called Extended Thinking, which carries four times the weight of the other math questions. Here's a sample multiple-choice problem:

If $xy - 12 = z$, and the value of x is 2, which of the following must be true?

(A) $z = xy$

(B) $y = 12 + z$

(C) $z = 2y - 12$

(D) $2y - z = 100$

Substitute 2 for x, and see which answer most closely resembles $2y - 12 = z$. The correct answer is Choice (C).

Scoring on the New SAT

The new SAT has a completely different scoring system. The goal is to give colleges an in-depth look at your performance. Scared? Don't be. If you take the exam more than once, as most people do, you can use the detailed information from your score reports to craft a personalized study program, zeroing in on the skills you need to *hone* (sharpen).

Types of scores

The redesigned SAT gives you many, many more scores than the older exam. Here's the deal:

- ✔ **Composite score:** This is the sum of Reading, Writing and Language, and Mathematics (400 to 1600 points). The maximum SAT score is 1600 (with a top score of 800 on Reading and Writing and Language and 800 on Mathematics). The minimum is 400, which you get for little more than showing up and bubbling in a few ovals *randomly* (without a plan or reason).

- ✔ **Area scores:** These are the scores for Reading and Writing and Language (200 to 800 points) and Mathematics (200 to 800 points). The optional essay receives separate scores for reading, analysis, and writing, each scored 1 to 4 points from two graders.

- ✔ **Test scores:** This name, *bestowed* (given) by the College Board, is a little surprising, because where else would your scores come from, other than the test? This is the term applied to the three branches of the exam. You get a score for Reading (10 to 40 points), Writing and Language (10 to 40 points), and Mathematics (10 to 40 points).

- ✔ **Cross-test:** These scores are determined by questions of a particular type in all three areas of the SAT (Reading, Writing and Language, and Mathematics). You get a score for analysis in history/social studies (10 to 40 points) and another for analysis in science (10 to 40 points).

- ✔ **Subscores:** A few skills on the new SAT are so important and *ubiquitous* (appearing everywhere) that the College Board provides separate scores for them. On the Reading and Writing and Language sections, you get a score for command of evidence (1 to 15 points) and understanding words in context (1 to 15 points). On the Writing and Language section, you get a score for expression of ideas (1 to 15 points) and Standard English conventions (1 to 15 points). The scoring of the essay will evolve as results from the first few new SATs come in. The current plan is to provide three subscores (reading, analysis, writing), each 2 to 8 points, based on adding the scores of two readers who grade your essay from 1 to 4 in those categories. The Mathematics section gives you three scores: 1 to 15 points each for algebra, advanced math, and problem solving/data analysis.

One happy, wonderful development is that the new SAT has no penalty for wrong answers! You get one point for each correct answer you supply, and no deduction for incorrect answers. This system does away with a "trick" of the old SAT — gaming the system by guessing when the odds favored you and skipping a question when they didn't. Now you can answer every question, even if you're clueless, unless you run out of time.

Score reporting

The basic fee for the test includes four score reports. Students who are eligible for a fee waiver can request an additional four free reports. You send these reports to colleges you're interested in. If you want to add still more colleges to your list, you can do so by paying $11.25 extra for each additional score report. (Prices, of course, are always subject to change, and don't expect any to go down. Check the College Board website at www.collegeboard.org for pricing changes.) You request additional score reports on the Additional Score Report Request Form (how do they think of these names?), which you can download from the website.

For a higher fee ($13.50), you can get a detailed analysis of your test performance — how many of each sort of question you answered right and wrong and how difficult each question was. Then you can tailor your prep hours to the stuff that's hard for you. Ask for the Student Answer Service when you register. For even more money ($18), the SAT sends you a copy of the questions and the correct answers. Fee waivers apply to this service.

If you're planning to take another SAT, pay the fee for the Student Answer Service. Seeing what you got wrong gives you a blueprint for review.

Score reports arrive in your mailbox and at your high school about five weeks after you take the test. If you're the antsy type and are willing to fork over a few more dollars, you can find out the good news by phone. Call Customer Service (within the U.S.: 866-756-7346; outside the U.S.: 212-713-7789; TTY 888-857-2477 for the U.S. or 609-882-4118 for outside the U.S.). Have a credit card, your registration number, and your birth date ready. The fee for a "rush" score is $15. If you're returning to academia after a break and want access to old scores, you pay $31 for the College Board to dig them up.

If you have access to the Internet, you can create a free (yes, something's actually free!) account on the College Board website (www.collegeboard.com). Look for My SAT Online Score Report. It tells you your 200 to 800 scores in Reading, Writing and Language, and Mathematics and some information on how well you did on various types of questions. The report also tells you how well your performance was in comparison with everyone else who took the exam when you did.

Chapter 2

Slow and Steady (Breathing) Wins the Race: Preparing for the Test

. . . .

In This Chapter

▶ Tailoring SAT prep to your life

▶ Using the time remaining before the test efficiently

▶ Dealing with last-minute nerves

▶ Ensuring success on the morning of the test

. . . .

"*A*ll things are ready, if our mind be so," wrote William Shakespeare. When you hit test day, the last thing you want is an unprepared mind. But you won't have one, because this chapter explains how to make "all things . . . ready," especially your mind, for the SAT.

SAT prep can start at many different points in your life and still be effective. In this chapter, you find long-term and short-term strategies for SAT prep as well as medium-length prep for the Average Joe and Josephine. And for those of you who suddenly realized that the test is *next week,* here you find a panic-button scenario. Lastly, this chapter tells you what to do to maximize your score the night before the test (speaking of panic) as well as the morning of SAT day.

Starting Early: A Long-Range Plan

You're the type of person who buys summer clothes in December. (By the way, thanks a lot. Because of you, all the department stores feature bikinis when normal people are trying to buy sweaters.) To put it another way, you're not in diapers, but the test isn't coming up within the next year. Congratulations. Check out the following long-range SAT-prep plan:

- **Sign up for challenging courses in school.** If you're in high school, *eschew* (reject) courses that require papers short enough to tweet and just enough math to figure out how many minutes remain before your next vacation. Go for subjects that stretch your mind. Specifically, stick it out with math at least through Algebra II. If high school is in your rearview mirror, check out extension or enrichment adult-ed courses.

- **Get into the habit of reading.** Cereal boxes, Internet pop-up balloons, and 1,000-page novels — they're all good, though they're not all equal. The more you read, and the more difficult the material you read, the more your reading comprehension improves. The new SAT places special emphasis on two reading skills — understanding vocabulary in context and analyzing evidence. In all your assigned or leisure reading, take note of unfamiliar words. Try to figure out the definition from the surrounding material, and then check yourself by looking up the word in a standard dictionary or online dictionary or by questioning a handy teacher or parent. (Your peers may know also, but they'll think you're strange if you ask vocab questions!) Also notice *how* the author makes a point — through description, quotations from experts, word choice, and so forth. Then when you encounter a question about evidence on the SAT, you'll know how to respond. Studying writing style also preps you for the optional SAT essay.

✔ **Write to the editor.** The editor of anything! Find a point of view and start sending off your prose — to the school or local paper, to websites, or to television stations. By practicing argumentative skills (and, yes, you can use them to fight with authority figures in your personal life!), you learn to recognize writing techniques in SAT reading and writing passages. As a side benefit, you may have a civic impact.

✔ **Be aware of graphics.** You don't have to be Picasso, but you do have to understand how tables, charts, graphs, diagrams, and other visuals *convey* (communicate) information. The new SAT awards many points to those who can correctly interpret graphic elements. Pay attention to illustrations when you're studying science, history, and math or reading something that has nothing to do with school.

✔ **Keep your math notebooks.** Resist the urge to burn your geometry text the minute the last class is over. Keep your math notebooks and (if you're really motivated!) folders of homework papers. Don't throw out any old exams. From time to time, go over the important concepts, because these are what you'll need on the SAT. Research shows that memory improves when concepts are reviewed after a period of time. The SAT math doesn't go in depth into any one topic, but the questions do require you to be *proficient* (skilled) with the basics. Review your notebooks to stay current with multiplying exponents, the Pythagorean theorem, and $y = mx + b$.

✔ **Read Parts II, III, and IV carefully so you understand the structure of each type of SAT question.** When SAT day dawns, you shouldn't be facing any surprises. Be sure that you're familiar with the directions for each section so that you don't have to waste time reading them during the actual exam.

✔ **Take the practice exams in Part V of this book.** Work your way through all those questions and then check the answers and explanations to everything you got wrong, skipped, or wobbled on. After you identify your weak spots (not that you actually have any — just areas where you could be even more excellent), you know what you have to practice.

✔ **Take the PSAT/NMSQT.** This "mini-SAT" gives you a chance to experience test conditions. It may also open the door to several pretty snazzy scholarships, such as the National Merit (the "NM" in the title of the test). The new PSAT/NMSQT, which is changing along with the SAT, debuted in October 2015. You'll get a preview of what you face on the redesigned SAT.

As the SAT approaches, you long-range planners can relax. You're in a fine position to *condescend* (act superior) to all the goof-offs who didn't even begin to think about the exam until junior year in high school. What? You're one of those goof-offs? Never fear. Hope and help arrive in the next section.

Avoiding Extremes: A Medium-Range Plan

In this category, you're conscientious but not obsessive. You have less than a year before SAT day, and you have a reasonable amount of time to devote to SAT prep. Here's your strategy:

✔ **Do all you can to sharpen your reading skills during your last school year before the SAT.** Remember that reading-comprehension skills matter in all three sections of the exam (Reading, Writing and Language, and Mathematics). When you're doing your homework or surfing the web, make friends with words (not to be confused with the app Words with Friends). Jot down unfamiliar words and examine the context. Can you determine the meaning? If not, hit the dictionary or *query* (question) someone who knows. If you have a spare hour, try a crossword puzzle — a great way to learn new words! *Peruse* (read thoroughly, scrutinize) the newspaper every day, either online or on paper, and check out the way in which statistics appear. Be sure to read the opinion columns and analyze how the author argues a point.

✔ **Work on your writing.** If your school offers an elective in nonfiction writing, go for it. Consider writing for the school newspaper. Send letters or emails to the editor (see a fuller explanation in the section "Starting Early: A Long-Range Plan"). Become comfortable with the sort of writing that makes a case for a particular point of view, because that's what you have to analyze on the new SAT — in the essay, multiple-choice writing, and reading sections.

✔ **Get a math study-buddy.** Not a tutor. Yes, you can learn a lot from someone who dreams quadratic equations, but you can also benefit from studying with someone who is on your own level of ability. As the two of you work together, solving problems and reviewing formulas, you can practice and set the knowledge firmly into your brain. All teachers know that you learn best what you have to explain to someone else. Plus, a study-buddy probably can explain what he or she knows in a different way. If the teacher's explanation didn't do it for you, your friend's may.

✔ *Resurrect* **(bring forth again) your Algebra II book or borrow one from a friendly math teacher.** Look through the chapters that you struggled with the first time you went through the book. Refresh your memory with a sample problem or two.

✔ **Study the illustrations in your science and history textbooks.** Many questions on all three parts of the new SAT include graphic elements. You may see a chart of voting preferences, a graph representing bacterial growth, or a map of cultivated land. Learning to decode these illustrations — as well as similar illustrations in material you read outside of school (you *do* read other material, right?) — helps you ace the SAT.

✔ **Look through Parts II, III, and IV.** Read the explanations of each type of question. Be sure that you know the directions and format by heart.

✔ **Take the practice exams in Part V of this book.** Pay special attention to the explanations accompanying each question that puzzled you (even if you accidentally got the right answer!). After you know which sort of question is likely to stump you, practice the skills underlying those questions. For example, you may discover that your grammar is a bit rusty. Time to hit your grammar book, or, if you don't have one, practice with *English Grammar Workbook For Dummies* or *1,001 Grammar Practice Questions For Dummies* (both published by Wiley).

✔ **Take the PSAT/NMSQT.** You can't pass up a chance to experience the exam in its native habitat (a testing center), even if the test is shorter than the real SAT. From October 2015 onward, the PSAT/NMSQT resembles the design of the new SAT.

If you follow this plan, you should be in fine shape for the SAT, and, as a bonus, you'll have time for an actual life, too.

Cutting It Close: A Short-Range Plan

The SAT is next month or (gulp!) next week. Not ideal, but not hopeless either. Use the following plan to get through it alive:

✔ **Skim through Chapters 3, 5, 7, and Part IV of this book carefully.** Find out what sort of questions are on the exam.

✔ **Do one practice exam from Part V.** Yes, it's terrible. Nearly four good hours gone forever. But you should do the exam anyway, just so you know what the SAT experience is like.

Should you take an SAT prep course?

Complete this sentence: SAT prep courses

(A) don't make a huge difference in your score

(B) employ Ivy League graduates who are paying off college loans until their blogs go viral

(C) provide jobs for unemployed doctoral candidates finishing dissertations on the lifestyles of bacteria

(D) keep underpaid high-school teachers from total *penury* (poverty)

The answer: All of the above. Choices (B) through (D) don't need an explanation, but you're probably wondering about Choice (A). The College Board, which makes the exam, has studied the effects of SAT prep courses and found that in general they have a minimal effect on your score. A few long-term courses do make a slightly bigger difference (25 to 40 points combined on the old SAT's verbal and math sections), but because you have to devote 40-plus hours to them, you get approximately one extra point per hour of study. Not a very efficient use of your time! You've already proved your brilliance by purchasing *SAT For Dummies*. If you work your way through this book and the online material with some care, you've done enough.

✔ **Read the explanations for *all* the questions on the practice test you took.** The explanations give you not only the correct answer but also some general information that will take your skills up a notch with minimal effort and time.

✔ **Clear the deck of all unnecessary activity so you can study as much as possible.** Don't skip your sister's wedding (or your physics homework), but if you can put something off, do so. Use the extra time to practice skills emphasized on the SAT.

Sometimes students put themselves in danger of failing a course in school because they're spending all their homework time on SAT prep. Bad idea. Yes, you want to send good scores to the colleges of your choice, but you also want to send a decent high-school transcript. Prepare for the test, but do your homework, too.

Coping with SAT-Night Fever

No matter what, don't study on SAT day minus one. The only thing that last-minute studying does is make you more nervous. What happens is simple: The closer you get to test day, the more you take notice of the stuff you don't know. On the eve of the test, every unfamiliar vocabulary word is outlined in neon, as is every *obscure* (not well known, hidden) math formula. And every time you find something that you don't know — or forget something that you did know at one time — your heart beats a little faster. Panic doesn't equal a good night's sleep, and eight solid hours of snoozing is the best possible prep for three-plus hours of multiple-choice questions.

Also, resist the urge to contact your friends who are also taking the test. Chances are they're nervous, and every text is a potential anxiety-propeller. Instead, place everything you need in the morning in one spot, ready and waiting for use. Lay out some comfortable clothes, preferably layers. If the test room is too cold, you want to be able to add a sweater. If it's too hot, you may find removing a jacket or sweater helpful without getting arrested for indecent exposure.

After you set up everything for SAT day, do something that's fun . . . but not too much fun. No parties or clubs for you! Find an activity that eases you through the last couple of pre-SAT waking hours. Go to sleep at a reasonable time (after setting your alarm clock) and dream of little, penciled ovals patting you gently on the shoulder.

Getting there is half the fun

On the morning of the SAT, what should you avoid more than anything?

(A) a relaxing session of your favorite cartoons

(B) a two-hour detour on the road to the test center

(C) a kiss from Grandma

(D) a slurp from your dog

The answer is Choice (B). Did you ever watch an old sitcom on television, one with a pregnancy plotline? Inevitably, the mad dash to the hospital is lengthened by a detour, a traffic jam, or a wrong turn. On SAT day, you don't want to be in that old sitcom. Make sure that your journey to the test center is event-free. Try the route there at least once before test day, preferably at the same time and on the same day of the week (that is, Saturday morning, unless you're taking the test on Sunday because of religious observances) so you know what sort of traffic to expect. Leave the house with plenty of time to spare. The idea is to arrive rested and as relaxed as someone who is facing 200-plus minutes of test can be.

Smoothing Out SAT-Day Morning

SAT day isn't a good time to oversleep. Set the alarm clock and ask a reliable parent/ guardian/friend to verify that you've awakened on time. If you're not a morning person, you may need a few additional minutes. Then, no matter how nutritionally challenged your usual breakfast is, eat something healthful. Unless it upsets your stomach, go for protein (eggs, cheese, meat, tofu, and so on). Stay away from sugary items (cereals made primarily from Red Dye No. 23, corn syrup, and the like) because sugar gives you a surge of energy and then a large chunk of fatigue. You don't want your sugar-high to *plummet* (fall sharply) right in the middle of a math section. Then hit the road for the test center.

If disaster strikes — fever, car trouble, uncle's arrest — and you can't take the SAT on the appointed day, call the College Board and request that they transfer your fee to the next available date.

Bringing the right stuff

Be sure to have these items with you:

- ✔ **Admission ticket for the SAT:** Don't leave home without it! If you registered online, print out the ticket. If you registered by mail or phone, check with the College Board a week or so before the test if your ticket still hasn't arrived. You can't get in just by swearing that you "have the ticket at home on top of the TV, really."

- ✔ **Photo identification:** The SAT accepts drivers' licenses, school IDs, passports, or other official documents that include your picture. The SAT doesn't accept Social Security cards or library cards. If you're not sure what to bring, ask your school counselor or check the College Board website (www.collegeboard.org).

- ✔ **No. 2 pencils:** Don't guess. Look for the No. 2 on the side of the pencil. Take at least three or four sharpened pencils with you. Be sure the pencils have usable erasers or bring one of those cute pink rubber erasers you used in elementary school.

- ✔ **Calculator:** Bringing a calculator is optional but recommended. You don't absolutely need a calculator to take the SAT, but it does help on some questions. A four-function, scientific, or graphing calculator is acceptable. The day before the exam, make sure the batteries in your calculator work. Anything with a keyboard (a mini-computer, in other words), a phone, or an iPad is barred, as are other tablets or any device that uses a stylus to input information. Also banned is anything that needs to be plugged in or that makes noise.

✔ **Handkerchief or tissues:** Experienced test-takers know that absolutely nothing is more annoying than a continuous drip or sniffle. Blow your nose and do the rest of the room — and yourself — a favor!

✔ **Snacks:** Bring some healthy snacks (some trail mix, cheese, or other non-candy items) in your backpack. You can eat them during your rest breaks.

✔ **Watch:** Yes, they still make watches, and no, you can't use your phone to check the time. Borrow a watch from somebody old enough to own one in case the wall clock is missing, broken, or out of your line of vision. Don't bring one that beeps because the proctor may take it away if it disturbs other test-takers.

After you arrive at the test center, take out what you need and stow the rest of the stuff in a backpack under your seat.

You're not allowed to bring a phone, camera, computer, or tablet to the testing room. Nor can you bring scrap paper, books, and other school supplies (rulers, compasses, highlighters, and so on). Leave these items behind. Also, no portable music devices. If your "watch" is one of those new, wearable computers, leave it home!

Easing test tension

You'll probably feel nervous when you arrive at the test center. Try a couple of stretches and head shakes to *dispel* (chase away) tension. During the exam, wriggle your feet and move your shoulders up and down whenever you feel yourself tightening up. Some people like neck rolls (pretend that your neck is made of spaghetti and let your head droop in a big circle). If you roll your neck or move your head to either side, however, be sure to close your eyes. Don't risk a charge of cheating. Just like an Olympic diver preparing to go off of the board, take a few deep breaths to calm yourself.

Recent studies have shown that some tension can actually boost your score. Before you begin the exam, visualize a time when you were nervous and had a good outcome — say, before riding a roller coaster or just prior to your entrance onstage. Setting a positive scene in your mind may channel your nervous energy to a higher score.

During your break, *stay away* from your fellow test-takers. You don't want to hear someone else's version of the right answer. ("I got negative twelve for that one! You didn't? Uh oh.") Test-chat won't help you and may increase your anxiety level. It's also against the rules.

Starting off

The test proctor distributes the booklets with, perhaps, a vindictive thump. (*Vindictive* means "seeking revenge," the sort of attitude that says, "Ha, ha! You're taking this awful test, and I'm not!") Before you get to the actual questions, the proctor instructs you how to fill in the top of the answer sheet with your name, date of birth, Social Security number, registration number, and so forth. Your admission ticket has the necessary information. You also have to copy some numbers from your test booklet onto the answer sheet. You must grid in all those numbers and letters. Filling in bubbles with a pencil is such a fun way to spend a weekend morning, don't you think?

Don't open the test booklet early. Big no-no! The proctor can send you home, scoreless and SAT-less, for starting early, working after time is called, or looking at the wrong section.

The proctor announces each section and tells you when to start and stop. The proctor probably uses the wall clock or his/her own wristwatch to time you. When the proctor says that you're starting at 9:08 and finishing at 9:33, take a moment to glance at the watch you brought. If you have a different time, reset your watch. Marching to a different drummer may be fun in real life, but not during the SAT.

Focusing during the test

Keep your eyes on your own paper, except for quick glimpses at your watch, so you can concentrate on the task at hand. If you glance around the room, you may see someone who has already finished. Then you'll panic: *Why is he done, and I'm only on Question 2?* You don't need this kind of idea rattling around in your head when you should be analyzing the author's tone in Passage 3. Also, wandering eyes open you to a charge of cheating.

If your eye wants to run around sending signals to your brain like *I glimpsed Number 15, and it looks hard,* create a window of concentration. Place your hand over the questions you've already done and your answer sheet over the questions you haven't gotten to yet. Keep only one or two questions in eye-range. As you work, move your hand and the answer sheet, exposing only one or two questions at a time.

You aren't allowed to use scrap paper, but you *are* allowed to write all over the test booklet. If you eliminate a choice, put an *X* through it. If you think you've got two possible answers but aren't sure which is best, circle the ones you're considering. Then you can return to the question and take a guess.

If you skip a question, be careful to skip that line on your answer sheet. When you choose an answer, say (silently, to yourself), "The answer to Number 12 is (B)." Look at the answer sheet to be sure you're on Line 12, coloring in the little oval for (B). Some people like to answer three questions at a time, writing the answers in the test booklet and *then* transferring them to the answer sheet. Not a bad idea! The answer sheet has alternating stripes of shaded and nonshaded ovals, three questions per stripe. The color helps you ensure that you're putting your answers in the correct spot. Take care not to run out of time, however. Nothing from your test booklet counts; only the answers you bubble in add to your score.

Pacing yourself

The SAT-makers do all kinds of statistical calculations to see which math questions stump most people and which are relatively simple. The test-makers place questions more or less in easy, medium, and hard order. The reading-comprehension and writing/language passages follow the order of the passage itself.

As you move through a section, you may find yourself feeling more and more challenged. When you approach the end, don't worry so much about skipping questions. You get the same amount of credit (one point) for each right answer from the "easy" portion of the test as you do for a correct response in the "hard" section. If you're stuck on an early question, take a guess, mark the question, and come back to it later. This way, you're sure to reach all the later questions that you're able to answer. Also, during the last minute of each section, bubble in an answer to every remaining question, perhaps choosing one letter and sticking with it for every blank. With no penalty for guessing, you may as well take a shot!

When you talk about easy and hard, one size doesn't fit all. A question that stumps 98 percent of the test-takers may be a no-brainer for you. Look at everything carefully. Don't assume that you can't answer a question at the end of a section; nor should you assume that you know everything in the beginning and panic if you don't.

Should you take the PSAT/NMSQT?

Complete this sentence: The PSAT/NMSQT is

(A) what you see on the bottom of the bowl when you don't eat all the alphabet soup

(B) the noise you make slurping the aforementioned soup

(C) a test that prepares you for the SAT and screens scholarship applicants

(D) a secret government agency that investigates music downloads from the Internet

The answer is Choice (C). The PSAT used to be short for the *Preliminary Scholastic Aptitude Test,* back when the initials SAT actually meant something. Now PSAT just means *Pre-SAT.* The NMSQT part still stands for something — *National Merit Scholarship Qualifying Test.* Though it has a two-part name, the PSAT/NMSQT is just one test, but it performs both the functions described in Choice (C). If you're a super brain, the PSAT/NMSQT may move you into the ranks of semifinalists for a National Merit Scholarship, a *prestigious* (high-status) scholarship program, or give you entry to other special programs. You don't have to do anything extra to apply for these scholarships and programs. Just take the test, and if you make the cut, the National Merit Scholarship Program and other organizations send you additional information. Some students who do not score high enough to become semifinalists will receive a Letter of Commendation, which also looks good on your college applications. Even if you think your chances of winning a scholarship or receiving a letter are the same as Bart Simpson's passing the fourth grade, you should still take the PSAT/NMSQT. The PSAT has changed along with the SAT and mirrors the SAT, though the PSAT is slightly shorter. Taking the PSAT gives you a feel for the SAT itself.

Part II
Comprehending SAT Reading Sections

Top Five Tips for a Better Reading Score

- ✔ Read the whole passage. Don't hop around looking for answers.
- ✔ Check the graphic element, if there is one.
- ✔ Define the vocabulary *in the context* of the passage.
- ✔ Identify lines in the passage that support your answers.
- ✔ Don't use your own experience or knowledge to answer the questions. Everything you need is in the text booklet!

Head to www.dummies.com/extras/SAT for a free article that covers how to answer reading questions on graphics.

In this part . . .

✔ Find out all you need to know about the SAT Reading section.

✔ Get some practice under your belt by trying out reading passages.

Chapter 3

Decoding the SAT Reading Section

....

In This Chapter

▶ Surveying the SAT Reading section

▶ Approaching science, history/social studies, and literary passages

▶ Honing techniques for each type of reading question

▶ Prioritizing the questions and increasing your reading speed

....

*W*hen you were little, you may have snuggled up to a story about a talking rabbit or a curious monkey, feeling safe and happy with reading. Now, reading may be (pardon the pun) an entirely different story, especially when it shows up on a high-stakes test. Never fear. In this chapter, you polish the skills that help you ace the SAT Reading section. You can also pick up some tips on how to read faster and zero in on the questions you're more likely to answer correctly.

Getting Acquainted with the Reading Section

The SAT *consists of* (is made up of) six short passages. In this way, the College Board attempts to relate 65 minutes of highly artificial reading to your ability to plow through 50 or 60 pounds of textbooks (or the electronic equivalent) each semester. Here's what to expect on the SAT Reading test:

✔ **Single passages:** You see four passages, each 500 to 750 words long. Attached to every passage are 10 to 11 multiple-choice questions.

✔ **Paired passage:** One pair, totaling 500 to 750 words, appears on every SAT Reading section. Most pairs offer two *distinct* (different) points of view on one issue, not necessarily for or against, but rather two ways of thinking about the same topic. Either 10 or 11 questions come with each pair.

✔ **Content:** You get one passage drawn from a work of literature, two passages (or one passage and one pair) from history/social studies, and two passages (or one passage and one pair) from science.

✔ **Purpose:** Passages may present an argument or theory, relate a series of events, describe a situation or a place, or reveal character and attitude.

✔ **Graphics:** You won't see a picture of the main character in a literary passage, but you will see charts, graphs, or diagrams similar to those that appear in textbooks. One or two graphic elements will be attached to science passages, and one or two to history passages.

✔ **Level:** The reading level of the passages ranges from 9th and 10th grade to just before college entry.

For information on types of passages, questions and strategy, read on.

Conquering Every Type of Question

When you enter SAT Reading-Passage World, be sure to take weapons — not swords and machine guns, but logic and comprehension skills. This section shows you how to answer the most common types of SAT reading questions, whether they're attached to single passages or pairs.

Speaking factually

It never hurts to have some real-world knowledge in your test-taking tool box, but don't panic when you encounter a passage and several fact-based questions about a topic you've never heard of. The SAT reading questions never require you to know anything beyond what's presented in the passage. So even though you run when you see a bug, you can still master all the questions related to a passage about beetles and flies.

Fact-based questions zero in on statements in the passage. They test whether you comprehend the meaning of what you're actually reading. For example, in a descriptive paragraph, a fact-based question may ask whether the neighborhood is crowded or sparsely populated. In a science passage, you may be asked the result of an experiment.

Fact-based questions are almost impossible to get wrong. Amazingly enough, the test-makers often refer you to the very line in the passage that contains the answer.

SAT fact-based questions *do* have a couple of traps built in. Sometimes the test-writers word the question in a confusing way. Successfully decoding a question's meaning depends on your ability to pick up the word clues embedded within it. Here are a few of the words SAT-makers love to use to keep you on your toes, and some explanations of what they really mean. (You may want to memorize these words so they're in neon lights in your brain.)

- **Except, but, not, in contrast to, otherwise, although, even though, despite, in spite of:** These words indicate contrast, identifying something that doesn't fit the pattern.

- **And, also, in addition to, as well as, moreover, furthermore, not only . . . but also, likewise, not the only:** When you see these clue words, you're probably looking for something that does fit the pattern.

- **Therefore, because, consequently, hence, thus, accordingly, as a result:** Now you're in cause-and-effect land. Look for something that causes or leads to something else (or something caused by something else).

- **Than, like, equally, similarly:** Time to compare two ideas, two quantities, two people, two actions — you get the idea.

- **Until, after, later, then, once, before, since, while, during, still, yet, earlier, finally, when:** You're watching the clock (or calendar) when you see these clue words. Think about the order of events.

Time for a sample question, based on this excerpt from a science passage about an unusual animal, taken from *The Dancing Mouse: A Study in Animal Behavior,* by Robert M. Yerkes.

Line   As a rule the dancing mouse is considerably smaller than the common mouse. All the dancing mice had black eyes and were smaller as well as weaker than the common gray house mouse. The weakness, indicated by their inability to hold up their own weight or to cling to an object, curiously enough does not manifest itself in their dancing; in this they are tireless. Frequently
(05)   they run in circles or whirl about with astonishing rapidity for several minutes at a time.

According to the passage, in what way is a dancing mouse superior to other types of mice?

(A) endurance

(B) muscle strength

(C) ability to cling

(D) weight

Line 4 tells you that the dancing mouse is "tireless," so Choice (A) is a good bet. Before you settle there, test the other choices. The passage tells you that these mice are "smaller as well as weaker" (Line 2), so you can rule out Choices (B) and (D). Because dancing mice are unable "to cling to an object" (Line 3), Choice (C) is wrong. You're left with Choice (A), the right answer.

Clue words show up in the questions, too, so be *vigilant* (on your guard) when reading the questions, not just while perusing the reading passage itself.

Defining as you read

Many SAT questions ask you to define a word as it's used in the passage. Teacher-types call this exercise *vocabulary in context.* The definition is often in the same sentence. Even if the definition is missing, figuring out the meaning of the word is usually easy. Consider what the sentence or paragraph as a whole is saying. Insert a logical word or phrase of your own choice in place of the word they're asking about. Match your word with an answer choice, and you're done.

Here's an example, based on the "dancing mouse" passage in the preceding section:

In Line 4, the best definition of "manifest" is

(A) emphasize

(B) prove

(C) discover

(D) show

Line 4 tells you that the weakness of dancing mice "does not manifest itself in their dancing." Mentally cross out *manifest* and throw in a possible replacement. The passage tells you that the mice can "dance" rapidly for several minutes at a time. That activity isn't weak. Okay, the activity doesn't *show* weakness, a match for Choice (D), which is your answer.

Vocabulary-in-context questions do contain one big sand trap, though. Many of these questions ask you for the definition of a word you probably already know. But — and this is a big *but* — the passage may use the word in an odd or unusual way. Of course, one of the choices is usually the word's definition that you know, just sitting there waiting for the unwary test-taker to grab it. For example, the word *deck* may be "a surface of a ship," "a wooden structure outside a house," or "to decorate." In the Christmas carol, "Deck the Halls," *deck* matches the last meaning. Don't settle for *any* definition of the vocabulary word. Look for the definition that works in the context of the sentence.

Identifying attitude and tone

An *attitude* in a reading passage goes way beyond the "don't take that attitude [or tone] with me" comment that parents repeat with depressing regularity. In SAT jargon, an attitude or tone can be *critical, objective, indifferent,* and so forth. The following clue words may pop up in the answer choices:

> ✔ **Pro, positive, in favor of, leaning toward,** *laudatory* **(praising), agreeable,** *amenable* **(willing to go along with), sympathetic:** The author is *for* a particular topic or argument.

> ✔ **Doubtful, offended, anti, resistant to, contrary to, counter to,** *adversarial* **(acting like an enemy), opposed, critical of, disgusted with:** The author is *against* a particular topic or argument.

> ✔ **Objective, indifferent, noncommittal, impartial,** *apathetic* **(not caring), unbiased,** *ambivalent* **(can't decide either way or has mixed feelings):** The author is *neutral* on a particular topic or argument.

To answer an attitude question, first decide where the author lands — for, against, or neutral — in relation to the topic. Check for clue words that express approval or disapproval.

A variation of the attitude question asks you to identify the author's *tone.* Tone and attitude overlap a little, but tone is closer to what you would hear if the passage were the words of someone speaking directly to you. You can use most of the same clues you use for attitude to help you figure out the author's tone. Just remember that tone questions include emotions, so check for irony, amusement, nostalgia, regret, and sarcasm.

In paired passages, you often run into questions comparing tone or attitude, such as

> In comparison with Passage I, Passage II is more . . .

> The author of Passage II would probably agree with the author of Passage I regarding . . .

To answer such a question, determine the tone or attitude separately and then compare the two. Be sure to read the question stem (the part preceding the multiple-choice answers) especially carefully. Words such as *more* or *less* really matter in comparisons!

Take a crack at this attitude question, based on an excerpt from a story by Virginia Woolf:

Line "Fifteen years ago I came here with Lily," he thought. "We sat somewhere over there by a lake and I begged her to marry me all through the hot afternoon. How the dragonfly kept circling round us: how clearly I see the dragonfly and her shoe with the square silver buckle at the toe. All the time I spoke I saw her shoe and when it moved impatiently I knew without
(05) looking up what she was going to say: the whole of her seemed to be in her shoe. And my love, my desire, were in the dragonfly; for some reason I thought that if it settled there, on that leaf, she would say "Yes" at once. But the dragonfly went round and round: it never settled anywhere — of course not, happily not, or I shouldn't be walking here with Eleanor and the children.

In this passage, the speaker's attitude may best be characterized as

(A) mocking

(B) confused

(C) nostalgic

(D) argumentative

In this paragraph, the speaker looks at the past, remembering an afternoon when he "begged" (Line 2) a woman to accept his marriage proposal. He's *nostalgic* (feeling pleasure and sadness at remembering the past), Choice (C). The sadness shows in Lily's refusal, which he now sees "happily" (Line 8).

Decoding figurative language

Appearances often deceive on the SAT. The passage may contain one or more symbols, similes, or metaphors (all types of *figurative* language) that have a deeper meaning. Questions about figurative language may resemble the following:

✔ In the second paragraph, the author compares his trip to Yankee Stadium to a treasure hunt because . . .

✔ The fly ball mentioned in Line 8 symbolizes . . .

The best strategy for answering symbol- or metaphor-based questions is to form a picture in your brain. Refer to the preceding questions and pretend that you're playing a video of the trip to Yankee Stadium featuring the fly ball or the wait for a hot dog. Then ask yourself *why* the author wanted to place that picture in your brain. Perhaps the trip to the ballpark (on your internal video) is bathed in golden light and accompanied by mellow violins. The comparison to a treasure hunt may show you that the author was searching for his lost youth, which he found unexpectedly at a baseball game. Or, when you run the video of the fly ball smacking into the author's forehead, you may realize that the incident embodies the shock of his realization that baseball is no longer the idyllic sport he once played.

The SAT-writers use metaphor-based questions to check whether you can grasp the big picture. Don't focus only on the detail; instead, look at the context to see what the detail represents.

Try your hand at a figurative language question, based on the Virginia Woolf excerpt in the preceding section:

In this passage, Lily's shoe most likely represents

(A) Lily's desire to protect others

(B) Lily's reluctance to settle down

(C) Lily's love for the narrator

(D) the narrator's attraction to Lily

Line 4 tells you that Lily's shoe "moved . . . impatiently." The narrator sees the dragonfly and the shoe together and notes that the dragonfly "never settled anywhere" (Lines 7 through 8). The shoe and Lily's mood are clearly related, so Choice (B) is the right answer here.

Relating style to content

A fair number of questions on the SAT ask you to examine *how* a particular passage is written and *why* the author wrote it that way — in other words, to relate style to content or purpose. Here are a few examples:

✔ The statistics about fish consumption demonstrate that . . .

✔ The marine biologist's quoted statement that the fishing should be regulated (Line 3) serves to . . .

✔ The description of the marine ecosystem exemplifies . . .

The key to this sort of question is to get inside the writer's mind. Why did the author put that particular example or quotation in that particular place? The example may be a small detail in a paragraph full of details. If so, try to decide what title you would give to the paragraph. Depending on the paragraph's contents, you may choose "why we should stop catching cod" or "the ocean is overrun with cod" as a good title for the list. After you get the title, you should be able to choose the answer choice that best explains why the writer chose to use the example in the passage. Alternatively, the example may be one complete paragraph out of many in the passage. In that case, what title would you give this passage? Chances are giving the passage a fitting title can lead you to the correct response.

Style and content often show up in paired-passage questions, because two authors may make the same point in completely different ways. To answer a question like this, determine the style and content separately, place your conclusions side by side, and notice the similarities and differences. Chances are that one of the answer choices will match your ideas. If not, take a guess and move on, unless you have a lot of extra time. This sort of question requires close reading, and you may do better by concentrating on an easier and less time-consuming question.

Try your hand at this style question, based on a history passage taken from *To and Through Nebraska,* by Frances I. Sims Fulton, describing settlers traveling to the West during the 19th Century:

Line During all this time, and despite the disagreeable weather, emigrants from the cities of the Northeast to the wilderness in the West keep up the line of march, traveling in their "prairie schooners," as the great hoop-covered wagon is called, into which, often are packed their every worldly possession, and have room to pile in a large family on top. Sometimes a (05) sheet-iron stove is carried along at the rear of the wagon, which, when needed, they set up inside and put the pipe through a hole in the covering. Those who do not have this convenience carry wood with them and build a fire on the ground to cook by; cooking utensils are generally packed in a box at the side or front. The coverings of the wagons are of all shades and materials. When oil cloth is not used, they are often patched over the top with (10) their oil-cloth table covers, saving them from the rain.

The details about the wagon serve to

(A) reveal the convenience of covered wagons

(B) emphasize the ingenuity of the travelers

(C) show that the travelers were ill-equipped for life on the frontier

(D) contrast life in the city with life in the wilderness

Why does the author describe the covered wagons in so much detail? Probably to tell you something about the travelers themselves. They seem clever (and *ingenuity* means "cleverness"): They pack everything they need into one wagon. Some have more than others, but those who, for example, lack stoves, "carry wood with them and build a fire on the ground" (Line 7). They protect themselves from the rain with either a wagon cover or a tablecloth. Did you fall for Choices (C) or (D)? You don't learn much about the land they're traveling through, except that the weather isn't great. Plus, the passage doesn't give any hints about the final destination or the travelers' previous situations. Yep, Choice (B) is best.

Unearthing the main idea

In reading terms, the questions on the SAT that address the main idea of a particular passage give you choices that fall into the too-broad, too-narrow, off-base, or just-right categories. A just-right choice includes all the supporting points and details in the passage, but it isn't so broad as to be meaningless. Imagine for a moment that you're trying to find a main idea for a list that includes the following: jelly, milk, waxed paper, light bulbs, and peaches. A main idea that fits is *things you can buy at the supermarket*. One that is too broad is *stuff*. A too-narrow choice is *food*, because very few people like the taste of light bulbs — and everyone who does is locked up in a padded room somewhere. A completely off-base main idea is *canned goods*.

Look back at the paragraph about covered wagons in the preceding section to answer this question:

Which of the following titles best fits the main idea of this passage?

(A) Cooking on the Frontier

(B) A Pioneering People

(C) Prairie Schooners

(D) Wilderness Encounters

The passage describes covered wagons, also known as "prairie schooners," according to Lines 2 through 3. Therefore, Choice (C) is perfect. Choice (A) is too narrow, and Choice (B) is too broad. Choice (D) is off topic because no one *encounters* anyone else in this passage.

Making inferences

You make inferences every day. (An *inference* is a conclusion you reach based on evidence.) Perhaps you come home and your mother is chewing on the phone bill and throwing your bowling trophies out the window. Even though she hasn't stated the problem, you can guess that the call you made to the bowling team in Helsinki wasn't included in your basic monthly calling plan.

The SAT Reading section features many inference questions. You get a certain amount of information, and then you have to stretch it a little. The questions may resemble the following:

- ✔ What may be inferred from the author's statement that "further study should include archaeological digs" (Line 66)?

- ✔ The author implies in Line 12 that the documents were . . .

- ✔ The author would probably agree with which of the following statements?

To crack an inference question, act like the famous fictional detective Sherlock Holmes. You have a few clues, perhaps some statements about historical documents: No one has decoded the writing system from that era. One document is missing key pages. The authors of that culture gave equal weight to mythological and governmental accounts. You get the picture? Then ask yourself what sort of conclusion you can come to, given the evidence. You may decide that the author recommends archaeological investigation because he or she sees what's lacking in other sorts of historical records. After you reach a conclusion, check the choices for one that matches your idea.

If you're asked to infer, don't look for a statement that's actually in the passage. By definition, inferences *reside* (dwell, live) between the lines. If you think you found a direct statement in the passage, it's the wrong answer.

Try your hand at this inference question, based on these sentences about the westward journey of settlers during the 19th century.

The women generally do the driving, while the men and boys bring up the rear with horses and cattle of all grades, from poor weak calves to fine, fat animals, that show they have had a good living where they came from.

With which statement would the travelers described in this passage probably agree?

(A) Gender distinctions are valid considerations in assigning work.

(B) All livestock should be treated equally.

(C) Only healthy animals can survive a long journey.

(D) Many pioneers are motivated by greed.

The passage tells you that women drive while "men and boys" are in the rear with "horses and cattle." Clearly, gender plays a part in *assigning work*, so Choice (A) is your answer here.

Supplying evidence

Two questions out of every set of 10 to 11 reading questions ask you to identify evidence for your answer. The wording will resemble this:

> Which lines support the answer to the preceding question?

These questions are so easy, they're practically freebies! Unless you're guessing, you always select an answer for a reason. All you have to do to answer an evidence question is to (1) get the answer to the first question right, and (2) find an answer choice that matches the *reason* you selected your answer to the first question. To see this technique in action, read the explanations accompanying the answers to every sample reading question in this chapter. See the lines and words cited as evidence? Those lines may form the answer to an evidence question.

If you are struggling to find a supporting reason, the answer to the previous question may be incorrect. Go back and check for another possible answer that does have supporting evidence.

Interpreting visual elements

Bowing to the real world, where visual elements — charts, tables, graphs, diagrams, and so forth — carry valuable information, the SAT includes graphic elements in science and history/social studies passages. (The SAT Writing and Language and Math questions have visuals, too; check out Chapters 5 and 9 for more information.) To *garner* (harvest) every scrap of information from a visual element, follow these guidelines:

✔ **Look at everything.** The title, the explanation on the top, bottom, or sides, the labels inside a diagram — *everything*. You never know which part may be relevant. Imagine the difference in a graph with bars reaching levels of 12, 18, and 11. Now imagine that you neglected to read the note telling you that each level represented 10,000 people. A bar drawn to level 12, then, represents not a dozen people but 120,000 — a fact you can be sure the SAT-makers will quiz on.

✔ **Note all the variables.** Depending on the type of graph you see, a *variable* (what changes) may be represented by a line, a section of a circle, or a bar. Some graphs include more than one factor — perhaps a solid line *depicting* (showing) peanut butter sales and a dotted line tracing jelly sales. Bars may appear in pairs, with one a deep shade and the other a little lighter, comparing peanut butter and jelly sales each year. You need all the information you can get to answer some questions.

✔ **Note the relationship between the visual element and the text.** Most of the time, these two parts work together. The imaginary bar graph referred to in the preceding bullet point may tell you how many people took the SAT in a particular year, while the text may explain how many test-takers sat for the SAT in a particular geographical area. Together, these statistics may help you answer a question about — well, SAT distribution, testing misery, or something else.

Visual elements are good sources for fact or inference questions. Try this one:

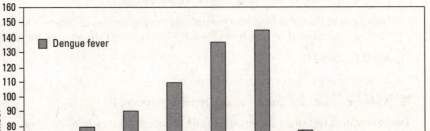
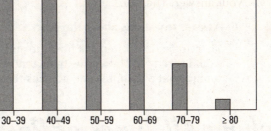

Cases of Dengue Fever, Confirmed or Suspected, 2010

Source: Centers for Disease Control, U.S. Government.

Which statement about Dengue Fever is true?

(A) Infants are less likely to contract Dengue Fever than the elderly.

(B) In 2010, most cases of Dengue Fever occurred in people aged 40 to 60.

(C) The risk of catching Dengue Fever rises with age.

(D) Dengue Fever is especially dangerous for infants and children.

The bar graph shows the number of cases of Dengue Fever, not the danger. A glance at the height of each bar tells the rest of the story: The bars for ages 40 to 49 and 50 to 59 are higher than those for other age groups. Therefore, Choice (B) is true.

Shining a Spotlight on Paired Passages

These two-fers, paired passages, may come from the *realm* (kingdom) of science, social science, history, or social studies. The questions, 10 or 11 of them, sometimes address one passage, sometimes the other, and sometimes both at the same time. To achieve the maximum number of points on a paired set, follow these steps:

1. **Read the introductory material.**

   Tucked into the directions you may find a description of the type of writing (diary, op-ed, speech, and so forth) and information about the author or time period. Often, you discover how the passages differ. One may be a first-person account of a historical event and the other, an interpretation of that event written at a later time. Or you may see that two different scientists write about the same topic. If so, they probably disagree or come at the subject from different angles.

2. **Read Passage I.**

As you read, annotate a bit. If you're a question-first sort of person (check out the section "Deciding Which to Read First, Passage or Questions," later in this chapter to find out), zero in on the information they're asking for. For instance, if you know one question addresses the attitude toward voting rights expressed in Passage I, underline any sentence that discusses this issue.

3. **Answer questions that deal solely with Passage I.**

Don't waste time reading every word of every question. Skip over anything that mentions both passages or that mentions Passage II. Concentrate on questions tied to Passage I.

4. **Read Passage II.**

Annotate again, as explained in Step 2.

5. **Answer questions that deal solely with Passage II.**

Now you're skipping questions about Passage I and again ignoring those that address both passages.

6. **Answer questions about the pair.**

These questions often ask how the authors' ideas or writing styles differ or what both would agree on. These questions tend to be time-consuming, so skip them if you're running out of minutes and go back to answer them later.

Cracking All Types of Passages

No matter what college major you decide on, you're bound to take courses in more than one *discipline* (branch of knowledge). The SAT therefore consciously pulls passages from several subject areas. Although many techniques apply to reading in general, you can improve your score by fine-tuning your approach to specific types of passages. This section provides advice on how to deal with science, social science and history, and literary passages.

Attacking science passages

Don't faint. No SAT question asks for previously memorized information from your biology, chemistry, environmental science, or physics class, or, for that matter, from any scientific discipline at all. Instead you get a discussion of an experiment, opposing theories about a particular *phenomenon* (observable event), and the like. Try these approaches to a science passage:

✔ **Search out the facts.** Whatever the topic, a science passage offers information gained from experiments, surveys, or observation (or a combination of all three). Some of the information is in the text and some in the graphic element, if the passage is illustrated. You don't need to know any math to answer a science-passage question, but you should pay close attention to numbers — percentages, populations, rates of growth or change, and so forth.

✔ **Don't worry about technical terms, but do know general science vocabulary.** If you see a strange word, the definition is probably tucked into the sentence. You won't encounter a question based on the definition of *Tephritidae* unless the passage explains what *Tephritidae* is. (It's a type of fruit fly.) Look for these definitions as you read. You should, however, know general terms that pop up frequently in science-related material, such as *control group* (a group that doesn't participate in an experiment and serves as a point of comparison) and *catalyst* (a substance that causes or increases the rate of a chemical process without being affected itself). As you work through the practice exam, notice the definitions in the answer explanations. Keep a list from your reading in science class, too.

✔ **Identify the argument.** Many SAT science passages, and especially paired passages, present a dispute between two viewpoints. The SAT questions may zero in on the evidence for each scientific *theory* (a claim, backed up by evidence gained from experiments) or *hypothesis* (an idea to be tested through the scientific method) and then quiz you about each author's stance. By the way, remember the definitions of *theory* and *hypothesis,* two important science terms.

✔ **Notice the examples, both in print and in graphics.** The SAT science passages are chock-full of examples. The questions may require you to figure out what the examples prove.

Hitting the history passages

If you're poring over a passage from history or social studies (anthropology, sociology, education, cultural studies, and so on), keep these tips in mind:

✔ **Go for the positive.** The SAT doesn't criticize anyone with the power to sue or contact the media. So if you see a question about the author's tone or viewpoint, look for a positive answer unless the passage is about war criminals or another crew unlikely to be met with public sympathy.

✔ **Take note of the structure.** The passages frequently present a claim and support it with sets of facts or quotations from experts. If you're asked about the significance of a particular detail in a passage, the detail is probably evidence in the case that the author is making. In a history passage, *chronology* (order of events) may be particularly important. Sketch a short timeline if the passage seems to focus on a series of linked events.

✔ **Check the graphics.** The information presented in tables, charts, diagrams, and other visuals is there for a reason. It may represent an opposing or a *corroborative* (supporting or confirming) point.

✔ **Identify cause and effect.** History and social studies passages often explain *why* something happens. Search for words such as *therefore, hence, consequently,* and others that signal a reason.

✔ **Look for opposing ideas.** Experts like to argue, and human nature — the ultimate subject of social studies passages — provides plenty of arguable material. Historians, too, have been known to face off like opposing teams in a hockey game, criticizing others' interpretations of archaeological discoveries or important events. Many history/social studies SAT passages present two or more viewpoints, in the paired passages and elsewhere. Look for the opposing sides, or identify the main theory and the objections to it.

Learning to love literary passages

If you face a literary passage on the SAT (one from fiction or a memoir) keep in mind the following tips:

✔ **Notice the details.** SAT literary passages often contain a great deal of description, as in "George toppled the structure, which was made of stacked, square pancakes soaked in maple syrup." Take note of the small stuff, because you may find a question addressing the symbolism of *maple syrup* or *square pancakes.*

✔ **Stay attuned to word choice.** A literary passage is perfectly suited to questions about the author's tone (*bitter, nostalgic, fond, critical,* and so forth). Pay attention to *connotation* — not the dictionary definition but the feelings associated with a word.

✔ **Keep in mind the big picture.** Literary questions frequently single out one example and ask you to explain its context or significance. Think about the big picture when you get to one of these questions. How does the detail fit into the whole?

✔ **Forget about plot.** Plot isn't important in fiction passages because not much can happen in 500 or so words. Concentrate on identifying scene, character traits, point of view, and symbols.

✔ **Listen to a literary passage.** Of course, you can't make any noise while taking the SAT, but you can let the little voice in your head read expressively, as if you were acting. Chances are you'll pick up some information from your mental reenactment that you can use when answering the questions.

Making the Most of Your Time

When you're barreling through the Reading section on the SAT, time is your *foe* (enemy). To maximize your score, you need to concentrate on questions you're fairly certain you can answer correctly. In general, follow these steps:

1. **Answer the factual questions.**

   (See the earlier section "Speaking factually.") These questions are usually straightforward, and the question usually supplies a line number so you know where to look for the answer.

2. **Go to the vocabulary-in-context questions.**

   (See the earlier section "Defining as you read.") These questions generally rely on your understanding of only one or two sentences and can be answered quickly.

3. **Answer all evidence questions.**

   This is a two-for-the-price-of-one deal. Unless the question preceding the evidence question stumped you, spend some time on the evidence questions. Don't just guess!

4. **If time is running out, guess the answers to questions that ask you to interpret the author's tone or attitude or to identify the main idea.**

   (See the earlier sections "Identifying attitude and tone" and "Unearthing the main idea.") These questions rely on a solid understanding of the entire passage. If anything is unclear and you don't have time to reread, guess and then move on to other questions.

5. **If the test-makers ask questions about relationships between paragraphs, style, inferences, and visual elements, do the ones that seem obvious to you and guess the answers for the rest.**

   (See the sections "Covering all your bases: The main idea," "Relating style to content," "Making inferences," and "Interpreting visual elements," earlier in this chapter.) Go back if you have time for the tough ones and try to refine your guess, if you can.

6. **In paired passages, work on each passage separately and then on questions about the pair.**

   See the previous section, "Shining a Spotlight on Paired Passages," for more information.

No matter which questions you answer first, remember one important rule: You get as many points for a correct answer to an easy question as you do for a correct answer to a hard question. It's not fair. But then again, this is the SAT. Fairness *isn't* part of the deal.

Deciding Which to Read First: Passage or Questions

Potential SAT-takers often wonder whether they should read the passage or the questions first. A variation of this query is whether to read the passages at all. The answer to the second question is easy: Never skip the passage. *Ever.* As for which to read first, make the decision based on your personal style. Are you good at keeping details in your head? If so, go for the read-the-question-first option. Don't read all the choices; just glance at the *question stem* (the beginning of the question) so you have a rough idea of what the testers want to know.

If you feel that your head is filled with too many facts already, settle in with the passage before you look at the questions. Keep your pencil handy and circle anything that looks particularly important. Write a word next to each paragraph, summing up its main idea ("hot dog line," "argument for the designated hitter," and so on). Then hit the questions and locate the answers. Many students who ace the SAT take marginal notes during the test, so give it a try!

Whether you read the passage or question first, never skip the italicized introduction to a passage. Many SAT passages are preceded by a short italicized description along the lines of *this passage comes from the diary of a 16th-century maniac* or *the author of this passage was locked in an SAT test site for 14 days before being rescued.* This description orients you to the passage and may help you decide the author's tone or attitude. You won't see a factual question based on the italicized introduction, but you may be sure that the SAT doesn't waste words, and whatever the test-writers say in italics is useful in some way.

Making a Long Story Short: Reading Quickly

The SAT Reading section asks you to read about 3,250 words in 65 minutes. If reading the passages were your only task, reading speed wouldn't be a problem, because (do the math!) you'd have to read only 50 words per minute to get through everything. Unfortunately, you also have to read and answer questions on those 3,250 words, raising the *optimal* (best) rate of words per minute *substantially* (significantly, by a large amount). You don't have to set your sights on becoming a Kentucky Derby winner, but if you usually plow through paragraphs at a turtle's pace, a few simple tricks may make a big difference in how many questions you have a chance to answer and, thus, how high you score on the SAT Reading section.

A few SAT prep courses advise you to save time by reading only bits of the passages in the Reading section. Bad idea, in our humble opinion. At least some of the questions in this section ask you to assess the entire piece, pinpointing the author's tone or overall point of view. If time is a problem, work on reading faster, not on reading less.

To increase your reading speed, try these techniques:

✔ **Wind sprint.** If you're a track star, you run a lot at a steady pace, but occasionally you let out all the stops and go as fast as possible for a short period of time. When you're reading, imitate the runners. Read at a steady pace, but from time to time push yourself through a paragraph as fast as you possibly can. After a couple of minutes, go back to your normal reading speed. Soon your "normal" speed will increase.

✔ **Read newspaper columns.** When you read, your eyes move from side to side. But you have *peripheral* (on-the-edge) vision that makes some of those eye movements unnecessary. To practice moving your eyes less (and, thus, speeding up your progress), read a narrow newspaper column. Printed material works best, but you can practice with on-screen material also. Try to see the entire column width without moving your eyes sideways. If you practice a couple of times, you can train your eye to grasp the edges as well as the center. Bingo! Your speed will increase.

✔ **Finger focus.** If you're reading something wider than a newspaper column, you can still reap gains from the peripheral-vision training described in the preceding bullet point. Just place your finger underneath the line you're reading, about a third of the way in. Read the first half of the line in one, stationary glance. Then move your finger to about two-thirds of the way across. Take in the second half of the line in just one more glance. There you go! Your eyes are moving less, you're staying focused, and you're reading faster.

✔ **Hit the high spots.** People who make a living analyzing such things as paragraph organization (can you imagine a more boring career?) have determined that nearly all paragraphs start with a topic sentence. If you want to get a quick overview of a passage, read the topic sentence of each paragraph slowly. Then go back and zoom through the details quickly. Chances are you can get everything you need.

The *mis*-ing link

Adding the *mis* family of words to your vocabulary is a surefire way to score higher on the SAT. Do you sometimes make a *mis*take and *mis*behave in front of the *mis*anthropic teacher who has a long, thick ruler and isn't afraid to use it because she totally hates people? Don't *mis*construe (misunderstand) the meaning: We're not that sort of teacher. We do, however, *mis*manage time, especially when we've been out partying when we should be home marking tests.

Welcome to the *mis* family, known for its bad manners and wrong ways. When you *mis*take, you take something wrong. When you *mis*behave, you behave badly. Here are a few more relatives in the *mis* family:

✔ *Misalign:* To deviate from the straight, or aligned course. A walk down a bumpy path illustrates what happens when the construction crew runs late and misaligns the paving stones.

✔ *Misanthropes:* Those who think people are basically bad. Picture a hermit on top of an alp, hiding in a cave. (*Misanthropic* is the adjective.)

✔ *Misconstrue:* A twin of misapprehend, meaning "misunderstand," as in "Hard-of-hearing Horatio misconstrued the command to blow his horn and instead saluted the captain by sewing a thorn."

✔ *Misnomer:* A wrong term, or wrong name, as in "Calling him *Honest Abe* is a misnomer, given that he has been arrested 569 times."

✔ *Misogynist:* Rounds out the I-hate-you category. A misogynist is someone who thinks women are bad and (in our experience) does everything possible to show it.

Chapter 4

Reading for Points: Practicing Critical Reading Passages

....

In This Chapter

▶ Attacking questions in single passages

▶ Taking a stab at paired passages

....

*I*f you're on a team, you know that for every "real" game — one that counts — you play four or five practice games. This chapter is a reading "practice game." The passages and questions are similar to those you face on the real SAT Reading test. To help you identify your Hall-of-Fame quality areas and skills as well as those requiring extra attention, each passage appears with a label (science, history/social studies, or literary) and every answer includes the correct choice, an explanation, and the type of question involved (factual, inference, main idea, and so forth). You won't work up a sweat, but you will strengthen your reading muscles and sharpen your comprehension. Batter up!

Hitting a Single (Passage)

Most SAT passages are singles; their only companions are 10 or 11 questions, which follow the order that information is presented in the passage, not the order of difficulty. In this section, you find science, history/social studies, and literary passages. Remember to check the introduction and visual element (if present) for helpful information.

History/social studies passage

Directions for Questions 1–11: Read this passage, which is an excerpt from Into the House of the Ancestors *by Karl Maier (Wiley). Based on what is stated or implied in the passage and accompanying chart, answer the questions that follow.*

Line   At first glance, there is little in Bamako, Mali, to suggest anything other than poverty and
       underdevelopment. The main road into the city from the north is filled with potholes and
       traffic jams of creaking minibuses and cars and goats and streams of people who walk the
       slow but steady pace dictated by the sun of the Sahel, that dry swath of scrub and savan-
(05)   nah, which shields the moist West African Coast from the furnace of the Sahara Desert.

       Cross the street from the bustling roadside market, walk through the university entrance,
       and take an immediate left, two flights up to the Department of Epidemiology and Parasitic
       Infections, and there is the latest equipment: computers, microscopes, scanners, and a host
       of other machines with jaw-breaking names, such as the Programmable Thermal Controller,
(10)   which analyzes the malaria parasite's DNA. Unlike those in some other major research

(15) centers in Africa, the scientists in Bamako are Africans, mostly Malian, but with a sprinkling of researchers from neighboring African countries. This is not a case of Europeans and Americans taking a mobile First World lab and setting it up in the African bush. Rather, it is a center of scientific excellence, which is administered by Malians, and where the most immediate benefits fall to Malians, though the ramifications are invaluable to Africa and the entire world.

(20) The stakes could not be higher. Malaria is the biggest killer in Africa today, more ruthless than cholera, yellow fever, and measles, far outdistancing the latest more highly publicized outbreaks, such as the *Ebola* virus, and even, at least for the time being, overshadowing AIDS. No one in Hollywood ever made a movie about malaria, but in Africa it claims the lives of nearly one million children each year. Ninety percent of the 300 million to 500 million clinical cases that occur each year are in Africa. In some parts of Mali, especially in the rice-growing area on the banks of the Niger River, one out of five children die before the age of five, most of them from malaria.

(25) What sets the center off from most other such bodies is its work in the villages and its close relationship with traditional leaders and healers. Dr. Ogobara Doumbo, head of the Department of Epidemiology and Parasitic Infections at the School of Medicine in Bamako, believes that not only must the research be relevant to the lives of ordinary Malians, but modern science has much to learn from them. "Traditionally in Africa, Western researchers (30) come for a while, secure the information they require, and then they are off. I wanted to create the link between the research and the communities which need health development. It is a philosophy of establishing field doctors in collaboration with the local communities. That is the dynamic that we have created here."

(35) Unselfish as Doumbo's views may seem, they reflect the cold calculation that village communities have as much to teach scientific researchers as the researchers have to teach the villagers. In effect, the center is attempting to do what so many universities, governments, and professional organizations have failed to do: build a bridge between the so-called traditional and modern faces of Africa. Only in-depth fieldwork can address some of the key questions that must be answered before there is real understanding of the malaria parasite and the (40) mosquito. From the point of view of pure research, the villages furnish the center with a constant supply of blood samples from the hottest malarial battlefronts, which allow the scientists to track how the parasite is mutating. By working with community elders, traditional healers, and especially important target groups, such as women, Doumbo's field workers are able to help people save their children's lives and to set up an unparalleled observation post.

(45) Rural Mali has provided more than a testing ground, however. Traditional healers have developed their own medicines, and unlike many Western and other African scientists, Doumbo and his colleagues are humble enough to admit that the healers often are way ahead of them. With [the usual drugs] losing the battle against malaria . . . the Mali center has discovered a traditional remedy. Malaria 5 is a combination of three herbal medicines (50) used for years by Malian healers. Together with the Ministry of Health, the center has tested Malaria 5 and proved that it has effectively battled malaria strains which [the usual drugs] can no longer fight. This discovery Doumbo cites as an example of cooperation between Western and African medicine.

Malaria in Africa, in Thousands, 2000–2012

	2000	*2001*	*2002*	*2003*	*2004*	*2005*	*2006*	*2007*	*2008*	*2009*	*2010*	*2011*	*2012*
Estimated deaths	802	804	804	800	791	779	737	714	677	647	608	575	562
Confirmed deaths	78	105	112	183	153	174	174	121	126	158	173	121	112

Source: World Health Organization

1. The description of Bamako, Mali, in paragraph one (Lines 1–5) serves primarily to

   (A) explain how challenging it is to work in Bamako

   (B) show the poverty of Mali

   (C) give the reader information about Mali's climate and economy

   (D) create a contrast between the research center and its surroundings

   The author lowers the reader's expectations by taking the reader through "the potholes and traffic jams of creaking minibuses and cars and goats and streams of people who walk" (Lines 2 through 3). Then, in the second paragraph, the scene changes completely to a high-tech paradise. Contrast is the point here, so Choice (D) is your answer. Question type: style.

2. All these statements about the Department of Epidemiology and Parasitic Infections are true EXCEPT

   (A) The center primarily investigates the *Ebola* virus, cholera, yellow fever, and measles.

   (B) The center's scientists take blood samples from rural residents.

   (C) The center studies traditional medicines.

   (D) The center uses computers to access research materials.

   Though the diseases listed in Choice (A) are mentioned in the passage, the focus of the center is malaria. Therefore, the center *primarily* deals with that disease. Choice (A) is untrue — and the answer you seek. Question type: fact.

3. Which of the following statements is true?

   (A) The number of malarial infections decreased steadily from 2000 to 2012.

   (B) Malaria is not always fatal.

   (C) The number of deaths from malaria fell every year from 2000 to 2012.

   (D) Many deaths from malaria do not appear in official records.

   The chart shows many more cases of malaria than deaths, so many people survive the infection, as Choice (B) indicates. Did you choose Choice (C)? If so, you skipped too quickly over the statistics for 2001 and 2002, among other years, which show a steady, not a decreasing, number of deaths. Question type: visual element.

4. The passage implies that the media

   (A) pays too much attention to illnesses in Africa

   (B) does not focus enough attention on African diseases

   (C) focuses on some diseases for a short period of time and then moves on

   (D) portrays African doctors incorrectly

   The fourth paragraph declares that malaria is ignored because the media pays attention to "highly publicized outbreaks" (Line 18), such as Ebola. An outbreak, however terrible, usually lasts for only a short period of time. The passage also states that Ebola "at least for the time being" (Line 19) gets more publicity than AIDS. These statements add up to a "disease of the week" mentality, which is expressed by Choice (C). Question type: inference.

5. Which of the following provides support for the answer to Question 4?

   (A) Lines 7–10: "Department of Epidemiology . . . malaria parasite's DNA."

   (B) Lines 10–12: "Unlike those in some other major research centers . . . neighboring African countries."

   (C) Lines 18–20: "far outdistancing . . . overshadowing AIDS."

   (D) Lines 25–26: "What sets the center off . . . leaders and healers."

As you see in the explanation for Question 4, malaria is a killer "far outdistancing the latest more highly publicized outbreaks, such as the *Ebola* virus, and even, at least for the time being, overshadowing AIDS" (Lines 18 through 20). The correct answer is Choice (C). Question type: evidence.

6. The reference to Hollywood is intended to illustrate

   (A) Western exploitation of Africa

   (B) the power of publicity

   (C) how the media misses important stories

   (D) a universal interest in healthcare

Because "no one in Hollywood ever made a film about malaria" (Line 20), the disease may not be the first thing that pops into your mind when you think about deadly threats. Yet the passage tells you that nearly a million African children die from malaria each year. One million! That's an important story, and the media misses it. Hence, Choice (C) is the best answer here. Question type: inference.

7. The quotation from Dr. Ogobara Doumbo (Lines 29–33) depicts Western researchers as

   (A) interested only in obtaining research data

   (B) better trained than African researchers

   (C) respectful of traditional healers

   (D) committed to extensive periods of research in Africa

The statement that "Western researchers come for a while, secure the information they require, and then they are off" (Lines 29 through 30) tells you that the scientists return to their country of origin after obtaining blood samples or whatever other information they need. Opt for Choice (A), and you're right. Question type: inference.

8. In the context of Line 33, which of the following is the best definition of "dynamic"?

   (A) energy

   (B) liveliness

   (C) change

   (D) pattern

Dynamic may be a description (an adjective) meaning "fast, energetic," but in Line 33, *dynamic* is a noun. As a noun, a dynamic is a system of behavior — in other words, a pattern, as Choice (D) indicates. Question type: vocabulary in context.

9. What is the most likely reason the author refers to "so-called" traditional and modern Africa (Lines 37–38)?

   (A) The definitions of the two are not clear.

   (B) Only one of the terms is accurate.

   (C) The "traditional" face of Africa is actually a recent development.

   (D) The author highlights the distinction between the two.

   The word *so-called* indicates disagreement. If someone refers to your so-called talent, he or she really means that you have no talent at all. The passage talks about the advantages of both traditional and modern medicine. "The traditional" may be more modern than the term implies, because the passage tells you that a new medicine was synthesized from three herbal medicines. "The modern" may be less than cutting edge, too, because many drugs created solely in labs have lost their effectiveness. All these facts add up to a blurry line between the two terms, and Choice (A) expresses that idea. Question type: vocabulary in context.

10. The discovery of Malaria 5 shows

    (A) that traditional healers know more than research scientists

    (B) the importance of investigating herbal compounds

    (C) the advantages of working with traditional healers

    (D) that malaria will soon be extinct

    The drug Malaria 5 is "an example of cooperation between Western and African medicine" (Lines 52 through 53). Without the healers, Malaria 5 wouldn't exist. But it also wouldn't exist without the research center, because scientists there figured out how to combine three traditional remedies. Because both are needed, Choice (A) doesn't work. Choice (B) is too broad, and nothing in the passage supports Choice (D). You're left with Choice (C), the right answer. Question type: inference.

11. The author's attitude toward the Department of Epidemiology and Parasitic Infections may best be characterized as

    (A) laudatory

    (B) critical

    (C) antagonistic

    (D) serious

    Everything about the Department in this passage is positive, so the author is praising it. *Laudatory,* handily enough, means "praising," so Choice (A) is correct. Question type: attitude.

Literary passage

Directions for Questions 12–21: In this excerpt from Dickens's 19th-century novel Great Expectations, *the narrator recalls a Christmas dinner. Answer the questions that follow based on what is stated or implied in the passage.*

Line   I opened the door to the company — making believe that it was a habit of ours to open that
door — and I opened it first to Mr. Wopsle, next to Mr. and Mrs. Hubble, and last of all to
Uncle Pumblechook. N.B.[1], I was not allowed to call him uncle, under the severest penalties.

(05)   "Mrs. Joe," said Uncle Pumblechook: a large hard-breathing middle-aged slow man, with a
mouth like a fish, dull staring eyes, and sandy hair standing upright on his head, so that he
looked as if he had just been all but choked, and had that moment come to; "I have brought
you, as the compliments of the season — I have brought you, Mum, a bottle of sherry
wine — and I have brought you, Mum, a bottle of port wine."

(10)   Every Christmas Day he presented himself, as a profound novelty, with exactly the same
words, and carrying the two bottles like dumb-bells. Every Christmas Day, Mrs. Joe replied,
as she now replied, "Oh, Un-cle Pum-ble-chook! This IS kind!" Every Christmas Day, he
retorted, as he now retorted, "It's no more than your merits. And now are you all bobbish[2],
and how's Sixpennorth of halfpence[3]?" meaning me.

(15)   We dined on these occasions in the kitchen, and adjourned, for the nuts and oranges and
apples, to the parlour; which was a change very like Joe's change from his working clothes
to his Sunday dress. My sister was uncommonly lively on the present occasion, and indeed
was generally more gracious in the society of Mrs. Hubble than in other company. I remember Mrs. Hubble as a little curly sharp-edged person in sky-blue, who held a conventionally
(20)   juvenile position, because she had married Mr. Hubble — I don't know at what remote
period — when she was much younger than he. I remember Mr. Hubble as a tough high-
shouldered stooping old man, of a sawdusty fragrance, with his legs extraordinarily wide
apart: so that in my short days I always saw some miles of open country between them
when I met him coming up the lane.

(25)   Among this good company I should have felt myself, even if I hadn't robbed the pantry, in a
false position. Not because I was squeezed in at an acute angle of the table-cloth, with the
table in my chest, and the Pumblechookian elbow in my eye, nor because I was not allowed
to speak (I didn't want to speak), nor because I was regaled with the scaly tips of the drumsticks of the fowls, and with those obscure corners of pork of which the pig, when living,
had had the least reason to be vain. No; I should not have minded that, if they would only
(30)   have left me alone. But they wouldn't leave me alone. They seemed to think the opportunity
lost, if they failed to point the conversation at me, every now and then, and stick the point
into me. I might have been an unfortunate little bull in a Spanish arena, I got so smartly
touched up by these moral goads.

1. Abbreviation for "note well." 2. Hungry. 3. A small quantity of British money.

12. Which statement may be inferred from Lines 1–3?

(A) The door that the narrator opens is normally locked.

(B) The door that the narrator opens is never used for company.

(C) The narrator is not normally allowed to open the door for visitors.

(D) Different doors are used on special occasions and for everyday entries.

Lines 1 through 3 contain the statement that the narrator was "making believe that it was a
habit of ours to open that door." *That door* implies a contrast with another door, so you can
rule out Choices (A) and (C). The two remaining choices present no real puzzle. Because
company is arriving, Choice (B) can't be correct. Bingo — Choice (D) is your answer.
Question type: inference.

13. The author's attitude toward Uncle Pumblechook and Mrs. Joe in paragraphs two and three (Lines 4–13) may best be characterized as

    (A) mildly critical

    (B) admiring

    (C) ambivalent

    (D) sharply disapproving

    The description of Uncle Pumblechook (isn't that one of the all-time greatest names?) clearly shows that Choice (B) won't do, because a mouth like a fish isn't an admiring comment. Choice (C) is possible, because clearly the author isn't sharply disapproving (Choice [D]), given that the negative comments are quite tame (*ambivalent* means "of two opinions"). Choice (A) is the best. If the two characters are pretending to do something that they've never done before and do so every year, the author is critical of them, but only mildly so. Question type: attitude.

14. Which of the following is the best evidence for the answer to Question 13?

    (A) Line 3: "I was not allowed . . . severest penalties."

    (B) Lines 4–5: "middle-aged slow man . . . upright on his head."

    (C) Lines 10–11: "Every Christmas Day . . . This IS kind."

    (D) Lines 16–17: "My sister was uncommonly . . . than in other company."

    Did you fall for Choice (B)? These comments about Uncle Pumblechook fall into the category of mildly critical, but Question 13 asks about two characters, Uncle Pumblechook and Mrs. Joe. Only Choice (C) does the job here. As you see in the explanation to Question 13, these lines show the false surprise of these two characters. Question type: evidence.

15. In the context of Line 5, which of the following is the best definition of "dull"?

    (A) boring

    (B) blunted

    (C) sharp

    (D) unattractive

    In the cited line, *dull* refers to Uncle Pumblechook's eyes. The opposite of dull is "sparkling and lively" — qualities that attract attention and admiration. Uncle Pumblechook definitely doesn't have an attractive face; he has a "mouth like a fish" and "hair standing upright on his head" (Line 5). Put it all together, and you arrive at *unattractive,* Choice (D). Question type: vocabulary in context.

16. The move from the kitchen to the parlour is compared to Joe's change of clothes because

    (A) Mrs. Joe is uncomfortable with both

    (B) both take place only on special occasions

    (C) the narrator is confused by each of these actions

    (D) Joe insists upon both of these changes

    Mrs. Joe is *uncommonly lively,* so Choice (A) is out. The passage gives no indication that Joe insists on anything, so you can rule out Choice (D). You see no evidence of the narrator's confusion about the move, so Choice (C) doesn't work. The best answer is Choice (B), because Joe's change is referred to as *Sunday dress* and Choice (B) refers to special occasions. Question type: figurative language.

17. The details in paragraph five (Lines 24–33) serve to

    (A) show how the author enjoys Christmas dinner

    (B) explain the behavior of the dinner guests

    (C) describe a 19th-century Christmas celebration

    (D) make the case that the narrator is not treated well

The author is certainly not enjoying dinner, so Choice (A) is out. The dinner guests' behavior (Choice [B]) is possible, but the details tell you more about how the narrator is treated than about the guests' general behavior. Choice (C) is too general. Choice (D) is the only one to make the cut. Question type: style.

18. In the context of Line 27, what is the best definition of "regaled"?

    (A) scolded

    (B) entertained

    (C) bothered

    (D) gifted

The narrator gets "the scaly tips of the drumsticks" (Line 27) and "obscure corners of pork" (Line 28). These don't sound like nice presents, but they are what he is given, so Choice (D) works best here. Question type: vocabulary in context.

19. The metaphor of "an unfortunate little bull in a Spanish arena" (Line 32) means that

    (A) the narrator, like a bull in a bullfight, is a target of teasing attacks

    (B) the narrator's table manners are more like those of an animal than a polite child

    (C) the narrator did not participate actively in the conversation

    (D) the dinner guests were the targets of the narrator's mocking comments

The guests are described as unwilling to leave the narrator alone, so you can rule out Choice (D) because the narrator isn't the attacker. Choice (C) is true but has no relationship to the bullfighting image and neither does the statement about table manners. The narrator is, however, described as the target of attacks by the guests' statements, just as the bull faces attacks in a bullfight. Thus, Choice (A) is the correct answer. Question type: figurative language.

20. The author of this passage would most likely agree with which statement?

    (A) Children should be seen and not heard.

    (B) The narrator has a happy life.

    (C) Holiday gatherings may be joyous occasions.

    (D) People often show off during holiday gatherings.

The change from one room to another, the use of a special door, the ceremonial exchange of gifts — all these details prove that the characters in this passage are showing off, putting on airs, pretending to be better than they really are, and in general acting like contestants on a reality show. Choice (D) fills the bill. Question type: inference.

21. Which lines provide the best evidence for the answer to Question 20?

    (A) Line 3: "I was not allowed to call . . . severest penalties."

    (B) Lines 4–6: "a large hard-breathing . . . choked."

    (C) Lines 14–16: "We dined . . . lively on the present occasion."

    (D) Lines 30–32: "They seemed to think the opportunity lost . . . into me."

As the explanation to Question 20 reveals, several details in the passage lead you to believe that these characters are showing off. Of the lines given to you as answer possibilities, only Choice (C) lists some of the ways that the characters *show off*. Question type: evidence.

Science passage

Directions for Questions 22–31: Read this excerpt from Reality's Mirror *by Bryan Bunch (Wiley) and answer the questions based on what is stated or implied in the passage.*

Line Human beings find some arrangements more appealing than others. When people trim the natural shapes of trees and herbs to produce a pleasing landscape, they are looking for, among other things, a balance. Putting all the tall delphiniums[1] off center in a border or the large yews[2] on one side of the walk and the small yews on the other just does not seem ade-
(05) quate. The same is true of ideas. When a philosopher, scientist, or mathematician puts ideas forward as something that will appeal to others in his or her field, it is generally considered good practice to make sure that the ideas have a kind of balance. The balance required, however, is not between large and small ideas; it is more complex yet simpler. Certain concepts or entities should have similar concepts or entities on the other side of
(10) the conceptual walk. Other concepts or entities can exist without requiring this balancing act. Why is this so? Let's look at an example.

A philosopher might think that since Being exists, Nonbeing must also exist; a scientist learns that for every action there is an equal and opposite reaction; a mathematician would be lost without negative numbers as well as positive ones. These are examples of concepts
(15) or entities that exhibit *balance*. The true, the good, and the beautiful all have their opposite partners.

Other concepts or entities, however, have no similar counterparts. For example, scientists have not found an opposite for mass — no entity that a scientist could label antimass. The need for balance is so strong, however, that some physicists predict that one day antimass
(20) will be found.

The nonexistent antimass should not be confused with the existing antimatter, about which more will be said later. The prediction of the existence of antimatter is one of the most spectacular examples of using mathematics to describe some previously unknown entity. In science, the conclusion that certain entities must have matching but opposite partners is a
(25) direct outcome of interpreting a mathematical treatment of the entities in question. Antimatter emerges as one of the consequences of equations that describe matter. Specifically, the equations that tell how the electron behaves imply the existence of a twin particle that is in some ways the direct opposite of the electron. When scientists found such a particle, the equations had already shown that it must be there.

(30) The belief among scientists in this kind of balance goes even deeper. If some sort of balanced pairing does not exist, scientists may say that at some earlier time or in some other physical state the balance once did exist. By reaching for a higher energy, for example, it is predicted that the balance will be recaptured. This line of thinking has led to the development of huge machines that can reach such high energies and temporarily restore the balance.

1. A type of flower. 2. A type of tree.

22. In the first paragraph (Lines 1–11), the author discusses a garden to

    (A) explain the attraction of Nature

    (B) advocate balance in Nature

    (C) show that scientific thought may be applied to commonplace things

    (D) provide a concrete image of symmetry

    The first paragraph "shows" the reader a garden that's lopsided, with all the "tall delphiniums off center . . . or the large yews on one side" (Lines 3 through 4). The garden image is preceded by the statement that "people trim the natural shapes" (Lines 1 through 2) because of a need for "balance" (Line 3). *Symmetry* is a fancy word for balance, so Choice (D) is your answer. Were you fooled by Choice (A)? True, the first paragraph talks about what human beings find "more appealing" (Line 1), but Choice (A) is too vague. Question type: style.

23. What is the best evidence for the answer to Question 22?

    (A) Lines 1–3: "When people trim . . . things, a balance."

    (B) Lines 10–11: "Other concepts or entities . . . balancing act."

    (C) Line 5: "The same is true of ideas."

    (D) Lines 7–8: "The balance required, however, is not between large and small ideas."

    Take a look at the explanation for Question 22. You see that all the garden comments support a need for balance, with the garden as an example. Choice (A) is correct. Question type: evidence.

24. In the context of Line 5, what is the best definition of "adequate"?

    (A) sufficient

    (B) satisfactory

    (C) enough

    (D) permissible

    The passage explains that a garden with all the tall plants on one side or all the big trees clumped together "just does not seem adequate" (Line 5). In other words, it's not satisfactory, and Choice (B) is your answer. Question type: vocabulary in context.

25. According to the passage, with which statement would a philosopher agree?

    (A) No one can define "true" or "good" or "beautiful."

    (B) Good can exist only if evil exists.

    (C) Nature tends toward imbalance.

    (D) Opposites attract.

    The second paragraph of the passage (Lines 12 through 16) is the only one to deal directly with philosophy. The author gives an example of balance in math, with positive numbers requiring the existence of negative numbers. The author also states that "[t]he true, the good, and the beautiful all have their opposite partners" (Lines 15 through 16). Put those two ideas together — as the author does in paragraph two — and you arrive at Choice (B). The other choices are all the sort of vague statement that philosophers love to debate, but only Choice (B) is justified in the passage. Question type: inference.

26. What is the best evidence for the answer to Question 25?

    (A) Line 5: "The same is true of ideas."

    (B) Lines 10–11: "Other concepts or entities can exist . . . balancing act."

    (C) Lines 15–16: "The true, the good, and the beautiful . . . their opposite partners."

    (D) Line 30: "The belief among scientists . . . even deeper."

    The explanation for the answer to Question 25 points you to the second paragraph, where the concept of balance is illustrated with examples from both math and philosophy. Choice (C) combines these ideas and is the correct answer. Question type: evidence.

27. According to the ideas expressed in the passage, all of the following are examples of symmetry EXCEPT

    (A) a forest

    (B) a butterfly

    (C) a human face

    (D) armies attacking and defending a fort

    The balanced garden of paragraph one (Lines 1 through 11) is similar to Choices (B) and (C) — both examples of visual symmetry. The passage also discusses balanced actions (Line 13: "an equal and opposite reaction"), so Choice (D) doesn't work. You're left with Choice (A). A forest doesn't necessarily grow in a balanced, patterned way, so it's not an example of symmetry. Question type: evidence.

28. One reason scientists predict that someday "antimass" (Line 19) will be found is that

    (A) antimatter exists

    (B) some evidence of antimass has already been discovered

    (C) the need for balance is extremely strong

    (D) antimass is a natural quality

    Antimass is called "nonexistent" in Line 21, but the passage states that "the need for balance is so strong . . . that one day antimass will be found" (Lines 18 through 20). Sounds like Choice (C) to us! The prize for runner-up goes to Choice (A), because antimatter balances out matter. However, Choice (C) addresses the balance issue directly, so it's a better answer. Question type: fact.

29. The author discusses antimatter in order to

    (A) show that mathematics is useful

    (B) explain why some entities appear unbalanced

    (C) focus the reader's attention on scientific theories

    (D) support the idea that Nature seeks balance

    The passage explains that by the time the existence of antimatter was proved experimentally, it had already been predicted mathematically because of a fundamental quality of Nature — its tendency to be balanced. Therefore, Choice (D) is your answer. Question type: style.

30. In the context of Line 24, which of these is the best definition of "conclusion"?

    (A) judgment

    (B) termination

    (C) goal

    (D) end

    Lines 23 through 25 describe the way in which scientists put ideas together ("interpreting a mathematical treatment") to reach a "conclusion," or judgment. Choice (A) is your answer. Question type: vocabulary in context.

31. Given "the belief among scientists in this kind of balance" (Line 30), with which of the following statements would scientists also agree?

    (A) A system may be unbalanced only for a limited period of time or under certain conditions.

    (B) Scientific theories are more often wrong than right.

    (C) Balance is always temporary.

    (D) Only the past can predict the future.

    The last paragraph talks about the lack of balance sometimes found in Nature and goes on to say that if balanced pairs don't exist now, "at some earlier time or in some other physical state the balance once did exist" (Lines 31 through 32). Therefore, Nature tends toward balance, and anything unbalanced now was unbalanced at some point or is balanced in some other way. Give it up for Choice (A), the correct answer. Question type: inference.

Doing Double Duty: Paired Passages

Paired passages double your trouble, but if you approach them the right way, they also double your score. Twice as many chances to get the answer right! Expect some questions on Passage I, some on Passage II, and a couple that address the similarities or differences between both passages.

Directions for Questions 32–41: Read the following passages and answer the questions that follow based on what is stated or implied in the passages. Passage I is from a history of ancient Egypt. Passage II is excerpted from The Ancient Egyptians For Dummies *by Charlotte Booth (Wiley).*

Passage I

Line   Hatshepsut was the daughter of the great warrior king, Thutmosis I, and, according to some historians, was during his later years associated with him in the government. Her father left two sons, as well as a daughter; and the elder of these, according to Egyptian law, succeeded him. He was, however, a mere youth, of a weak and amiable temper; while

(05)   Hatshepsut, his senior by some years, was a woman of great energy, clever, enterprising, vindictive, and unscrupulous. The contrast of their portrait busts is remarkable, and gives a fair indication of the character of each of them. Thutmosis has the appearance of a soft and yielding boy. Hatshepsut holds her head erect, giving her an air of vigor and resolution. She took the direction of affairs under her brother's reign, her influence paramount in every

(10)   department of the government.

The joint reign of Hatshepsut and Thutmosis II did not continue for more than a few years. The king died while he was still extremely young, and after his death Hatshepsut showed her hostility to his memory by erasing his name wherever it occurred on the monuments, and substituting for it either her own name or that of her father. She appears also at the
(15) same time to have taken full possession of the throne, and to have been accepted as actual sovereign of the Egyptian people. She assumed male apparel and an artificial beard and gave herself on many of her monuments the style and title of a king. She took the titles of "*son* of the sun," "the good *god*," "*lord* of the two lands," "beloved of Amun, the protector of *kings*." A curious anomaly appears in some of her inscriptions, where masculine and femi-
(20) nine forms are inextricably mixed up; though spoken of consistently as "the king," and not "the queen," yet the personal and possessive pronouns which refer to her are feminine for the most part, while sometimes such perplexing expressions occur as "His Majesty herself."

The legal position which Hatshepsut occupied during the sixteen years that followed the death of Thutmosis II was probably that of regent for Thutmosis III, his (and her) younger
(25) brother; but practically she was full sovereign of Egypt. It was now that she formed her grand schemes of foreign commerce. She caused to be built a fleet of ships, propelled both by oars and sails, and each capable of accommodating some sixty or seventy passengers. Of these, thirty were the rowers, whose long sweeps were to plough the waves and bring the vessels into port, whether the wind were favorable or not.

Passage II

(30) A spectacular event of the reign of Hatshepsut was a shopping expedition to the city of Punt. The expedition was very profitable for Egypt, and Hatshepsut was remembered for her participation — even though it was an act of a king and not a queen.

The excursion is recorded on Hatshepsut's mortuary temple at Deir el Bahri in Luxor. The location of Punt has been questioned over the years. Many places, from the Indian Ocean to
(35) Ethiopia, have been suggested as the location; the only thing that is known is that it was reached via the Red Sea.

The trading expedition was primarily for incense trees. Incense was used extensively in Egypt by the cult of the god Amun as well as by ordinary people as a fumigator. Because incense was not a natural resource of Egypt, it had to be imported. Ever industrious,
(40) Hatshepsut wanted to plant the trees in Egypt and make incense a natural resource. She did indeed plant these trees along the causeway leading to her mortuary temple, and some of the pits can still be seen today.

32. In the context of Line 4, what is the best definition of "temper"?

    (A) anger

    (B) annoyance

    (C) nature

    (D) moderation

The sentence speaks of Thutmosis I as someone of "weak and *amiable* (friendly) temper" (Line 4). His older sister, on the other hand, is described as "clever, enterprising, vindictive, and unscrupulous" (Lines 5 through 6), all words that describe her personality or *nature*. Choice (C) is correct. Question type: vocabulary in context.

33. Information about Hatshepsut's character in Passage I and Passage II relies upon all the following types of evidence EXCEPT

    (A) comments from her peers

    (B) sculpture

    (C) titles

    (D) items at her burial site

In Lines 6 through 7 in Passage I, you see a description of a "portrait bust" (sculpture) of Hatshepsut, which the author says "gives a fair indication of [her] character." Out goes Choice (B). You also learn that she "took the titles" of a king (Line 17), so you can rule out Choice (C). In Line 41 of Passage II, you learn that pits of incense trees may be seen at her "mortuary temple" (tomb), so Choice (D) isn't the answer. You're left with Choice (A), the answer. Question type: fact.

34. In the context of Line 5, what is the best definition of "senior"?

    (A) older one

    (B) aged person

    (C) retiree

    (D) person of higher rank

You're probably used to seeing the word *senior* as a name for a high-schooler who bosses around — oops, who helps — younger kids. You've also run into the word *senior* attached to citizen. So perhaps Choices (C) and (D) tempted you. In Passage I, though, Hatshepsut is "senior by some years" (Line 5). The phrase "by some years" tips you toward the real answer, Choice (A). Question type: vocabulary in context.

35. The information in the second paragraph of Passage I (Lines 11–22) serves to

    (A) explain why Thutmosis II died

    (B) show that Thutmosis II was not a good ruler

    (C) illustrate gender roles in ancient Egypt

    (D) defend Hatshepsut's actions

In this paragraph, you hear that Hatshepsut wore a fake beard and took masculine titles. In other words, she had to take masculine attributes (characteristics) to act as a ruler — indications of the gender roles of ancient Egypt, Choice (C). Question type: style.

36. Hatshepsut's "fleet of ships" (Line 26) was intended for

    (A) defense

    (B) trade

    (C) luxury travel

    (D) ceremonies

Line 26 refers to Hatshepsut's "grand schemes of foreign commerce" and is followed by the statement that she "caused to be built a fleet of ships" (Line 26). The side-by-side placement of these two statements shows you that the fleet was meant for trade, as Choice (B) indicates. Question type: fact.

37. With which statement would the author of both passages agree?

    (A) Hatshepsut overpowered her male relatives.

    (B) Hatshepsut was a forward-thinking ruler.

    (C) Hatshepsut's priority was always the needs of her subjects.

    (D) Hatshepsut traveled extensively.

Passage I gives you information about Hatshepsut's "grand schemes" (Line 26) and the fleet of ships she had built. Passage II goes into more detail on her "shopping expedition" (Line 30) to Punt. Put these ideas together and you see that she was planning for the future by building boats and trading for the seeds of incense trees. Choice (C) works well here. The other choices are possible, but you don't have enough information to know for sure. Question type: inference.

On the SAT, you're looking for the *best* answer, not just a possible answer.

38. Which lines are the best evidence for the answer to Question 37?

    (A) Lines 8–9 and 12: "an air of vigor . . . brother's reign" and "the king died . . . extremely young."

    (B) Lines 14–15 and 32: "erasing his name . . . her own name" and "act of a king and not a queen."

    (C) Lines 26 and 40: "grand schemes . . . fleet of ships" and "make incense . . . resource."

    (D) Lines 28–29 and 34–36: "plough the waves . . . favorable or not" and "from the Indian Ocean . . . Red Sea."

As you see in the explanation for Question 37, Hatshepsut planned ahead by building ships and using them for trade, bringing back seeds of incense trees, as Choice (C) says. Question type: evidence.

39. In contrast to the author of Passage I, the author of Passage II

    (A) relies more on unproven assumptions

    (B) disapproves of Hatshepsut's assumption of male privileges

    (C) has a less favorable opinion of Hatshepsut

    (D) has a more favorable opinion of Hatshepsut

In Passage I, the author calls Hatshepsut "clever, enterprising, vindictive, and unscrupulous" (Lines 5 through 6). The first two descriptions are positive, but not the last two. Vindictive people hold grudges and seek revenge; unscrupulous people don't spend much time worrying about right and wrong. Nothing in Passage II is negative. The author portrays Hatshepsut's journey to Punt as an attempt to make Egypt less dependent on imported goods, something a good ruler should do. In fact, Passage II calls Hatshepsut "ever industrious" (Line 39). True, the author mentions that Hatshepsut's trip was something "a king and not a queen" would do (Line 32), but you see no evidence that the author opposes this act. Choice (D) is best here. Question type: inference.

40. Which of the following forms the best evidence for the answer to Question 39?

    (A) Lines 4–5 and 30–31: "He was, however, a mere . . . great energy" and "A spectacular event . . . to the city of Punt."

    (B) Lines 5–6 and 39–40: "clever, enterprising . . . unscrupulous" and "Ever industrious . . . natural resource."

    (C) Lines 12–13 and 32: "The king died . . . erasing his name" and "act of a king . . . queen."

    (D) Lines 17–19 and 41–42: "She took the titles . . . protector of kings" and "plant these trees . . . seen today."

As the explanation to Question 39 states, the author of Passage I drops two negative words into the list of descriptions. Passage II, on the other hand, calls her "ever industrious" and portrays her more positively. Choice (B) is the answer. Question type: evidence.

41. Which of the following would make the best addition to Passage II?

    (A) a photo of an incense tree

    (B) a diagram of Hatshepsut's mortuary temple

    (C) a map showing sites in ancient Egypt as well as possible locations of Punt

    (D) a family tree showing Hatshepsut's lineage

Most of Passage II concerns Hatshepsut's trip to Punt, and the passage also refers to "Deir el Bahri in Luxor" (Line 33). Do you know where these sites are? Many readers wouldn't, so a map would be helpful. Choice (C) is the answer. Question type: style.

Directions for Questions 42–52: Read the following passages and answer the questions that follow based on what is stated or implied in the passages. Passage I discusses the relationship between geography and human culture. Passage II comes from The Secret Life of Dust *by Hannah Holmes (Wiley). The author addresses climate change. (**Note:** An* oviraptor *is a type of dinosaur. Mount Pinatubo was a volcano that erupted in 1991.)*

Passage I

Line Human culture is invariably rooted in the site in which it flourishes. Thus human history is also the study of land and water formations, climate, and characteristics of the physical world. Climate, of course, is neither a constant nor a sole factor in human development. The earth's climate has undergone many variations in its long history. So too are there shifts in
(05) civilizations. Today's fertile soil, verdant forests, and prosperous empire may very well be tomorrow's ruins, as the fall of classic Mayan civilization following a prolonged drought in the ninth century illustrates.

Acknowledging the influence of climate, scientists today study the gradual rise in average temperature, preparing for major shifts in trade, population density, and political affinity.
(10) Modern science has in some sense inherited the mantle of ancient seers. One historian declared that climatologists have taken up the role of ancient priests — those in Egypt, for example, whose prayers to the gods were designed to ensure that the annual flood of the Nile River was sufficient for agriculture but not so extensive as to cause damage to settlements.

(15) Yet anyone studying the effect of climate change on human culture must also take into account the consistency and resiliency of human life. Archaeologists at some sites have found similarities in artifacts and settlement patterns before and after major climate changes. More than 73,000 years ago, for example, the eruption of Mt. Toba, a volcano in Indonesia, ejected so much dust into the atmosphere that sunlight was dimmed and the

(20) earth entered an ice age. If climate change is such a powerful force, how is it that humanity survived this period with its culture largely intact?

Passage II

One very clear message in the ice is that the Earth's climate is naturally erratic. According to the dust and gases trapped in the ice, the climate is always — always — in flux. If it's not getting warmer, it's getting colder. Year to year the shifts may be masked by an El Niño, a La
(25) Niña, a Mount Pinatubo, or some other temporary drama. But decade to decade, century to century, the world's temperature is in constant motion.

On a grand scale, our moderate, modern climate is abnormal. Through most of the dinosaur era the planet's normal state was decidedly steamier. When the oviraptor perished in the Gobi Desert, the world may have been eleven to fourteen degrees hotter, on average.

(30) Then, just 2.5 million years ago, the planet entered a pattern of periodic ice ages, punctuated by brief warm spells. The ice caps, as a result, have taken to advancing and retreating intermittently. The glaciers have ruled for the lion's share of time, with the warm "interglacials" lasting roughly ten thousand years each. We inhabit an interglacial known as the Holocene, which ought to be coming to an end any day now. The thermometer, however,
(35) does not seem poised for a plunge.

All things being equal, no climatologist would be surprised if the Holocene persisted for another few thousand years — climate change is that erratic. But all things are not equal. Human industry has wrought profound changes in the Earth's atmosphere since the last warm period.

42. Based on the statements in the first paragraph (Lines 1–7) of Passage I, which position would the author most likely support?

   (A) History is intertwined with geography.

   (B) Human beings shape their environment, not the other way around.

   (C) Climate and prosperity are completely unrelated.

   (D) Dramatic climate changes always cause dramatic cultural shifts.

Most of the choices are as extreme as a category-five hurricane, but the author's position is closer to a moderate summer breeze. Lines 1 through 3 make clear that *the site* (that is, the geography and climate) where people live is a factor in human culture, a belief expressed by Choice (A). Did Choice (C) entrap you? Lines 6 through 7 refer to the fall of the Mayan Empire because of extreme drought, but Line 3 firmly asserts that climate isn't the *sole factor* determining the stability of a civilization. Question type: inference.

43. Which lines provide the best evidence for the answer to Question 42?

   (A) Lines 1–3: "Human . . . physical world."

   (B) Lines 3–4: "The earth's climate . . . history."

   (C) Lines 5–6: "Today's fertile soil . . . ruins

   (D) Lines 6–7: "as the fall of the . . . ninth century illustrates."

Check out the answer explanation to Question 42, and you see that the lines in Choice (A) support the idea that history is intertwined with geography. Question type: evidence.

44. In the context of Line 4, what is the best definition of "shifts"?

    (A) transfers

    (B) modifications

    (C) swings

    (D) transfers

Lines 4 through 5 tell you that "climate has undergone many variations . . . [s]o, too, are there shifts in civilizations." The word *too* tells you that you're looking for a synonym of *variations,* which Choice (C) provides. Choice (B) is close, but a modification usually refers to a small change to an existing thing, and the paragraph describes more extreme changes. Question type: evidence.

45. The example of the Mayan civilization serves to

    (A) emphasize the importance of water conservation

    (B) clarify how history and climate are related

    (C) show that no empire is immune to climate change

    (D) reveal how human behavior influences climate

The Mayan empire fell because of a prolonged drought (Line 6), so you can immediately eliminate Choices (C) and (D). To choose between the remaining two answers, examine the whole paragraph, which discusses the effect of climate on human culture. In that context, Choice (B) is the best answer. Question type: style.

46. Which of the following best expresses the meaning of this statement: "Modern science has in some sense inherited the mantle of ancient seers" (Line 10)?

    (A) Much scientific knowledge is as imprecise as magic.

    (B) Scientific knowledge isn't accessible to ordinary people.

    (C) Science attempts to predict future events.

    (D) Scientists today are expected to understand the past.

Ancient seers tried to predict the future, and Lines 8 through 9 tell you that today's scientists are "preparing for major shifts in trade, population density, and political affinity" — future trends, in other words. Hence, Choice (C) is the answer you seek. Question type: figurative language.

47. The author mentions Mt. Toba (Lines 18–20)

    (A) as an example of human endurance in the face of climate change

    (B) to warn of the dangers of natural forces

    (C) to show that volcanoes can do damage

    (D) as an illustration of the way human behavior changes when climate changes

The third paragraph of Passage I (Lines 15 through 21) talks about climate and culture. The passage states that the eruption of Mt. Toba brought on an ice age, but — and this is an important but — human culture survived intact (not damaged or broken). Therefore, Choice (A) is your best answer here. Question type: inference.

48. In Passage II, the author mentions the oviraptor (Line 28) to illustrate

   (A) the difference between human and animal responses to climate

   (B) how living creatures adapt to many climates

   (C) a creature that became extinct because of climate shifts

   (D) a dinosaur that lived during a warm period

   The author doesn't develop the oviraptor example. Choices (A), (B), and (C) are out because they call for a more extensive discussion of the dinosaur in question. Choice (D) is the correct answer. Question type: style.

49. In Passage II, which phrase most nearly defines "any day now" (Line 34)?

   (A) within a month

   (B) within a year

   (C) during our lifetime

   (D) within a thousand years

   The author of Passage II certainly takes the long view. Paragraph four specifically says that even a few thousand years would be possible, but that amount of time is labeled as erratic, or without a consistent pattern. So the best answer is Choice (D). Question type: vocabulary in context.

50. Compared to the authors of Passage I, the author of Passage II

   (A) describes volcanic eruptions as more important factors in climate change

   (B) believes that climate change has less effect on human behavior

   (C) is more concerned with human beings' effect on climate than the effect of climate on human beings

   (D) sees climate as having greater historical importance

   Lines 38 through 39 state that "[h]uman industry has wrought profound changes in the Earth's atmosphere since the last warm period." Thus the author considers how human beings affect climate, not the other way around, as is the case in Passage I. Go for Choice (C). Question type: attitude.

51. Evidence from both passages supports the idea that

   (A) climate change is inevitable

   (B) human beings cannot withstand radical climate changes

   (C) human activity affects climate

   (D) climate changes very little

   Passage I makes a point of stating that climate isn't "a constant" (Line 3), and Passage II flat out tells you that climate is always changing. Therefore, Choice (A) fits perfectly. Choice (C) may have lured you because the author of Passage II does state that human activity is a factor; Passage I, however, ignores the human effect on the weather. Question type: evidence.

52. The title that best fits both passages is

    (A) Global Warming

    (B) Climate Change

    (C) Volcanoes and Climate

    (D) Human Effects on Climate

Choice (A) is out because Passage I talks about Mt. Toba, an example of colder temperatures. Passage II doesn't really deal with volcanoes, so Choice (C) is also out. Passage I ignores human effects on climate, so the answer can't be Choice (D). As a result, Choice (B) is the correct answer. Question type: main idea.

Part III
Getting the "Write" Answers: The Writing and Language Section

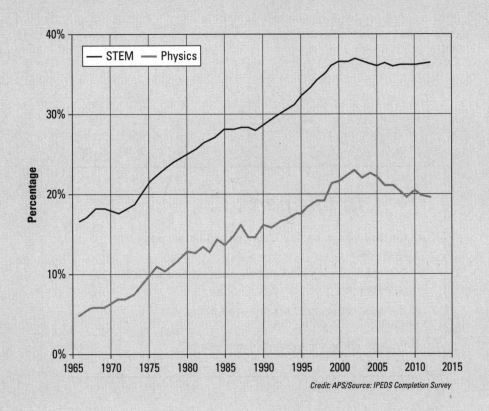

Credit: APS/Source: IPEDS Completion Survey

In this part . . .

✔ Get the scoop on multiple-choice writing and language questions.

✔ Practice answering some multiple-choice writing and language questions.

✔ Find out what you need to know about writing your SAT essay.

✔ Practice writing some essays of your own.

Chapter 5

Getting It in Writing: Answering Multiple-Choice Writing and Language Questions

....

In This Chapter

▶ Surveying the SAT Writing and Language section

▶ Developing effective approaches for each type of question

▶ Reviewing the most frequently tested grammar errors

....

Whether you're headed for the Nobel Prize in Literature or ideas expressed only with emoticons (those little drawings that take the place of words), you still have to conquer the Writing and Language section of the SAT. One part of this section is a required set of multiple-choice questions about grammar, style, logic, and structure, all based on passages that are well written but not quite perfect. The other part is an optional essay. For information about the essay question, turn to Chapter 7. To score big on multiple-choice, passage-based questions, read on.

Surveying Multiple-Choice Writing and Language Questions

The SAT Writing and Language section sounds like a test of two separate areas. Not so! The College Board acknowledges that content, style, and grammar all play a part in the act of writing and that questions about those elements make the most sense when they appear in context. Therefore, the SAT Writing and Language multiple-choice questions accompany short passages. The test-makers want to know how you'd revise the passage if you were the author. Get ready for some details:

✔ You must answer 44 questions in 35 minutes.

✔ Each passage is 400 to 450 words long.

✔ You see one passage in each of these categories: science, history/social studies, careers, and humanities (writing about literature, art, and the like).

✔ One or two passages make an argument, one or two give information, and one narrates a series of events.

✔ Graphics (tables, charts, diagrams, and so forth) appear with one or more passages.

- Eleven questions accompany each passage. In the entire section, 20 questions cover Standard English conventions — better known as grammar and punctuation. An additional 24 questions address style, what the College Board calls "expression of ideas." This last category is broad and may include word choice (selecting the right word for a particular context), concise writing, organization, logic, and effective use of evidence.

- The complexity of language and graphics ranges from 9th to 10th grade through post-high-school level.

The title of this section of the SAT sounds scary, but the work isn't. You write essays, reports, and papers for your teachers all the time. When you're working on the Writing and Language section of the SAT, imagine that you're reworking a rough draft of a piece that you'll eventually hand in. What would you change? Do you see any errors to correct? The questions that the SAT asks you are the same as the questions you ask yourself.

Devising a Strategy for All Types of Multiple-Choice Questions

Passage-based, multiple-choice questions are relatively easy if you approach them in the right way. In this section, you discover the best strategy for the most common types of questions.

Correcting grammar and punctuation errors

Even if you've always wanted to tear a grammar book into tiny little pieces, you can still do well on grammar and punctuation questions. The SAT concentrates on the most important *principles* (rules) of Standard English — the way educated people speak and write. You see an underlined word or phrase and must decide whether a change is needed. If so, you select an alternative. (The same format shows up in style questions.) In the "Nailing Nouns and Capturing Commas: The SAT Grammar Review" section, later in this chapter, you find a *comprehensive* (all-inclusive) review of the grammar topics you should know for the exam — and for life! Here's what to look for in grammar and punctuation questions:

- **Keep an eye open for incorrect punctuation.** Always check apostrophes and commas, which may show up where they shouldn't or be absent from a spot where they're needed.

- **Be sure every sentence is complete.** *Run-ons* (incorrectly joined sentences) and *fragments* (half sentences) are incorrect in Standard English. If you're asked how best to combine two ideas, steer clear of these common mistakes.

- **Don't worry about spelling and capitalization mistakes.** The SAT doesn't test spelling except when it comes to commonly confused words (*too, to,* and *two,* for example), and very infrequently takes on capitalization. Assume that capital letters are in the right spots unless a glaring mistake jumps out at you.

- **Watch out for verbs.** Verb tense is a big deal on the SAT, so make a mental timeline when you're reading and check that the verb tense expresses the right time for an event or state of being. Another SAT favorite is subject-verb agreement (choosing a singular or plural verb to pair with a singular or plural subject). Be sure the subject-verb pairs match.

- **Pay attention to pronouns.** The SAT-ists often mix singular and plural forms incorrectly. The test-makers also throw in some questions that revolve around pronoun *case;* be sure that an object pronoun functions as an object, a subject pronoun as a subject, and possessive pronouns as, well, possessives!

> ✔ **Notice parallel structure.** In English-teacher terminology, *parallel structure* means that everything doing the same job in the sentence must have the same grammatical identity. "Listen" to the sentence as you read it (silently, of course). Does it sound balanced? If not, you may have a parallelism error.
>
> ✔ **Check the placement of descriptions.** Every description must be clearly attached to one word and only one word. If the meaning of a sentence is unclear, you've probably found an error.

If you locate a grammar or punctuation mistake, be sure that your answer choice doesn't contain a *different* error. You must be able to plug in the new version and end up with a proper sentence.

Ready to practice? Try this sample question, excerpted from a science passage.

Samples taken every quarter mile along the river show the extent of the problem. The water five miles downstream <u>not only was polluted but also laden with debris</u>, including tires, chunks of wood, and plastic trash bags.

(A) NO CHANGE

(B) was not only polluted but also laden with debris

(C) not only polluted but also debris was laden there

(D) not only polluted but also laden with debris

The paired conjunction *not only/but also* should trigger an immediate check for parallelism. After *not only* you have a verb, *was*. After *but also,* you don't have a verb. Choice (D) removes the verb, but now you're left with a "sentence" lacking a verb — which is a fragment, not a sentence at all! Choice (B) moves the verb. Now *not only* and its partner *but also* join parallel elements — two descriptions, *polluted* and *laden*.

The SAT Writing and Language test has two columns, one with the passage and the other with a set of answer choices (often with no question stem) roughly at the level of the portion of the passage you are to address. If you don't see a question stem, the question is always the same: "How should the underlined words be changed, if at all?" The first choice, (A), is always *NO CHANGE*. Choices (B), (C), and (D) offer different wordings or punctuation.

Note: If you need a full-scale grammar course, take a look at *English Grammar For Dummies*, 2nd Edition, *English Grammar Workbook For Dummies*, 2nd Edition, or *1,001 Grammar Practice Questions For Dummies*, all published by Wiley.

Selecting the right word: Vocabulary in context

No section of the SAT tests vocabulary directly, but every section checks whether you grasp the ***nuances*** (shades of meaning) of an expression in a particular context. Several questions in the Writing and Language passages highlight one word — usually a fairly sophisticated word — that appears where it doesn't quite fit. The answer choices offer alternatives. These questions arise from the fact that English is rich in words, many with nearly the same meaning. Nearly, though, isn't good enough when you're writing. For instance, your eyelids don't *tremble* when you're flirting; they *flutter*. Both words refer to quick, small movements, but only one is appropriate for a sentence about attracting a romantic partner.

The best long-term preparation for writing/language vocabulary-in-context questions is reading. When you read, you probably run across unfamiliar words. Make a note of every new word, along with the sentence or phrase the words appears in. The context helps you remember the meaning and gives you a head start in *deciphering* (figuring out) vocabulary questions.

To answer a vocabulary-in-context question in the SAT Writing and Language section, be sure you know both the definition and the *connotation* (feelings or situations associated with the word). Time for you to try one, which is *embedded* (implanted, set firmly) in a sentence that would be part of a longer passage:

Few in the community are pleased with the plan to construct a sewage plant on First Street. Opponents <u>detract</u> the proposed facility despite claims that it will bring much-needed jobs to the area.

(A) NO CHANGE

(B) criticize

(C) degrade

(D) diminish

To detract is "to take value away from," a definition that is related to criticism but not exactly the same. Orange sequins may *detract from* the elegant outfit you're trying to assemble, and if you wear them, someone may *criticize* you, but no one will *detract* you. Go for Choice (B). By the way, *to degrade* is "to treat with disrespect," as in *an advertisement that degrades women,* and *to diminish* is "to lessen in value or amount," as in *his appetite diminished after he saw what the chef had prepared.*

Answering style, logic, and organization questions

Correct writing is not necessarily good writing. In "expression of ideas" questions, you may see an underlined word, phrase, or sentence and must determine whether it's the best possible way to *convey* (communicate) the intended meaning. You may also be asked whether additional evidence is needed to support a point or whether a sentence should be deleted or moved to maintain the focus of a paragraph or of the passage as a whole. At least a couple of questions relate to the visual element.

When you approach a question in the "expression of ideas" category, keep these points in mind:

- ✔ **Underlined material may be grammatically correct but wordy or awkward.** The answer choices may include a more mature or fluid version.

- ✔ **Briefer is usually better.** It takes a long time to learn to write *concisely* (with few words), and the SAT tries to *distinguish* (recognize the difference between) whether you're a mature writer or a beginner. If you can cut repetitive words from the sentence *without* creating a grammar mistake, go for it!

- ✔ **Unity is crucial.** Everything in a paragraph should revolve around one idea. If a sentence hops off topic, it has to go.

- ✔ **The flow of logic is essential.** Check for smooth transitions between one paragraph and another. The reader should immediately realize why the writer moved in a particular direction. If not, look for an answer choice that reveals the logical thread.

- ✔ **Interpret visual information correctly.** The text may refer to information that a chart, graph, or diagram contains. Be sure that the text says the same thing as the graphic element. If not, look for an answer choice that does.

✔ **Arguments need evidence.** If the passage puts forth a point of view, supporting facts or quotations should appear. Look for these additions in the answer choices if the original is lacking.

Do you have any old compositions stuffed in a drawer somewhere? Perhaps something that you wrote a few years ago? If so, you have ready-made SAT practice material. Take out those sheets of paper and see how you could have improved the writing. Revision prepares you for SAT Writing and Language questions.

Don't expect to be thrilled by the subject matter in passage-revision questions. The material is boring, but the questions are reasonably easy. Keep these strategies in mind to score maximum points:

✔ **Read the whole passage before you hit the questions.** Don't skip over any text because you may miss something essential.

✔ **Generally ignore everything the SAT-writers don't ask you about.** Even if you're itching to make a particular sentence better, don't. But when you choose the best revision for something they *do* ask you about, be sure that your new sentence fits well with the sentences before and after it.

✔ **Start with the easier questions.** Questions that refer to one sentence are easier, in general, than questions that refer to the entire passage. If you're pressed for time, go for the one-sentence questions first. You can always go back later to the whole-passage or whole-paragraph questions.

Here's a sample writing of a typical writing passage (the real ones are longer), with a couple of questions to go with it.

Can animals predict earthquakes? Since ancient times, strange or unusual behavior in fish, birds, reptiles, and [1] <u>animals has been reported</u>. In modern times, too, people have noticed what they believe to be early warning signals from their pets. In 1975, for example, snakes awoke from hibernation just before a major earthquake in China. [2] <u>The snakes froze to death, the weather was still too cold for them to survive.</u>

Many pet owners firmly believe that their dogs or cats have advance knowledge of the terrifying event that is a major earthquake. Because many animals can see, hear, and smell things beyond the range of human senses, [3] <u>it may be the case in which they are detecting</u> small changes in air pressure, gravity, or other phenomena associated with earthquakes. Researchers know that earthquakes [4] <u>breed</u> two types of waves, P waves and S waves. The P wave travels faster than the S wave, which is stronger and more easily felt. Animals that predict earthquakes may be reacting to the P wave that humans can't feel.

[5] <u>Every year more and more people die from earthquakes.</u> If animals are indeed able to warn of earthquakes, and if scientists find an effective way to monitor the animals' signals, many lives will be saved.

Estimated Number of Deaths from Earthquakes, Worldwide, 2000–2012

Year	2000	2001	2002	2003	2004	2005	2006	2007	2008	2009	2010	2011	2012
Estimated deaths	231	21,357	1,685	33,819	228,802	88,003	6,605	712	88,011	1,790	320,120	21,953	768

U.S. Geological Survey

1. (A) NO CHANGE

   (B) animals reported

   (C) other animals have been reported

   (D) other animals has been reported

This question tests your knowledge of two things: comparisons and matching subject-verb pairs. Fish, birds, and reptiles are animals, so the logic of comparing them with animals is faulty. Insert "other" and that problem goes away. Now your choices are narrowed to Choices (C) and (D). Look at the subject, which is *behavior,* a singular word. (The *animals* are part of a prepositional phrase beginning with *of,* so they don't count as a subject.) The singular subject requires a singular verb, *has,* making Choice (D) your answer.

2. (A) NO CHANGE

   (B) Change the comma to a semicolon.

   (C) Add *Because* at the beginning of the sentence and lowercase the *t* in *The.*

   (D) Add *being that* after the comma.

The original sentence is actually a *run-on* — two complete thoughts joined by a comma, a grammatical felony. Replace the comma with a semicolon, and you're fine.

3. (A) NO CHANGE

   (B) it may be the case in which they are detecting

   (C) they may detect

   (D) it may be that they detect

Concise writing is what you want in a revision, as long as the original meaning comes across. The original has no grammar errors, but it's wordy. The revision in Choice (C) gets the point across with fewer words.

4. (A) NO CHANGE

   (B) generate

   (C) propagate

   (D) spawn

The earthquake causes the waves, and if you were speaking as a poet, you could say that the quake *gives birth to* the *P* and *S* waves. *Breed* is similar to *give birth to,* but *breed* usually applies to animals' producing offspring. The word you want is *generate,* which means "to cause or produce." The best answer, therefore, is Choice (B).

5. (A) NO CHANGE

   (B) Now, the number of people who die from earthquakes is always increasing.

   (C) People currently die from earthquakes at an increasing rate.

   (D) In 2004, more than 200,000 people died from earthquakes, as did more than 300,000 in 2010.

The chart accompanying this passage doesn't show a steady increase in deaths. Two terrible years — 2004 and 2010 — accounted for half a billion deaths, but the number dropped to 768 in 2012. Choice (D) correctly interprets the data.

The Writing and Language section addresses grammar — and more! Don't forget to check for accuracy, style, and organization.

Nailing Nouns and Capturing Commas: The SAT Grammar Review

This grammar review is quick and painless, and if you're pretty good at grammar, you can ignore this section entirely. Here are the most commonly tested topics on the SAT.

Agreeing with the grammar cops

Stop nodding your head! *Agreement* isn't about comments like "yes, I also think we should defrost Antarctica." It's about matching singular to singular, plural to plural. In the grammar world, you can't mix singular and plural without risking war.

In terms of agreement, the SAT loves to ask you about

- Subject-verb pairs
- Pronoun-antecedent pairs

Subject-verb agreement

A *verb* expresses action or state of being; the *subject* is whoever or whatever is *doing* the action or *in* the state of being. Think of the subject-verb pair as a marriage: The two have to be compatible or potted plants start sailing across the room. In grammarland, compatibility means that a singular subject takes a singular verb, and a plural subject takes a plural verb. Check out these examples:

Felicia flounders in the face of an SAT test. (*Felicia* is a singular subject; *flounders* is a singular verb.)

All Felicia's *friends* happily *help* her. (*Friends* is a plural subject; *help* is a plural verb.)

The SAT doesn't spend much time on simple subject-verb pairs. Instead, the exam concentrates on the ones that may be confusing, such as the following:

- *There/here:* Neither of these words are subjects. The real subject comes *after* the verb. Match the verb to the real subject.

  "Here are three crayons." *Crayons* is the subject.

- *Either/or* and *neither/nor:* These words may join two subjects. Match the verb to the closest subject.

  "Neither Mary nor her parakeets are eating that leftover lettuce." *Parakeets* is the closest subject.

- **Interrupters between the subject-verb pair:** If a description or an addition without the word *and* comes between the subject and the verb, ignore it.

  "Barry, not his parakeets, likes honey-flavored seed." *Not his parakeets* is an interrupter.

Don't ignore anything tacked on with *and*. Two singular words joined by *and* make a plural subject. ("Frank and his partners are investing in that bird-cage factory." *Frank and his partners* is a plural subject.)

Pronoun-antecedent agreement

An *antecedent* is a word that a pronoun replaces. In the sentence "Mary told John that he was a drip," *he* is a pronoun, and *John* is the antecedent because *he* stands for *John.* The rule on antecedents is super simple: Singular goes with singular and plural with plural. You probably already know all the easy applications of this rule. In the *Mary/John* sentence, you'd never dream of replacing *John* with *they.* The SAT-makers, however, go for the confusing spots.

- ✔ **Pronouns containing *one, thing*, or *body* are singular.** Match these pronouns with other singular pronouns.

  "Everyone brought his or her cheat sheet to the SAT." *His or her* is singular.

- ✔ ***Either, neither, each,* and *every* are singular.** These words are sometimes followed by phrases that sound plural (*either of the boys* or *each father and son*), but these words are always singular.

  "Neither of the boys has brought his cheat sheet to the SAT." *His* is singular.

As in the preceding examples, when you're deciding singular or plural for a pronoun, you may be deciding the same issue for a verb. Check both!

Tensing up

On the SAT Writing and Language section, tense isn't just what's happening to your muscles. *Tense* is the quality of verbs that indicates time. Remember these rules:

- ✔ **The helping verbs *has* and *have* connect present and past actions.** When you see these helping verbs, something started in the past and is still going on. ("Rodney has been bubbling in SAT answers for about ten minutes.")

- ✔ **The helping verb *had* places one past action before another past action.** ("Rodney had bubbled only three answers when the proctor called time.")

- ✔ **Don't change tenses without a reason.** You may see a sentence that veers suddenly from past to present or vice versa. If the meaning justifies the shift, fine. If not, you've found an error.

Verbs also have moods. The only mood you have to worry about on the SAT is subjunctive (forget the name) and in only one situation: condition contrary to fact. Look for sentences that make statements that aren't true. (*If I were making the SAT, I would dump all the grammar questions. If I had known about the grammar, I would not have burned my English textbook.*) The *if* part of the sentence — the untrue part — gets *were* or *had,* and the other part of the sentence features *would.* The SAT-makers sometimes incorrectly place a *would* in the *if* part of the sentence to trip you up. Your job, of course, is to identify and fix the mistake.

Casing the joint

Pronouns, bless their little hearts, have case. *Case* makes the difference between *me, my,* and *I, him, he* and *his,* and so forth. The rules are actually quite easy. Use a subject pronoun (*I, he, she, we, they, who, whoever*) when you need a subject. Object pronouns (*me, him, her, us, them, whom, whomever*) cover almost everything else. To show possession, try *my, his, her, its, our, your, their,* and *whose.* Naturally, the SAT tries to throw you curveballs, but the following strategies help you keep everything straight:

- **Isolate the pronoun and check the sentence.** By placing pronouns with nouns (in a list, perhaps), the pronoun gets lost. You have a better chance of "hearing" the correct pronoun if you ignore the distractions.

    For example, if you see "The proctor gave the test to three boys and she," you may not notice the error. Cut out "the three boys," however, and you have "The proctor gave the test to she." Now the error may be easier to spot: The sentence should read "to the three boys and her."

- **Pronouns and nouns preceding *-ing* words, such as *swimming, skiing,* and *crying,* should be possessive**. The possessive shifts the emphasis to the *-ing* word. ("Gonzo's parents did not object to *his* taking the SAT fifteen times.")

Between you and I is a common error, so the SAT-writers like placing it on the test. The correct phrase is *between you and me.*

One cardinal rule of pronouns: Confusing pronouns (*she* in a sentence with two female names, perhaps) are a no-no. Be sure that the meaning isn't **ambiguous** (open to more than one interpretation).

Punctuating your way to a perfect score

A few punctuation rules show up on the SAT Writing and Language test. These rules help keep you on your toes:

- **Sentences must be joined together legally.** Sometimes a comma and a conjunction (joining word) — *and, or, but,* and *nor,* for example — do the job, and sometimes you need a semicolon. Some tricksters (*consequently, therefore, nevertheless, however*) look strong enough to join two sentences, but they really aren't. When you have one of these guys stuck between two sentences, add a semicolon.

- **Be careful to punctuate descriptions correctly.** If the description is essential to the meaning of the sentence — you don't know what you're talking about without the description — don't use commas. ("The play that George wrote makes no mention whatsoever of the SATs.") If the description is interesting but nonessential, place commas around it. ("George's first and only play, which he called *The SAT Blues,* flopped at the box office.")

- **Know the rules governing quotation marks.** The SAT won't ask you about obscure rules (one quotation inside another, for example), but you may run into a quotation without quotation marks or one with improper capital letters or commas. Be sure you know the basics. If you see *Don said I don't want to paint and you can't make me,* look for an answer choice with quotation marks (*Don said, "I don't want to paint and you can't make me."*) Be sure not to enclose words in quotation marks if they serve only as an introduction, not as part of what was said or written. Also, don't use quotation marks for paraphrases — reported but not quoted material. (Wrong: *Don said "that he was prepared to sketch but not paint."* Right: *Don said that he was prepared to sketch but not paint.*)

- **Check apostrophes.** You may find a missing possessive form in front of an *-ing* word. (See the section "Casing the joint" for more information.) You may also find an apostrophe where it doesn't belong, in a possessive pronoun or in a simple, non-possessive plural, perhaps.

No possessive pronoun (*whose, its, theirs, his, hers, our,* and so on) ever has an apostrophe in it.

Choosing the right word

The SAT places great emphasis on vocabulary in context, so you may see a word that is almost correct. Unfortunately, in grammarland, not quite right is completely wrong. You probably don't know every single word in the dictionary (and if you do, you need to get a life). Nothing can prepare you for every possible vocabulary-in-context question, but a couple of word pairs are frequent fliers on the exam:

✔ **Affect and effect:** The SAT *affects* your life; its influence is inescapable. The *effect* of all this SAT prep is a high score. See the difference? The first is a verb and the second a noun. But — and the SAT loves this trick — *effect* can sometimes be a verb meaning "to bring about" as in "Pressure from the colleges effects change."

✔ **Except and accept:** I *accept* all the awards offered to me *except* the one for Nerd of the Year.

✔ **Fewer and less:** *Fewer* is for stuff you can count (shoes, pimples, cavities) and *less* for stuff you measure (sugar, ability, toothache intensity).

✔ **Good and well:** In general, *good* describes nouns, and *well* describes verbs. To put it another way, a person or thing is *good,* but you do something *well.* The SAT is *good,* and you study *well* for the exam. One exception: *Good* can be used with sensory verbs. The ice cream tastes *good,* for example.

✔ **Lie and lay:** Two words created by the devil. You *lie* down when you plop yourself on the sofa, and you *lay* a book on a shelf. But in the past tense, you *lay* down for a few hours yesterday, and you *laid* your SAT-prep book on the bonfire.

✔ **Sit and set:** *Sit* is what you do to yourself, and *set* is what you do to something else. Therefore, "May sits down as soon as Al sets a chair on the floor."

Along with these pairs of commonly confused words, be on the lookout for the following "words" or phrases that you should never use because they don't exist in Standard English:

✔ Irregardless (use *regardless*)

✔ Different than (the correct version is *different from*)

✔ The reason is because (should be *the reason is that*)

✔ Could of/should of/would of (use *could have, should have, would have*)

This list obviously doesn't contain all the misused words or expressions you may encounter on the SAT tests, because English has thousands and thousands of words and a lot can go wrong. But now that you've read this section, these tricky words won't trap you on the SAT.

Staying between the parallel lines

A favorite SAT question concerns *parallelism,* the way a sentence keeps its balance. The basic principle is simple: Everything doing the same job in a sentence must *be* the same type of grammatical element. You can't "surf and soak up sun and playing in the sand" because *playing* breaks the pattern. You can "surf and soak up sun and play in the sand" without any problems — well, without any grammatical problems. Don't forget about sunblock! To parallel park in the high-score spots, keep these ideas in mind:

✔ **Look for lists.** Whenever you have two or three things bunched together, they probably have the same job. Make sure they match.

✔ **Be wary of paired conjunctions.** Conjunctions are joining words. Three common paired conjunctions are *either/or, neither/nor,* and *not only/but also.* When you encounter one of these pairs, examine what follows each conjunction. If a subject-verb combo follows *either,* a subject-verb combo should follow *or.* ("Either I will go to the store or I will order the sweater online.") If only a noun follows *either,* only a noun should follow *or.* ("Either the store or the Internet will have the sweater I want.")

✔ **When two complete sentences are joined together, usually the verbs are both active or both passive.** In an active-verb sentence, the subject is doing the action or is in the state of being expressed by the verb. ("Archie flies well." "Archie is happy.") In a passive-verb sentence, the subject receives the action of the verb. ("The window was broken by a high-speed pitch.") A parallel sentence generally doesn't switch from active to passive or vice versa.

Chapter 6

Bragging "Writes": Practicing Multiple-Choice Writing and Language Questions

. . . .

In This Chapter

▶ Practicing passage-based, multiple-choice Writing and Language questions

▶ Improving your score by focusing on challenging topics

. . . .

This chapter helps you get in the mood (terminally bored, ready to glue your toes together rather than think about the SAT) for the multiple-choice Writing and Language section. Here, you find four passages similar to those on the real exam, along with questions to tone your grammar and style muscles. All are accompanied by answers and explanations as well as labels indicating what's being tested (punctuation, logic, verb tense, evidence, and so forth). As you practice, keep track of your strengths and weaknesses. After you find out what tends to stump you, concentrate your attention on those topics. You'll improve faster than you can say "SAT Writing and Language!"

The explanations here will *suffice* (be enough) for readers who have studied some grammar already. If you need a more complete review, turn to Chapter 5 . If your grammar skills need additional polishing, you may want to consult *English Grammar For Dummies,* 2nd Edition, *English Grammar Workbook For Dummies,* 2nd Edition, and *1,001 Grammar Practice Questions For Dummies,* all published by Wiley.

When you take the SAT Writing and Language test, you'll see a two-column format, with the passage in the first column and the answer choices in the second column, more or less on the same level as the portion of the passage you are to address. Often, the answer choices are not attached to a question. In that case, the question is always the same: "How should the underlined portion of the sentence be changed, if at all?" The first answer, Choice (A), is always *NO CHANGE*. Choices (B), (C), and (D) offer alternatives.

Passage I

At least one passage in the Writing and Language section focuses on careers and one on science. This passage has a little bit of both. Put on your business suit (or a lab coat, given the career discussed) and try this one, which describes one woman's career as a scientist.

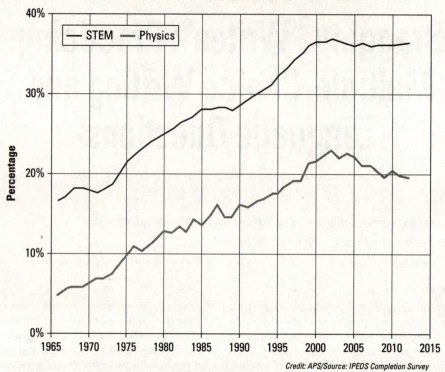

Percentage of Bachelor's Degrees Earned by Women in the STEM Fields, 1965–2015

Credit: APS/Source: IPEDS Completion Survey

Jocelyn Bell [1] says, "that she started by failing." [2] When eleven years old, a standardized national exam used in Great Britain to determine a student's academic future proved difficult for her. Fortunately, her parents believed in her ability to learn. They were also firmly committed to education. [3] Instead of withdrawing her from school, they enrolled her in boarding school rather than accept an end to her education. Bell went on to earn advanced degrees in physics and to make important contributions to her field. Today, she is one of two full-time female professors of physics (out of 150) in Britain.[4]

While she was studying at Cambridge University, Bell, along with her professors and fellow graduate students, [5] has built a radio telescope. Bell's main duty was to analyze data from this telescope. She pored over miles of data from the telescope. Her hard work and sharp powers of perception paid off. She discovered some fast and regular bursts of radio waves that she initially called "scruff." [6] She analyzed these radio waves. She ruled out several possible sources, including orbiting satellites and French television broadcasts. At one point Bell called them "LGM" — little green men — and considered whether they were signals from alien life forms. Eventually, Bell and her colleagues proved that the "scruff" arose from a particular type of fast-spinning neutron star. The media named the signals, which occurred in predictable patterns, "pulsars." Jocelyn Bell's discovery of the first pulsar, named CP 1919 ("Cambridge Pulsar Number 1919"), was followed by more, some found by Bell herself and others by researchers around the world. [7] A neutron star is a dense mass that comes into existence when an extremely large star explodes.

In 1974, Jocelyn Bell's professors received the Nobel Prize in Physics, one of the world's most prestigious awards, for their work on pulsars. Because Bell was only a student when she discovered CP 1919, Bell did not share the prize. Some protested this [8] deletion, but Bell did not. Student work should not be recognized, she believes, unless there are special circumstances. She doesn't think that her discovery falls into that category. However, some critics believe that gender bias played a role in the decision to exclude her. [9] Statistics show that while the number of women studying physics is rising steadily, women are still a minority in the field.

After this early achievement, Jocelyn Bell continued her research work and teaching at other universities. [10] She has received many awards in which she studied almost every wave spectrum in astronomy and gained an unusual breadth of experience. At Southampton University, she was awarded a grant to study gamma ray astronomy. She also studied and taught X-ray astronomy in London and infrared astronomy in Edinburgh. She currently teaches at the Open University, which enrolls many students who, like Bell, did not pass the traditional exams. [11]

1. (A) NO CHANGE
   (B) says, "I started by failing."
   (C) says "that she started by failing."
   (D) started by failing is what she says.

The word *that* may introduce a quotation, but when it does so, it isn't part of the quotation. Choice (B) removes *that,* properly enclosing Jocelyn Bell's remarks inside quotation marks. Question type: punctuation.

2. (A) NO CHANGE
   (B) At the age of eleven
   (C) When she was eleven years old
   (D) When eleven

To make sense, an introductory statement with an implied subject must share the subject that appears in the next portion of the sentence. In this case, the stated subject is *exam.* If you insert *exam* into the introductory statement, though, you end up with an 11-year-old *exam* — not the intended meaning. The solution is simple: Add a subject *(she)* to the introductory statement, Choice (C). Now Jocelyn Bell is 11, not the exam. Question type: illogical descriptions.

3. (A) NO CHANGE
   (B) Instead of withdrawing her from school and they enrolled her in boarding school and did not accept an end to her education.
   (C) They enrolled her in boarding school rather than accept an end to her education.
   (D) They enrolled her in boarding school rather than except an end to her education.

The original sentence has no grammatical errors, but it's repetitive. *Instead of withdrawing her from school* means exactly the same thing as *rather than accept an end to her education.* One of these statements has to go. Choices (C) and (D) solve the repetition problem, but Choice (D) incorrectly substitutes *except* for *accept.* Choice (C) is correct. Question type: repetition, vocabulary in context.

4. Which of the following additions, if any, should be made to the first paragraph of this passage?
   (A) NO CHANGE
   (B) information about the careers of Bell's parents
   (C) a detailed description of the exam Bell failed
   (D) a history of radio astronomy

The passage focuses on Bell and her achievements. Her parents played a role in Bell's life, of course, but they're not the stars of this piece. Therefore, you can rule out Choice (B). The fact that Bell failed a standardized test (do you sympathize with her?) is an interesting detail, but it isn't important enough to *warrant* (deserve) a ton of information about the exam. Bang, Choice (C) is out! Radio astronomy is Bell's field, but because the focus is Bell's achievement, you don't need to know anything beyond the fact that she made a significant discovery. Choice (A) is the answer you want. Question type: logic and organization.

5. (A) NO CHANGE

   (B) built

   (C) has been building

   (D) have built

The present perfect tense, which is formed with the helping verb *has* or *have,* connects the past to the present. The second paragraph mentions several activities, all in the past. They don't continue into the present, so *has built* is the wrong tense. The simple past tense, *built,* is what you want, making Choice (B) the correct answer. Question type: verb tense.

6. What is the best way to combine the underlined sentences?

   (A) Ruled out several possible sources, including orbiting satellites and French television broadcasts, Bell analyzed these radio waves.

   (B) She analyzed these radio waves, she ruled out several possible sources, including orbiting satellites and French television broadcasts.

   (C) She analyzed these radio waves, but she ruled out several possible sources, including orbiting satellites and French television broadcasts.

   (D) As she analyzed these radio waves, she ruled out several possible sources, including orbiting satellites and French television broadcasts.

Choice (A) starts with a *participle* (a verb form used as a description), which is often a fine way to tuck ideas into a sentence. However, Choice (A) doesn't express the same meaning as the original. Choice (B) is a run-on (two complete sentences linked by a comma). Nope! A run-on is a grammatical felony. Choice (C) is legal in Standard English, but the conjunction *but* signals a change in direction and makes no sense in this sentence. Go for Choice (D), which places two events at the same time with the conjunction *as.* Question type: logic, complete sentences.

7. Which of the following changes, if any, should be made to the underlined sentence?

   (A) (A) NO CHANGE

   (B) Place it before the sentence beginning "The media named. . . ."

   (C) Delete the sentence.

   (D) Place it at the beginning of the next paragraph, before the sentence beginning "In 1974. . . ."

The most logical spot for a definition of the term *neutron star* is right after the term is introduced, making Choice (B) the best answer. Question type: logic and structure.

8. (A) NO CHANGE

   (B) exemption

   (C) exception

   (D) omission

Bell wasn't named, so what happened to her wasn't a deletion, which is what you do when you cross out or erase. Because she was never on the prize list, *omission* (the term for something that's overlooked or left out) is a better word. Question type: vocabulary in context.

9. (A) NO CHANGE

    (B) Statistics show that while the number of women earning degrees in physics is rising, though not steadily, women are still a minority in the field.

    (C) According to statistics, more and more women are earning degrees in physics every year, but men earn more degrees in physics.

    (D) The number of women studying physics is rising steadily, but women are still a minority in the field.

The graph accompanying this piece shows an increase, but not a steady increase. Here and there you see a drop. Only Choice (B) makes this fact clear. Question type: interpretation of visual evidence.

10. (A) NO CHANGE

    (B) Receiving many awards, studying almost every wave spectrum in astronomy and gained an unusual breadth of experience.

    (C) She studied almost every wave spectrum in astronomy and gained an unusual breadth of experience, receiving many awards.

    (D) She has received many awards and studied almost every wave spectrum in astronomy and gained an unusual breadth of experience.

The original sentence doesn't quite make sense because of the phrase *in which*. To fix the sentence, you have many options. Choice (B) doesn't work because it's not a complete sentence. Choice (D) is childish, stringing together a bunch of ideas with the word *and*. Choice (C) is more mature. Question type: complete sentence, style, logic.

11. Which of the following should be added at the end of the last paragraph?

    (A) Bell's discovery of pulsars was impressive.

    (B) Jocelyn Bell has had a great career.

    (C) The little girl who once failed now helps others achieve success.

    (D) Bell should receive a prize for her work.

The best addition to the end of the passage is Choice (C). The passage comes full circle with this added sentence, a nice bookend to *she started by failing* in the first paragraph. Question type: structure, style.

Passage II

How tired are you? Are you too drowsy to work on this passage about lack of sleep? Prop your eyelids open with toothpicks and give it a go.

Percentage of Adults in the United States Reporting Sleep Behaviors, 2009		
Age (in Years)	Fell Asleep Unintentionally During the Day at Least Once During the Past Month	Fell Asleep while Driving in the Past Month
18 to 25	43.7	4.5
25 to 35	36.1	7.2
35 to 45	34.0	5.7
45 to 55	35.3	3.9
55 to 65	36.5	3.1
65 and up	44.6	2.0

Source: Centers for Disease Control

The prevalence of screens may be a contributing factor to the epidemic of sleep disorders we are now witnessing. According to one researcher, "The higher use of these potentially sleep-disruptive technologies among younger generations may have serious consequences for physical health, cognitive development, and other measures of wellbeing." Artificial light, including glowing screens, [12] suppress melatonin, a hormone that aids sleep. When a person looks at a screen during the hour before bedtime, [13] they may become more alert and find it harder to fall asleep.

[14] Sleep deprivation is a problem. Sleep deprivation has been linked to a number of health issues, such as obesity, high blood pressure, irregular heartbeat, cancer, and diabetes. Lack of sleep also damages the immune system, which protects the body from infection. Tired people are more likely to have car accidents or make mistakes at work; many medical errors and industrial disasters [15] are the result of sleep deprivation. One study found that drivers [16] who were younger than 25 were more likely to fall asleep while behind the wheel, a particularly [17] exciting number given that these drivers may not be able to react from instinct if they suddenly awake in a dangerous traffic situation. Students don't learn as well if they lack sufficient rest. [18] Research subjects, who slept after learning a new task, retained the knowledge and scored higher on tests than those who did not sleep. Scientists say that this "memory consolidation" takes place during sleep; for this reason babies, who learn at a phenomenal rate, need more sleep than adults. According to the National Institutes of Health, elementary school children need at least 10 hours of sleep a night, teens 9 to 10 hours, and adults 7 to 8 hours. Yet in a recent year, nearly 30% of adults reported that they slept less than 6 hours a night, and only 31% of high school students got at least 8 hours of sleep on an average weekday night. [19]

Sleep deprivation is being caused by many factors. A condition called apnea is [20] another. Someone with apnea stops breathing while asleep and wakes up gasping for air many times each night. Work schedules, which may [21] swing, and the assumption that employees will check e-mail or be on call even when they're not physically at the office are also problems. Working more, though, is not the same as working efficiently. Researchers in Finland studied 4,000 men and women for a period of 7 years. The number of sick days was remarkably higher for those who slept less than 6 hours or more than 9 hours a night. Researchers caution that underlying illness may cause lack of sleep or superfluous sleep, not the other way around. [22] Irregardless, sleeping an adequate amount of time is clearly important.

12. (A) NO CHANGE

    (B) has suppressed

    (C) suppresses

    (D) are suppressing

The subject of the sentence is *light,* not *screens,* which is part of a participial phrase. (Don't worry about the grammar terminology. Just know that the subject is *light*). Because the subject is singular, it pairs with the singular verb *suppresses.* Choices (B) and (C) are singular, but the simple present tense (Choice [C]) is best for an ongoing action. Question type: subject-verb agreement, verb tense.

13. (A) NO CHANGE

    (B) he or she may become more alert

    (C) you may become more alert

    (D) more alert occurs

Take a look at the first part of this sentence. *A person* is a singular, third-person expression. (*Third person* is the grammatical term for talking about someone.) The pronoun *they* in the original is plural, so it doesn't match *a person.* Choice (B) substitutes the singular pronouns *he or she* and is the correct answer. The pronoun *you,* by the way, may be either singular or plural. The problem with Choice (C) is that *you* is *second person* (talking to someone) and therefore not a proper match for the third-person reference to *a person.* Choice (D) is an attempt to avoid the pronoun problem, but it isn't Standard English. Question type: pronoun agreement.

14. How should the underlined sentences be combined?

    (A) Sleep deprivation is a problem; sleep deprivation has been linked to a number of health issues, such as obesity, high blood pressure, irregular heartbeat, cancer, and diabetes.

    (B) Sleep deprivation is a problem, and sleep deprivation has been linked to a number of health issues, such as obesity, high blood pressure, irregular heartbeat, cancer, and diabetes.

    (C) Sleep deprivation, a problem, which has been linked to a number of health issues, such as obesity, high blood pressure, irregular heartbeat, cancer, and diabetes.

    (D) Sleep deprivation is a problem that has been linked to a number of health issues, such as obesity, high blood pressure, irregular heartbeat, cancer, and diabetes.

Choices (A) and (B) create grammatically correct sentences, but both repeat *sleep deprivation.* Concise writing is generally better. Choice (C) eliminates the repetition, but it isn't a complete sentence. Choice (D), the best answer, solves the repetition problem and creates a complete sentence. Question type: concise writing, complete sentences.

15. (A) NO CHANGE

    (B) result from

    (C) are what results when there is

    (D) result when there is

Short, sweet, and complete — these are the qualities you want in writing, and Choice (B) provides them. Question type: concise writing.

16. (A) NO CHANGE

    (B) who were between 25 and 35

    (C) aged younger than 25

    (D) aged 25 to 35

This question is easy if you look at the chart carefully and stick to the correct column. The last column on the right reports the number of drivers who reported falling asleep while behind the wheel: 7.2 percent of drivers aged 25 to 35, compared to 4.5 percent of drivers aged 18 to 25. Okay, now you know that Choices (A) and (C) are inaccurate. Both Choices (B) and (D) correct the error, but Choice (D) is phrased more concisely and is thus the better answer. Question type: interpretation of visual evidence, concise style.

17. (A) NO CHANGE

    (B) agitating

    (C) disturbing

    (D) moving

The thought that so many drivers are snoozing at 40 miles an hour (or any speed!) would certainly keep anyone up at night, so it's *disturbing*. Question type: vocabulary in context.

18. (A) NO CHANGE

    (B) Research subjects who slept after learning a new task retained

    (C) Research subjects, who slept after learning a new task retained

    (D) After learning a new task and sleeping, research subjects

Not all *research subjects retained* knowledge, only those *who slept after learning a new task*. The description *who slept after learning a new task* is essential to your understanding of the sentence and shouldn't be surrounded by commas so Choice (B) is correct. Question type: punctuation of essential/nonessential elements.

19. Which of the following change, if any, should be made to the second paragraph of the passage?

    (A) NO CHANGE

    (B) Make this the first paragraph.

    (C) Add information on the number of traffic accidents not caused by sleep problems.

    (D) Divide it into two paragraphs, with the second beginning "According to the National Institutes of Health . . ."

The first paragraph of the original discusses one cause of sleep problems (too much screen time). The third paragraph returns to the topic of causes. In between is a paragraph about the consequences of sleep deprivation. The logical flow improves when you place paragraphs one and three next to each other. Choice (B) does so by making this paragraph the beginning of the passage. Question type: structure and logic.

20. (A) NO CHANGE

    (B) another one

    (C) one

    (D) an additional one

The first sentence of the paragraph refers to *many factors*. Because no *factor* is cited, *another* makes little sense. *One* (Choice [C]), on the other hand, simply introduces the concept of *apnea*. Question type: logic.

21. (A) NO CHANGE

    (B) fluctuate

    (C) adapt

    (D) reorganize

If you were inserting a word into the sentence to replace *swing,* you might choose *change,* because here you need a general word that allows for different times of day, days of the week, and number of hours. *Swing* involves movement and change, but it works better for physical motion. Choice (B), *fluctuate,* is a synonym for *change* and is the answer you seek. Question type: vocabulary in context.

22. (A) NO CHANGE

    (B) Regardless, you should sleep an adequate amount of time.

    (C) Either way, sleeping an adequate amount of time is clearly important.

    (D) Sleeping an adequate amount of time, either way, is shown to be important.

In Standard English, *irregardless* is always wrong. You can substitute *regardless,* as Choice (B) does, but then you have another problem — an unjustified shift to the second-person pronoun *you.* Choice (D) includes an unnecessary passive verb *(is shown to be).* Choice (C) is correct, substituting *either way* for *irregardless* and staying in third person. Question type: word choice.

Passage III

Would you like to visit Spain? How do you feel about time-travel to the 16th century? In this passage, you enter the land of Miguel de Cervantes.

On the stage, the actor bowed his head. The setting was a prison cell. [23] The actor began to tell his fellow inmates a story. The story was about a man, a man from the region of La Mancha, Spain. Soon the set [24] malformed into a country inn and the character, Don Quixote, came to life.

Don Quixote is the central figure in *Man of La Mancha,* a Broadway play. The character is based on the novel *Don Quixote,* written by Miguel de Cervantes in the 16th century. The novel is loosely based on Cervantes' life story. [25] Having been born in 1547 in Alcala de Henares, a small city near Madrid, Cervantes grew up in poverty. Little is known of Cervantes' education, though some say he attended the University of Salamanca. Around 1570 Cervantes enlisted in the Spanish navy and [26] soon after was wounded in the Battle of Lepanto. In his autobiography, Cervantes wrote that he "had lost the movement of the left hand for the glory of the right," a pun based on the fact that [27] Cervantes he believed that he was fighting for what was right. He added, "If my wounds have no beauty . . . they are, at least, honorable in the estimation of those who know where they were received, for the soldier shows to greater advantage dead in battle than alive in flight."

After Lepanto, Cervantes [28] fought battles and was captured by pirates and taken to Algiers, where he was enslaved for five years. He was freed after ransom was paid, and he [29] returned to Spain and devoting much of his time to writing while he worked as an accountant and tax collector. He died in 1616; his novels and plays were only moderately successful. [30]

Today Miguel de Cervantes is recognized as one of the first great novelists. *Don Quixote,* [31] noted a masterpiece, has inspired generations of writers and many modern reinterpretations, such as Broadway's *Man of La Mancha*. The title character is a country gentleman obsessed with the age of chivalry. He puts on rusty armor, mounts a broken-down old horse, [32] and riding off in search of adventure with a peasant, Sancho Panza, as his squire. Don Quixote lives in a world of illusion, seeing windmills as murderous giants and a shaving basin as a gold helmet. Cervantes intended his novel as a satire of chivalric romances, a style of writing popular in his time. [33] For centuries, *Don Quixote* has been a symbol of the human need for idealistic heroes, willing to risk their lives to do what is right.

23. How should the underlined sentences best be combined?

   (A) The actor began to tell his fellow inmates a story about a man from La Mancha, Spain.

   (B) The actor began to tell his fellow inmates a story, which was about a man, and the man from the region of La Mancha, Spain.

   (C) Telling his fellow inmates a story, the actor spoke about a man who was from the region of La Mancha, Spain.

   (D) The actor began to tell his fellow inmates a story, that was about a man, from the region of La Mancha, Spain.

The first three choices are correct, but because Choice (A) is the most concise, it's the correct answer. Choice (D) has punctuation problems, throwing in commas where they aren't needed. Question type: concise writing.

24. (A) NO CHANGE

   (B) transformed

   (C) distorted

   (D) redesigned

The set changed completely, or *transformed*, from a jail cell to a country inn, so Choice (B) is correct. The original word, *malformed*, refers to something *badly shaped*, as does Choice (C), *distorted*. Neither meaning is justified by the context. Choice (D) fails because the set isn't being *redesigned* during the show. The design process took place before the play began. Question type: vocabulary in context.

25. (A) NO CHANGE

   (B) Being born

   (C) Born

   (D) He was born

The introductory verb form, a *participle*, gives you information about Cervantes. The simple participle, *born*, is better than *having been born* or *being born*. The more complicated forms imply a time line *(Having sealed the envelope, Kerinna couldn't insert the photo I just gave her)* or a cause-and-effect relationship between the statements in the sentence *(Being forgetful, Kerinna relied on her planner to keep track of her many appointments)*. You don't need either situation here, because the events of Cervantes' youth (birth and growing up in poverty) are simply listed. The order is understood (how can you grow up before you're born?), and one event didn't cause the other. Go for Choice (C), the correct answer. Question type: verb tense.

26. (A) NO CHANGE

    (B) soon after he had enlisted

    (C) more time went by when he

    (D) after

The original phrase establishes the order of events clearly and concisely. No change is needed, so Choice (A) is the answer. Question type: concise writing.

27. (A) NO CHANGE

    (B) Cervantes believed that

    (C) Cervantes, what he believed was that

    (D) Delete the entire underlined expression.

The original is faulty because the pronoun *he* should replace the noun *Cervantes,* not sit next to it in the sentence. Doubling up isn't necessary. Choices (B) and (D) both solve the problem. Dropping the whole expression, though, changes the meaning — something you shouldn't do on the SAT. *Cervantes believed* is important information, because those he fought may have had an entirely different view of the situation. Choice (B) is correct. Question type: pronoun use.

28. (A) NO CHANGE

    (B) was fighting battles

    (C) went on to battles, where he fought

    (D) fought other battles

The passage says that Cervantes fought in the Battle of Lepanto, but the statement that he *fought battles* implies a new activity. Add *other,* as in Choice (D), and the situation becomes clear. Question type: logic.

29. (A) NO CHANGE

    (B) returning to Spain and devoting much of his time

    (C) returned to Spain where he was devoting much of his time

    (D) returned to Spain and devoted much of his time

When you join two elements of a sentence with the conjunction *and,* they must have the same grammatical identity. The original links *returned* and *devoting.* Do you hear the mismatch? Change *devoting* to *devoted,* as Choice (D) does, and you've solved the problem. Are you wondering why you can't change *returned* to *returning,* as Choice (B) offers? The new version of an underlined portion of the sentence must fit smoothly with everything else in the sentence. *He returning* doesn't work as a subject-verb pair. Question type: parallelism.

30. Which of the following changes would improve the third paragraph of the passage?

    (A) Delete references to Cervantes' success as a writer.

    (B) Add information about Cervantes' writing.

    (C) Include more details about the ransom.

    (D) Describe Cervantes' work as an accountant and tax collector.

The passage as a whole discusses Cervantes' life, but he is worthy of attention because of his career as a writer. The third paragraph gives very little information beyond the fact that Cervantes was "only moderately successful." Choice (B) is the best answer. Question type: evidence.

31. (A) NO CHANGE

    (B) regarded

    (C) seen

    (D) deemed

The concept you need here is *judged* or *considered.* Those aren't answer choices, but a synonym, *deemed* is, so Choice (D) is your answer. Did you fall for Choices (B) or (C)? Those words include the right idea, but they need the word *as (regarded as, seen as)* to work. Question type: vocabulary in context.

32. (A) NO CHANGE

    (B) he rides

    (C) and he rides

    (D) and rides

When a sentence contains a list, everything on the list must match. The three verbs in the original *(puts, mounts, riding)* don't match, so *riding* has to go. You don't want a subject for the third verb, because they're all paired with the initial *he.* If you stick another *he* in front of *rides,* your list is *he puts, mounts, he rides* — not a match! The answer is Choice (D). Question type: parallelism.

33. (A) NO CHANGE

    (B) For centuries, though, *Don Quixote*

    (C) *Don Quixote* for centuries,

    (D) Lasting for centuries *Don Quixote*

To keep the chain of logic strong, you need to guide the reader to see the contrast between Cervantes' intention and the actual effect of his novel. The word *though* signals a change in direction (in this case, from intention to effect). The answer is Choice (B). Question type: logic.

Passage IV

One more practice set for you, if you're still awake after working through the previous three! Try your hand at this passage.

Circles show the range of various missiles based in Cuba

Source: JFK Library

On October 16, 1962, the United States Secretary of State informed President John F. Kennedy that American spy planes had discovered a construction site in Cuba. Analysts determined that it was a base to launch long-range nuclear missiles capable [34] <u>of reaching all of the United States</u>, much of South America, and most of Canada. [35] <u>Cuba a communist country about 90 miles from the southern tip of Florida was</u> an ally of the Soviet Union. [36]

For one week the President and his advisors debated several [37] <u>possible potential strategies</u>. The U.S. [38] <u>could invade Cuba, bomb the missile bases, establishing a naval blockade around the island, or deal</u> with the Soviet Union diplomatically. Within a few days, aerial photographs showed more missile launching sites, with 16 to 32 missiles in place.

Finally, Kennedy called Nikita Khrushchev, the Soviet leader, to tell him that the United States was [39] <u>adjoining</u> Cuba with warships, creating a ring around the island. He told Khrushchev, [40] <u>"I have not assumed that you or any other sane man would, in this nuclear</u>

age, deliberately plunge the world into war, which it is crystal clear no country could win and which could only result in catastrophic consequences to the whole world, including the aggressor." Kennedy informed the American public on October 22nd of the missiles and the United States' demand that they be [41] stripped. The next day, Soviet submarines moved toward Cuba, but most ships carrying building material for the bases stopped en route. One ship, an oil tanker, continued its journey.

The world waited. What if a Soviet ship challenged the blockade and fired on an American vessel? Would full-scale war break out? As Kennedy noted in his conversation with Khrushchev, no one [42] could of won a nuclear war. No ships fired, but in Cuba construction work continued. At least some of the missiles were launch-ready. On October 27, Robert Kennedy, the Attorney-General and brother of the President, met secretly with the Soviet ambassador. [43] They reached an agreement, the United States promised not to invade Cuba, and the Soviet Union agreed to remove its missiles from Cuba. The U.S. agreed to remove some of its missiles from Turkey, a country close to the Soviet Union.

The blockade was lifted, and the world breathed a sigh of relief. Nuclear war had been averted. In June 1963, Kennedy referred to the [44] crisis, saying, "In the final analysis, our most basic common link is that we all inhabit this small planet. We all breathe the same air. We all cherish our children's future. And we are all mortal."

34. (A) NO CHANGE

(B) to reaching all of the United States

(C) of reaching most of the United States

(D) where it could reach the United States

The map shows that not all of the United States was in range of Cuban missiles. The Pacific Northwest lies beyond the edge of the largest circle. Only Choice (C) accurately reports this fact. Question type: evidence, visual element.

35. (A) NO CHANGE

(B) Cuba was a communist country about 90 miles from the southern tip of Florida was

(C) Cuba a communist country about 90 miles from the southern tip of Florida, was

(D) Cuba, a communist country about 90 miles from the southern tip of Florida, was

The information that Cuba is *a communist country about 90 miles from the southern tip of Florida* is interesting, but it's not essential. In grammar terms, an *essential* element identifies what it describes. You already know which country you're talking about: Cuba. *Nonessential* elements should be set off from the rest of the sentence by commas, as you see in Choice (D). Question type: punctuation of essential/nonessential elements.

36. Which of the following would be the best addition to the first paragraph?

(A) Explain that the Soviet Union was then a communist superpower engaged in a cold war with the United States.

(B) Identify John Kennedy's political party.

(C) Give the name of the Secretary of State.

(D) Describe how a nuclear missile works.

The passage as a whole describes a clash of two nations, the United States and the Soviet Union. Information about the relationship between these nations fits well with the overall meaning of the passage. It's especially well suited to the first paragraph, which sets up the basis of the dispute. None of the other information is as important. Political parties aren't discussed, nor is the focus on the Secretary of State (McGeorge Bundy, in case you're interested). The inner workings of a nuclear missile don't matter; only the effect of a missile strike is relevant. Choice (A) is the best answer. Question type: logic, evidence.

37. (A) NO CHANGE

    (B) potential strategies

    (C) possible potential strategy

    (D) possible strategy

    Possible and *potential* are synonyms, so you don't need both. The word *several* indicates that you need *strategies* (plural), not *strategy* (singular). Choice (B) works best. Question type: repetition, concise writing, agreement.

38. (A) NO CHANGE

    (B) could invade Cuba, bombing the missile bases, establishing a naval blockade around the island, or deal

    (C) could invade Cuba, bomb the missile bases, establish a naval blockade around the island, or deal

    (D) invading Cuba, bombing the missile bases, establishing a naval blockade around the island, or dealing

    When you see a list, think about *parallelism*, the English-teacher term for balance. The original list of verbs *(invade, bomb, establishing, deal)* is faulty. *Establishing* doesn't fit. Change that verb to *establish*, as in Choice (C), and you're fine. Did you select Choice (D)? The list matches, but changing everything to the *-ing* form creates another problem, because then the sentence has no subject-verb pair. Question type: parallelism, complete sentences.

39. (A) NO CHANGE

    (B) surrounding

    (C) encasing

    (D) enclosing

    The blockade is a *ring*, so *surrounding*, Choice (B), is the word you want. *Adjoining* (next to, bordering on) doesn't work. *Encasing* and *enclosing* are better for physical objects that are completely covered. Question type: vocabulary in context.

40. (A) NO CHANGE

    (B) that, "he had not

    (C) that he "have not

    (D) he "have not

    The original sentence is correct. The quotation from Kennedy is introduced by a *speaker tag* (a label identifying the speaker). After the speaker tag, you have a comma and then the opening quotation marks, which enclose Kennedy's words. *That* sometimes introduces a quotation, and Choice (B) may have been tempted you. However, the pronoun *he* is unclear in Choice (B), because two men, Kennedy and Khrushchev, are potential antecedents. Question type: punctuation with quotation marks.

41. (A) NO CHANGE

    (B) ended

    (C) concluded

    (D) dismantled

The meaning you want is "taken apart," a fine definition of *dismantled,* Choice (D). Question type: vocabulary in context.

42. (A) NO CHANGE

    (B) could have won

    (C) could be winning

    (D) couldn't win

The contraction *could've* sounds like *could of,* but *could of* isn't Standard English. Choice (B) expands the contraction *could've* to the proper words, *could have,* and is the correct answer. Question type: word choice.

43. (A) NO CHANGE

    (B) They reached an agreement; the United States promised not to invade Cuba, and

    (C) Reaching an agreement where the United States promised not to invade Cuba, and

    (D) They reached an agreement. The United States promised not to invade Cuba,

The original is a run-on, with one complete sentence tacked onto another with just a comma. To solve the problem, change the comma to a semicolon. Did Choice (D) catch your eye? That selection illustrates the importance of reading carefully. The period after *agreement* solves one problem, but the deletion of *and* from the end creates another run-on. Choice (B) is the correct answer. Question type: complete sentences.

44. (A) NO CHANGE

    (B) crisis, and he said

    (C) crisis, when he was saying

    (D) crisis, and what he said was

The original is concise and correct. No changes needed! Choice (A) is your answer. Question type: concise writing.

Here's looking at *Eu, Anthro*

The *eu* family has nothing in common with *ew,* the sound you make when a bug crawls up your sleeve. *Eu* is a Greek prefix that means *good* or *pleasant.* Easy-listening tunes are *euphonious* (they sound good) and *eulogies* are speeches in which all (and only) good things are said about someone who died. A *euphemism* is a more pleasant term that may substitute for a word you don't like to say, such as the substitution of *restroom* for *toilet.*

The anthros are the family of man (and woman). An *anthropologist* studies human behavior and society, but a *misanthrope* hates people. If you dress your dog in little dresses (pause for a shudder and a call to the humane society), you're guilty of *anthropomorphism* — projecting human qualities onto nonhumans.

Chapter 7

Writing Your Way to a High Score: The Essay

The SAT features only one question that requires you to write something in your very own words — the essay — and that question is optional. You can add 50 minutes to the end of your SAT morning by writing the essay, which is the last section of the exam, or you can go home. By the way, your words will probably flow from a No. 2 pencil onto paper. The College Board has begun computer-based testing in only a *miniscule* (extremely small) number of testing sites, though they've promised more in the future. Assume you're working without a screen or keyboard unless you've been granted accommodations because you have a documented learning disability, such as *dysgraphia,* the term for difficulty in producing readable penmanship. (For more information on accommodations, turn to Chapter 2.) In this chapter, you find information on the standard SAT essay format and the best approach to this section, along with a sample question and answers.

The Write Thing? Deciding Whether to Tackle the Essay

Hamlet famously asked, "To be or not to be?" The SAT presents you with a different question: "To write or not to write?" Before you answer, take a moment to become familiar with the task you face. Read through this chapter, and then *reflect on* (think about) yourself. Do you have the *stamina* (energy, endurance) to undertake an extra 50 minutes of work after you've been in the testing room for more than three hours already? If you droop in the middle of an hour of homework, the essay is probably not for you. Also think about your *prior* (earlier) work on ordinary tests. If you generally do well on in-class writing assignments, you should probably take a crack at the SAT essay. If you freeze when you're given a timed essay, consider opting out.

Check with your English teacher, if you have one who knows you fairly well, for advice. Look through essays you wrote in the past. The most *relevant* (appropriate to the situation) are essays about literature, but history essays in which you analyzed a historical document or speech are also good material. Read the teacher's comments. Have you improved in the areas your teacher noted? If you have time, rewrite an old piece and ask a friendly teacher to read it. No matter how busy, most teachers respect students who are trying to improve and will squeeze out enough time to read your work. If the teacher tells you that you've done a good job, go for the SAT essay.

The colleges you intend to apply to should also factor into your decision on whether to write the essay. Will they look at your essay score or not? Many admissions officers saw the pre-2016 SAT essay as a waste of time. The "old" SAT essay required test-takers simply to take a position on a random topic. Some SAT-takers wrote and memorized essays in advance, filled with "evidence" they'd made up to fit their views, and then transcribed the previously written work onto the answer sheet. The graders were not permitted to downgrade the essay score because of obvious factual errors. The current essay section may be more popular with admissions offices because it is passage-based. The 2016 version of the essay is *rigorous* (thorough and difficult). Colleges that ignored the old essay may be eager to see your response to the new version.

Bottom line: Check with the college(s) on your list about essay preferences.

Decoding the Prompt

Every essay on the SAT has the same basic *prompt,* or question, which you can study in advance. The prompt is split into two parts, one before and one after a passage that is about 650 to 750 words long. The passage is always an opinion piece, making an argument for a particular point of view on a real-life situation.

Before the passage, you see a box with the following information, with the real name of the writer or a gender-appropriate pronoun taking the place of "Author."

As you read the passage, consider how Author uses

- Evidence such as facts or examples to support Author's ideas

- Logic to develop the argument and link claims and supporting evidence

- Style choices — appeals to emotion, figurative language, word choice, and so forth — to add to the persuasive power of the argument

The prompt mentions a couple of possible writing techniques, which vary from passage to passage. Certainly, your first task is to think about the techniques cited in the prompt, but use those only as a starting point. If you notice a technique that isn't listed, go for it! (Check out the next section, "Identifying Writing Techniques," for elements of style you may see.)

Following the passage is another box for the prompt with the author's name or a pronoun replacing "Author." In the blank, you'll see a brief statement summarizing the author's main idea:

Write an essay in which you explain how Author constructs an argument to persuade the reader that _____. In your essay, discuss how Author uses one or more of the elements of style listed above, or other elements, to strengthen the logic and persuasiveness of Author's argument. Focus on the most important features of the passage. Do not explain whether you agree or disagree with Author's ideas. Instead, concentrate on how Author builds a persuasive case.

This two-part prompt looks complicated, but it's not. Your job is to analyze the author's argument and, most important, to discuss the writing techniques the author employs to convince readers of his or her point of view. In other words, you have to relate content to style — *what* the author says, *how* the author says it, and *why* saying it that way is effective. The prompt gives you the *what* (the main idea in the second box). The prompt also hints at the *how* (the elements of style listed in the first box). You have to *amplify* (add to) the *how* and then figure out the *why*. (The next section, "Identifying Writing Techniques," helps you with the *how* and *why*.)

Because you're learning everything about the prompt now, don't waste time reading it carefully during the exam. Glance briefly at the style points in the first box and the main idea in the second box. Take note of those two *variables* (things that change) and skip the rest of the question. You know it already!

Identifying Writing Techniques

Every passage is different, but many techniques appear frequently when the author makes an argument. Here are several things to look for when you read the SAT essay passage.

Appeals to logic, authority, and emotion

Ancient Greeks, who valued the art of persuasion, named three general strategies for argument:

- **Logos** is an appeal to logic or reason. Factual evidence and examples may be part of logos. Perhaps the writer cites statistics on the rate of car crashes when the speed limit is lowered and refers to accident rates in neighboring areas with different traffic laws.

- **Ethos** relies on the character and qualifications of the writer (perhaps a highway patrol officer who regularly handled crash sites) or, in some cases, quotations from experts (perhaps urban planners). Look for references to authorities on the subject if you suspect that the writer is relying on *ethos* to make a point.

- **Pathos** hits the emotions. The writer may present a story about one particular accident victim, hoping to tug the readers' heartstrings.

You can probably identify at least one in the passage you're assigned, and you may see two or even three in different parts of the reading.

Diction and tone

Diction, or word choice, may have a huge effect on the readers' reaction. Consider the difference between "privacy" and "loneliness" in an essay about solitude. One of those words (privacy) creates a positive impression, and the other (loneliness) a negative.

Tone is influenced by all the words in the passage as well as the way they're put together (*syntax,* in English-teacher terminology). Sophisticated vocabulary and sentence structure tells you that the writer sees the reader as educated and aware; simpler vocabulary and shorter, more straightforward sentences may create a "just us folks" impression of innocence. Meaning contributes to tone also. If the writer says one thing, knowing that the reader receives the opposite impression, the tone may be *sarcastic* or *mocking*. Check for tone by "hearing" the passage in your mind.

As you read, underline a few words or sentences that are typical of the passage as a whole; circle any words that seem to break the pattern. You may find that the exceptional words highlight significant points or emphasize a particular emotion. In your essay, mention both the dominant style and any variations, explaining the effect of each.

Organization

A good writer always has a plan to organize the arguments — and SAT essay passages come from good writers. Your job is to figure out the underlying structure, or organizing principle, for the material. Check these possibilities, both for the passage as a whole and for individual paragraphs within the passage:

- **Comparison:** In an argument about lowering the speed limit, you may see accident rates in Germany compared to those in the United States, a paragraph describing differing driving patterns or laws, and so forth.

- **Cause and effect:** You may find a paragraph (or an entire passage) about the consequences of a particular action. Continuing with the speed limit example from the preceding bullet point, you would see that a law was passed changing the speed limit from 65 to 55 miles per hour, and statistics on the decrease in traffic fatalities.

- **Observations and conclusions:** This pattern resembles a mosaic. You read seemingly random facts that gradually forge a chain of logic drawing the reader to the writer's point of view.

- **Chronological order:** The author describes series of events, in order, perhaps *extrapolating* (extending through logic) into the future. This organizational tactic may be coupled with cause and effect or observations and conclusions.

- **Concession and reply:** This tactic appears when the author assumes that the reader doesn't agree with the argument. Useful in written arguments (not to mention personal quarrels), this writing technique acknowledges and responds to the opposing point of view. Using the speed-limit example mentioned in the first bullet point, the author may concede that driver inattention has more influence on the accident rate than speed limits do. Then the writer will go on to argue that lower speed limits save *some* lives and are therefore still desirable.

As you read, try to *discern* (detect, perceive) the organizing principle of the passage.

Other techniques

Keep your eyes out for these style points, which show up often in arguments:

- **Repetition:** Normally, writers avoid repetition. When you see repetition of words or a set of strikingly similar expressions, figure out what the writer is emphasizing. For example, a section of the Declaration of Independence lists the actions of King George III that the colonists object to. The writers use the expression "he has" more than 20 times. The result resembles a criminal *indictment* (formal charge of wrongdoing). Each time you read "he has," the writer's case becomes stronger.

- **Parallel structure:** Writing teachers and editors look for variety in sentence length and pattern. However, sometimes a string of similar elements makes an appearance. When you see a list within a sentence or paragraph, the items on the list have equal weight and importance. The same principle holds true for comparisons.

> ✔ **Figurative language:** Imaginative comparisons, even in nonfiction passages, add depth to the writer's arguments. In his magnificent "I Have a Dream" speech, Martin Luther King Jr. refers to "the bank of justice" and a check returned from the bank marked "insufficient funds" to show the unmet demands for equal rights. These *metaphors* (comparisons made without the words *like* or *as*) relate King's argument for equality to a situation everyone with a bank account can understand.

If you run across any of these techniques, identify them in your essay and analyze their impact on the reader.

Preparing, Writing, and Proofing the Essay

No matter how pressed for time you feel, your score will rise if you spend a few minutes (about 5 to 7) preparing before you write the essay and more minutes (5 to 6) proofreading your work after you've written it. All the minutes in between are for the writing itself.

Don't even think about touching the answer sheet until you have all your thoughts in order. The SAT test booklet is a fine spot for prewriting. Remember, however, that nothing you write on the test booklet counts toward your essay. Only the answer sheet is graded.

Here's more detail on how to approach the essay:

1. **Read the passage, annotating as you go.**

   The *annotations* (notes or marks) should be very brief — an important feature underlined or circled, a word or abbreviation in the margin (for example, "sent struc" where you notice something interesting about *sentence structure* or "wc" when *word choice* matters).

2. **Be sure you understand the author's argument.**

   The second part of the prompt summarizes the author's position very briefly. Let that statement guide you, but before you write, expand the idea. Suppose the prompt says that the author favors lower speed limits, for example. Ask yourself *why* or *in what way.* The fuller version may be that the author favors lower speed limits on roads also used by cyclists and pedestrians or in limited-visibility conditions because accidents are more likely in those situations. If you grasp exactly what the writer believes, you have a better chance of understanding how the writer tries to convince the reader.

3. **Quickly decide which points are most important.**

   With a strict time limit, you may not have time to write about everything you notice. Don't agonize. Select the most relevant points and move to the next step.

4. **Choose a structure.**

   The simplest structure follows the passage; you discuss the writing techniques you see in the passage in the order in which they appear, first analyzing something in paragraph one, then something in paragraph two, and so on. A little more complicated but also a more mature approach is to group similar elements. You may have a paragraph about diction, for instance, analyzing the author's choice of words throughout the passage. Next up, perhaps, is a paragraph about the author's reliance on expert opinions *conveyed* (communicated) through quotations.

5. **Make an outline.**

   You don't have time for a formal outline, complete with roman numerals and fancy indentations. Jot down the points you will make and letter them *A, B, C,* and so on. Now you know what comes first, what's second, and so on.

6. **Write the essay.**

Sounds easy, right? It isn't. But as one sneaker company says, "Just do it." As you write, take care to analyze, not just list. The graders give you little credit for saying that similes appear in paragraphs two, four, and eight. They give you much more credit for explaining the effect of those similes on the reader. Also, avoid general statements such as "This essay contains a lot of similes." Instead, quote the similes as you discuss them. Every point you make about the passage should be firmly attached to the text of the passage, either through a quotation or a specific reference (for example, "the anecdote about the snake in paragraph two . . .").

7. **Proofread.**

Look for misspelled words, awkward sentences, grammar mistakes, repetition, and the like. Correct your mistakes by crossing them out *neatly* (one line is enough!) and inserting the proper word or punctuation.

When you proofread, you may think of a great addition to your essay. With limited space and time, you can't rewrite. So place your new idea at the end. Label it "insert A." Then make a note ("see insert A") at the spot in the essay where this point logically belongs.

Understanding Your Essay Scores

The SAT pays desperate-for-cash or have-no-life English teachers (some fall into both categories) to score the essays. The graders used to sit in windowless rooms, scoring essays until their eyeballs went on strike. Now modern technology allows them to sit in their very own living rooms, where their eyeballs still fry. An image of each essay is also posted on the web, where colleges that you apply to can view it, warts and all (a reason it's so important to write neatly).

The score for the SAT essay is *holistic* (meaning that it's seen as one item in its entirety; it isn't broken into parts). Therefore, the graders don't award a tenth of a point for grammar, a half-point for organization, and so on. They just read the essay and enter numbers based on the whole thing.

So what do the essay graders look for as they score your essay? The College Board, as of this moment, is still fine-tuning the essay question. Current plans call for two readers working independently of each other. Most likely, a third "super-reader" with special training will also read your work if scores from the first two readers disagree by more than one point. Both teachers, the College Board says, will award 1 to 4 points in three categories:

- ✔ **Reading:** Comprehending the main idea of the passage, noting details and their relationship to the main idea, grasping the structure of the passage

- ✔ **Analysis:** Evaluating the author's use of evidence, logic, and persuasive techniques

- ✔ **Writing:** Supporting your statements in a well-organized essay that employs evidence (quotations or paraphrased examples) and shows mature writing style (varied sentence patterns, consistent tone, grammatically correct sentences) and higher level vocabulary

The College Board's *criteria* (standards) in the preceding list are quite broad. Here are more details to help you understand what SAT-graders are looking for:

- ✔ **Has the test-taker understood the subtleties of the passage?** Most people get the main idea, but to rise to the top of the scoring chart, you have to dig into the small stuff.

Graders look for at least three or four specific points about the author's argument. Check for exceptions to the principle the author argues for. Note the time frame (in modern society, in the last two years, looking to the future, and so forth). Examine the context: what special situation(s) the author describes (within a family, worldwide, and everything in between; person-to-person or on social media, and the like). If the passage expresses a disagreement, who takes each point of view, and where does the author's *stance* (position) fall?

✔ **Does the test-taker understand the elements of style the author employs?** The first prompt box lists a couple of possible things to consider, perhaps word choice or parallel structure. If you can legitimately move beyond the list in the prompt, you're on your way to a better score. (The section "Identifying Writing Techniques," earlier in this chapter, tells you what to look for.) Most of the time, you should be able to identify and discuss three or four elements of style. True, sometimes you have two dominant techniques and sometimes five. If you find yourself straying from the three-four range, though, check whether you've omitted something important or spread yourself too thin.

✔ **Has the test-taker analyzed how each element of style contributes to meaning?** They don't want a list; they want an analysis. If you've explained the effect on the reader of an anecdote or a metaphor, you're doing well. For example, if the author compares a happy memory to a diamond, you know that the memory is beautiful, precious, and durable. A comparison to a fluffy cloud suggests beauty, too, but this time the author has added *transience* (impermanence) and haziness. One simile tells you that the memory will never go away, and the other suggests that it probably will drift from consciousness. Making points like these raises the level of your essay.

✔ **Is the essay organized? Does it move logically from one idea to the next?** Great SAT essays are like guided tours; readers never have to wonder where they are or how they got there. One paragraph leads clearly to the next. A middle-of-the-road essay has a dead end or a wrong turn in it. A poor essay leaves readers wandering around without a clue. One important element, transitions, strengthens the logical chain. If you begin a paragraph with *however, nevertheless,* or a similar word, you signal an exception to the point you just made. *Also, then, moreover,* and the like tell the reader that you're building on an idea you just expressed. Be sure that you provide these helpful markers for your graders.

✔ **Is the vocabulary appropriate?** Academic writing is formal, so stay away from slang words. You don't need to insert a dictionary into your essay, but your word choice should show some variety, and at least some of the words need to have more than one syllable.

Be careful to use only words that you're comfortable with. Every English teacher groans when a student-writer selects a word from a vocabulary list or thesaurus without understanding more than its surface meaning. For example, *beneficial* and *favorable* are synonyms, but you can hold a *favorable opinion of a project* but not a *beneficial opinion.* If you're not sure, go with a simpler expression (*a good opinion,* perhaps).

✔ **Is the writing fluent, with varied sentence structure?** An excellent essay matches sentence structure and meaning. Less important ideas, for example, show up in subordinate clauses or *verbals* (verb forms used as descriptions), and main ideas appear in independent clauses. An acceptable but unremarkable essay strays only occasionally from the usual subject-verb-object pattern. In a poor essay, the sentences sound short and choppy.

✔ **Is the writing grammatical, with good spelling and punctuation?** The idea here is simple: Follow the rules of Standard English, and your score rises. The better essays have some mistakes, but not enough to make a lasting impression on the reader. Weaker essays would draw a lot of red ink from the graders' pens, if they actually corrected your work. (If grammar isn't your *forte,* or strong point, turn to Chapter 5 for help.)

The essay will probably evolve in the next couple of years as the College Board receives feedback from graders, test-takers, and college admissions officers. The best preparation for this moving target is to pay attention to the material you read in school or for pleasure and to *hone* (sharpen) your own essay-writing skills as you do your homework and school exams. Also, check www.dummies.com/go/sat for updates.

No one can write a perfect essay — not even with unlimited time, and certainly not in the pressurized atmosphere of a high-stakes exam. The graders understand this fact. They're looking for a good first draft, evidence of a thoughtful and fairly accomplished student writer, not the product of a Nobel Prize for Literature candidate. Relax and concentrate on showing your best reading and writing ability. Don't worry about the scores until they arrive, and maybe not even then!

Examining a Sample Essay Question

Reconnaissance (advance scouting) is always a good idea before facing an enemy. The SAT essay isn't exactly an enemy, but checking out a sample question and answer gives you an idea of what you're up against. In this section, you find a sample essay question along with a grid to score the response. You also see examples of a poor, medium, and great answer, so you have a sense of how the graders evaluate a response. If you're feeling energetic, go ahead and write your own essay. Don't peek at the answers and explanations until you're finished. If you want to conserve your strength, simply read the question along with the answers and analysis. When you're ready for practice, turn to Chapter 8.

The question

As you read the passage, consider how Keith Sawyer uses

- Evidence such as facts or examples to support his ideas
- Logic to develop the argument and link claims and supporting evidence
- Style choices — appeals to emotion, figurative language, word choice, and so forth — to add to the persuasive power of the argument

The following passage is taken from Zig Zag: The Surprising Path to Great Creativity *by Keith Sawyer (Wiley).*

Most successful creativity comes through the process you begin without knowing what the real problem is. The parameters aren't clearly specified, the goal isn't clear, and you don't even know what it would look like if you did solve the problem. It's not obvious how to apply your past experience solving other problems. And there are likely to be many different ways to approach a solution.

These grope-in-the-dark situations are the times you need creativity the most. And that's why successful creativity always starts with asking.

It's easy to see how business innovation is propelled by formulating the right question, staying open to new cues, and focusing on the right problem. But it turns out the same is true of world-class scientific creativity. "The formulation of a problem is often more essential than its solution," Albert Einstein declared. "To raise new questions, new possibilities, to regard old problems from a new angle, requires creative imagination and marks real advances in science." Einstein went on to say, "For the detective the crime is given," he concluded. "The scientist must commit his own crime as well as carry out the investigation."

If the right "crime" — the right puzzle or question — is crucial for business and scientific breakthroughs, what about breakthroughs in art or poetry or music? A great painting doesn't emerge from posing a good question — does it?

The pioneering creativity researcher Mihaly Csikszentmihalyi of the University of Chicago decided to answer that question. He and a team of fellow psychologists from the University of Chicago spent a year at the School of the Art Institute of Chicago, one of the top art schools in the United States. "How do creative works come into being?" they wanted to know. They set up an "experimental studio" in which they positioned two tables. One was empty, the other laden with a variety of objects, including a bunch of grapes, a steel gearshift, a velvet hat, a brass horn, an antique book, and a glass prism. They then recruited thirty-one student artists and instructed them to choose several items, position them any way they liked on the empty table, and draw the arrangement.

After observing the artists, Csikszentmihalyi was able to identify two distinct artistic approaches. One group took only a few minutes to select and pose the objects. They spent another couple of minutes sketching an overall composition and the rest of their time refining, shading, and adding details to the composition. Their approach was to formulate a visual problem quickly and then invest their effort in solving that problem.

The second group could not have been more different. These artists spent five or ten minutes examining the objects, turning them around to view them from all angles. After they made their choices, they often changed their minds, went back to the table, and replaced one object with another. They drew the arrangement for twenty or thirty minutes and then changed their minds again, rearranged the objects, and erased and completely redrew their sketch. After up to an hour like this, the students in this group settled on an idea and finished the drawing in five or ten minutes. Unlike the first group — which spent most of the time *solving* a visual problem — this group was *searching* for a visual problem. The research team called this a "problem-finding" creative style.

Which artists' work was more creative: that of the problem solvers or that of the problem finders? Csikszentmihalyi asked a team of five Art Institute professors to rate the creativity of each drawing. With few exceptions, the problem finders' drawings were judged far more creative than the problem solvers' — even though their exploratory process left them much less time to devote to the final image, which was all the judges (who knew nothing of the process involved) were evaluating.

The most creative artists were those who focused on asking the right question.

Six years after the students graduated, the most successful of the students had become well known in the art world, with work in leading New York galleries and even in the permanent collections of famous museums. And these successful artists were by and large the problem finders back when they were in art school. They were the artists who focused on asking the right question.

Write an essay in which you explain how Sawyer constructs an argument to persuade the reader that creativity comes from asking the right question. In your essay, discuss how Sawyer uses one or more of the elements of style listed above, or other elements, to strengthen the logic and persuasiveness of his argument. Focus on the most important features of the passage. Do not explain whether you agree or disagree with Sawyer's ideas. Instead, concentrate on how he builds a persuasive case.

The answer

Many paths lead to a good answer to this essay question. Here are some possible ideas you might mention in your essay, broken down into three categories, and some loose guidelines for awarding points. *Note:* Sample graded responses follow the general points listed here.

Reading

The essay graders check to see whether you understood everything in the passage. This passage centers on one idea, developed in several ways:

- "Formulating the right question" is crucial to creativity.

- Your "past experience" may not help you with a new problem.

- When you're confused, in a "grope-in-the-dark" situation, creativity matters most.

- The "real advances" that Einstein mentions come only when you're open to "new questions, new possibilities."

- The author states that this idea holds true for business, where he says that "it's easy to see" that innovation comes with the correct question and "staying open to new cues, and focusing on the right problem."

- The author extends the idea to science with the quotation from Einstein.

- Creativity in art also comes from "a problem-finding creative style."

Give yourself 4 points for this category if you mentioned six to seven of these items. If you hit only four or five items, give yourself 3 points. If you discussed two or three items in the bulleted list, award yourself 2 points. If all you did was restate the main idea, give yourself 1 point.

Analysis

SAT graders also want to see a good analysis of the argument in which you explain *how* the author makes his or her case. Here are some points about this passage:

- The author provides no proof for his assertions about business. His statements in that regard are untested assumptions and overall weaken the author's case.

- Appeal to ethos: The essay quotes Albert Einstein, a widely known genius who came up with startling new ideas about the nature of space and time. He shows up in a paragraph about the need for scientists to formulate questions. Einstein was a scientist, so his opinion is *authoritative* (reliable, from a trusted source).

- Appeal to logos: The art experiment is factual, explaining how the artists worked and how their creations were evaluated. The use of a factual example is classic *logos*. You can argue with opinions, but it's much harder to *contest* (fight) the results of a well-designed experiment.

- The essay structure moves logically from point to point. Right in the first paragraph, Sawyer explains the problem — which is that you often don't know what the problem actually is. Next Sawyer moves to Einstein's views on creativity and finally to the art experiment, both of which confirm that the most creative people fiddle around with the question before they seek the answer.

- The crucial point appears as a single sentence that itself is a single paragraph: "The most creative artists were those who focused on asking the right question." To add emphasis, Sawyer places that line in italics.

- Sawyer's diction is simple and straightforward; few words are above elementary-school level, though the concepts Sawyer discusses are fairly sophisticated. He speaks directly to readers with the second-person pronoun *you*. The result is a recommendation that any reader can understand and adopt.

- By mentioning "business innovation," Einstein, and art, Sawyer underlines the universality of his view of creativity.

Scoring yourself on analysis is similar to scoring your reading. Give yourself a 4 if you wrote something resembling six to seven of the points in the bulleted list or a point we didn't mention that you're sure is relevant. If you discussed only four or five points, give yourself a 3. If you hit two or three points in the bulleted list, award yourself 2 points. If your essay mentions only one idea about the author's writing style, give yourself 1 point.

Writing

This category is the toughest one to self-score, because you have to step back and examine your own work as if a stranger had written it. (If you can, show your essay to an English teacher or a friendly adult. A pair of expert eyes can evaluate your work more effectively.) You, as well as your helper, if you have one, should check these factors:

- **Structure:** Does your essay have a solid, logical structure? One possibility is to work in order from the first paragraph of the passage, where the author states the *thesis* (idea to be proved), and then move through paragraph after paragraph until you reach the end of the passage. A more mature organization of ideas might begin by stating Sawyer's views on creativity in greater detail. An analysis of *logos* and *ethos* could be grouped in paragraph two. A discussion of the Sawyer's structure, including the single-sentence paragraph, forms the main idea of the third paragraph. Finally, examples of simple diction and second-person point of view create a fourth paragraph.

- **Evidence:** Do you back up every statement you make with quotations or specific references to the passage? Count how many times you zeroed in on details. You should have at least two in every paragraph you write and maybe more.

- **Language:** Does your essay sound formal, as if a teacher were explaining the passage? If you lapsed into slang or informal word choice, your essay is weaker.

- **Mechanics:** English teachers group grammar, spelling, and punctuation in this category. As you reread, underline any sentence fragments or run-ons, misspelled words, and faulty commas or quotation marks.

Adding up points to evaluate your writing is tricky. In general, give yourself 1 point (up to a total of 4) for every category in the bulleted list in which you excelled. If you stumbled slightly in a category (say, three or four grammar or spelling mistakes), give yourself 3/4 of a point. If you feel your performance in one of these categories was poor (perhaps you drifted off topic or made seven or eight grammar errors), take only 1/2 point.

Scoring your own essay

You probably aren't a professional grader. (Lucky you! Watching grass grow is a more interesting profession.) You can, however, get a fair idea of how your essay measures up to College Board standards if you fill in this grid.

Category	Reading	Analysis	Writing
Number of Points			

Now double the number in each of the three boxes. The results are your essay reading, analysis, and writing scores.

Examining graded responses

To help you evaluate your work, here are three sample responses illustrating poor, average, and great essays.

Response 1: A "poor" essay

Keith Sawyer said, "creativity comes from asking the right question". He talked about how you don't really know what the answer is unless you ask the right question. Creative people ask the right question. If they struggle for a while sometimes.

Keith Sawyer appeals to your emotions because everyone wants to be creative. If you are in business, you want to sell products. Creativity is important in business. If you are an artist, they want to make art. Art is creative. Keith Sawyer did an experiment where artists had to use some things to make a painting. Some artists worked with a plan. Others erased again and again, like me writing an essay. The second group did better. Sawyer wrote about the experiment so you would feel what the artists felt. The example shows how you have to ask the right question.

The words in Keith Sawyer's writing are simple, mostly. He quotes Albert Einstein, who is famous for being a genius. This quote shows that Einstein agrees with Keith Sawyer. He thinks that you have to commit a crime to be creative, which is to ask the question. The word "crime" shows that it can be dangerous to be creative.

Keith Sawyer tells you to take a chance, and he uses examples (like the artists), authorities like Einstein, and simple words to convince you that "creativity comes from asking the right question."

Here are the scores for this essay:

- ✔ **Reading:** 1 point. The writer understands the main idea — that creativity comes from asking the right question — but not much else. The writer makes a couple of reading-comprehension errors. Keith Sawyer did not do the experiment at the University of Chicago; a professor named Csikszentmihalyi did. Einstein did refer to a crime, but he did not see creativity as dangerous. Instead, the "crime" is the puzzle to be solved, the question to be asked.

- ✔ **Analysis:** 1 point. The writer mentions the appeal to authority (Einstein) but doesn't explore the way that scientific authority might influence the reader. Neither does the writer discuss the way the example of the art experiment adds to Sawyer's argument. The writer also discusses the *metaphor* (imaginative comparison) of the crime but misinterprets its purpose. The quotation ("Creativity comes from asking the right question") comes from the prompt, not from the passage.

- ✔ **Writing:** 2 points. The essay could be better — much better! — but the spelling and grammar are fairly good. The sentences are complete, with the exception of "If they struggle for a while sometimes." The sentences are short and show little variety. The writer has some immature habits, such as labeling evidence ("___ shows that").

The total scores for this essay are 2 (Reading), 2 (Analysis), and 4 (Writing).

Response 2: A "medium" essay

"The most creative artists were those who focused on asking the right question." Keith Sawyer places this sentence alone in a paragraph, in different letters, to show how important the idea is. In this passage, Sawyer talks about how creative artists, business people, and scientists are creative.

First Sawyer explains the problem is what you want to find. He says that there are many ways to find a solution. "Grope in the dark" is a metaphor, so the reader connects to the experience of trying to find something without the benefit of visual clues. This connects to the idea that what you knew in the past may not help you. Sawyer makes his point broad when he mentions business. He appeals to authority, the scientist Albert Einstein to back up his idea. If a genius thinks that it is important "to raise new questions, new possibilities, to regard old problems from a new angle," then regular people should think so too. Plus, most people think of science as factual, not an opinion that you can argue about. Scientific fact becomes part of Sawyer's argument this way.

Next Keith Sawyer explains an experiment with artists at the University of Chicago. The artists who spent most of their time defining a problem by starting and then restarting to draw did better than those who made a plan and could not give up the plan. He even talks about the success of these artists after school. The group that had to make a question first did better. This example convinces the reader that questioning and creativity go hand in hand together. The experiment has a factual outcome, how successful the artists are. Again, you can't say that Sawyer's main idea is just an opinion. It was tested in a scientific way. The results were real.

The experiment takes up most of the passage, so you can see that it is really important to Sawyer's argument. He wants you to imagine you in a way that you are a problem solver. He wants you to see success for yourself. He makes the experiment real, he makes the reader understand that questioning is real and possible. Some people may think that the people in the experiment were not creating questions the way Sawyer said they were, but his explanation is believeable.

All over the passage, the evidence is found. Sawyer makes his point, and he convinces you that questions are more important than anything else.

Here are the scores for this essay:

- ✔ **Reading:** 3 points. The writer got the main idea (creativity comes from asking the right questions) and some of the smaller points about "past experience," Einstein's references to "new possibilities," and the broadening of the argument from business to science and the arts. The writer correctly interprets the experiment and its importance in the essay.

- ✔ **Analysis:** 2 points. The writer interprets the significance of the single-sentence paragraph in italics and the importance of the experiment's being described at length. The writer also understands what the quotation from Einstein adds to the argument. The discussion of "grope in the dark" is fairly well done, too.

- ✔ **Writing:** 2 points. This essay isn't very well organized, and at times the writer repeats information or ideas. The essay doesn't show mature style and includes very few quotations from the passage. However, you see few grammar mistakes.

The total scores for this essay are 6 (Reading), 4 (Analysis), and 4 (Writing).

Response 3: A "great" essay

Albert Einstein, the epitome of genius in most people's minds, said that "to raise new questions, new possibilities, to regard old problems from a new angle, requires creative imagination." Einstein's authority adds weight to Keith Sawyer's examination of the relationship between questioning and creativity. Sawyer's analysis takes into account business, science, and art, hitting the topic from several angles so that one is sure to relate to the reader's own experience.

Sawyer's discussion of business is not supported by ample evidence. He states that "business innovation is propelled by formulating the right question," but he gives no examples from marketing or the creation of a new gadget or company. This weakness in his argument, though, is more than made up for by his lengthy discussion of an experiment with art students at the University of Chicago. Faced with the chance to create something from a limited number of objects, one group make a plan and stuck to it. The more successful group, that was judged by outside experts and by success in their careers later in life, spent most of the time deciding what to create, experimenting with the creation of the "question," in Sawyer's interpretation. This factual example supports the main point and brings the reader along. The experimental design can be criticized, but not the results, and certainly not the idea that "six years after the students graduated . . . these successful artists were by and large the problem finders back when they were in art school." Sawyer emphasizes the connection with his final sentence: "They were the artists who focused on asking the right question."

Sawyer's enthusiastic tone comes across with italicized statements and words. The reader's eye is pulled to the single sentence paragraph, "The most creative artists were those who focused on asking the right question." The passage revolves around that striking effect. Sawyer's figurative language, such as his reference to "grope-in-the-dark," evoke strong reactions from the reader. The "dark" can be a scary place, the unknown. Yet the dark can also hide mistakes and encourage risk, an element of creativity. In the same way, quoting Einstein's reference to a detective and a crime brings in another element of risk, and another element of creativity.

Sawyer's simple vocabulary and use of the second person (you) connects his ideas to the reader's experience, showing that anyone can be creative, as long as they are "focused on asking the right question."

Here are the scores for this essay:

- ✔ **Reading:** 4 points. The writer grasped the main idea and many nuances of Sawyer's argument.

- ✔ **Analysis:** 4 points. The essay discusses the appeal to authority (Einstein), the lack of evidence for the relationship between creativity and business, and the role of the art experiment. The essay also touches on tone, word choice, paragraph structure, and figurative language ("grope-in-the-dark" and "crime").

- ✔ **Writing:** 3 points. The essay is fairly well organized, though the points analyzed could be grouped together more logically. The writing shows a mature style and is nearly error-free.

The total scores for this essay are 8 (Reading), 8 (Analysis), and 6 (Writing).

Chapter 8

Practicing Essays

• •

In This Chapter
▶ Trying your hand at some sample SAT essays
▶ Evaluating your responses to SAT essay questions

• •

If you're reading this chapter, and especially if you're trying your hand at any of the three practice SAT essay questions it contains, you've probably decided to write the optional, 50-minute essay. Good for you! But if you're going to do it, do it well. *Simulate* (imitate) real test conditions. Lock the cat in the garage. Plop your little sister in front of the television with enough snacks to last an hour. Turn off the phone. Set a timer for 50 minutes and tear out four sheets of lined paper from a notebook. (Loose-leaf is also acceptable.) Sharpen a No. 2 pencil. (The SAT doesn't allow you to write with a pen, and so far computerized testing is available only in a tiny percentage of testing sites. Unless you know for sure that your SAT location has computer-based testing, stay away from screens and keyboards.)

We suggest you write your essay(s) after reading Chapter 7. Once you complete an essay, take a break and then evaluate it, measuring your work against the scoring guidelines in the answer section.

Practice Essay 1 — Momentum: Igniting Social Change

Are you constantly holding your phone or tablet while staring at a computer screen? Do you want to change the world? If so, this question is for you.

The question

Read this excerpt from *Momentum: Igniting Social Change* by Allison Fine (Wiley 2007).

As you read the passage, consider how Fine uses

▶ Evidence such as facts or examples to support her ideas

▶ Logic to develop the argument and link claims and supporting evidence

▶ Style choices — appeal to emotion or authority, word choice, and so forth — to add to the persuasive power of the argument

In 1999 the ruler of Kuwait, Sheikh Jabir al-Ahman al-Jabir as-Sabah, issued a decree granting women full political rights. Advocates of women's suffrage in this small Arab country were hopeful that legislation would soon follow to codify the decree. Six years passed in vain while legislation stalled. Suddenly, in May 2005, the Kuwaiti legislature voted by a surprisingly large margin of 35 to 23, with one abstention, to remove the word *men* from Article One of the election laws, thereby guaranteeing women the right to vote and the opportunity to run for elected office. Who voted for the legislation was clear. Why they voted for it was something of a mystery. So what happened? Privately, often beneath their burkas (the full-length robes often worn by women in conservative Muslim countries), women used their Blackberries and cell phones to send text and e-mail messages urging legislators to vote in favor of full women's suffrage. Kuwaiti legislators learned that e-mails don't wear skirts or burkas.

In the click of a mouse or the touch of a screen, we have traveled from the Information Age to the Connected Age, from silent majorities to connected activism. The passion for social change is colliding with the reality that we are increasingly connected to one another through social media. Social media are important not only for their wizardry but because they are inexpensive and accessible and can make interactions, and therefore social change, massively scalable. Connectedness does not come from technology but is facilitated and strengthened by it. Being successful in the Connected Age means using technology to achieve an end. All people, in every aspect of their work, will have to know how and when to use various tools to inform and unite people and to fuel collective action.

Digital technology continues to develop at a ferocious pace, and whether and how we embrace these developments will determine how successful we are as activists. The policies that are debated and the decisions that are made will determine how open or closed our society will be. Do we believe that personal privacy trumps the needs and interests of the government and corporations? How do we view common spaces in cyberspace: as opportunities to meet and exchange ideas and things or as potential places for theft and deceit?

Perhaps the gravest barrier to participation in the Connected Age is the ongoing threat to our security and privacy caused by the aggregation, and in some cases the outright theft, of our personal information. The dampening effect of privacy concerns, including the ongoing onslaught of spam, cannot be underestimated, and neither can the damage it can cause to broad participation and the use of social media to effect social change. The process of developing societal and legal norms for privacy and communal behavior in the Connected Age will be messy, even maddening at times. It will range from simple social interactions (When and how can one use cell phones in public?) to far more serious issues (Who owns my health care information?). A tug of war among industries, consumers and their advocates, and governments around the world is unfolding, and activists must be a part of it. Activist organizations must participate in this public-policy debate, and they must inform and educate their members to ensure that the overall direction is toward open access and away from closed and proprietary tendencies.

We must move with a sense of urgency to incorporate connected activism into social-change efforts. We need to get better at taking a few problems off the table before new problems get crowded onto it. . . As long as we have social problems to solve, we need to keep searching for a better way. Broad, positive, sustainable change is possible in the Connected Age. Kaliya Hamlin, an activist, advocate, and blogger, perhaps put it best when she said, "Social change is happening. People are exchanging ideas, learning from one another and learning to trust one another in new and different ways, particularly . . . strangers. This process will lead to new and different ways of tackling existing problems. We don't have to come with solutions; we just have to get out of the way of passionate people and good ideas will emerge."

Write an essay in which you explain how Allison Fine constructs an argument to persuade the reader that social media can bring about constructive change. In your essay, discuss how Fine uses one or more of the elements of style listed above, or other elements, to strengthen the logic and persuasiveness of her argument. Focus on the most important features of the passage. Do not explain whether you agree or disagree with Fine's ideas. Instead, concentrate on how Allison Fine builds a persuasive case.

The answer

Allison Fine raises many important issues in her essay and argues persuasively for her view that social media can *effect* (bring about) positive change.

Showing that you grasped these points contributes to your "reading" score:

- Fine mentions texts and email but also refers to "digital technology." She sees these means of communication as powerful tools.

- The women of Kuwait, who normally have fewer rights than men, employed social media to obtain *suffrage* (the right to vote).

- Social media gives voice to people who would otherwise not be heard because these tools are "inexpensive and accessible."

- Social media is also a means of communication between activists, what Fine calls "the Connected Age."

- Activists *not* using social media are at a disadvantage.

- Privacy concerns are real (though Fine doesn't give details), and figuring out "societal and legal norms for privacy and communal behavior" is tough. Activists must play a part in this debate.

- Regardless of how "messy" the debate is, the movement should be toward "open access."

- Social media isn't going away, so activists and others must deal with it.

How did you do? If you mentioned six or seven of the bullet points, give yourself a 4 for "reading." If you hit four or five of the point, take 3 points for reading. Only two or three? Award yourself 2 points. If you stayed on the main idea, take 1 point for reading.

These guidelines are flexible. If you discussed these ideas in different terms, or if you came up with something we didn't mention, take credit — and points — for reading.

Now consider Allison Fine's writing style. All these ideas (and some we didn't list here) may be part of your "analysis" score:

- Beginning with an anecdote draws the reader into a real situation, one that gives a positive spin to the effect of social media. The women of Kuwait can vote! This success story sets the scene for Fine's *advocacy* (promotion of) social-media activism. Because the story is somewhat emotional, this may be labeled *pathos*.

- The first paragraph ends with a dramatic statement: "Kuwaiti legislators learned . . . burkas." The reference to *burkas,* robes that cover a woman's head and body, powerfully illustrates the old order (women without power) and the new (the activism through email).

- The second paragraph sets up several parallel sentences creating comparisons: "from the Information Age to the Connected Age, from silent majorities to connected activism." The parallel structure gives them equal historical importance. Fine implies that the forward movement is inevitable; there's no going back.

- The third paragraph raises questions that the reader (and society) must answer: "Do we believe . . . corporations? How do we view . . . deceit?" The questions set up opposing ideas — "open or closed," "personal privacy" versus "needs and interests of the government and corporations," "exchange of ideas" versus "theft and deceit."

- ✔ Paragraphs four and five are an example of concession and reply. Fine acknowledges the dangers and disadvantages of new media, but she sees as crucial the "overall direction . . . toward open access."

- ✔ The final paragraph is an example of *ethos,* as Fine quotes an "activist, advocate, and blogger" who presumably knows the power of social media.

- ✔ The diction is often extreme: Fine mentions "barrier" and "threat" in paragraph five.

Evaluate your analysis. If you mentioned five or six of the bullet points, give yourself a 4 for "analysis." If you hit three or four, take 3 points for analysis. Only two? Award yourself 2 points. If you discussed only one technique, take 1 point for analysis.

These guidelines are flexible. If you discussed other style points or grouped several together, adjust your analysis score.

Your final category is writing and applies to your own essay. Evaluating your own writing may be difficult. If you can find a friendly teacher or a helpful adult, ask for assistance in checking your grammar and style. Pay attention to these factors:

- ✔ **Structure:** Does your essay have a solid, logical structure? One possibility is to work in order from the first paragraph of the passage, where the author states the *thesis* (idea to be proved), and then move through paragraph after paragraph until you reach the end of the passage. Another possibility is first to examine Fine's ideas on social media, including her acknowledgement of the problems associated with it. Then you might discuss her appeal to pathos (the Kuwaiti example) and ethos (the blogger quotation). Finally, examples of extreme diction and parallel structure create a third paragraph.

- ✔ **Evidence:** Do you back up every statement you make with quotations or specific references to the passage? Count how many times you zeroed in on details. You should have at least two in every paragraph you write and maybe more.

- ✔ **Language:** Does your essay sound formal, as if a teacher were explaining the passage? If you lapsed into slang or informal word choice, your essay is weaker.

- ✔ **Mechanics:** English teachers group grammar, spelling, and punctuation in this category. As you reread, underline any sentence fragments or run-ons, misspelled words, and faulty commas or quotation marks.

Adding up points to evaluate your writing is tricky. In general, give yourself 1 point (up to a total of 4) for every category in the bulleted list in which you excelled. If you stumbled slightly in a category (say, three or four grammar or spelling mistakes), give yourself 3/4 of a point. If you feel your performance in one of these categories was poor (perhaps you drifted off topic or made seven or eight grammar errors), take only 1/2 of a point.

For sample graded responses that may assist you in your grading, turn to Chapter 7.

Scoring your essay

To get a fair idea of how your essay measures up to College Board standards, fill in this grid.

Category	*Reading*	*Analysis*	*Writing*
Number of Points			

Double the points for Reading, Analysis, and Writing and place the number in the appropriate box. The results are your essay scores.

Practice Essay II — Addressing Mathematical Innumeracy

Innumeracy is the mathematical equivalent of *illiteracy*. The first term refers to ignorance of math and the second, to the inability to read and write. Here's a passage that explores why so many Americans are clueless when faced with a number — any number!

The question

Read the following excerpt from *200% of Nothing* by A.K. Dewdney (Wiley).

As you read the passage, consider how Dewdney uses

- Specific statements to develop his ideas

- Logic to develop the argument and link claims and supporting evidence

- Style choices — appeal to emotion, figurative language, word choice, and so forth — to add to the persuasive power of the argument

What if you are already a mathematician and don't know it? We all use logic (of a largely unconscious kind) to take us through everything from business meetings to family dinners. If only we could be good *conscious* mathematicians!

At the conscious level, too many of us are still innumerate, the mathematical twin of illiterate, the term for people who cannot read. Because we are innumerate, we cannot deal with fractions, large numbers, percentages, and other relatively simple mathematical concepts. Meanwhile we are beset more than ever by the abuses that stem from this innumeracy. And those who abuse and misuse mathematics also abuse us. We become prey to commercial trickery, financial foolery, medical quackery, and numerical terrorism from pressure groups, all because we are unable (or unwilling) to think clearly for a few moments. In almost every case, the mathematics involved is something we learned, or should have learned, in elementary school or high school.

Suppose you grant that we are all mathematicians in some sense of that, at a very minimum, we all have this innate, largely unconscious logical ability. Why, then, do we continue to exhibit such awful innumeracy and why, for that matter, is mathematics education in such a crisis? The answer is already implicit in what I have said about mathematics in life. Mathematics itself is too simple!

By this I don't mean that the subject is simple. Far from it! No subject of human thought has anything like the stunning depth and complexity of mathematics. But the elements of mathematics, primary concepts like numbers, sets, relations, and even functions, are really quite simple. Paradoxically, it is only this simplicity (and clarity) that makes the complexity of mathematics possible.

Those of us with little or no familiarity with formal mathematics are nevertheless used to thinking complex thoughts about complex subjects, namely other people. When we come to study mathematics, we find it hard, perhaps, because we cannot get used to thinking about such simple subjects. It's much harder, for a mind that readily analyzes Aunt Mary's strange behavior at the reception, to realize that A, B, and C have no character or personality whatever.

In mathematical concepts, all unnecessary details have been stripped away by the process of abstraction. The naked idea stands before you and your first temptation is to clothe it with some detail, even if it means missing the whole point of the concept. Deep down you want A, B, and C to have human dimensions. Instead, they simply stand for numbers, sets, or some other apparently barren concept. . . .

As Sheila Tobias, author of *Overcoming Math Anxiety,* has pointed out, people who are introduced to mathematical problem solving for the first time routinely try to add dimensions to the problem that simply aren't there. Used to bringing an enormous array of data to the mental table, they simply aren't ready for the utter simplicity of it all. They may attempt to fill in enough lifelike elements to make the characters real and, therefore, manageable by a mind used to more complex situations. Otherwise, the terrain is all too alien.

If mathematics is so hard for people, it may not be due to a lack of innate ability at all, but rather to a cognitive style that demands a certain level of complexity that just isn't there! If this idea holds any truth at all, it may help people learn mathematics better by inspiring them with a sense of confidence. Sometimes expectation paves the way to a completely new learning experience. If the theory holds water, it suggests that the best way to teach mathematics, at least to students encountering it for the first time, is to move gradually toward simple, abstract situations from complicated, real-life ones. Not apples and oranges at the supermarket shelf nor transactions at the cash register, but the shoppers themselves, and the logic of their social interactions.

Write an essay in which you explain how Dewdney constructs an argument to persuade the reader that math education is poorly designed. In your essay, discuss how Dewdney uses one or more of the elements of style listed above, or other elements, to strengthen the logic and persuasiveness of his argument. Focus on the most important features of the passage. Do not explain whether you agree or disagree with Dewdney's ideas. Instead, concentrate on how he builds a persuasive case.

The answer

A. K. Dewdney argues that math is too simple for human beings to understand. This *premise* (hypothesis, idea to be proved) leads Dewdney to the conclusion that math education must change. Okay, that's the main idea, but Dewdney's argument is more complicated. Discussing these ideas in your essay contributes to your "reading" score:

- Dewdney believes that everyone can be a mathematician; *innate* (inborn) ability isn't the problem.

- Mathematical ability is largely "unconscious"; we all do math without realizing it.

- When math become conscious, as in a school or test problem, we overcomplicate the issue.

- Too many Americans suffer from "innumeracy," a complete misunderstanding of mathematical concepts, when they approach math with preconceived notions.

- People think about people, and people are complicated. Faced with a simple math problem, solvers apply the same sort of thinking to math as they do to other human beings. This technique doesn't work well.

- We tend to take an abstract idea and "clothe it with some detail." Unnecessary detail makes solving the math problem much more difficult, if not impossible.

- Confidence is key. If people expect to fail, they will. If they expect to succeed, they have a greater chance of doing so. (Remember this as you approach the SAT!)

- Beginning with real-life situations and gradually moving toward simpler, more abstract math problems is easier.

- The more math is related to people and personality, the easier it is.

Time for you to do some math. Add up the number of ideas from the bulleted list. If you mentioned seven or eight of the bullet points, give yourself a 4 for reading. If you hit four, five, or six points, take 3 points for reading. Only got two or three? Award yourself 2 points. If you stayed on the main idea, take 1 point for reading.

These guidelines aren't set in stone. If you discussed the ideas in different terms, or if you discovered something in the passage that we overlooked, add more points to your reading score.

Now consider A.K. Dewdney's writing style. Here are some ideas that may be part of your "analysis" score:

- ✔ The passage begins with a rhetorical question — a question with an answer the author anticipates. As Dewdney asks, "What if you are already a mathematician and don't know it?" he sets you up for a "yes." Then he goes on to prove the answer true.

- ✔ The second paragraph lists details of innumeracy — fractions, large numbers, and percentages — that most people can't deal with. This list gives an idea of the scope of the problem.

- ✔ Next, Dewdney explains the consequences — "commercial trickery, financial foolery, medical quackery, and numerical terrorism from pressure groups." These parallel items are all terrible, and Dewdney uses this structure to emphasize the importance of this problem.

- ✔ Dewdney uses an extreme word, "abuse," to describe how math is used improperly. The diction here takes the problem to a new and more serious level.

- ✔ Two pairs appear in the second paragraph: "unable (or unwilling)" and "learned or should have learned." The second half of each pair places responsibility on the person. This structure supports Dewdney's point that math ability can be developed.

- ✔ The passage as a whole is organized as a straight, logical line, leading the reader from one idea (you can do math) to another (math teachers make it harder) and then to still another (math should be taught differently).

- ✔ Using the pronouns *we* and *us* links the author to the reader.

- ✔ In the sixth paragraph, Dewdney ventures into figurative language. A "naked idea" is something you want to "clothe in some detail." Dewdney illustrates the concept he's discussing. He personifies the process of thinking, just as people personify math.

- ✔ With the example of "Aunt Mary," Dewdney takes his abstract concept and makes it real.

- ✔ The reference to Sheila Tobias stems from ethos, an appeal to authority.

- ✔ Mentioning "cash registers" and "the shoppers" illustrates Dewdney's recommendations for a better way to teach math.

How did you do? If you mentioned 8 to 10 of the 11 bullet points, give yourself a 4 for "analysis." If you hit six to eight points, take 3 points for analysis. If you discussed three to five ideas, take 2 points. Fewer than three? Give yourself 1 point for analysis.

If you discussed other style points or grouped several together, adjust your analysis score.

Your final category is writing and applies to your own essay. Grading your own work is like performing your own dentistry — hard to do! If you can enlist a teacher or other educated adult, do so. Check these factors:

- ✔ **Structure:** Does your essay have a solid, logical structure? One possibility is to work in order from the first paragraph of the passage, where the author asks whether you are "already a mathematician" and then move through the logical thread of his argument. Another way to organize your thoughts is to devote a paragraph to Dewdney's structure, another to the examples and appeals to ethos, and another to diction and parallel structure.

- **Evidence:** Do you back up every statement you make with quotations or specific references to the passage? Count how many times you zeroed in on details. You should have at least two in every paragraph you write, and maybe more.

- **Language:** Does your essay sound formal, as if a teacher were explaining the passage? If you lapsed into slang or informal word choice, your essay is weaker.

- **Mechanics:** English teachers group grammar, spelling, and punctuation in this category. As you reread, underline any sentence fragments or run-ons, misspelled words, and faulty commas or quotation marks.

To evaluate your writing, try to see the big picture. Then give yourself 1 point (up to a total of 4) for every category in the bulleted list in which you excelled. If you stumbled slightly in a category (say, three or four grammar or spelling mistakes), give yourself 3/4 of a point. If you feel your performance in one of these categories was poor (perhaps you drifted off topic or made seven or eight grammar errors), take only 1/2 of a point.

Scoring your essay

To get a fair idea of how your essay measures up to College Board standards, fill in this grid.

Category	Reading	Analysis	Writing
Number of Points			

Double the points for Reading, Analysis, and Writing and place the number in the appropriate box. The results are your essay scores.

Practice Essay III — Nonsexist Language

Are you a fan of grammar? How do you feel about stereotypes? Take a look at this essay by Margaret Spicer to see if your views match hers.

The question

As you read the passage, consider how Spicer uses

- Specific statements to develop her ideas

- Logic to develop the argument and link claims and supporting evidence

- Style choices — exaggeration, figurative language, word choice, and so forth — to add to the persuasive power of the argument

Today's paper has a full-page ad for a type of investment product I've been considering for some time. The advertisement, which must have cost several thousand dollars, detailed why I should leave my current financial advisor and switch to the guy whose smiling photo appears in a sidebar. I was halfway to writing "follow up on this" on my to-do list when I crashed into a recommendation about what I should "ask the salesman when evaluating his product." Excuse me? No females sell investment products? I could accept this sentence if it referred to Smiling Guy's company, because presumably he'd know the gender composition of his sales force. However, the recommendation was to ask *my* advisor. My advisor could be anywhere and therefore could be anyone, including a female.

I imagine that Smiling Guy (or his copy editor) was taught that a masculine pronoun includes both men and women. This principle, the "masculine universal," was in effect for many years. In fact, in the 19th century, the British Parliament passed a law stating that masculine references were understood to include females. This quirk of language, though, has practical effects. Studies show that children hearing about careers tend to accept and apply stereotypes if language reinforces traditional gender roles. Job advertisements referring to both "he and she" tend to attract men and women in more or less equal numbers; those referring only to one gender draw far fewer responses from the gender that was omitted. Plus, inclusiveness costs nothing and brings huge advantages. Leaving out half the human race (notice that I didn't say "mankind") isn't good business. This fact I know for sure, as there's no way I'm giving my money or time to Smiling Guy, because to him I don't exist. I'd rather speak with a *broker, investment counselor,* or *agent* (all gender-neutral words) than with a company that attaches the word *sales* only to a *man* and *his* product.

The problem Smiling Guy faces is rooted in Standard English grammar. One unbreakable rule, agreement, holds that singular forms must be paired with singular forms and plural with plural. A *table* has stains on *its* legs; *tables* have stains on *their* legs. The singular noun *table* pairs up with the singular pronoun *its,* and the plural noun *tables* pairs with the plural pronoun *their*. So far, so good, because *its* is neither masculine nor feminine, but "neuter," in grammar terminology. The plural pronoun *their* wins the hospitality award, because this useful pronoun pairs with plurals of nouns that are masculine, feminine, and neuter.

Their was once considered a good match for both singular and plural nouns, and it still is in conversation. In formal writing, though, *their* is plural only. Until a few decades ago, most grammarians saw no problem with the masculine universal; the proper match for a noun such as *student* was *he* (singular, masculine), and any females in the vicinity were expected to understand their supposed inclusion in that pronoun.

Enter feminism, sometime in the late 60s and early 70s. It became obvious that Standard English, when dealing with a singular noun that could apply to either gender, had a pronoun problem. Some radicals urged the adoption of *per* or other manufactured words to replace, for example, *his* or *her*. Other grammarians opted for *their,* arguing that this now firmly plural term should revert to its singular/plural, all-inclusive nature. Still others urged a 50-50 split, alternating the masculine universal with the feminine universal (*she* and *her,* referring to both sexes), paragraph by paragraph. Personally, I find it jarring to read about giving a baby *his* bottle and changing *her* diaper shortly thereafter. Most English teachers adopted this rule: Use *his or her* or *he or she* when you refer to a mixed group of males and females or when you don't know which genders are represented in the group. That's the solution I prefer.

Smiling Guy, avoid sexist language, and perhaps your company will appear on my to-do list after all.

Write an essay in which you explain how Spicer constructs an argument to persuade the reader that avoiding sexist language is important. In your essay, discuss how Spicer uses one or more of the elements of style listed above, or other elements, to strengthen the logic and persuasiveness of her argument. Focus on the most important features of the passage. Do not explain whether you agree or disagree with Spicer's ideas. Instead, concentrate on how she builds a persuasive case.

The answer

The main idea of this blog post is that sexist language is a problem with serious consequences. Beyond that central ***contention*** (argument), here are other reading points from the passage that you might mention in your essay:

- ✔ Spicer reacts negatively to an advertisement that refers only to males and refuses to do business with a company that uses sexist language.

- The advertisement is based on an assumption, but its wording stems from a problem with the English language.

- Studies show that language influences perception and has "practical effects" (reinforcing stereotypes and gender roles, gaining or losing customers or job applicants).

- Grammar rules calls for singular pronouns, but English has no gender-neutral singular pronouns for people, only the masculine *he* or the feminine *she*.

- The pronoun problem can be solved in several ways, none of which is clearly superior.

- Historically, females were represented by masculine words, a practice confirmed by law.

- Many people, including Spicer, now see the "masculine universal" as sexist.

- Movement toward gender-inclusiveness can have positive effects, such as increased sales.

How did you do? If you mentioned six or seven of the bullet points, give yourself 4 points for reading. If you hit four or five, take 3 points for reading. Only got two or three? Award yourself 2 points. If you stayed on the main idea, take 1 point for reading.

You probably found things we haven't listed, and you may have discussed these ideas in different terms. Take credit — and points — for every accurate idea you grasped from this reading.

Now consider Margaret Spicer's writing style. All these ideas (and some we didn't list here) may be part of your analysis score:

- The opening anecdote draws the reader into a real-life situation.

- Although the passage refers to a real person, whose photo appears in the advertisement, Spicer calls him "Smiling Guy," making his attitude and personality more universal. The implication is that other advertisements or situations include sexist language.

- Within the anecdote lies an appeal to logos, or logic. Spicer reasons that "my advisor could be anywhere and therefore could be anyone, including a female."

- The appeal to logos continues with an explanation of the effects of gendered language in children and job applicants. Because these statements come from "studies," the implication is that the findings are factual and not simply opinions. The studies, however, aren't cited specifically.

- *Juxtaposing* (placing next to each other) the term "human race" and "mankind" shows that nonsexist terms can easily replace the masculine universal.

- In the third and fourth paragraphs, Spicer gives a short grammar lesson on pronouns and gender. This information explains why avoiding sexist pronoun usage is difficult.

- In the fifth paragraph, you see some historical background and possible solutions. Taken together with the two preceding paragraphs, you have a "problem/solution" structure, which is a variation of the "cause-and-effect" pattern of organization.

- The third, fourth, and fifth paragraphs also create a concession and reply. The concession to opposing arguments is that English lacks a singular, nonsexist pronoun for people. The reply is the suggestion to return *they* and *their* to singular and plural status or to use *him or her* or *he or she* as needed.

- The passage comes full circle with a reference to "Smiling Guy" and the initial advertisement. The single-sentence paragraph adds emphasis to the point.

Evaluate your analysis. If you mentioned seven or eight of the bullet points, give yourself a 4 for analysis. If you hit five or six, take 3 points for analysis. If you settled on three or four ideas, take 2 points. If you discussed only one or two techniques, give yourself 1 point for analysis.

If you discussed other style points or grouped several together, adjust your analysis score.

Your final category is writing and applies to your own essay. Ask any educated adult with a good grasp of grammar and style to help you, if you can. Check these factors:

- ✔ **Structure:** Does your essay have a solid, logical structure? One possibility is to work in order from the first paragraph of the passage, where the author's anecdote sets forth the problem, and then move through paragraph after paragraph until you reach the end of the passage. Another possibility is first to examine Spicer's ideas on nonsexist language, including her acknowledgement of the grammar problems associated with pronouns. Then you might discuss her appeal to logos (reference to her rejection of the investment and studies on children and job applicants). Next up could be a discussion of concession and reply, coupled with an examination of the problem/solution structure of the passage.

- ✔ **Evidence:** Do you back up every statement you make with quotations or specific references to the passage? Count how many times you zeroed in on details. You should have at least two in every paragraph you write and maybe more.

- ✔ **Language:** Does your essay sound formal, as if a teacher were explaining the passage? If you lapsed into slang or informal word choice, your essay is weaker.

- ✔ **Mechanics:** English teachers group grammar, spelling, and punctuation in this category. As you reread, underline any sentence fragments or run-ons, misspelled words, and faulty commas or quotation marks.

Give yourself 1 point (up to a total of 4) for every category in the bulleted list in which you excelled. If you stumbled slightly in a category (say, three or four grammar or spelling mistakes), give yourself 3/4 of a point. If you feel your performance in one of these categories was poor (perhaps you drifted off topic or made seven or eight grammar errors), take only 1/2 of a point.

Scoring your essay

To get a fair idea of how your essay measures up to College Board standards, fill in this grid.

Category	Reading	Analysis	Writing
Number of Points			

Double the points for Reading, Analysis, and Writing and place the number in the appropriate box. The results are your essay scores.

Part IV
Take a Number, Any Number: The Mathematics Sections

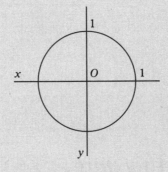

In this part . . .

✔ Discover the ins and outs of the SAT Math sections.

✔ Strengthen your knowledge and understanding of algebra and work on algebra-related practice questions.

✔ Get the scoop on problem solving and data analysis and then test your skills on some practice questions.

✔ Find out what you need to know about advanced math as it pertains to the SAT.

✔ Become comfortable with other types of math topics found on the SAT.

Chapter 9

Meeting Numbers Head-On: The SAT Math Section

....

In This Chapter

▶ Surveying the Mathematics portion of the SAT

▶ Choosing the right calculator and using it efficiently during the exam

▶ Tackling time constraints

▶ Getting good at grid-ins

▶ Adopting the best strategies for SAT math questions

....

*I*f you're one of those people who whined to your ninth-grade math teacher, "No one in the real world ever has to calculate the value of $6x - y$," the SAT is about to prove you wrong. You can't get much more real world than a test that helps to determine where you go to college and maybe even what sort of job you get afterward. And on the SAT, the value of $6x - y$ is fair game. So are absolute value (and I'm not talking about the great price you got on that orange sweater), exponential growth (the kind your tuition payments will display), and plenty of other stuff. In this chapter, we show you what's where, how to prepare, and most important, how to survive the SAT Math section.

Having Fun with Numbers: SAT Math 101

The SAT that you begin one chilly morning in the near future will contain two sections of math that count toward your score: one 55-minute section and one 25-minute section. You may also encounter an unscored section that allows the SAT-makers to try out new questions. In other words, you pay them to try out experimental questions on you. Nice, huh?

The experimental section doesn't count toward your final score, but because you may not know which section is equating, don't blow off anything. You could be ignoring a section that matters.

Each Math section begins with a little gift basket: a set of formulas to help you solve the problems — the area and circumference of a circle, the area of a square, the angles and sides of "special" triangles, and so forth. As you plod through an SAT Math section, look back whenever you need this information so you're sure that your nerves haven't changed, say, the area of a rectangle from $A = lw$ to $A = lw^2$.

Outside the possible unscored experimental section, 45 SAT Math questions are multiple-choice with four answer choices. Thirteen questions are *grid-ins,* which require you to bubble in the numbers you come up with, thus, giving you no hint whatsoever about the correct answer. Two of these 13 grid-ins are *Extended Thinking,* meaning they're more complicated and worth 2 points each. They are also related and based on the same information. (Check out the section "Knowing When to Grid and Bear It," later in this chapter, for everything you need to know about these questions.) Expect to see problems relating to topics commonly covered in the first three years of high-school math. In other words, you'll see questions on numbers and operations, algebra and functions, geometry, trigonometry, statistics, probability, and data interpretation. For more specifics, read on.

Algebra and functions

These problems account for 35 percent of your math score. They ask you to analyze and solve equations, create expressions to represent quantity relationships, and rearrange and interpret formulas. They include the following:

- **Absolute value:** How far away from a particular point on the number line is another number? That's the absolute value, which may show up in equations or functions.

- **Inequalities:** No, it's not social injustice. It's whether one number is larger than another, or if x is greater than 2, or what happens when you multiply both sides by –1.

- **Exponents:** These little numbers tell you how many times to multiply something by itself, as in x^4. You may see positive, negative, and fractional exponents.

- **Factoring:** Factoring is the math equivalent of extracting the cocoa powder and flour from a brownie after it's baked. Here's a typical factoring problem: If a rectangle has a width of $x+3$ and an area of $x^2+8x+15$, what is its length, in terms of x?

- **Functions:** We're not talking about cousin Thelma's fundraiser for impoverished beekeepers but about problems in which you take a number, do some stuff to it, and end up with a new number. Functions, which are written as $f(x)$ or other letters, including $g(h)$, appear in a number of forms, including the graphs of linear and quadratic functions.

- **Special symbols:** These strange figures have been created just for the SAT; in other words, they don't exist in *normal* math. You have to figure out, given the definition, how to manipulate these symbols.

Problem solving and data analysis

These problems, worth 28 percent of your math score, examine whether you can analyze relationships by using ratios and proportions as well as interpret and summarize graphs. They include the following:

- **Arithmetic:** You have to add, subtract, multiply, and divide, plus show understanding of even and odd numbers, positive and negative numbers, consecutive integers, and primes.

- **Arithmetic sequences:** You have to see how numbers fit together to make a sequence, or pattern. For example, if you get 20, 24, 28, 32, and 36 on your five most recent math quizzes, what will you get on the next one, assuming that the sequence stays the same?

- **Coordinate geometry:** The SAT asks about slopes of lines, including parallel and perpendicular lines. Also, if point G has the coordinates (x_1, y_1) and point W has coordinates (x_2, y_2), what is the midpoint or the distance between the points? You may also have to interpret the graph of a function and to answer questions about transformations of a function. An example: If $f(x)$ measures how much time Gloria spends on her cellphone, how will $f(x)$ change the day after her unlimited calling plan starts?

✔ **Exponential growth sequences, also known as geometric sequences:** These questions require you to multiply by a certain number to get to the next term in the sequence. For example, the number of bent wire hangers at the bottom of your closet increases by a factor of 3 each day: 4, 12, 36, 108, 324 . . . you get the idea. You may be asked to create a mathematical statement expressing the way this wire hanger collection grows.

✔ **Percents:** You will be asked to find the amount that you pay if your book bill increases by 4,000 percent and books are 10 percent of your budget.

✔ **Ratios and proportions:** The SAT asks about values that are in proportion. If the ratio of tuba players that try out for Prestigious University to those who get in is 200 to 3, how many tuba players are accepted out of the 400 who apply?

✔ **Sets, including union, intersection, and elements:** The SAT may ask you to identify common elements or ask other questions about two or more sets. The set of all the dog treats given and the set of all the dog treats that the dogs will actually eat (instead of strew around the living room) overlap slightly.

Passport to advanced math

Problems here, worth 27 percent of your math score, ask you to solve quadratic equations and rewrite expressions based on the math structure. It's also a useful bucket for questions that don't fall into the other three categories.

✔ **Averages:** Make friends with the three *m*'s — mean, median, and mode.

✔ **Geometric probability:** If you're hanging a picture on the kitchen wall, what's the probability that you'll drive the nail right through a hot-water pipe?

✔ **Logic:** This topic covers those horrible problems you never see in real life, such as *What is the seating plan if Mr. Green can't sit next to Ms. Red but must sit across from Violet and behind Orchid or he throws popcorn. . . .* Wait, this sounds like the seating plan at a wedding. You *do* use this stuff in real life!

✔ **Equations and inequalities:** Equal signs represent what things are, as in $h = 3w + 4$ represents the number of hours you work while learning stuff like this. Or, if $3w + 4$ isn't enough time, your hours are represented with the inequality $h > 3w + 4$. This category also includes quadratic equations, which have x^2 in them, such as $x^2 + 8x + 15 = 0$.

✔ **Probability:** If you have 12 pairs of black socks and one pair of white socks, what is the likelihood that you'll match two socks right out of the drawer?

✔ **Graphs and charts:** These are data represented in a drawing. The test-writers may show you a bunch of dots or some other pattern, where the *x*-axis represents the amount of time students spend reading this book and the *y*-axis shows their SAT scores. You may have to answer questions on this, such as exactly how it was the right move to pick up this new edition of *SAT For Dummies*.

Anything here sounds like a foreign language? Probably, because math has its own language. If you need to brush up on one or more of these topics, check out the relevant chapters in Part IV for review and practice problems.

Additional topics in math

The SAT calls this category "Additional Topics in Math," but it's really just basic geometry: lines and angles, flat shapes, three-dimensional shapes, and trigonometry. Problems here are worth 10 percent of your math score.

- ✓ **Areas, perimeters, and volume:** This topic covers the basic how-much-carpet-do-you-need-to-cover-the-floor or how-much-water-do-you-need-to-fill-the-gas-can questions for common shapes as well as weird forms.

- ✓ **Parallel and perpendicular lines:** This topic questions you about what parallel and perpendicular lines do when they're alone in the dark, what kind of angles cut into them, how they behave under pressure (when they have to take the SAT, for example), and so forth.

- ✓ **Quadrilaterals and other polygons:** The SAT folks may throw you a quadrilateral quiz or a polygon problem.

- ✓ **Triangles:** You find everything you ever wanted to know about triangles, especially the properties of right, isosceles, equilateral, and "special" ones. (Why are they special? Because they're on the SAT. Kidding. Check out Chapter 16 for the lowdown on special triangles.)

- ✓ **Trigonometry:** There's a chilling word. You could just use "Trig." Actually it's not bad at all because the SAT keeps it at a very basic level. Your friend *SOH-CAH-TOA* guides you through almost all the trigonometry that you need, and the unit circle provides the rest. More on this in Chapter 16.

Calculating Your Way to SAT Success

When **pundits** (wise guys, like the intellectuals sitting around tables discussing politics on TV) blather on about the decline of civilization, they often mention the fact that students today are allowed to bring calculators to the SAT and other standardized tests. "In our day," they say, "we had to work with our heads, not with machines." Yeah, right. As if any of them even knows how to turn on a calculator, let alone figure out the square root of 324. (P.S. It's 18.)

So you can use a calculator on part of the math. Big deal. The SAT-makers declare that you can solve every problem on the test with brainpower alone, and they're right. But you're not against a little help, are you? In fact, a calculator may not be the absolute number-one requirement for doing well on the Math section, but it's pretty high on the list. Let us tell you a little secret of success: Become best friends with your calculator *before* the exam. Don't waste time on SAT day trying to find the right buttons.

You're allowed to bring a battery-operated graphing or scientific calculator to the exam. In addition to the four functions (addition, subtraction, multiplication, and division), a graphing or scientific calculator also lets you figure out useful stuff like square roots, combination problems involving π, and more. Most also calculate fractions, so adding 1/4 to 1/2 is less traumatic. You aren't allowed to bring anything with a QWERTY keyboard, a touchscreen, or anything that connects to the outside world. (For more information on what's prohibited, turn to Chapter 1.)

In addition to doing everything a scientific calculator accomplishes, a graphing calculator also lets you draw graphs. If you have one you're comfortable with, bring it along to the test. If you don't own a graphing calculator, don't rush out and buy one, because the instruction manual is about 100 pages long, and you need to spend that time reading this book. Besides, you don't really need graphing capability on the SAT.

Practice using your calculator, especially with the more complicated-looking procedures with problems from a math book or from this book. Fractions, decimals, and percents should be first on your list. If you're not getting the right answers, ask a fellow student or your math teacher for help. Last thing you need is to get stuck on how to calculate an exponent *while you're taking the exam*. Know this in advance, so you can push the right buttons, save time, and choose more correct answers.

If you don't own a calculator, don't worry. Although the SAT doesn't supply calculators, some schools do provide loaners to students who don't have their own. Talk with your math teacher. (Home-schoolers, call the local high school to inquire about access to their supply.) You can also pick up a cheap calculator that doesn't draw graphs but does handle almost all the functions you'll need on the SAT.

Knowing when *not* to use a calculator is almost as important as knowing how to tap in numbers. Sometimes a question presents you with a long string of numbers. You *can* find the answer with a calculator, *if* you don't make a mistake typing everything in. But often you can solve the long-string-of-numbers question much more quickly without a calculator by carrying out a simple math operation in your head or with paper and pencil. (As you work out the practice problems in Part IV, read the explanations that accompany the answers, even if you correctly answered the problem. Tucked into the explanation you may find a statement telling you how a calculator could have helped.)

Also, a calculator simply crunches numbers, but it doesn't help you see the pattern, logic, or underlying concept of the question. For a high math score, you have to understand how the question works, not how the numbers add together; and for this, the calculator doesn't help. It's all you.

Don't let your batteries run out during the test — that's a silly way to hurt your score. Have fresh batteries in your calculator before SAT-day morning.

Taking Your Time versus Getting It Right

Finishing every problem on the Math section of the SAT in the time you're given is certainly possible. However, finishing every question *and* getting them all correct is more challenging. Furthermore, if you're in a mad rush to finish a section, you're going to make mistakes that you would never have made had you worked at a slower pace. Your goal is not to get them *all* right. (Almost no one gets a perfect SAT score.) Your goal is to do better than enough of the other test-takers so you can get accepted to the school of your choice.

Now that you've resolved that you're not going to worry about getting all the problems, focus on how you can get the *most* problems. Decide to spend as much time as you need on each problem to be reasonably sure that you answer it correctly. Also, cut your losses. Move on past a problem if you spend two or three minutes on it without getting anywhere. Take a guess in your answer sheet, circle the question number in the test booklet (or write the question number down), and go back to it if you have time at the end of the section.

Make sure to answer *all* the questions, even if it just means guessing through the end of the section. Because wrong answers are no worse than unanswered, you may as well take a shot at getting it right.

Is it just me, or are there more exponents on the bottom of the page?

Complete this sentence: SAT math problems are placed in order

(A) with the hardest topics first

(B) by grade level, with 9th-grade material first and 11th-grade material last

(C) by throwing the questions down a flight of stairs

(D) from easiest to hardest (more or less)

The correct answer is Choice (D). The SAT-makers arrange the problems roughly in the order of difficulty. (How do they know what's difficult and what's easy? They gather data on test-takers and experimental questions, that's how.) Don't assume that all the arithmetic questions are easy and all the third-year math problems are tough. The SAT-makers try to include varying levels of difficulty for each topic, regardless of when it shows up in your high-school curriculum.

Knowing When to Grid and Bear It

Twelve of the most fun questions (kidding — they're as boring as anything else on the exam) are grid-ins. Sadly, you don't get four convenient multiple-choice answers for a grid-in. Figure 9-1 shows a sample blank grid-in.

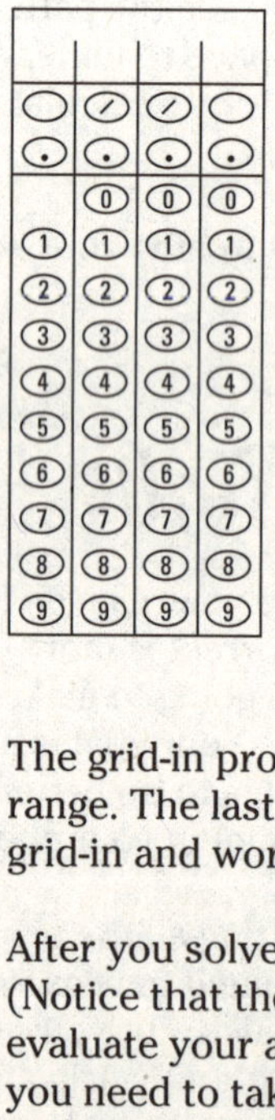

Figure 9-1:
A blank
grid-in.

The grid-in problems are normal questions of any type but tend to be in the higher difficulty range. The last question of the long Math section, Question 37, is an especially challenging grid-in and worth 4 points, unlike the other questions worth 1 point each.

After you solve the problem, you have to darken the ovals that correspond to your answer. (Notice that the SAT-makers cleverly avoid spending money on graders who could actually evaluate your ability to solve a math problem.) Before you start filling in those little ovals, you need to take note of some built-in traps. Beware of the following:

- ✔ **Write your answer and then darken the ovals.** Grid-ins have little boxes in which you can write your answer, but the scanner doesn't read the boxes, just the darkened ovals. But even though only the bubbles are scored, don't skip the writing part, because you may "bubble" inaccurately.

- ✔ **You can't grid in negative numbers.** The grid has no minus sign. Hence, all answers are positive or zero.

✔ **Don't grid in a mixed number.** If you grid in 51/2, the scanner reads "51 over 2," not "five and one-half." Solution: Convert your answer to an improper fraction. Grid in 11/2 (11 over 2), as shown in Figure 9-2a. You may also grid your answer as a decimal: 5.5.

✔ **You can start from the left, right, or middle.** Just be sure that you have enough boxes for the answer you want to record.

✔ **Don't place zeroes before a decimal point.** If your answer is .5, darken the oval for the decimal point and the five, not 00.5 (Figure 9-2b).

✔ **If your answer is a repeating decimal, fill in all the boxes, rounding off the last number only.** In other words, darken the ovals for .333 or .667 (1/3 and 2/3 expressed as decimals), not .3 or .67 (Figure 9-2c).

✔ **If your answer isn't a repeating decimal (.4, for example), you don't have to fill in all the boxes.** Just darken a decimal point followed by a 4.

Don't agonize over *the* perfect, correct answer. Some grid-ins have several possible right answers. (Usually those problems say something like "one possible value of *x* is . . .") Just find one answer and you're all set.

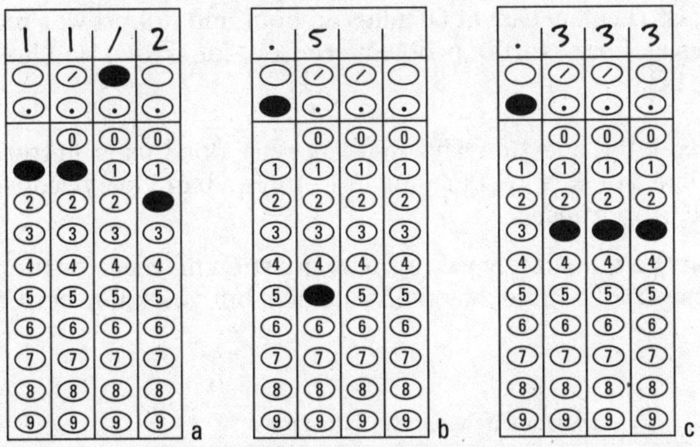

Figure 9-2:
Three
grid-ins,
properly
filled in.

Planning for the Battle: Some Effective Math Strategies

In other chapters in Part IV, you find the best way to attack each type of question in the SAT Math section. Here are some general math strategies to help you get off on the right foot. Try these on for size:

✔ **Read the question and figure out what the SAT-makers want to know.** Circle significant words, such as *greater than, percentage,* and so forth.

✔ **Use the test booklet as scrap paper.** Write your calculations in the extra blank space, but take time to bubble in your answers. Even though the proctor collects the test booklet, the information in it doesn't count toward your score.

✔ **Don't overuse the calculator.** Trust your ability to do simple math, like 3×4. Also, see if a simple math approach to a complicated-appearing problem gets you to the right answer.

✔ **Keep an eye on the clock.** You get as many points for each correct answer to an easy question as you do for a correct answer to a hard question. Don't spend five minutes on one hard question and miss out on 11 easy questions because you run out of time.

✔ **Try out the multiple-choice answers and see which one works.** With only four options, this can be fast. If the SAT-writers ask something like "Which number is divisible by both 13 and 14?" start plugging in the answers until one of them works. SAT multiple-choice answers are usually in order from smallest to largest. When you plug in, start with Choice (C), and check whether you end up above or below the target. Then try Choice (B) or (D), depending on the direction you need to go.

✔ **Think of realistic answers.** The SAT Math section isn't tied tightly to the real world, but it's not from Mars, either. If you're looking for a person's weight, for example, don't go with "5,098 pounds" unless you have a truck on the scale. Think about the range of human body sizes and concentrate on answers in that category. Similarly, if you're looking for a discount and come up with a negative sale price, try again.

✔ **Don't assume that the provided diagram will solve the problem.** SAT figures aren't created purposely to deceive you, but they may not be drawn to scale. They're usually close enough to be useful, but if the notes say, "Not drawn to scale," then they're *way* off.

✔ **Use your own drawings to illustrate problems to help visualize them.** For example, the classic "Evelyn was traveling east at 60 miles an hour and Robert was moving toward her at 30 miles an hour" sort of problem cries out for arrows and lines like the ones shown in Figure 9-3.

✔ **Plug in numbers for x.** If the question says that x is even, don't use x in the question; try an even number, like 2 or 4. Note: Plugging in 1 or 0 is a bad idea, because those numbers have unique properties.

✔ **Pay attention to what the question is asking.** The question may ask for the value of $2x$ or $x + y$. A trap answer, of course, has the value of x, but you know better than to go for that answer.

Figure 9-3:
A diagram like this one may help you solve SAT math problems.

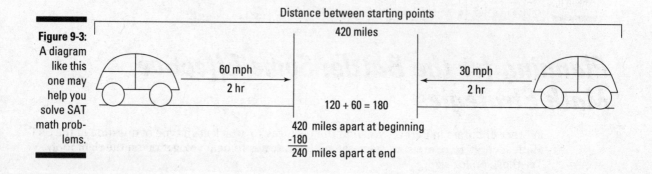

Distance between starting points

420 miles

60 mph
2 hr

30 mph
2 hr

120 + 60 = 180

420 miles apart at beginning
-180
240 miles apart at end

Chapter 10

Numb and Numbering: The Ins and Outs of Numbers and Operations

*O*nce upon a time, you could take care of all the numbers you needed for school purposes with ten fingers and, in a pinch, a couple of toes. Sadly, life has changed. For the SAT, you need to know what's prime and what's not as well as how to calculate and manipulate percents, ratios, means, and the like. Not to mention sets and sequences! Never fear. Even though you've moved way beyond body-part math, this chapter tells you everything you need to know about numbers and operations, at least as they appear on the SAT.

Meeting the Number Families

Mathematics is based on numbers, and different groups of numbers work in different ways. It helps to know about these before taking the exam, so in this section we explore the variations.

You may be wondering why you need a vocabulary lesson to do well on SAT math. The fact of the matter is, the SAT-makers love to tuck these terms into the questions, as in "How many prime numbers are . . ." or "If the sum of three consecutive integers is 99, what is . . ." and the like. If you don't know the vocabulary, you're sunk before you start.

Check out these different groups of numbers:

✔ **Whole numbers:** *Whole numbers* aren't very well named, because they include 0, which isn't a whole lot of anything. The whole numbers are the ones you (hopefully) remember from grade school: 0, 1, 2, 3, 4, 5, 6 . . . you get the idea. Whole numbers, by definition, don't include fractions or decimals.

Whole numbers can't be negative, but they can be even or odd. *Even numbers* are divisible by 2, and *odd numbers* aren't.

↙ **Prime numbers:** *Prime numbers* are whole numbers divisible only by themselves and by 1. The first few prime numbers are 2, 3, 5, 7, 11, 13, 17, and 19. Zero and 1 aren't prime numbers. They're considered "special." (The kids in grade school said that about us, too.) Two is the only even prime number. No negative number is ever prime because all negative numbers are divisible by –1.

One common misconception is that all odd numbers are prime. Don't fall into that trap. Tons of odd numbers (9 and 15, for example) aren't prime, because they're divisible by at least one other number besides 1 and itself.

↙ **Composite numbers:** Any whole number that's not prime or special is *composite*. If you can divide a number by some smaller whole number (other than 1) without getting a remainder, you have a composite number. A few composite numbers are 4, 6, 8, 9, 10, 12, 14, 15, 16, 18, 20, 21, and so on.

Speaking of divisibility, remembering these points will win you SAT points:

- All numbers whose digits add up to a multiple of 3 are also divisible by 3. For example, the digits of 789 add up to 24 ($7 + 8 + 9 = 24$); because 24 is divisible by 3, so is 789.

- Ditto for multiples of 9. If the digits of a number add up to a multiple of 9, you can divide the number itself by 9. For example, the digits of 729 add up to 18; because 18 is divisible by 9, so is 729.

- All numbers ending in 0 or 5 are divisible by 5.

- All numbers ending in 0 are also divisible by 10.

Consider the number 365. It's not even, so it can't be divided by 2. Its digits add up to 14, which isn't divisible by 3 or 9, so it's not divisible by either 3 or 9. Because 365 ends in 5, it's divisible by 5. Because it doesn't end in 0, it's not divisible by 10.

↙ **Integers:** The whole numbers and all their opposites — also known as *negative numbers* — are *integers*. The whole numbers go all the way up to infinity, but the integers are even more impressive. Integers reach infinity in both directions, as the number line in Figure 10-1 shows.

Figure 10-1: Integers go on forever.

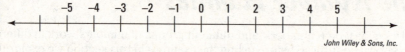

John Wiley & Sons, Inc.

When you're asked to compare integers, remember that the farther to the right a number is, the greater it is. For example, –3 is greater than –5.

↙ **Rational numbers:** All integers are *rational numbers*. In addition, any number that can be written as a fraction — proper or improper — is a rational number. (In a *proper fraction*, the number on top is smaller than the number on the bottom, and in an *improper fraction*, the top number is greater than the bottom number.) Plus, any decimal that either ends, such as 1.2, or repeats, such as $0.\overline{33}$ (the decimal for 1/3), is a rational number. The following are also rational: –2, 0.234, 787/23, $3.21\overline{33}$.

↙ **Irrational numbers:** These are numbers for which a padded room is necessary. Kidding. *Irrational numbers* have decimals that never end or repeat. Practically speaking, you need to worry about only two kinds of irrational numbers:

- Radicals (such as $\sqrt{2}$ and $\sqrt{3}$)

- π, which you've seen from working with a circle

Every type of number in this chapter is a *real* number. This means that it can be found on the number line, and it includes both rational and irrational numbers. You may be wondering, "Are some numbers *not* real?" The bad news: Yes, these are called "imaginary numbers," and you may have to work with them someday, perhaps at the college where you're sending your SAT scores. The good news: That day isn't today, because every number on the SAT is real.

Getting Your Priorities Straight: Order of Operations

How many times has your mom told you to turn off the PlayStation and start your homework because you "have to get your priorities straight"? We won't comment on the annoyance that authority figures generate, especially when they're right, but we're going to tell you that in math, priorities matter.

Consider the problem $3 + 4 \times 2$. If you add $3 + 4$, which of course equals 7, and multiply by 2, you get 14. Nice answer, but wrong, because you forgot about Aunt Sally. "Aunt Sally," or more accurately, "**P**lease **E**xcuse **M**y **D**ear **A**unt **S**ally" — *PEMDAS* — is a mnemonic device you can use to help you remember what mathematicians call *order of operations*. When faced with a multipart problem, just follow the order of operations that "Aunt Sally" calls for. Note the italicized letters in the following step list, which tells you what "Aunt Sally" really means:

1. Do everything in *p*arentheses.
2. Calculate all *e*xponents.
3. *M*ultiply and *d*ivide, from left to right.
4. *A*dd and *s*ubtract, from left to right.

Back to the sample problem, $3 + 4 \times 2$. No parentheses or exponents, so the first operations up are multiplication and division. Because there's no division, you're left with 4×2, which equals 8. Onward to addition and subtraction (in this problem, subtraction isn't present, so forget about subtracting). Just add 3 to 8, at which point you arrive at 11, the correct answer.

Many calculators know the "Aunt Sally" rules, but on older ones, sometimes you have to input the numbers according to the "Aunt Sally" rules to ensure the right answer. Be sure to figure out which kind of calculator you have before test day.

Here's another chance to visit Aunt Sally:

The expression $20 - (40 \div 5 \times 2) + 3^2$ equals

(A) −5

(B) 7

(C) 10

(D) 13

The answer is Choice (D). Start with what's in the parentheses: $40 \div 5 \times 2$. Don't fall into the trap of multiplying 5×2 first; proceed from left to right: $40 \div 5 = 8$ and $8 \times 2 = 16$. Next, tackle the exponent: $3^2 = 9$. At this stage, you have $20 - 16 + 9$. Again, resist the temptation to start by adding; just go left to right ($20 - 16 = 4$ and then $4 + 9 = 13$).

Playing Percentage Games

The SAT loves percentages, perhaps because math teachers who are sick of the question "Am I ever going to use this stuff in real life?" actually write the math portion of the exam. With percentages, the answer is yes if you're taking out a loan (interest rates) or investing the earnings from your part-time job in mutual funds (still interest, but this time it's a good thing) or buying something on sale (15 percent off the regular price). *Percents* represent how much of each hundred you're talking about.

Taking a percentage of a number is a simple task if you're using a calculator with a "%" button. Just hit the "%" and "×" buttons. For example, to find 60 percent of 35, multiply 60% by 35. The answer is 21. If you're not blessed with such a calculator, you can turn a percent into a decimal by moving the decimal point two spaces to the left, as in 60% = 0.60. (Other examples of percents include 12.5% = 0.125, 0.4% = 0.004, and so on.) Or turn the percent into a fraction. The "cent" in *percent* means hundred, (as in a *century* is 100 years,) so 60 percent literally means, "60 per 100," or 60/100.

For more complicated problems, fall back on the formula you mastered in grade school:

$$\frac{is}{of} = \frac{\%}{100}$$

Suppose you're asked "40% of what number is 80?" The number you're looking for is the number you're taking the percent *of,* so x will go in the *of* space in the formula:

$$\frac{80}{x} = \frac{40}{100}$$

Now cross-multiply: $40x = 8,000$. Dividing by 40 gives you $x = 200$.

You can also consider that the percent of the whole equals the part. In other words, 40% of x is 80. Set up the equation and solve for x:

$$40\%x = 80$$
$$0.4x = 80$$
$$x = \frac{80}{0.4}$$
$$x = 200$$

One subtopic of percentages is a problem that involves a percent increase or decrease. A slight variation of the percentage formula helps you out with this type of problem. Here's the formula and an example problem to help you master it:

$$\frac{amount\ of\ change}{starting\ amount} = \frac{x}{100}$$

The value of your investment in the winning team of the National Softball League increased from $1,500 to $1,800 over several years. What was the percentage increase of the investment?

(A) 300

(B) 120

(C) 50

(D) 20

The correct answer is Choice (D). The key here is that the number 1,800 shouldn't be used in your formula. Before you can find the *percent* of increase, you need to find the *amount* of increase, which is $1,800 - 1,500 = 300$. To find the percentage of increase, set up this equation:

$$\frac{300}{1,500} = \frac{x}{100}$$

Cross-multiply to get $1,500x = 30,000$. Dividing tells you that $x = 20$ percent.

The SAT-makers often try to confuse you by asking about something that doesn't appear in the original question, as in this example:

At one point in the season, the New York Yankees had won 60 percent of their games. The Yanks had lost 30 times and never tied. (As you know, there are no ties in the world's noblest sport, baseball.) How many games had the team played?

(A) 12

(B) 18

(C) 50

(D) 75

The answer is Choice (D). Did you find the catch? The winning percentage was 60 percent, but the question specified the number of losses. What to do? Well, because ties don't exist, the wins and losses must have represented all the games played, or 100 percent. Thus the percentage of losses must be $100\% - 60\%$, which is 40%. Putting the formula to work:

$$\frac{30}{x} = \frac{40}{100}$$

As always, cross-multiply: $40x = 3,000$, and $x = 75$

Keeping It in Proportion: Ratios

After you know the tricks, ratios are some of the easiest problems to answer quickly. Here are the points to remember:

- A ratio is written as $\frac{of}{to}$ or of:to.
  - The ratio *of* sunflowers *to* roses = $\frac{sunflowers}{roses}$.
  - The ratio *of* umbrellas *to* heads = umbrellas : heads.
- A possible total is a multiple of the *sum* of the numbers in the ratio.

You may have to confront a proportion problem like this on the test:

At a party, the ratio of blondes to redheads is 4:5. What could be the total number of blondes and redheads at the party?

This one's easy. Just add the numbers in the ratio: $4 + 5 = 9$. The total must be a multiple of 9, such as 9, 18, 27, 36, and so on. If this "multiple of" stuff is confusing, think of it another way: The sum must divide evenly into the total. That is, the total must be divisible by 9. Can the total, for example, be 54? Yes, 9 goes evenly into 54. Can it be 64? No, 9 doesn't go evenly into 64.

Check out another example.

While creating his special dish, Thomas uses 7 teaspoons of whipped topping for every 5 teaspoons of chocolate mousse. Which of the following could be the total number of teaspoons of whipped topping and chocolate mousse in his special dish?

(A) 75

(B) 57

(C) 48

(D) 35

The correct answer is Choice (C). Add the numbers in the ratio: $7 + 5 = 12$. The total must be a multiple of 12. (It must be evenly divisible by 12.) Here, only *48*, Choice (C), is evenly divisible by 12. Of course, 75 and 57 try to trick you by using the numbers 7 and 5 from the ratio.

Notice how the question has been what *can be* the *possible* total. The total can be *any* multiple of the sum. If a question asks you which of the following *is* the total, you have to answer, "It cannot be determined." You know only which *can be* true.

Another ratio headache strikes when you're given a ratio and a total and asked to find a specific term. To find a specific term, do the following, in order:

1. **Add the numbers in the ratio.**

2. **Divide that sum into the total.**

3. **Multiply that quotient by each term in the ratio. (The *quotient* is the answer you get when you divide.)**

4. **Add the answers to double-check that they sum up to the total.**

Pretty confusing stuff. Take it one step at a time. Look at this example problem:

> To congratulate his team, which had just won the last game for an undefeated 21-in-0 season, the ecstatic coach took his team to the local pizza joint, where each player ordered either a deep dish pizza or a calzone. If there were 3 deep dishes for every 4 calzones, and if every member of the 28-man squad ordered either one or the other, how many deep dishes were there?

Here's how to solve it:

1. **Let $3x$ be the number of players who ordered a pizza.**

2. **Let $4x$ be the number of players who ordered a calzone.**

3. **Together they ordered 28 meals: $3x + 4x = 28$.**

4. **Solve for x: $x = 4$.**

5. **Plug in 4 for x to get your numbers: $3(4) = 12$ pizzas and $4(4) = 16$ calzones.**

Now you have all the information you need to answer a variety of questions: How many deep dish pizzas were there? 12. How many calzones were there? 16. How many more calzones than deep dish pizzas were there? 4. How many additional calzones would have to be eaten for the number of calzones and deep dish pizzas to be equal? 4. The SAT-writers can ask all sorts of things, but if you have this information, you're ready for anything they throw at you.

The SAT-writers may throw in extra numbers that aren't used at all to solve the problem. In the preceding example, the team's impressive 21-in-0 win/loss record is interesting but irrelevant in terms of the question you're answering. Don't get distracted by extra information.

Getting DIRTy: Time, Rate, and Distance

Time to dish the dirt, as in D.I.R.T. **D**istance **I**s **R**ate × **T**ime or D = *RT*. When the SAT throws a time, rate, and distance problem at you, use this formula. Make a chart with the formula across the top and fill in the spaces on the chart. Here's an example to help you master this formula:

> Jennifer drives 40 miles an hour for $2\frac{1}{2}$ hours. Her friend Ashley goes the same distance but drives at $1\frac{1}{2}$ times Jennifer's speed. How many *minutes* longer does Jennifer drive than Ashley?

Don't start making mad formulas with *x*'s and *y*'s. Make the DIRT chart using the distance formula: Distance = Rate × Time.

When you fill in the 40 miles per hour and $2\frac{1}{2}$ hours for Jennifer, you can calculate that she went 100 miles. Think of it this way: If she goes 40 miles per hour for 1 hour, that's 40 miles. For a second hour, she goes another 40 miles. In a half hour, she goes $\frac{1}{2}$ of 40, or 20 miles. (See? You don't have to write down $40 \times 2\frac{1}{2}$ and do all that pencil-pushing; use your brain, not your yellow No. 2 pencil or your calculator.) Add them together: $40 + 40 + 20 = 100$. Jennifer drives 100 miles.

	Distance	=	Rate	×	Time
Jennifer	100		40 mph		$2\frac{1}{2}$ hours

Because Ashley drives the same distance, fill in 100 under distance for her. She goes $1\frac{1}{2}$ times as fast. Uh-uh, put down that calculator. Use your brain: 1×40 is 40; $\frac{1}{2} \times 40$ is 20. Add $40 + 20 = 60$. Ashley drives 60 miles per hour. Now this gets really easy. If Ashley drives at 60 miles per hour, she drives one mile a minute (60 minutes in an hour, 60 miles in an hour). Therefore, to go 100 miles takes her 100 minutes. Because your final answer is asked for in minutes, don't bother converting this to hours; leave it the way it is.

	Distance	=	Rate	×	Time
Ashley	100		60 mph		100 minutes

Last step. Jennifer drives $2\frac{1}{2}$ hours. How many minutes is that? Do it the easy way, in your brain. One hour is 60 minutes. A second hour is another 60 minutes. A half hour is 30 minutes. Add them together: $60 + 60 + 30 = 150$ minutes. If Jennifer drives for 150 minutes and Ashley drives for 100 minutes, Jennifer drives 50 minutes more than Ashley.

	Distance	=	Rate	×	Time
Jennifer	100		40 mph		150 minutes
Ashley	100		60 mph		100 minutes

Be careful to note whether the people are traveling in the same direction or opposite directions. Suppose you're asked how far apart drivers are at the end of their trip. If you're told that Jordan travels 40 miles per hour east for 2 hours and Connor travels 60 miles per hour west for 3 hours, they're going in opposite directions. If they start from the same point at the same time, Jordan has gone 80 miles one way, and Connor has gone 180 miles the opposite way. They're 260 miles apart. The trap answer is 100, because careless people (not *you*) simply subtract 80 from 180.

Demonstrating the Value of Radicals

In math-speak, a *radical* is a square root as well as the symbol indicating square root, $\sqrt{}$. The *square root* of number x, written as $\sqrt{x}$, is the positive number, which, multiplied by itself, gives you x. As a classic example, $\sqrt{9} = 3$, because $3 \times 3 = 9$. Although most numbers have square roots that are decidedly not pretty, ($\sqrt{7}$, for example, equals approximately 2.646), most of the radicals you encounter on the SAT will either simplify nicely (such as $\sqrt{25} = 5$) or can be left in the radical form (such as $\sqrt{2}$ or $3\sqrt{5}$).

The rules for multiplication and division of radicals are simple. Just multiply and divide the numbers normally: $\sqrt{5} \times \sqrt{6} = \sqrt{30}$ and $\sqrt{21} \div \sqrt{7} = \sqrt{3}$. However, you can't add or subtract radicals. For example, $\sqrt{3} + \sqrt{5}$ doesn't equal $\sqrt{8}$. You can break down any radical by factoring out a perfect square and simplifying it, so $\sqrt{27} = \sqrt{9}\sqrt{3} = 3\sqrt{3}$, and $\sqrt{12} = \sqrt{4}\sqrt{3} = 2\sqrt{3}$. Also, you can add and subtract radicals that have the same number under the square root symbol, so $2\sqrt{3} + 3\sqrt{3} = 5\sqrt{3}$. In a sense, radicals work like variables. When the variables or radicals are the same, you can add or subtract their coefficients: $5x + 3x = 8x$ and $5\sqrt{2} + 3\sqrt{2} = 8\sqrt{2}$ work the same way.

A few squares show up all the time on the SAT. Scan Table 10-1 so you're familiar with these numbers when you see them.

Table 10-1					Simple Square Roots								
Numbers	$-x$	-1	0	1	2	3	4	5	6	7	8	9	x
Squares	x^2	1	0	1	4	9	16	25	36	49	64	81	x^2

Notice how the square of both x and $-x$ is x^2? Conveniently, when you multiply two negative numbers, the result is positive, as it is when you multiply two positive numbers. So the square of the same negative and positive number is always the same: $(-8)^2 = 64$ and $(+8)^2 = 64$.

A couple of notes on this. First of all, the exponent affects only what it's touching. For example, $5x^2$ is equivalent to $5 \cdot x \cdot x$. You may wonder why the 5 isn't also squared: It's because the exponent is only touching the x. If you want to square the 5 also, put the expression in parentheses, and then put the exponent on it: $(5x)^2 = 5 \cdot x \cdot 5 \cdot x = 25x^2$. This is also true with the negative sign: Put -5^2 in the calculator, and it returns -25. This is because the calculator reads -5^2 as $-5 \cdot 5 = -25$. In other words, it squares the 5 and places the negative on it: -25. To square the entire -5, place it in parentheses. The calculator reads $(-5)^2$ as $(-5) \times (-5)$ and returns the answer you were expecting: 25.

Secondly, if $x^2 = 64$, x could equal either 8 or -8. However, the square root of a number always has the positive value. For example, $\sqrt{64}$ equals 8 but never -8. This is because the square root can only be on a positive number.

Computing Absolute Value

Absolute value is a simple concept that's annoyingly easy to mess up. *Absolute value* is the number, shorn of its positive or negative value. The number has pipes on either side, like this: $|-15|$. The absolute value of 3 is written $|3|$, which equals 3; the absolute value of –3 is written $|-3|$, which also equals 3.

On the SAT, you may see a number or algebraic expression inside the absolute value symbol. If you do, follow these steps:

1. **Simplify whatever is inside the absolute value symbol, if possible.**

2. **If the answer is negative, switch it to positive.**

Some people have the (incorrect) idea that absolute value changes subtraction to addition. Nope. If you're working with $|3-4|$, don't change the quantity to $3+4$. Calculate whatever is inside the absolute value symbols first, $|3-4| = |-1|$, and only *then* change the result to a positive number, in this case 1.

Finding the Pattern

Math sometimes involves recognizing patterns and seeing where those patterns lead. The SAT occasionally asks you to play mathematician with two types of patterns: *arithmetic* and *geometric*. The math word for pattern, by the way, is *sequence*.

Check out this arithmetic sequence: 2, 5, 8, 11, 14. . . . Notice how each number is 3 more than the previous number? In an arithmetic sequence, you always add or subtract the same number to the previous term to get the next term. Another example of an arithmetic sequence is 80, 73, 66, 59. . . . In this one, you're subtracting 7 from the previous term.

A geometric sequence is similar to an arithmetic sequence, but it works by multiplication or division. In the sequence 2, 6, 18, 54, . . . every term is multiplied by 3 to get the next term. In 88, 44, 22, 11, . . . each term is divided by 2 to get the next term.

Often, the best way to solve these problems is just to make a list and follow the pattern. However, if the test writers ask you for something like the 20th term of the sequence, this process can take forever. Each type of sequence has a useful formula, which is worth memorizing if you have the time and the room in your head:

✔ For an arithmetic sequence, the *n*th term = a (the first term) + $(n-1)d$, where d is the difference between consecutive terms in the sequence. In the sequence 2, 5, 8, 11, 14, the difference between consecutive terms is +3, because you add 3 each time. What would be the 20th term? Take 2, the first term, and add 3 nineteen times, so it's $2 + 19(3) = 2 + 57 = 59$.

✔ For a geometric sequence, the *n*th term = a (the first term) $\times r^{(n-1)}$, where r is the ratio of one term to the next. Huh? Well, you probably remember that taking something to a power (that's what the exponent stands for) means multiplying it by itself a bunch of times. For example, 4 to the 3rd power = $4 \times 4 \times 4$, which equals 64. You can do powers on most calculators by using either the "y^x" or the "$\wedge$" button.

✔ Check out this sequence: 2, 6, 18, 54. The ratio is 3, because you multiply by 3 each time. To find the 10th term (the 20th would be way too big to handle), take 2×3^9 (that's 3 to the 9th power): $3^9 = 19,683$, and $2 \times 19,683 = 39,366$, so that's the answer.

To find the *n*th term, you always use $n-1$, no matter what kind of sequence it is.

As if your life weren't tough enough, the SAT folks often hide these sequences inside a word problem, such as the following:

The bacteria population in my day-old wad of chewing gum doubles every 3 hours. If there are 100 bacteria at 12:00 noon on Friday, how many bacteria will be present at midnight of the same day?

(A) 200

(B) 300

(C) 800

(D) 1,600

The right answer is Choice (D). To solve this problem, make a chart. Because the population doubles every 3 hours, count off 3-hour intervals, doubling as you go:

> 12:00 (noon) = 100 bacteria
>
> 3:00 p.m. = 200 bacteria
>
> 6:00 p.m. = 400 bacteria
>
> 9:00 p.m. = 800 bacteria
>
> 12:00 (midnight) = 1,600 bacteria

Or use the formula for $100 \times 2^4 = 100 \times 16 = 1,600$.

And here's another example in which the formulas come in handy:

Author A, an extraordinarily fast writer who zips through a chapter a day, gets paid $100 for her first chapter, $200 for her second, $300 for her third, and so on. Author B, also a member of the chapter-a-day club, gets paid $1 for his first chapter, $2 for his second, $4 for his third, $8 for his fourth, and so on. On the 12th day,

(A) Author A is paid $76 more.

(B) Author B is paid $24 more.

(C) Author A is paid $1,178 more.

(D) Author B is paid $848 more.

The correct answer is Choice (D). Author A's plan is an arithmetic sequence, increasing by $100 each time, so on the 12th day she's paid $100 + 11(100) = 100 + 1,100 = \$1,200$. Author B's plan is a geometric sequence, multiplied by 2 each time, so on the 12th day, he's paid $1 \times 2^{11} = 1 \times 2,048 = \$2,048$. Because $\$2,048 - \$1,200 = \$848$, author B is paid $848 more.

Setting a Spell

A *set* is just a collection of things — marbles, hockey pucks, Legos, whatever. In math, a set is a collection of *elements,* usually numbers, which you find inside brackets: $\{\ldots\}$. For example, the set of positive integers less than 6 is a set with five elements: $\{1, 2, 3, 4, 5\}$. Some sets go on forever, and three dots at the end tell you so. The set of positive odd numbers is $\{1, 3, 5, 7, \ldots\}$

because it reaches infinity. A set may have nothing inside of it; this is the "empty set" or "null set," and it's written either $\{\ \}$ or, more commonly, $\varnothing$.

For the SAT, you need to know about two specific things when it comes to sets — the union and the intersection of sets. The *union* of two sets is just the two sets put together; thus, the union of $\{1, 2, 3\}$ and $\{5, 7, 8\}$ is $\{1, 2, 3, 5, 7, 8\}$.

Even if something shows up in both sets, it shows up only once in the union. Thus, the union of $\{2, 3, 4\}$ and $\{3, 4, 5\}$ is $\{2, 3, 4, 5\}$, *not* $\{2, 3, 3, 4, 4, 5\}$. The following steps help you find the number of elements in the union of two sets:

1. **Add up the number of elements in each set.**

2. **Subtract the number of elements that show up in both.**

To count the elements in the preceding example, $3 + 3 = 6$; but because 3 and 4 show up in both sets, you have to subtract 2. The union has 4 elements. The *intersection* of two sets, on the other hand, contains only those elements that show up in both sets. The intersection of $\{1, 2, 4\}$ and $\{4, 6, 7\}$ is $\{4\}$; the intersection of $\{3, 5, 7\}$ and $\{2, 4, 6\}$ is $\varnothing$.

Chapter 11

Practicing Problems in Numbers and Operations

. . . .

In This Chapter

▶ Trying your hand at SAT questions involving numbers and operations

▶ Figuring out which problems give you the most trouble

. . . .

*T*hat old saying, "Practice makes perfect," is annoying yet true. In this chapter, we hit you with two sets of numbers and operations questions along with explanations of the answers.

After you practice each question in the first set, check your answers and read the explanations for any questions you answered incorrectly. (The answers immediately follow each question. Use a piece of paper to cover the answers as you work.) If you're confused about any point, check Chapter 10 for more details on the kind of problem that's stumping you.

The second set is set up like the real test: You do all the problems and then check your work with the answer key that follows the last question.

Set One: Trying Out Some Guided Questions

1. If you invest $2,000 for one year at 5% annual interest, the total amount you would have at the end of the year would be

    (A) $100

    (B) $2,005

    (C) $2,100

    (D) $2,500

    Solve the question like this: 5% = 0.05, so 5% of $2,000 = 0.05 × $2,000 = $100. But wait! Before you choose $100 as your answer, remember that you still have the $2,000 that you originally invested, so you now have $2,000 + $100 = $2,100. Choice (C) is correct.

2. Which number is an element of the set of prime numbers but not of the set of odd numbers?

    (A) 0

    (B) 1

    (C) 2

    (D) 3

    Because 2 is the only prime number that isn't odd, Choice (C) is correct.

3. 100 percent of 99 subtracted from 99 percent of 100 equals

    (A) –1

    (B) 0

    (C) 0.99

    (D) 1

Keep in mind that 100 percent of anything is itself, so 100 percent of 99 is 99. And 99 percent of 100 equals $0.99 \times 100 = 99$ (not a big surprise because percent means "out of one hundred"). And $99 - 99 = 0$, so Choice (B) is the correct answer.

4. The tenth number of the sequence 50, 44.5, 39, 33.5, . . . is

    (A) –4

    (B) 0.5

    (C) 1

    (D) 1.5

The numbers decrease by 5.5 every time. The simplest way to do this problem is to continue the pattern: 50, 44.5, 39, 33.5, 28, 22.5, 17, 11.5, 6, 0.5. You can also use the following formula to find the tenth term: the nth term = the first term $+(n-1)d$, where d is the difference between terms in the sequence. Therefore, $50+9(-5.5) = 50-49.5 = 0.5$ $50+(10-1)(-5.5) = 50-49.5 = 0.5$. Choice (B) is the correct answer.

5. If E represents the set of even numbers and N represents the set of numbers divisible by 9, which number is in the intersection of E and N?

    (A) 99

    (B) 92

    (C) 66

    (D) 54

An element is in the intersection of two sets only if it's in both of them. You can go through the choices until you find the right one: 99 isn't even; 92 isn't divisible by 9; 66 isn't divisible by 9; 54 is even *and* divisible by 9. Thus, 54 is the only one that works, and Choice (D) is the right answer.

6. The first three elements of a geometric sequence are 1, 2, and 4. What is the eighth element of the sequence?

    (A) 14

    (B) 16

    (C) 29

    (D) 128

The formula for geometric sequences tells you that the answer is $1 \times 2^7 = 1 \times 128 = 128$. (Remember that in this formula, the exponent is one less than the number of the term you're being asked for.) Go with Choice (D).

7. The expression $3^2 - 4 + 5\left(\frac{8}{2}\right)$ equals

    (A) –27

    (B) –15

    (C) 5

    (D) 25

    "Aunt Sally" can help with this problem. (See Chapter 10 for the lowdown on our favorite relative.) First, do the operation in parentheses, $\frac{8}{2} = 4$, and then calculate 3^2, which equals 9. That leaves you with $9 - 4 + 5(4)$. Next, multiply $5 \times 4 = 20$. Now the expression is $9 - 4 + 20$. You have a trap to avoid: Did you see it? Don't do addition before subtraction; just go left to right: $9 - 4 = 5$, and $5 + 20 = 25$. Aunt Sally says Choice (D) is correct.

8. Which of the following numbers is rational?

    (A) π

    (B) $0.12112111211112\ldots$

    (C) $\sqrt{8}$

    (D) $\sqrt{9}$

    To do this problem, you need to remember the definitions of rational and irrational numbers. π is irrational by definition. (Yes, it's worth memorizing this fact.) The number $0.12112111211112\ldots$ is irrational because the decimal never ends or repeats. (For those of you who are still awake, it doesn't repeat because the number of 1s keeps increasing.) All radicals are irrational if the number underneath the radical symbol isn't a perfect square, so $\sqrt{8}$ is irrational. However, because $\sqrt{9} = 3$, it's rational. Choice (D) is correct.

9. Given that there are 30 days in April, the ratio of rainy days to sunny days during the month of April could *not* be

    (A) 5:3

    (B) 3:2

    (C) 5:1

    (D) 4:1

    The rule for ratios states that the total must be divisible by the sum of the numbers in the ratio. Because $5 + 3 = 8$, and 30 isn't divisible by 8, Choice (A) is correct. Just to be sure, check that all the other possible sums do go into 30.

10. At a sale, a shirt normally priced at $60 was sold for $48. What was the percentage of the discount?

    (A) 12%

    (B) 20%

    (C) 25%

    (D) 48%

    Use the percentage formula, $\frac{is}{of} = \frac{x}{100}$, but, as always, be extra careful. The problem asks for the percentage of the discount, so don't just plug in 48. Instead, first figure out the amount of the discount, which was $60 - 48 = 12$. Using 12, write $\frac{12}{60} = \frac{p}{100}$, where p is the percentage of the discount. Cross-multiplying, you get $1,200 = 60p$, and $p = 20$. You can still get the right answer using 48. If you use 48 in the formula, you get 80%. Because the shirt now costs 80% of what it used to, the discount is $100\% - 80\% = 20\%$. Choice (B) is correct.

Set Two: Practicing Some Questions on Your Own

Note: Two questions (2 and 6) are grid-ins. On the blank grids in this section, write and bubble in your answers. (See Chapter 9 for the proper way to bubble in your answers for grid-in questions.)

1. The total number of even three-digit numbers is

   (A) 49

   (B) 100

   (C) 449

   (D) 450

2. Evaluate $\left|10 - \left(42 \div |1-4|\right)\right|$.

3. A shark is eating the fish in a certain lake. Every eight days, exactly half of the fish in the lake are eaten. If there are 1,000 fish in the lake on March 3, how many remain on March 27?

   (A) 0

   (B) 100

   (C) 125

   (D) 250

4. If a number n is the product of two distinct primes, x and y, how many factors does n have, including 1 and itself?

   (A) 2

   (B) 3

   (C) 4

   (D) 5

5. Which number is 30% greater than 30?

    (A) 27

    (B) 30.9

    (C) 33

    (D) 39

6. A recipe for French toast batter calls for 1/2 teaspoon of cinnamon for every 5 eggs. How many teaspoons of cinnamon would be needed if a restaurant made a batch of batter using 45 eggs?

7. Which of the following is *not* equivalent to $\sqrt{40}$?

    (A) $2\sqrt{10}$

    (B) $\sqrt{30} + \sqrt{10}$

    (C) $\sqrt{5} \times \sqrt{8}$

    (D) $\sqrt{90} - \sqrt{10}$

8. Janice wrote down all the numbers from 11 to 20. Darren wrote down all the positive numbers less than 30 that are divisible by 6. How many numbers are in the union of their two lists?

    (A) 2

    (B) 12

    (C) 14

    (D) 15

9. Elena drove for one hour at 60 miles per hour and for half an hour at 30 miles per hour. Returning home along the same route, she maintained a constant speed. If the journey home took the same total amount of time as the original drive, what was her speed on the journey home?

    (A) 40 mph

    (B) 42 mph

    (C) 45 mph

    (D) 50 mph

$$ABC$$
10. $\underline{+6BC}$
$$1,B5A$$

In the correctly solved addition problem above, *A*, *B*, and *C* all stand for different numbers from 1 to 9. The value of *C* must be

(A) 8

(B) 7

(C) 6

(D) 5

Answers to Set Two

1. **D.** Counting all the even three-digit numbers would take a really long time, so try to figure out this question logically. The three-digit numbers start with 100 and end with 999. How many numbers do you have? It's 900, not 899. (Yes, there is a formula you can use here: Subtract the numbers and add 1. Works every time.) How many of these numbers are even? Well, because even and odd numbers alternate on this list, half of them are even, and half are odd. So you have 450 of each type. Choice (D) is right.

2. **4.** When doing an absolute value problem, treat the absolute value symbols as parentheses when trying to figure out the order of operations. Because this problem has a bunch of parentheses and absolute values, work from the inside out:

$$\left|10-\left(42\div|1-4|\right)\right|$$
$$\left|10-\left(42\div|-3|\right)\right|$$
$$\left|10-\left(42\div3\right)\right|$$
$$\left|10-\left(14\right)\right|$$
$$\left|-4\right|$$
$$4$$

3. **C.** On March 3, 1,000 fish exist. On March 11, 500 fish are alive. On March 19, 250 fish are swimming. And on March 27, 125 fish remain. Choice (C) is correct.

4. **C.** Prime numbers have only two factors: 1 and themselves. Pretend in your problem that $x = 5$ and $y = 7$. Then $n = 5 \times 7 = 35$. The factors of 35 are 1, 5, 7, and 35. Because you can't break down 5 or 7, there are no other factors. As long as you pick prime numbers for x and y, you'll always get four factors for n. Choice (C) is correct.

5. **D.** Solve it like this: 30% of $30 = 0.30 \times 30 = 9$. Because the answer is 30% greater than 30, add $30 + 9 = 39$. Go with Choice (D).

6. **4.5 or 9/2.** If 1/2 teaspoon is needed for 5 eggs, then 9 times that (because $9 \times 5 = 45$) is needed to make 45 eggs: $9 \times 1/2 = 4.5$ or 9/2. (Don't grid in $4\frac{1}{2}$. The machine will read it as 41/2, which is wrong.)

7. **B.** You could use a calculator to figure out what each choice equals, but it's better to work with the radicals, because you'll catch mistakes easier. Start with $2\sqrt{10}$. To multiply these,

turn 2 into $\sqrt{4}$; now, $\sqrt{4} \times \sqrt{10} = \sqrt{40}$. On to Choice (B): You can't add radicals, and there's no way to break down $\sqrt{30}$ or $\sqrt{10}$, because no perfect square goes into either one. So you're stuck on this one. In Choice (C), $\sqrt{5} \times \sqrt{8} = \sqrt{40}$. In Choice (D), which is $\sqrt{90} - \sqrt{10}$, $\sqrt{90}$ becomes $\sqrt{9} \times \sqrt{10}$ and then $3\sqrt{10}$. Now $3\sqrt{10} - \sqrt{10} = 2\sqrt{10}$, which matches Choice (A), which you already know is equivalent to $\sqrt{40}$. Bottom line: They all equal $\sqrt{40}$, except for Choice (B). If you check it out on a calculator, $\sqrt{40} \approx 6.32$, but $\sqrt{30} + \sqrt{10} \approx 8.64$. Thus, Choice (B) is correct.

8. **B.** Janice's list has 10 numbers: $\{11, 12, 13, 14, 15, 16, 17, 18, 19, 20\}$. Darren's list has 4 numbers: $\{6, 12, 18, 24\}$. Now, don't fall into the trap of thinking that there are 14 numbers in the union; even though 12 and 18 show up in both sets, you're not allowed to count them twice in the union. The total number of elements in the union is $14 - 2 = 12$. Choice (B) is correct.

9. **D.** The original trip took $1\frac{1}{2}$ hours. Elena traveled 60 miles plus half of 30, which is $60 + 15$ or 75 miles. The return trip took the same amount of time: 1 hour $+ \frac{1}{2}$ hour $= 1\frac{1}{2}$ hours. And 75 miles divided by $1\frac{1}{2}$ hours equals 50 miles per hour. Choice (D) is correct.

10. **A.** You know that

$$
\begin{array}{r}
ABC \\
+6BC \\
\hline
1,B5A
\end{array}
$$

This problem takes some inductive reasoning. A must be an even number because you get it by adding $C + C$, but A can't be 2, because then the two numbers wouldn't add up to something bigger than 1,000. So A = 4, 6, or 8.

Now look at the tens column. The sum of $B + B$ can't be 5 unless you carried a "1" from the ones column. That means that $C + C$ = 14, 16, or 18, so C = 7, 8, or 9.

What about B? The sum of $B + B + 1$ (you carried, remember) gives you 5. So B could be either 2 or 7, because $7 + 7 + 1 = 15$. But if B = 7, then the hundreds column makes no sense. (Try it and you'll see why.) So B must be 2. Because B = 2, A must be 6 to make the hundreds column work, and that makes C = 8. Check the original problem:

$$
\begin{array}{r}
628 \\
+628 \\
\hline
1,256
\end{array}
$$

It works: Choice (A) is correct.

Hitting a vocabulary homer

Had enough math for the moment? Take a TV break. Have you ever seen anyone less *hirsute* (hairy) than Homer Simpson? This famous *gourmand* (someone who loves to eat and drink a large quantity) isn't exactly a fan of *gourmet* cooking (featuring excellent or high-quality food and drink). Homer is *gullible* (he'll believe anything) and *indolent* (don't wake him up when he's "working"). Three words you'll never use to describe Homer are *adroit* (clever), *lithe* (graceful), and *emaciated* (starving). Yet he is lovable.

Chapter 12

X Marks the Spot: Algebra and Functions

If x is the value of the present your mom expects for her birthday and y is the amount of money in your piggybank, what equation best represents your chances of staying on her good side this year? Don't worry. This problem won't appear on the SAT, but it's a good example of algebra: You play with letters, even though you're solving a math problem.

If you love algebra, or even if you'd prefer to shred the pages of your algebra text, this chapter's for you. Here, you find a quick and dirty review of the basics of SAT algebra, plus a spin through functions, where $f(x)$ rules.

Note: Throughout this chapter and this book, the × multiplication symbol is used in problems that involve two or more numbers; whenever the problem involves variables, the · multiplication symbol is used instead.

Powering Up: Exponents

Many SAT questions require you to know how to work with bases and exponents. Here's the lowdown on some of the most important concepts:

▶ **The *base* is the big number (or letter) on the bottom. The *exponent* is the little number (or letter) in the upper-right corner.**

- In x^5, x is the base; 5 is the exponent.
- In 3^y, 3 is the base; y is the exponent.

▶ **A base to the zero power equals one.**

- $x^0 = 1$
- $129^0 = 1$

There is a long, *soporific* (sleep-causing) explanation as to why a number to the zero power equals one, but you don't really care, do you? For now, just memorize the rule.

▶ **A base to the first power is just the base. In other words, $4^1 = 4$.**

▶ **A base to the second power is *base* × *base*.**

- $x^2 = x \cdot x$
- $5^2 = 5 \times 5 = 25$

✔ **The same is true for bigger exponents.** The exponent tells you how many times the number repeats. For example, 3^4 means that you write down four 3s and then multiply them all together.

- $3^4 = 3 \times 3 \times 3 \times 3 = 81$

- Remember that an exponent tells you to multiply the base times itself as many times as the exponent, so 2^3 does *not* equal 6 ($2^3 = 2 \times 2 \times 2 = 8$).

TIP

On most calculators, you can do powers with either the "y^x" or the "$\wedge$" button. Just type the base, the appropriate button, the exponent, and the trusty "=" button. However, almost all the exponents you encounter on the SAT are simple enough that you don't need a calculator.

✔ **A base to a negative exponent is the reciprocal of the base to a positive exponent.**

A *reciprocal* is the upside-down version of a fraction. For example, $\frac{4}{3}$ is the reciprocal of $\frac{3}{4}$. An integer (except 0) can also have a reciprocal: $\frac{1}{3}$ is the reciprocal of 3. When you have a negative exponent, just put base and exponent under a 1 and make the exponent positive again.

- $x^{-4} = \dfrac{1}{x^4}$

- $5^{-3} = \dfrac{1}{5^3} = \dfrac{1}{125}$

The answer isn't negative. When you flip it, you get the reciprocal, and the negative goes away. Don't fall for the trap of saying that $5^{-3} = -5^3$ or -125.

Also, if a number or variable with a negative exponent, such as x^{-4}, appears in the denominator of a fraction, such as $\dfrac{2}{3x^{-4}}$, you can make the exponent positive and move it to the numerator, like this: $\dfrac{2x^4}{3}$.

✔ **A base to a fractional exponent is a root of the base.** Ah, more confusion. You're already familiar with the standard square root of a number: $\sqrt{25} = 5$ because $5^2 = 25$. Because it takes two 5s to make 25, you can also write $25^{1/2} = 5$.

✔ **To multiply like bases, add the exponents.**

- $x^3 \cdot x^2 = x^{(3+2)} = x^5$

- $5^4 \times 5^9 = 5^{(4+9)} = 5^{13}$

- $p^3 \cdot p = p^3 \cdot p^1 = p^{(3+1)} = p^4$

- $129^3 \times 129^0 = 129^{(3+0)} = 129^3$

WARNING!

You can't multiply numbers with *unlike* bases. (Actually you can, by making the exponents the same, but that's not something you do on the SAT.)

- $x^2 \cdot y^3$ stays $x^2 \cdot y^3$

- $5^2 \times 7^3$ stays $5^2 \times 7^3$ (you actually have to work it out)

✔ **To divide like bases, subtract the exponents.** You can divide two bases that are the same by subtracting the exponents.

- $x^5 \div x^2 = x^{(5-2)} = x^3$

- $5^9 \div 5^3 = 5^{(9-3)} = 5^6$

- $x^3 \div x^7 = x^{(3-7)} = x^{-4} = \dfrac{1}{x^4}$

- $129^2 \div 129^0 = 129^{(2-0)} = 129^2$

(That last one should make sense if you think about it. Any base to the zero power is 1. Any number divided by 1 is itself.)

Did you look at the second example, $5^9 \div 5^3$, and think that it was 5^3? Falling into the trap of dividing instead of subtracting the exponents is easy, especially when you see numbers that just beg to be divided, such as 9 and 3. Keep your guard up.

✔ **Multiply exponents that appear inside and outside of parentheses, like this:**

- $\left(x^2\right)^3 = x^{(2 \cdot 3)} = x^6$
- $\left(5^4\right)^3 = 5^{(4 \times 3)} = 5^{12}$

✔ **You can add and subtract bases with exponents if the bases and exponents are the same.** Remember, the *base* is the number or letter tied to the exponent.

- **x^3:** The base is x, and the exponent is 3.

- **$x^3 + x^3 = 2x^3$:** This works the same way as $x + x = 2x$.

- **$37x^3 + 10x^3 = 47x^3$:** Because the bases are the same and the exponents are the same, just add the numbers (also known as numerical coefficients) to count the x^3: $37 + 10 = 47$.

- **$15y^2 - 10y^2 = 5y^2$:** Just subtract the numbers to count the y^2: $15 - 10 = 5$.

You can't count bases with different exponents or different bases. In other words, $13x^3 - 9x^2$ stays $13x^3 - 9x^2$, and $2x^2 + 3y^2$ stays $2x^2 + 3y^2$. The bases and exponents must be the same for you to combine them.

Putting It Together and Taking It Apart: FOIL and Factoring

One of the most common tasks that you probably remember from algebra class is the multiplication of expressions. These expressions come in several varieties:

✔ **One term times one term:** To multiply two terms, multiply their coefficients and *add* the powers of any common variables being multiplied; for example, $\left(3a^3\right)\left(-2a\right) = \left(3 \times -2\right)\left(a^{3+1}\right) = -6a^4$. Check out the earlier section "Powering Up: Exponents" for more details about exponents.

✔ **One term times two (or more) terms:** Use the familiar distributive law: Multiply the single term by each of the terms in parentheses. Be sure to take your time and work out each product individually before combining them for the final answer.

To simplify $3b^3\left(2b^2 - 5\right)$, write each multiplication task separately:

- $\left(3b^3\right)\left(2b^2\right) = 6b^5$
- $\left(3b^3\right)\left(-5\right) = -15b^3$

And your answer is $6b^5 - 15b^3$.

✔ **Two terms times two terms:** Now, you FOIL: Multiply in the order *First, Outer, Inner, Last*.

To work out $\left(x - 3\right)\left(2x + 5\right)$:

1. Multiply the **First** terms: $\left(x\right)\left(2x\right) = 2x^2$.

2. Multiply the **Outer** terms: $\left(x\right)\left(5\right) = 5x$.

3. Multiply the **Inner** terms: $\left(-3\right)\left(2x\right) = -6x$.

4. Multiply the **Last** terms: $-3 \times 5 = -15$.

5. Combine like terms: $5x - 6x = -x$.

And your solution is $2x^2 - x - 15$.

Memorize the following three special cases of FOIL. Don't bother to work them out every time you see them. If you know them by heart, you can save valuable SAT minutes on test day.

✔ $(a+b)(a-b)=a^2-b^2$. You can use this shortcut only when the two terms are exactly the same *except for their signs*. For example, $(x+5)(x-5)=x^2-5^2=x^2-25$.

✔ $(a+b)^2=(a+b)(a+b)=a^2+2ab+b^2$.

✔ $(a-b)^2=(a-b)(a-b)=a^2-2ab+b^2$. Check out the following example to see the rule in action.

The expression $(x-3)^2$ is equivalent to

(A) x^2-9

(B) x^2+9

(C) x^2+6x-9

(D) x^2-6x+9

The correct answer is Choice (D). Choices (A) and (B) are wrong, because you don't just distribute the exponent. If you FOIL it out, you get $(x-3)(x-3)=x^2-3x-3x+9=x^2-6x+9$. Or you could just use the formula: $(x-3)^2=x^2+2(-3)x+(-3)^2=x^2-6x+9$.

Now that you know how to do algebra forward, are you ready to do it backward? You need to be able to factor down a quadratic equation, taking it from its final form back to its original form of two sets of parentheses.

For example, given $x^2+13x+42=0$, solve for x.

Take this problem one step at a time:

1. **Set up your answer by drawing two sets of parentheses.**

    $(\quad)(\quad)=0$.

2. **To get x^2, the *first* terms have to be x and x. Fill those in.**

    $(x\quad)(x\quad)=0$.

3. **Look now at the *last* term in the problem.**

    You need two numbers that multiply together to be +42. Well, there are several possibilities such as 42×1, 21×2, or 6×7. You can even have two negative numbers: -42×-1, -21×-2, or -6×-7. You aren't sure which one to choose, so go on to the next step.

4. **Look at the *middle* term in the problem.**

    You have to add two values to get +13. What's the first thing that springs to mind? Probably $6+7$. Hey, that's one of the possibilities in the preceding step! Plug it in and try it.

    $(x+6)(x+7)=x^2+7x+6x+42=x^2+13x+42$

Great, but you're not done, yet. The whole equation equals 0, so you have $(x+6)(x+7)=0$. Because any number times 0 equals 0, either $(x+6)=0$ or $(x+7)=0$. Therefore, x can equal either -6 or -7, not both and *not* +6 or +7. These possible values of x are known as the *roots* of the equation.

You may also have to factor an expression like $y^2 - 49 = 0$. This sort of problem probably looks familiar to you if you remember the formula (discussed earlier in this section): $(a+b)(a-b) = a^2 - b^2$. The expression $y^2 - 49 = 0$ is known as a *difference of squares* because it equals $y^2 - 7^2 = 0$. Any difference of squares can be factored like this: $y^2 - 49 = (y+7)(y-7) = 0$, and just as with $y^2 = 49$, y equals either 7 or –7. This is why $y^2 = 49$ is known as a *square root*. SAT factoring is usually simple.

Solving Equations: Why Don't They Just Tell Me What X Is?

You've probably spent a lot of time in school solving the two most basic types of equations: *linear* (for example, $3x + 5 = 5x - 7$, whose solution is $x = 6$) and *quadratic* (for example, $x^2 + 13x + 42 = 0$, solved in the preceding section by factoring). Every once in a while, the SAT-makers also hit you with more complex algebraic equations: absolute value equations, rational equations, and radical equations. This section provides you a brief overview of these topics so they look familiar if you run into any of them on SAT day.

Remember that most of the SAT is a multiple-choice test. When you're presented with an equation that you're not sure how to solve, you can often fall back on plugging in the answers one at a time.

Absolute value

Absolute value presents you with a number, letter, or expression inside of two lines, as explained in Chapter 10. Here is what you do when one pops up in an equation. Check out this problem:

In the equation $|x - 4| = 3$, x could equal

(A) 7 only

(B) 1 only

(C) 7 or 1

(D) 7 or –1

The correct answer is Choice (C). Because an absolute value symbol turns everything into a positive number, the expression inside the absolute value could equal either 3 or –3. This is the key to solving an equation with an absolute value. If $|something| = n$, then either *something* $= n$ or *something* $= -n$. You must solve each of these equations separately to get two answers. But there's a catch: You also must check each answer in the original equation. Only solutions that make the original equation true count in your final answer.

Now back to the preceding example:

$$|x - 4| = 3$$
$$x - 4 = 3 \quad \text{or} \quad x - 4 = -3$$
$$x = 7 \qquad\qquad x = 1$$

Check your work:

$$|(7)-4| = 3 \qquad |(1)-4| = 3$$
$$|3| = 3 \quad \text{and} \quad |-3| = 3$$
$$3 = 3 \qquad\qquad 3 = 3$$

Because both checks work, your answer is Choice (C): 7 or 1.

You could, of course, just plug in the choices to solve the problem. Remember those pesky grid-ins, though! Because not every problem is multiple-choice, take the time to figure out how to solve each type of equation from scratch.

The value of x can't be both 7 *and* 1. x has one value, and that's why the problem says, "*x could* equal."

Radical equations

Radical equations are equations that contain square roots. Check out this example:

Find the solution to the equation $3\sqrt{x} + 5 = 17$.

Because this question isn't multiple-choice (yep, it's a grid-in), you have to solve this problem the long way. In a normal linear equation, you start by isolating x; here, you must first isolate $\sqrt{x}$:

$$3\sqrt{x} + 5 = 17$$
$$3\sqrt{x} = 12$$
$$\sqrt{x} = 4$$

Now don't make the mistake of thinking that x should be 2; $\sqrt{2}$ doesn't equal 4. Instead, square both sides, and $x = 16$.

Rational equations

Rational equations have fractions in them. Sometimes, when the denominators of the fractions contain only numbers, removing the fractions and dealing with a simpler problem is easier. To solve $\frac{x}{3} + 1 = \frac{x}{2} - 3$, you multiply every term by 6, because that's the smallest number that eliminates both the 2 and the 3 (officially, 6 is the *least common denominator*, or LCD, of 2 and 3). Assuming you cancel correctly, your new equation is $2x + 6 = 3x - 18$, and x equals 24. (We're letting you do the steps by yourself; practice makes perfect scores.)

When the denominator contains variables, your best bet is to combine terms with like denominators and then cross-multiply:

$$\frac{12}{x} + \frac{15}{x-1} = \frac{25}{x-1}$$
$$-\frac{15}{x-1} \quad -\frac{15}{x-1}$$
$$\frac{12}{x} = \frac{10}{x-1}$$

Cross-multiplying gives you $12(x-1)=10x$. Then $12x-12=10x$, and $x=6$. If you plug back into the original equation, you get

$$\frac{12}{6}+\frac{15}{5}=\frac{25}{5}, \text{ or } 2+3=5$$

So your answer checks out.

Direct and inverse proportion

In a direct or inverse proportion problem, instead of being given an equation to work with, the SAT-makers tell you that two quantities "are directly proportional" or "inversely proportional." These expressions represent two specific types of equations that you're already familiar with under other names.

A *direct proportion* problem is just another type of ratio problem. If a and b are directly proportional, then the ratio $\frac{a}{b}$ is always equal to a certain constant. Thus, you can solve a direct proportion problem by setting up the ratio $\frac{a_1}{b_1}=\frac{a_2}{b_2}$, cross-multiplying, and solving as usual, as you do in this example:

x and y are directly proportional. If $x=10$ when $y=6$, what does x equal when $y=21$?

Let $x_1=10$ and $y_1=6$. Then x_2 is what you're looking for, and $y_2=21$. Set up the ratio

$\frac{x_1}{y_1}=\frac{x_2}{y_2}$ or $\frac{10}{6}=\frac{x_2}{21}$, and cross-multiply to get $6x_2=210$, so $x_2=35$.

Notice that as one variable increases, the other variable also increases. This feature of direct proportion problems helps you do a common-sense check of your answer.

When two variables vary *inversely*, their product is always equal to the same number. For example, suppose that p and q vary inversely, and $p=3$ when $q=12$. Because $pq=(3)(12)=36$ in this case, pq must equal 36 for all values of p and q. When $p=2$, $q=18$ (and vice versa); when $p=6$, $q=6$ as well. This strategy works for all inverse proportion problems.

Barely Functioning

By the time you get to functions on the SAT, you may think that you can't . . . function, that is. But think of a function as a simple computer program: You give it an input, and it produces an output. For example, $f(x)=2x-1$ is a function. You put in a number for x (5, for example) and get out $2x-1$ or $2(5)-1$ as a result (9, in this case). The input and output can then be written as an ordered pair: $(5, 9)$ is a member of this function, as are the pairs $(1, 1)$ and $(0.5, 0)$, along with infinite others.

Consider the example $f(x)=x-4$: $f(9)=5$, $f(4)=0$, and $f(1)=-3$. In other words, when you put in 9 for x, you get out 5; when you put in 4, you get out 0; and when you put in 1, you get out –3. Notice that $f(x)$ and y are the same thing.

Notice that the number replaces x when evaluating the function. When x is 9, for example, just replace x with 9 throughout the equation. So $f(x) = x - 4$ becomes $f(9) = 9 - 4$, and you know that $f(9) = 5$.

On the SAT, you may be given a function and be asked what *can't* go into it. Keep in mind two things that you can't do in a function:

✔ Divide by zero.

✔ Take the square root of a negative number.

So if you see a function like $y = \sqrt{x - 4}$, numbers like 4, 5, 6, and so on are okay, but numbers less than 4 aren't, because then you'd have a negative number under the radical. For a function like $f(x) = \dfrac{x + 2}{(x - 4)(x + 1)}$, x could be any number except 4 or –1, because plugging in those numbers gives you a denominator of zero, which doesn't work. Notice, by the way, that plugging in –2 is fine, because it's okay for the *numerator* of a fraction to be zero.

Functioning at a Higher Level

At this point, you may be wondering, "Why are functions such a big deal?" After all, functions seem like a pretty abstract concept. However, it turns out that a huge number of real-life situations can be modeled using functions. To do well on the Math section of the SAT, you definitely want to be good friends with two of the most common types of functions: linear and quadratic.

Figuring out linear functions

You've probably worked a lot with linear functions, especially in graphing. All linear functions have the form $y = mx + b$ or $f(x) = mx + b$. In graphing terms, m represents the slope of the line being drawn, while b represents its y-intercept. Take a look at this example:

If $f(x)$ is a linear function with a slope of 2, passing through the point $(-2, -3)$, $f(x)$ must also pass through the point

(A) $(1, 2)$

(B) $(1, 3)$

(C) $(2, 2)$

(D) $(2, 3)$

The correct answer is Choice (B). The best way to solve this problem is to draw a graph. To get it right, you have to remember the meaning of slope: Slope $= \dfrac{\text{rise}}{\text{run}}$. A slope of $\dfrac{2}{5}$, for example, tells you to move 2 spaces up (the rise) and 5 spaces to the right (the run). You don't have to be a great artist, just count the spaces. The function in this problem has a slope of 2, which is the same as $\frac{2}{1}$. Starting at $(-2,-3)$ and following these directions yields this graph:

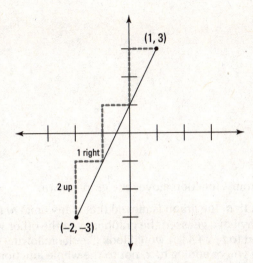

Instead of simply giving you numbers, the SAT-writers may present a real-world situation and ask you to model it with a function. For example, if an express mail package costs $1.50 plus $0.40 per pound, you can write $c = 1.50 + 0.40p$, where c is the cost and p represents the number of pounds.

Thinking through quadratic functions

Quadratic functions, on the other hand, have the form $y = ax^2 + bx + c$ or $f(x) = ax^2 + bx + c$. Graphically, they're represented by a *parabola,* a shape that resembles the basic roller-coaster hump. You certainly won't be asked to graph any of these, but you may be asked some graph-based questions. Keep these points in mind as you work with quadratic functions:

✔ The roots or solutions of a function are the x-values that make $f(x) = 0$. On a graph, these roots are the points where the graph crosses the horizontal x-axis.

✔ The number of solutions of $f(x) = a$ is the number of points where the graph has a height of a. On the following graph, $f(x) = 3$ twice, at the marked points.

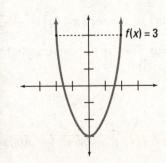

✔ If a number is added to a function, the graph is moved up that many units. If the function above were changed from $f(x)$ to $f(x)+4$, the new graph would be:

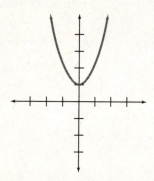

Note that subtracting a number from a function moves the graph down.

✔ If a number is added to x in a function, the graph is moved that many units *to the left*. This rule is tricky because you may have guessed the graph moved the other way. If the original function were changed to $f(x+4)$, it would look like the following graph. Notice that this rule is used when you're adding to x, not to the whole function. As you may guess, if you were to graph $f(x-4)$, you'd move four units to the right.

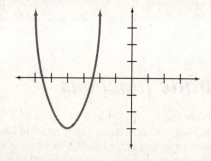

Some graphing problems don't involve equations; instead, you may be given a pair of points and be asked about the line connecting them. In these types of problems, three formulas are crucial:

✔ The slope of the line connecting the points (x_1, y_1) and (x_2, y_2) is $\frac{y_2 - y_1}{x_2 - x_1}$.

✔ The distance between the points (x_1, y_1) and (x_2, y_2) is $\sqrt{(x_2 - x_1)^2 + (y_2 - y_1)^2}$.

✔ The midpoint of the line connecting the points (x_1, y_1) and (x_2, y_2) is $\left(\frac{x_2 + x_1}{2}, \frac{y_2 + y_1}{2} \right)$.

You probably learned these formulas some time ago. They're not exciting, but they are useful. Try using them on the points $(-1, 2)$ and $(5, -6)$:

$$\text{Slope} = \frac{(-6)-(2)}{(5)-(-1)} = \frac{-8}{6} = -\frac{4}{3}$$

$$\text{Distance} = \sqrt{[(5)-(-1)]^2 + [(-6)-(2)]^2} = \sqrt{(6)^2 + (-8)^2} = \sqrt{36+64} = \sqrt{100} = 10$$

$$\text{Midpoint} = \left(\frac{(5)+(-1)}{2}, \frac{(-6)+(2)}{2} \right) = \left(\frac{4}{2}, \frac{-4}{2} \right) = (2, -2)$$

Thanks, you've been *grat*

Did your favorite grandparent send you a reward to ensure success on the SAT? If so, you probably expressed your *gratitude* (thanks) because you were *grateful* (thankful) and not an *ingrate* (someone who thinks the whole world owes him or her a living and, therefore, never appreciates anything). Waiters and bartenders, on the other hand, always appreciate *gratuities* (tips). Other *grat* words include *gratis* (free — you'll be thankful for the gift, right?) and *gratuitous* (given freely but not necessary, like your mom's criticism of your latest dating partner). You may find the *grat* words *gratifying* (filling one's needs or desires) when they show up on the SAT.

Decoding symbolism

One of the most popular (to the test-makers, that is) types of function problems on the SAT involves symbols. In these problems, the SAT-makers create a new symbol for a function. Look over this example, which uses $\wedge$ as a symbol.

If $a \wedge b = 2a - b$, which of the following is equal to $3 \wedge 4$?

(A) 1

(B) 2

(C) 3

(D) 4

Choice (B) is the answer. Just as in a normal function problem, where you plug in a number for x, here you plug in 3 and 4 for a and b. It's actually very simple. To solve $3 \wedge 4$, plug in those numbers, in order:

$$a \wedge b = 2a - b$$
$$3 \wedge 4 = 2(3) - (4)$$
$$= 6 - 4$$
$$= 2$$

And the answer is Choice (B).

Chapter 13

Practicing Problems in Algebra and Functions

In This Chapter

▶ Practicing algebra and functions with some guided problems

▶ Troubleshooting your problem areas with some practice questions

In this chapter, you hone your skills for SAT algebra and function problems. Try ten, see how you do, and then try ten more if you're a glutton for punishment (or algebra, which in some people's minds is the same thing).

Be sure to check all your answers. Don't forget the explanations, which may help you understand what went wrong or a faster, better way to work a question you got right.

In the first practice set, each answer immediately follows the question. Don't cheat. Cover the answer with a piece of paper until you're ready to read the explanation. The second set is set up like the real test: You go through all the questions and then check your answers in the next section.

For more information on any of the topics in these questions, check out Chapter 12.

Set One: Getting Started with Some Guided Questions

Note: Question 3 is a grid-in, so you don't get any answers to choose from. See Chapter 9 for more on answering grid-ins correctly.

1. If k is a positive integer, which of the following is a possible value for k^2?

    (A) –1

    (B) 0

    (C) 6

    (D) 9

Choice (A) is impossible because any number, when squared, is positive. Choice (B) is 0 squared, but the problem said that the original number had to be positive. Choice (C) isn't a perfect square; no number multiplied by itself gives you 6 as an answer. That leaves you with Choice (D), which is 3^2.

2. If $y = \frac{x+5}{2}$, then increasing the value of y by 2 will increase x by

   (A) 1

   (B) 2

   (C) 3

   (D) 4

   This problem is good for picking your own numbers. For example, say that y was originally 10; then you would have $10 = \frac{x+5}{2}$. Multiplying both sides by 2 gives you $20 = x+5$, or $x = 15$. Now the problem tells you to increase y by 2, making it 12. If you do the math, you find that x is now 19, so it increased by 4. This result makes sense because the equation tells you that you need to divide $x+5$ by 2 to get y; y increases half as quickly as x. Thus, your answer is Choice (D).

3. In his will, a man left his land to his three children: $\frac{2}{3}$ of the estate to his oldest child, $\frac{1}{4}$ to his middle child, and 15 acres to his youngest. How many acres were in the original estate?

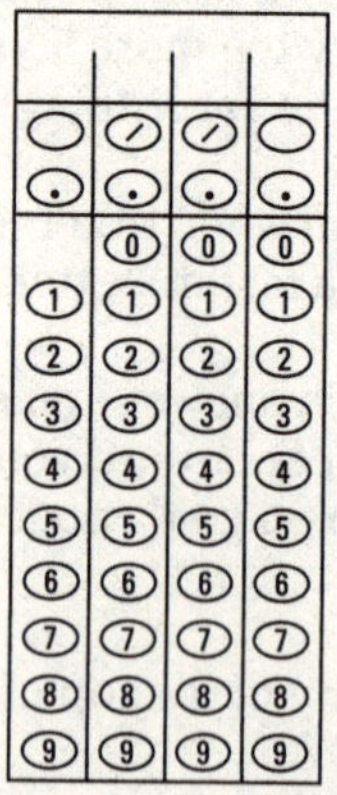

   A word problem? With no multiple-choice answers? And fractions? Okay, deep breaths. Now get to work. In any word problem, list the various things you need to know to solve the problem. Four important things pop up in this one: the original estate and the amount left to the three children. Because the original estate is what you're looking for, call it x. Remembering that the word *of* usually indicates multiplication, you can then make a list:

   x = original estate

   $\frac{2}{3}x$ = oldest child

   $\frac{1}{4}x$ = middle child

   15 = youngest child

   Because the three children's shares made up the whole estate, you can write $\frac{2}{3}x + \frac{1}{4}x + 15 = x$.

With a common denominator of 12:

$$\frac{8}{12}x + \frac{3}{12}x + 15 = x$$

$$\frac{11}{12}x + 15 = x$$

$$15 = x - \frac{11}{12}x$$

$$15 = \frac{1}{12}x$$

Finally, multiplying both sides by 12, you get $x = 180$.

That's a lot of work for one problem. If you're a visual person, you may prefer to solve it with a graph:

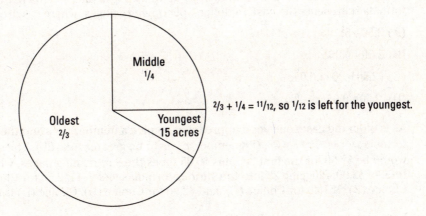

$\frac{2}{3} + \frac{1}{4} = \frac{11}{12}$, so $\frac{1}{12}$ is left for the youngest.

4. If x and y are both integers, $x > 3$, and $y < 2$, then $x - y$ could be

    (A) 3

    (B) 2

    (C) 1

    (D) –1

After the last problem, this one's a breeze. x is an integer greater than 3, so it must be at least 4. y is an integer less than 2, so it must be at most 1. To find $x - y$, just plug in those numbers: $4 - 1 = 3$, so Choice (A) is correct. Notice that making x bigger or y smaller would make $x - y$ greater than 3, so all the other choices are impossible.

5. If n and p are directly proportional, and $n = 12$ when $p = 9$, which of the following pairs is a possible set of values for n and p?

    (A) $n = 9, p = 12$

    (B) $n = 18, p = 15$

    (C) $n = 18, p = 6$

    (D) $n = 20, p = 15$

If n and p are directly proportional, the ratio of n/p must remain the same. That ratio is 12/9, which reduces to 4/3, so find an answer choice with that same ratio. Only Choice (D), at 20/15, reduces to 4/3.

6. If $a^2 - b^2 = 40$ and $a - b = 10$, then $a + b =$

   (A) 4

   (B) 10

   (C) 14

   (D) 30

When you see a quadratic expression in a problem, see whether it can be factored. $a^2 - b^2$ should look familiar to you. (If not, turn to Chapter 12.) Keep in mind that $a^2 - b^2$ factors out to $(a - b)(a + b)$. Because $a^2 - b^2 = 40$ and $a - b = 10$, $(10)(a + b) = 40$ so $a + b = 4$. Notice that you didn't even have to figure out what a and b are to solve the problem, which happens a lot on the SAT. The correct answer is Choice (A).

7. A copying service charges $2.50 to copy up to 20 pages plus 5 cents per page over 20. Which formula represents the cost, in dollars, of copying c pages, where c is greater than 20?

   (A) $2.50 + 5c$

   (B) $2.50 + 0.05c$

   (C) $(2.50)(20) + 0.05c$

   (D) $2.50 + 0.05(c - 20)$

As is often the case, one good approach is to pick a number for c and then see which formula works. Try $c = 28$. (Remember, c has to be greater than 20). The cost for 28 pages would be $2.50 for the first 20, plus $0.05 times the 8 remaining pages, which is $0.40, for a total of $2.90. Plugging 28 into the various formulas yields $142.50 for Choice (A), $3.90 for Choice (B), $51.40 for Choice (C), and $2.90 for Choice (D). Choice (D) is correct.

8. Let $*a$ be defined as one more than a if a is odd and as one less than a if a is even. Which of the following would result in the lowest value of $*a$?

   (A) –2

   (B) –1

   (C) 0

   (D) 1

Test out each answer choice. Choice (A), –2, is even, so one less than –2 is –3. The other choices give you 0, –1, and 2, in that order. Thus, Choice (A) is correct.

9. If $(2g - 3h)^3 = 27$, then $(2g - 3h)^{-2} =$

   (A) $\frac{1}{9}$

   (B) $\frac{1}{6}$

   (C) 6

   (D) 9

First, give up on trying to figure out the values of g and h. The key is the expression $(2g - 3h)$, which shows up in both parts of the problem. Replace it with something simpler, like q. (Why use x all the time?) So you know that $q^3 = 27$. A little trial and error (or your calculator) reveals that $q = 3$. Now you need to find $q^{-2} = (3)^{-2} = \dfrac{1}{(3)^2} = \dfrac{1}{9}$. Choice (A) is correct.

10. A party supplier charges a flat rate plus a certain amount per person. If supplies for 12 people cost $140 and supplies for 20 people cost $180, then supplies for 40 people would cost

    (A) $220

    (B) $280

    (C) $300

    (D) $360

    First, find the cost per person. If 12 people cost $140 and 20 people cost $180, then 8 people cost $40 (because $20 - 12 = 8$ and $180 - $140 = 40). Divide $40 by 8 for a per-person cost of $5. Now take the 20-person cost and add the cost of 20 more people. You know that 20 people cost $180 and that 20 additional people cost $100 (because $20 \times $5 = 100), so add the two together: $180 + $100 = 280, and the answer is Choice (B).

Set Two: Practicing Some Questions on Your Own

Note: Question 1 is a grid-in. Turn to Chapter 9 for help on answering that type of question.

1. If $(x+2)^2 + (x-1)^2 = ax^2 + bx + c$, find the value of b.

2. A gas's pressure and volume are inversely proportional. If a certain gas has a pressure of 120 kilopascals (kPa) when its volume is 250 cubic centimeters (cc), what is its pressure when its volume is 200 cc?

    (A) 170 kPa

    (B) 150 kPa

    (C) 100 kPa

    (D) 96 kPa

3. Given the function $f(x) = \dfrac{5x}{x^2 - 4x + 4}$, which is not a possible value of x?

    (A) 4

    (B) 2

    (C) 0

    (D) −2

4. Below is the graph of the equation $y = -x^2$.

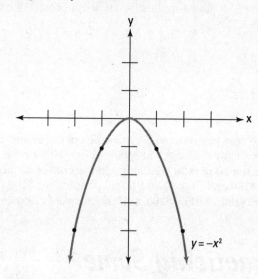

Which of the following choices represents the graph of $y = -x^2 + 4$?

(A)

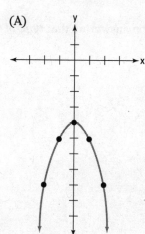

(B)

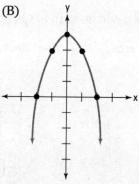

(C)

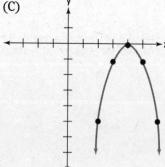

(D)

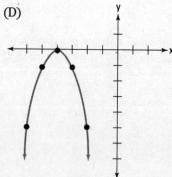

5. The solution set to the equation $|x+3| = 5$ is

   (A) $\{2\}$

   (B) $\{2, -8\}$

   (C) $\{-8\}$

   (D) $\{-2, -8\}$

6. If $f(x)$ is a linear function passing through the points $(2, 5)$ and $(6, 3)$, then the y-intercept of $f(x)$ is

   (A) 7

   (B) 6

   (C) 5

   (D) 3

7. If $x \otimes y$ is defined as $x^2 - y$ for all integers x and y, which of the following is always true?

   (A) $1 \otimes y = y$

   (B) $x \otimes 2$ is positive

   (C) $x \otimes 3 = x \otimes -3$

   (D) $4 \otimes y = (-4) \otimes y$

8. If $k^{1/2} - 3 = 5$, then $k =$

   (A) 64

   (B) 16

   (C) 8

   (D) 4

9. The population of a certain city can be modeled by the function $p(y) = 20,000(2^{y/20})$, where $p(y)$ represents the population and y measures years since 1975. If the city had a population of 40,000 in 1995, then its population in 2015 is

   (A) 40,000

   (B) 60,000

   (C) 80,000

   (D) 100,000

10. In the equation $5 - \dfrac{2x+2}{x+1} = \dfrac{9}{x+1}$, x is equal to

    (A) 0

    (B) 1

    (C) 2

    (D) 3

Answers to Set Two

1. **2.** This problem is an easy one to mess up, but not if you use the formulas from Chapter 12: $(a+b)^2 = a^2 + 2ab + b^2$. It's also fine to just do FOIL, rewriting the problem as $(x+2)(x+2)+(x-1)(x-1)$. Either way, the problem becomes $x^2 + 4x + 4 + x^2 - 2x + 1$, which equals $2x^2 + 2x + 5$, so $b = 2$.

2. **B.** When two quantities are *inversely proportional,* their product is always the same number. Usually, finding that number is the key to getting the right answer. You're told that a pressure of 120 corresponds to a volume of 250, and $120 \times 250 = 30,000$. Thus, your missing pressure (call it p) times 200 must equal 30,000. Solving $200p = 30,000$ gives you $p = 150$. Common-sense double-check: If quantities vary inversely, one goes up when the other goes down. Notice that the volume went down from 250 cc to 200 cc and that the pressure went up from 120 kPa to 150 kPa. Choice (B) is correct.

3. **B.** Don't bother trying the answer choices. Use your head. You know that dividing by 0 is against the rules. The denominator can be factored to $(x-2)(x-2)$, which means that 2 is the only number that makes the denominator 0, so it's the only number that can't be a value of x. Choice (B) is correct.

4. **B.** Adding 4 to a function raises its graph by four units, so Choice (B) is correct. If you're not sure, eliminate wrong answers by finding the x, y coordinates of one point on each graph, and plugging them into the equation $y = -x^2 + 4$. The equation only works with the correct answer.

5. **B.** You could just plug in all the choices, but, for practice, go through the official steps:

Create two equations:

$$x + 3 = 5 \quad \text{and} \quad x + 3 = -5$$

Solve them separately:

$$\begin{matrix} x+3=5 \\ x=2 \end{matrix} \quad \text{and} \quad \begin{matrix} x+3=-5 \\ x=-8 \end{matrix}$$

Check your answers:

$$\begin{matrix} |x+3|=5 \\ |(2)+3|=5 \\ |5|=5 \\ 5=5 \end{matrix} \quad \text{and} \quad \begin{matrix} |x+3|=5 \\ |(-8)+3|=5 \\ |-5|=5 \\ 5=5 \end{matrix}$$

So the answers that work are 2 and –8. Choice (B) is correct.

6. **B.** A sketch can help you see what's going on here, so draw something like this:

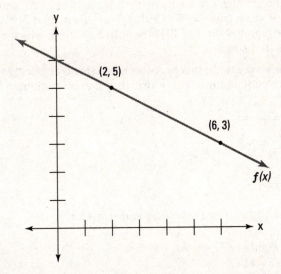

The graph suggests that the answer is either Choice (A) or Choice (B). To be sure, use the formula for linear equations, $y = mx + b$. First, find the slope of the line:

$$m = \frac{y_2 - y_1}{x_2 - x_1} = \frac{3-5}{6-2} = \frac{-2}{4} = -\frac{1}{2}$$

So the equation is $y = -\frac{1}{2}x + b$. Plug in $(2, 5)$ to find b:

$$(5) = -\frac{1}{2}(2) + b$$
$$5 = -1 + b$$
$$6 = b$$

The y-intercept is 6, and the answer is Choice (B).

7. **D.** No cool solving methods here. You just have to check all the possibilities.

Choice (A): $1 \otimes y = 1^2 - y = 1 - y$, which equals y only if y is 1/2. Moving on to Choice (B): $x \otimes 2 = x^2 - 2$. This is positive if x is 2 or more, but if x is 1 or 0, then it's negative. Now for Choice (C): $x \otimes 3 = x^2 - 3$ and $x \otimes -3 = x^2 - (-3) = x^2 + 3$. They're not equal. Which leaves Choice (D): $4 \otimes y = 4^2 - y = 16 - y$ and $(-4) \otimes y = (-4)^2 - y = 16 - y$. At last.

8. **A.** Start by isolating the $k^{1/2}$:

$$k^{1/2} - 3 = 5$$
$$k^{1/2} = 8$$

Because $k^{1/2}$ means $\sqrt{k}$, square both sides:

$$k = 8^2 = 64$$

So Choice (A) is correct.

9. **E.** Put away your calculator. SAT functions are simple, even if they look mad. The expression $2^{y/20}$ isn't so bad when y is a multiple of 20, and in this case it's 40 (the number of years from 1975 to 2015). This means that $2^{y/20}$ is really just $2^{40/20}$, or 2^2, which of course equals 4. And $p(40)$ is simply $20,000(4)$, which equals 80,000. It's really no fun when it's that simple.

10. **D.** The best way to do this problem is to start by noticing that the two fractions have common denominators. Therefore, they can be combined if you get them on the same side:

$$5 = \frac{9}{x+1} + \frac{2x+2}{x+1}$$
$$5 = \frac{9+2x+2}{x+1}$$
$$5 = \frac{11+2x}{x+1}$$

Now, multiply $x+1$ on both sides and solve for x:

$$(x+1)5 = 11+2x$$
$$5x+5 = 11+2x$$
$$3x = 6$$
$$x = 2$$

Choice (C) is correct.

Chapter 14

Checking More Figures Than an IRS Agent: Geometry and Trigonometry

- -

In This Chapter

▶ Getting acquainted with angles

▶ Solving problems containing triangles, quadrilaterals, and polygons

▶ Zeroing in on circles: Calculating circumference, area, and more

▶ Thinking in 3-D: Looking at volume and surface area

▶ Working with trigonometry

- -

Think of geometry as a mini art lesson. The key to doing well on geometry problems is this: Draw a picture for every geometry problem that you face. Include every measurement that you know on the diagram, and get a sense of what the problem is describing.

After you get a clear illustration on paper, you're ready to get through the problem. Even if a problem seems to be incredibly easy, draw a quick diagram anyway. It doesn't have to be perfect, but it will get you to the right answer.

Fair warning: This chapter has a lot of information to memorize, but don't panic. Much of what's covered in this chapter appears in the box of formulas printed at the beginning of each Math section on the SAT. Here's what the box looks like:

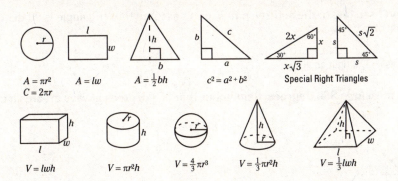

There are 360 degrees of arc in a circle. The number of radians of arc in a circle is 2π.

There are 180 degrees in the sum of the interior angles of a triangle.

Knowing What Makes One Angle Different from Another

Angles are a big part of the SAT geometry problems, so pay attention to this section. Finding an angle is usually a matter of simple addition or subtraction, provided you remember these key facts.

When it comes to angles, these three rules pretty much apply to the SAT math questions:

- ✔ There are no negative angles.

- ✔ There are no zero angles.

- ✔ Fractional angles rarely appear on the test. For example, an angle is unlikely to measure $19\frac{7}{8}$ degrees or $23\frac{4}{5}$ degrees.

Now that you know what you won't find in the SAT geometry questions, take a look at the important facts you need to remember for the problems you will find:

- ✔ **Angles that equal 90 degrees are called *right angles*.** They're formed by perpendicular lines and are indicated by a box in the corner of the two intersecting lines.

A common SAT trap is to have two lines appear to be perpendicular. Don't assume you're looking at a right angle unless you see one of the following:

- • The words "This is a right angle" in the question

- • The perpendicular symbol ⊥, which indicates that the two lines form a 90-degree angle

- • The box in the corner of the two intersecting lines

If you don't see one of these three notes, don't assume that the angle is 90 degrees.

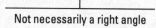

Not necessarily a right angle

- ✔ **A circle measures 360 degrees.** Remember that 360 degrees always creates a complete circle.

360 degrees

- ✔ **Angles that are opposite each other are *congruent* (they have equal measures) and are called *vertical angles*.** The name sticks even if the angles aren't positioned vertically. Just remember that vertical angles are across from each other, whether they're up and down or side by side.

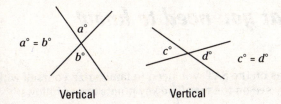

Vertical   Vertical

✔ **A line crossing two parallel lines creates two sets of four angles having the same measures.** This actually creates four sets of vertical angles, with the odd-numbered angles having one measure and the even-numbered angles having another.

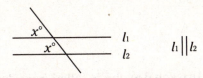

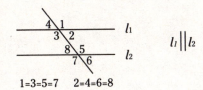

$1=3=5=7$ $2=4=6=8$

✔ **The *exterior angles* of any figure are supplementary to the interior angles and sum up to 360 degrees.** Exterior angles can be very confusing; keep in mind that they *always* sum up to 360 degrees, no matter what type of figure you have.

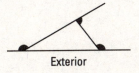

Exterior

REMEMBER

An exterior angle is *supplementary* to an interior angle; in other words, the two angles must form a straight line with a side of the figure. The following isn't an exterior angle:

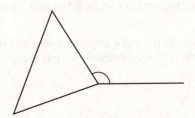

Increasing Your Polygon Knowledge

A fair number of math problems you face when you take the SAT deal with *polygons* — figures with three or more straight sides. Triangles take a star role on the test, but quadrilaterals (four-sided shapes) also appear fairly regularly, and exotic figures (such as pentagons or hexagons) also show up. Never fear: This section prepares you for all sorts of polygon questions that may appear on the SAT.

Figuring out what you need to know about triangles

Before learning about triangles on the SAT, you need to familiarize yourself with the different types of triangles you may see on the test. The key points are as follows:

✔ **A triangle with three equal sides and three equal angles is called *equilateral*.**

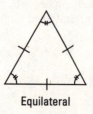

Equilateral

✔ **A triangle with two equal sides and two equal angles is called *isosceles*.**

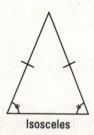

Isosceles

✔ **Angles opposite equal sides in an isosceles triangle are also equal.**

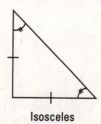

Isosceles

✔ **In any triangle, the largest angle is opposite the longest side.** Similarly, the smallest angle is opposite the shortest side, and the medium angle is opposite the medium-length side.

Note: In a right triangle, this largest angle is the right angle because the other two angles total 90 degrees. The longest side is the *hypotenuse,* which is always opposite the right angle.

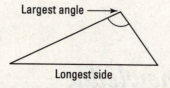

Largest angle ⟶

Longest side

✔ **In any triangle, the sum of the lengths of two sides must be greater than the length of the third side.** This is written as $a + b > c$, where a, b, and c are the sides of the triangle.

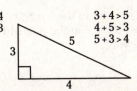

✔ In any type of triangle, the sum of the interior angles is 180 degrees.

  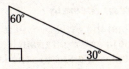

✔ The measure of an exterior angle of a triangle is equal to the sum of the two opposite interior angles.

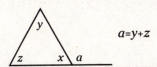

When you think about this rule logically, it makes sense. The sum of supplementary angles is 180 degrees, and the sum of the triangle angles is 180 degrees. In the preceding triangle, angle $x = 180 - (y + z)$ and angle $x = 180 - a$. Thus, $a = y + z$.

Identifying what makes two triangles (or other figures) similar

Two triangles are *similar* if they are exactly the same shape but different sizes. This also means that their sides are in proportion. For example, if the heights of two similar triangles are in a ratio of 2:3, the bases of those triangles are in a ratio of 2:3 as well.

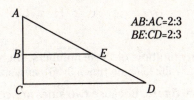

Calculating the area of triangles

The formula for finding the area of a triangle is: $A = \frac{1}{2} base \times height$. The height (also known as the *altitude*) is always a line perpendicular from any vertex to the opposite base. It may be a side of the triangle, as in a right triangle:

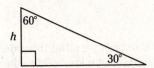

The height may be inside the triangle, in which case it's often represented by a dashed line and a small 90-degree box:

The height may also be outside the triangle. This configuration is very confusing, but you may find it in trick questions. On the plus side, the problem will usually show you the altitude, as in this drawing:

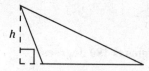

Using the Pythagorean theorem

You've probably studied the *Pythagorean theorem* (PT) at some point in your math career. The theorem says that in any right triangle, you can find the lengths of the sides using the formula $a^2 + b^2 = c^2$, where a and b are the legs of the triangle and c is the hypotenuse. The hypotenuse is always opposite the 90-degree angle and is always the longest side of the triangle.

Keep in mind that the Pythagorean theorem works only on right triangles. If a triangle doesn't have a 90-degree angle, you can't use it.

Simplifying things with Pythagorean triples

Going through the whole PT formula every time you want to find the length of a side in a right triangle can be a pain. To help you simplify your work, memorize the following three common PT ratios:

- **Ratio 3:4:5.** In this ratio, if one leg of the triangle is 3, the other leg is 4, and the hypotenuse is 5.

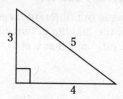

  Because this is a ratio, the sides can be in any multiple of these numbers, such as 6:8:10 (two times 3:4:5), 9:12:15 (three times 3:4:5), 27:36:45 (nine times 3:4:5), and so on.

- $s : s : s\sqrt{2}$, **where s stands for the side of the figure.** Because two sides are congruent, this formula applies to an isosceles right triangle, also known as a 45-45-90 triangle. If one side is 2, then the other leg is also 2, and the hypotenuse is $2\sqrt{2}$.

  This formula is great to know for squares. If a question tells you that the side of a square is 5 and wants to know the diagonal of the square, you know immediately that it is $5\sqrt{2}$. Why? A square's diagonal cuts the square into two isosceles right triangles (isosceles because all sides of the square are equal; right because all angles in a square are right angles). What is the diagonal of a square with sides of 64? $64\sqrt{2}$. How about a square with sides of 12,984? $12,984\sqrt{2}$.

- $s : s\sqrt{3} : 2s$. This ratio is a special formula for the sides of a 30-60-90 triangle.

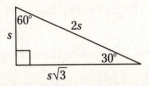

This type of triangle is a favorite of the test-makers. The important thing to keep in mind here is that the hypotenuse is twice the length of the smallest side, which is opposite the 30-degree angle. If you get a word problem saying, "Given a 30-60-90 triangle of hypotenuse 20, find the area" or "Given a 30-60-90 triangle of hypotenuse 100, find the perimeter," you can do so because you can find the lengths of the other sides:

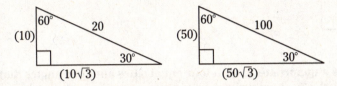

Two 30-60-90 triangles are formed whenever an equilateral triangle is cut in half. If an SAT question mentions the altitude of an equilateral triangle, you almost always have to use a 30-60-90 triangle to solve it.

Time to stretch those mental triangular muscles. Try this sample problem:

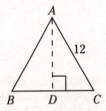

In this equilateral triangle, the length of altitude *AD* is

(A) 6

(B) 9

(C) $6\sqrt{2}$

(D) $6\sqrt{3}$

The answer is Choice (D). Look at the 30-60-90 triangle formed by *ABD*. The hypotenuse is 12, the original side of the equilateral triangle. The base is 6 because it's half the hypotenuse. That makes the altitude $6\sqrt{3}$, according to the ratio.

Remember that the 45-45-90 and 30-60-90 triangle patterns are included in the formula box at the beginning of each Math section, in case you forget them. Don't hesitate to refer to this formula box as you move through the Math sections.

Taking a quick look at quadrilaterals

Think you know everything there is to know about squares and rectangles? Well, think again! We're here to give you a few more oh-so-interesting rules to add to your geometry toolbox. These rules all have to do with four-sided figures, or *quadrilaterals:*

✔ **Any four-sided figure is called a *quadrilateral.*** The sum of the interior angles of any quadrilateral equals 360 degrees.

✔ **A *square* is a quadrilateral with four equal sides and four right angles.** The area of a square is *side²*.

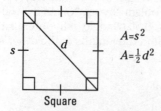

$$A=s^2$$
$$A=\tfrac{1}{2}d^2$$

Square

✔ **A *rhombus* is a quadrilateral with four equal sides and four angles that aren't necessarily right angles.** A rhombus looks like a square that's slipping sideways (unless it is a square — every squares is a rhombus but not every rhombus is a square). The area of a rhombus is $\frac{1}{2}d_1d_2$ (that is, $\frac{1}{2}$ *diagonal₁* × *diagonal₂*).

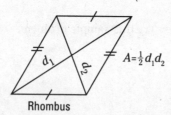

$$A=\tfrac{1}{2}d_1d_2$$

Rhombus

✔ **A *rectangle* is a quadrilateral with four equal angles, all of which are right angles.** The top and bottom sides are equal, and the right and left sides are equal. All angles in a rectangle are right angles. (The word *rectangle* means "right angle.") The area of a rectangle is *length* × *width* (which is the same as *base* × *height*).

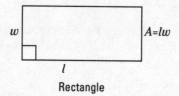

$$A=lw$$

Rectangle

✔ **A *parallelogram* is a quadrilateral with two opposite and equal pairs of sides.** The top and bottom sides are equal, and the right and left sides are equal. Opposite angles are equal but not necessarily right. The area of a parallelogram is *base* × *height*. (***Note:*** The height is a perpendicular line from the tallest point of the figure down to the base.)

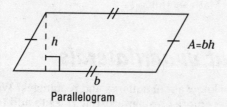

$$A=bh$$

Parallelogram

✔ A *trapezoid* **is a quadrilateral with two parallel sides and two nonparallel sides.** The area of a trapezoid is $\frac{1}{2}(base_1 + base_2) \times height$. The bases are the two parallel sides, and the height is the perpendicular distance between them.

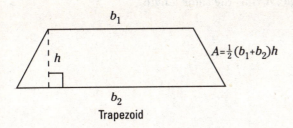

Trapezoid

Considering some other polygons

Triangles and quadrilaterals are the most common polygons tested on the SAT; however, they're certainly not the only ones out there. Table 14-1 notes a few other polygons you may see on the test.

Table 14-1	Some Polygons
Number of Sides	**Name**
5	Pentagon
6	Hexagon (think of *x* in six and *x* in hex)
8	Octagon (like a stop sign)

A polygon with all equal sides and all equal angles is called *regular*. For example, an equilateral triangle is a regular triangle, and a square is a regular quadrilateral.

The SAT-writers won't ask you to find the area of any of these polygons, but they may ask you to find the *perimeter,* which is just the sum of the lengths of all the sides. They may also ask you to find the exterior angle measure, which is always 360 degrees. If they ask you about other angles, divide the shape into triangles, as in the following figure. Then try your hand at the sample grid-in question that follows the illustration.

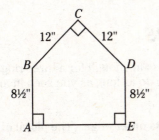

As the diagram shows, an official major league home plate has the shape of a pentagon. Given the measurements shown, the length of *AE,* to the nearest inch, must be

(A) 10

(B) 12

(C) 17

(D) 20

The answer is Choice (C). The key to solving this problem is in shape *BCD*. Because angle *C* is a right angle, and the two sides adjacent to *C* are the same length, *BCD* is an isosceles right triangle, also known as a 45-45-90 triangle, with the side-length ratio $s : s : s\sqrt{2}$. Therefore, the hypotenuse, or *BD*, must be $12\sqrt{2}$, which multiplies out to 16.97, or 17. Because *ABDE* is a rectangle, *AE* has the same length.

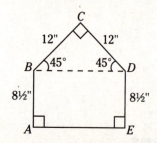

Sometimes you have to use several different shapes to solve a problem, especially when the SAT throws a strange diagram at you and asks you to find the area of a shaded section, a very popular question (popular with the test-makers, not with the test-takers). In the following diagram, a circle of radius 7 is surrounded by a square. How would you find the area of the shaded section?

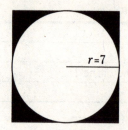

In any problem like this one, the shaded area is equal to the area of the larger shape minus the area of the smaller shape — in this case, the area of the square minus the area of the circle. Because the circle has a radius of 7, its diameter is 14, which must be the same as the side of the square. The area of the square, then, equals $14 \times 14 = 196$. You can find the circle's area by using the formula $\pi r^2 = \pi (7)^2 = 49\pi$. The shaded area, then, equals $196 - 49\pi$. (This calculates to 42.06, but you can usually leave the answer as $196 - 49\pi$.)

Getting the Lowdown on Circles

The SAT-makers love asking about circles, and they toss in enough for a three-ring circus. But don't panic. Problems involving circles are easy to do as long as you keep in mind the following points:

> ✔ A *radius (r)* goes from the center of a circle to its outer edge. (The plural of *radius* is *radii*, in case you're curious.)

Radius

✔ A *diameter (d)* connects two points on the outside or edge of the circle, going through the center. A diameter is equal to two radii.

Diameter

✔ **The perimeter of a circle is called the *circumference*.** The formula for circumference (C) is C = $2\pi r$, but you can also use πd, because 2 radii = 1 diameter.

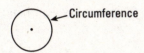

You may encounter a wheel question in which you're asked how much distance a wheel covers or how many times a wheel revolves. The key to solving this type of question is knowing that one rotation of a wheel equals one circumference of that wheel. There's an example problem like this later in this section.

✔ **The formula for the area of a circle is *A* = πr^2.**

✔ A *chord* is a straight line segment that connects any two points on a circle. The longest chord in a circle is the diameter.

✔ A *tangent* is a line that touches the circle at exactly one point. When a tangent line meets a radius of the circle, a 90-degree angle is formed.

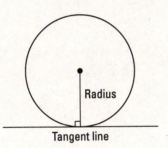

✔ An *arc* is a portion of the circumference of a circle. The degree measure of an arc is the same as its central angle. (A *central angle* is an angle with endpoints on the circumference of the circle and its vertex at the center of the circle.)

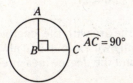

The SAT may ask you to find the length of an arc. To do so, follow these steps:

1. **Find the circumference of the entire circle.**

2. **Put the degree measure of the arc over 360 and reduce the fraction.**

3. **Multiply the circumference by the fraction.**

✔ **A *sector* is a portion of the area of a circle.** To find the area of a sector, do the following:

1. **Find the area of the entire circle.**

2. **Put the degree measure of the sector over 360 and reduce the fraction.**

3. **Multiply the area by the fraction.**

Finding the area of a sector is very similar to finding the length of an arc. The only difference is in the first step. Whereas an arc is a part of the circle's circumference, a sector is a part of the circle's area.

Now that all these rules are circling in your head (so to speak), try your hand at a few example problems.

A child's wagon has a wheel of radius 6 inches. If the wagon wheel travels 100 revolutions, approximately how many feet has the wagon rolled?

(A) 325

(B) 314

(C) 255

(D) 201

The answer is Choice (B). One revolution of the wheel is equal to its circumference: $C = 2\pi r = 2\pi(6) = 12\pi$ = approximately 37.68 inches, which is 37.68 inches $\div 12 = 3.14$ feet. Multiply that by 100, and $3.14 \times 100 = 314$ feet.

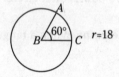

Find the length of minor arc *AC*.

(A) 36π

(B) 60

(C) 18π

(D) 6π

The answer is Choice (D). Take the steps one at a time. First, find the circumference of the entire circle: $C = 2\pi r = 36\pi$. Don't multiply 36π out; SAT math problems usually leave it in that form. Next, put the degree measure of the arc over 360. The degree measure of the arc is the same as its central angle, $60° = 60/360 = 1/6$. The arc is 1/6 of the circumference of the circle. Multiply the circumference by the fraction: $36\pi \times 1/6 = 6\pi$.

Be very careful not to confuse the degree measure of the arc with the length of the arc. The length is always a portion of the circumference, typically with π in it, and always in linear units. If you chose Choice (B) in this example, you found the degree measure of the arc rather than its length.

If point *B* is at the center of the circle, what's the area of the shaded sector?

(A) $\frac{1}{4}\pi$

(B) 16π

(C) 64π

(D) 90π

The answer is Choice (B). To do this problem, first, find the area of the entire circle: $A = \pi r^2 = 64\pi$. Second, put the degree measure of the sector over 360. The sector is 90 degrees, the same as its central angle: $90/360 = 1/4$. Third, multiply the area by the fraction: $64\pi \times 1/4 = 16\pi$.

Avoiding Two-Dimensional Thinking: Solid Geometry

Almost every SAT has a couple of problems dealing with a box, a cylinder, a sphere, a cone, or a prism. The key formulas you need to know regarding these 3-D figures are included in the direction text at the start of each Math section, but we also offer you a quick review here.

Volume

The volume of most SAT 3-D shapes is area of the *base × height*. This should help you memorize the following more-specific formulas:

✔ **Volume of a cube:** $V = s^3$

Cube

A cube is a 3-D square. Think of a die (one of a pair of dice). All a cube's dimensions are the same; that is, *length = width = height*. In a cube, these dimensions are called *edges* or *sides*. The volume of a cube is edge cubed: $V = side \times side \times side = side^3 = s^3$.

✔ **Volume of a rectangular solid:** $V = l \cdot w \cdot h$

Rectangular solid

A rectangular solid is a box, sometimes called a prism. The base of a box is a rectangle, which has an area of *length × width*. Multiply that area by height to fit the original volume formula: *Volume* = area of *base × height* or $V = l \cdot w \cdot h$.

✔ **Volume of a cylinder:** $V = \pi r^2 h$

Cylinder

Think of a cylinder as a can of soup. The base of a cylinder is a circle. The area of a circle is πr^2. Multiply that by the height of the cylinder to get this formula: *Volume* = area of *base × height*, or $V = \pi r^2 h$. Note that the top and bottom of a cylinder are identical circles. If you know the radius of either the top base or the bottom base, you can find the area of the circle.

✔ **Volume of a sphere:** $V = \frac{4}{3} \pi r^3$

A sphere is a perfectly round ball, like a basketball. Like a circle, it has a radius. Simply plug the radius into the equation, and you have the volume.

✔ **Volume of a cone:** $V = \frac{1}{3} \pi r^2 h$

A cone has a circular base and sides that taper toward a point. Like a cylinder, you find the area by multiplying the area of the circle by the height, but with the cone, you divide this product by 3.

✔ **Volume of a pyramid:** $V = \frac{1}{3} lwh$

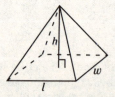

A pyramid has a square base and four identical triangular sides. Like a rectangular solid, you find the area by multiplying the length, width, and height, but with a pyramid, you divide this product by 3.

Although it may be helpful to memorize these formulas, fortunately, you don't have to. They are always right there in the formula bar that starts each Math section.

Surface area

On rare occasions, the SAT-writers may ask you to find the surface area of a solid object. The surface area is, sensibly enough, the total area of all the sides (surfaces) of the object. To find the surface area of a box with six sides, calculate the area of each of the rectangles that form a side, and then add them all up. If the test-makers were in a particularly bad mood when they wrote the test, you might see a problem like the following example:

Find the surface area of the square-based pyramid shown below:

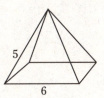

(A) 60

(B) 84

(C) 96

(D) 120

Choice (B) is the right answer. The area of the bottom square is $6 \times 6 = 36$. You know that the area of one of the triangular sides can be found by using the formula area $= 1/2 \; base \times height$, but you don't yet know the height of each triangle. So take a moment to draw one of the triangular sides by itself:

The dashed line is the height, which makes a right angle with the base and cuts it in half. Thus, you have a right triangle with a leg of length 3 and a hypotenuse of 5. Does that sound familiar? Of course: It's a 3-4-5 triangle! So the height is 4, making the area of one triangle $1/2 \times 6 \times 4 = 12$. And because there are four such triangles, their total area is $4 \times 12 = 48$, which you can now add to the 36 from the base to get Choice (B), or 84.

Trying Trigonometry

Many students clamp their teeth when they hear that the SAT has trigonometry questions. If you're clamping right now, relax and breathe easy. The SAT has only a few trig questions, and this section covers what you need to know to answer them, even if you've never stepped foot in a trigonometry classroom.

SOH CAH TOA: The trigonometric ratios

Most SAT trigonometry questions are based on *trigonometric ratios,* which are the relationships between the angles and sides of a right triangle in terms of one of its acute angles. (An *acute angle* is less than 90 degrees, so the ratio questions aren't based on the right angle.) You can answer almost every SAT trig question by using the mnemonic device for the three basic trigonometric ratios: SOH CAH TOA.

SOH CAH TOA stands for

$$\text{Sine} = \frac{\text{Opposite}}{\text{Hypotenuse}}$$

$$\text{Cosine} = \frac{\text{Adjacent}}{\text{Hypotenuse}}$$

$$\text{Tangent} = \frac{\text{Opposite}}{\text{Adjacent}}$$

Opposite, adjacent, and *hypotenuse* refer to the sides of a right triangle in relation to one of the acute angles. Take a look at this right triangle:

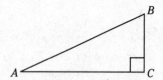

As you know, side *AB* is the *hypotenuse* of the triangle. (The hypotenuse is opposite the right angle and the longest side of the right triangle.) For angle *A,* side *BC* is *opposite,* and side *AC* is *adjacent.* For angle *B,* the opposite and adjacent switch: Side *AC* is opposite, and side *BC* is adjacent.

Use SOH CAH TOA to quickly find the sine, cosine, or tangent of any acute angle in the right triangle.

✔ **To find sin *A* (the sine of angle *A*), use the SOH part of SOH CAH TOA.** Place the length of the side opposite angle *A* (in this case, side *BC*) over the hypotenuse (side *AB*).

$$\sin A = \frac{\text{Opposite}}{\text{Hypotenuse}}$$

$$\sin A = \frac{\overline{BC}}{\overline{AB}}$$

✔ **To find cos *A* (the cosine of angle *A*), use the CAH part of SOH CAH TOA.** Place the length of the side adjacent angle *A* (in this case, side *AC*) over the hypotenuse (side *AB*).

$$\cos A = \frac{\text{Adjacent}}{\text{Hypotenuse}}$$

$$\cos A = \frac{\overline{AC}}{\overline{AB}}$$

✔ **To find tan *A* (the tangent of angle *A*), use the TOA part of SOH CAH TOA.** Place the length of the side opposite angle *A* over the side adjacent angle *A.*

$$\tan A = \frac{\text{Opposite}}{\text{Adjacent}}$$

$$\tan A = \frac{\overline{BC}}{\overline{AC}}$$

SOH CAH TOA applies only to a *right triangle* and only to an *acute angle,* never the right angle.

When you work with sine and cosine, keep this simple rule in mind: Sine and cosine can never be greater than 1.

$$\sin 90° = 1 \text{ and } \sin 0° = 0$$
$$\cos 90° = 0 \text{ and } \cos 0° = 1$$

Find the sine of angle A in right triangle shown below:

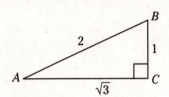

(A) 2

(B) $\sqrt{3}$

(C) 1

(D) $\frac{1}{2}$

Choice (D) is the right answer. Using the SOH in SOH CAH TOA, you know that the sine of angle A comes from the opposite (1) over the hypotenuse (2), for an answer of 1/2.

Three additional ratios aren't directly covered by SOH CAH TOA. They appear less frequently than sine, cosine, and tangent but are just as easy to find. These are cosecant (csc), secant (sec), and cotangent (cot). Basically, you find the sine, cosine, or tangent by using SOH CAH TOA and take the reciprocal to find cosecant, secant, or cotangent. The angle is usually represented by the Greek letter theta, θ:

$$\csc\theta = \frac{1}{\sin\theta}$$
$$\sec\theta = \frac{1}{\cos\theta}$$
$$\tan\theta = \frac{1}{\cot\theta}$$

Using the same right triangle, find the cotangent of angle A:

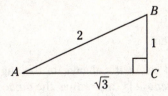

(A) 3

(B) 2

(C) $\sqrt{3}$

(D) 1

Choice (C) is the right answer. Using the TOA in SOH CAH TOA, you know that the tangent of angle A comes from the opposite (1) over the adjacent ($\sqrt{3}$), for a tangent of $1/\sqrt{3}$. Take the reciprocal of this to find the cotangent of the angle A: $\sqrt{3}$.

Going around in unit circles

The *unit circle* is a circle drawn on the *x-y* graph. The circle has a center at the origin of the graph — that is, coordinates $(0,0)$ — and a radius of 1.

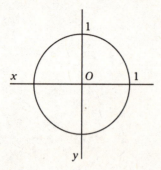

Starting with the radius of the circle at $(1,0)$, the angle θ is measured going counterclockwise.

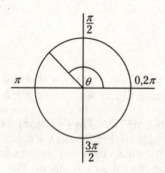

In this drawing, $\theta = 135°$. However, the angle isn't always measured in degrees; rather, it's in *radians,* which means that it's in terms of π, where $\pi = 180°$.

An angle measuring 45° also measures $\pi/4$ radians. An angle measuring 270° also measures $3\pi/2$ radians. More importantly, or the way it's used on the SAT, you can tell which quadrant an angle is in from the range of radians. In other words, an angle between $\pi/2$ and π is in the second quadrant. For the angle θ,

✔ $0 < \theta < \frac{\pi}{2}$ places the angle in the first quadrant.

✔ $\frac{\pi}{2} < \theta < \pi$ places the angle in the second quadrant.

✔ $\pi < \theta < \frac{3\pi}{2}$ places the angle in the third quadrant.

✔ $\frac{3\pi}{2} < \theta < 2\pi$ places the angle in the fourth quadrant.

When SOH CAH TOA is applied to an angle in the unit circle, it's always for the angle θ, which comes from the radius of the circle. The *hypotenuse* is this radius, the *adjacent* is the *x*-value, and the *opposite* is the *y*-value. Consider this example, where $\theta = 60°$ and the radius meets the circle at $\left(\frac{1}{2}, \sqrt{3}\right)$, where on the *xy* graph, $x = \frac{1}{2}$ and $y = \sqrt{3}$.

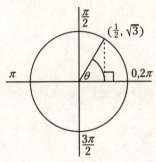

The sine of θ is the opposite over the hypotenuse, which in this case is $\dfrac{\sqrt{3}}{2}$. The cosine of θ is the adjacent over the hypotenuse, $\dfrac{1/2}{1}$, or $\dfrac{1}{2}$. The tangent of θ is the opposite over the adjacent, which is $\dfrac{\sqrt{3}}{1}$, or $\sqrt{3}$.

Knowing the quadrant and the sine, cosine, or tangent of an angle on the unit circle, you can find exactly where the angle is and solve almost any problem about it.

If $\dfrac{\pi}{2} < \theta < \pi$ and $\cos\theta = -\dfrac{3}{5}$, what is $\sin\theta$?

(A) $-\dfrac{4}{5}$

(B) $-\dfrac{3}{5}$

(C) $\dfrac{3}{5}$

(D) $\dfrac{4}{5}$

The answer is Choice (D). The first expression, $\dfrac{\pi}{2} < \theta < \pi$, places the angle in the second quadrant, and $\cos\theta = -\dfrac{3}{5}$ means the ratio of the x-value of the endpoint to the radius is $-\dfrac{3}{5}$. Because the hypotenuse (or radius) is always positive, the x-value is negative.

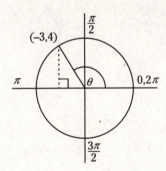

The $\sin\theta$, being the opposite over hypotenuse, is therefore $\dfrac{4}{5}$.

Chapter 15

Practicing Problems in Geometry and Trigonometry

. . . .

In This Chapter

▶ Practicing a few guided geometry and trigonometry problems

▶ Focusing on angles, shapes, and distances in some sample questions

. . . .

Even if you'd rather squash a polygon than calculate its measurements, bite the bullet and check out the practice questions in this chapter. You get two sets. In the first set, move through each problem by solving it and then immediately checking your answer using the explanation that follows. Don't cheat: Cover the answers with a blank sheet of paper until you come up with your own solutions. Then, try your hand at the second set, which is set up like the actual test. In that set, solve all the questions *before* checking your answers with the explanations in the section that follows the questions. (Turn to Chapter 14 for more information on any of the topics covered in these practice questions.)

The following diagrams appear at the beginning of each Math section of the SAT to help you work through the geometry problems. Don't hesitate to use them as you answer the practice problems in this chapter.

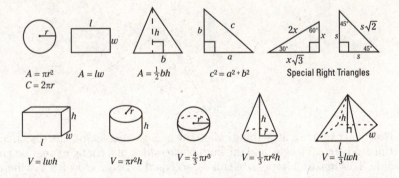

Set One: Getting Started with Some Guided Questions

Note: Questions 3 and 6 are grid-ins, so you don't get any answers to choose from. See Chapter 9 for a quick review of grid-ins.

1. In the following square, what is the length of side *s*?

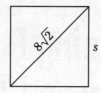

(A) 8

(B) $8\sqrt{2}$

(C) $8\sqrt{3}$

(D) 16

Choice (A) is correct. When you cut a square in half, you get a 45-45-90 triangle, with the square's diagonal as the hypotenuse. The freebie information at the beginning of each Math section (nice of them to help you, don't you think?) tells you that in a 45-45-90 triangle, the length of the hypotenuse equals $\sqrt{2}s$, where *s* is the length of a side of the square. Because the hypotenuse equals $8\sqrt{2}$, the side equals 8.

2. In triangle *ABC*, if the distance between points *A* and *B* is 5 and the distance between points *B* and *C* is 7, then the distance between points *A* and *C* may not equal

(A) 1

(B) 3

(C) 4

(D) 6

Choice (A) is correct. To answer this question, draw a line connecting *A* and *B* and another one connecting *B* and *C*, like so:

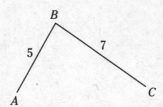

Now you can use a little thing called the *triangle inequality*. The distance from *A* to *C* forms the third side of a triangle, and the sum of two sides of a triangle must be greater than the third side. This makes it impossible for *AC* to equal 1, because $1 + 5 = 6$, which isn't bigger than 7. Before moving on, take a minute to make sure the other three answers do satisfy the triangle inequality.

3. In the following drawing, $\overline{BE} \parallel \overline{FI}$. Find the measure, in degrees, of the angle marked x.

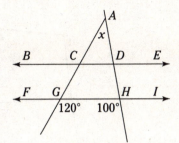

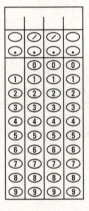

Because this drawing contains parallel lines cut by transversals (the two lines meeting at point A), you can fill in a whole lot of angles right off the bat. Each transversal creates eight angles, and these angles come in two groups of four pairs of vertical and supplementary angles. (Remember, a pair of *vertical angles* is two angles opposite each other and equal to each other. Supplementary angles total 180 degrees.) Here they are, filled in:

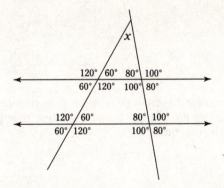

After you determine the angles, the problem becomes simpler. Because ACD is a triangle, its angles must add up to 180 degrees. With a 60-degree and an 80-degree angle already accounted for, the missing angle must be 40 degrees — your correct answer.

Don't grid-in the degree symbol, just the number.

4. What is the sum of the angles marked *a*, *b*, *c*, and *d* in the following diagram?

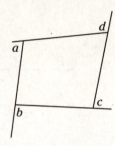

   (A) 180 degrees

   (B) 360 degrees

   (C) 540 degrees

   (D) 720 degrees

Choice (B) is correct. This one you just have to memorize. The sum of the exterior angles of any shape is always 360 degrees. Remember that fact.

5. If an equilateral triangle has sides of length 6, then its altitude has a length of

   (A) 3

   (B) $2\sqrt{3}$

   (C) $3\sqrt{2}$

   (D) $3\sqrt{3}$

Choice (D) is correct. This one's a special-triangle problem in disguise. Here's the equilateral triangle with its altitude drawn:

(Of course, you drew this triangle as soon as you were done reading the problem, right?) Each half of the original triangle forms a 30-60-90 triangle. Making a second drawing just to be clear is worth your time.

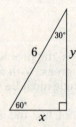

From the box of formulas and diagrams at the beginning of this chapter, you know that the side marked *x* must be half of 6, or 3, which means that *y*, the altitude, must equal $3\sqrt{3}$. Thus, Choice (D) is correct.

6. In the following diagram, O is the center of the circle, and angles A and B have the same measure. Find the measure, in degrees, of the angle marked x.

The easiest way to think about this problem is to cut the arrowhead shape into two triangles, like so:

Notice that the line segments OA, OB, and OC are all radii, making them all the same length. That means both triangles are isosceles. In any isosceles triangle, the base angles must have equal measures; because you were told that A and B have the same measure, all the angles marked in the following figure are congruent:

You're almost there. Because angle AOB is 90 degrees, the other side of the angle (dark line in the following figure) must measure 270 degrees to make 360 degrees around a point. That means that half of 270, or 135 degrees, is the top angle of the isosceles triangle. That leaves 45 degrees for the other two angles. And, because two of these angles together made up x, x must equal 45. Whew!

7. For this right triangle, if $\tan B = \frac{4}{3}$, find $\cos A$.

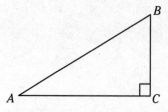

(A) $\frac{4}{3}$

(B) $\frac{5}{4}$

(C) $\frac{3}{4}$

(D) $\frac{4}{5}$

Choice (D) is the answer. If $\tan B = \frac{4}{3}$ and tangent is opposite over adjacent (the TOA from SOH CAH TOA), then draw the triangle like this:

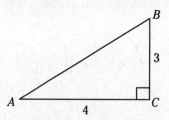

Spotting this as one of the Pythagorean triples (more on these in Chapter 14), you automatically throw the 5 down onto the hypotenuse:

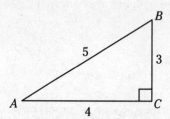

Cosine is CAH, which is adjacent over hypotenuse. Therefore, $\cos A = \frac{4}{5}$.

Set Two: Practicing Some Questions on Your Own

Note: Refer to the box of formulas and diagrams at the beginning of this chapter to help you answer these questions. Remember that those diagrams appear at the beginning of the Math sections on the real SAT.

1. In this triangle, the measure of angle x is greater than the measure of angle y. Which of the following statements must be false?

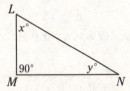

(A) $MN > LM$

(B) $(LN)^2 - (LM)^2 = (MN)^2$

(C) $LN > MN$

(D) $LN - LM = MN$

2. A car has wheels with radii of 1.5 feet. If the car is backed down a driveway that is 95 feet long, about how many complete turns will the wheels make?

(A) 10

(B) 13

(C) 15

(D) 20

3. In the following diagram, O is the center of the circle, and $\overline{AP}$ and $\overline{CP}$ are tangents. If $OA = 8$ and $BP = 9$, find CP.

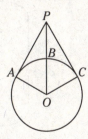

(A) $\sqrt{17}$

(B) 9

(C) $\sqrt{145}$

(D) 15

4. In the following diagram, a square is inscribed in a circle. If one side of the square has a length of 10, then the shaded area equals

(A) $100\pi - 100$

(B) $50\pi - 100$

(C) $100\pi - 50$

(D) $50\pi - 50$

5. In the following drawing, *ACDE* is a parallelogram with an area of 36. Find the length of *AC*.

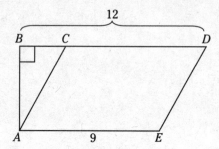

(A) 3

(B) 4

(C) 5

(D) 6

6. This cylindrical gas tank, originally empty, has a radius of 2 meters and a height of 3 meters. At 11 a.m., gas starts being added to the tank at a rate of 10 meters^3 per hour. The tank will be completely full closest to

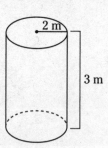

(A) 2 p.m.

(B) 2:30 p.m.

(C) 3 p.m.

(D) 3:30 p.m.

7. If $\frac{3\pi}{2} < \theta < 2\pi$ and $\sin\theta = -\frac{4}{5}$, what is $\cos\theta$?

(A) $\frac{4}{5}$

(B) $\frac{3}{5}$

(C) $-\frac{3}{5}$

(D) $-\frac{4}{5}$

Answers to Set Two

1. **D.** As you often should do in this type of problem, go through the answers one by one. Choice (A) is true because, in any triangle, the shortest side is opposite the smallest angle. Because y is smaller than x and both of them must be smaller than 90 degrees, y is the smallest angle and LM is the shortest side. Choice (B) is just a fancy way of writing the Pythagorean theorem. Because LN is the hypotenuse of a right triangle, $(LM)^2 + (MN)^2 = (LN)^2$, so $(LN)^2 - (LM)^2 = (MN)^2$. Choice (C) is true for essentially the same reason as Choice (A): LN must be the longest side of the triangle because it's across from 90 degrees, the largest angle. Choice (D) wins the "False Award" because of the triangle inequality. In any triangle, the sum of the two short sides must be *greater* than the longest side. That fact means that $LM + MN > LN$, so $LN - LM$ can't equal MN. The correct answer — the false statement — is Choice (D).

2. **A.** This one is a classic SAT problem. The key is knowing that one complete rotation equals the circumference of the wheel. Because circumference = $2\pi r$, you have $2(3.14)(1.5) \approx 9.42$ feet. Dividing 95 by 9.42 gives you 10.08, so your answer is 10. The correct answer is Choice (A).

3. **D.** Because $\overline{AP}$ and $\overline{CP}$ are tangents, the angles at A and C must be right angles. (If this fact is a surprise, turn back to Chapter 14. We can almost guarantee that this concept will show up in some form on the test). Triangles OPC and OPA are right triangles, so the Pythagorean theorem comes into play (and hits the ball out of the park). Because $OA = 8$, OB and OC are also 8 because all radii are equal. That makes $OP = 8 + 9 = 17$. OP is the hypotenuse, OC is a leg, and CP is a leg. So $(CP)^2 + (8)^2 = (17)^2$; $(CP)^2 + 64 = 289$; $(CP)^2 = 225$; and $CP = 15$. Choice (D) is correct.

4. **B.** This one is a shaded-area problem, so your answer must be the circle's area minus the square's area. The square's area is pretty simple to figure out: It's $(10)^2 = 100$. To find the circle's area, you need to know its radius. You can make a diameter by drawing the diagonal of the square, like so:

Look familiar? The diagonal of a square creates a 45-45-90 triangle, so the length of the diagonal is $10\sqrt{2}$. (The SAT-makers love special triangles.) The radius is half of the diameter, $\frac{10\sqrt{2}}{2}$, or $5\sqrt{2}$. Bingo. The area of the circle is $\pi\left(5\sqrt{2}\right)^2 = \pi(25 \times 2) = 50\pi$. So your answer is $50\pi - 100$, Choice (B).

Circling in on a better vocabulary

Lots of vocabulary words — the kind you may find in reading-comprehension passages or even in normal conversation — pop out of math lessons and land in the real world. For example, the line that touches a circle but doesn't pierce it (a *tangent*) gives rise to the expression *going off on a tangent* (moving away from the main topic to something that is only marginally related), as in "Coop went off on a tangent about eggs when he was supposed to be discussing feather boas." A related word, *tangential,* shows up in sentences such as "The dry cleaners' association and the United Featherworkers of America criticized Coop's tangential remarks."

You probably know how to find the *circumference* of a circle (the distance around the edge). Well, the following words are all in the same family:

✔ **Circumlocution:** To talk around by speaking indirectly and avoiding a clear statement, as in "Politicians use more circumlocutions than usual during an election year."

✔ **Circumnavigate:** To sail around, as in "Some say Phileas circumnavigated the globe in a hot air balloon."

✔ **Circumscribe:** To limit; picture a warden drawing a circle around someone and forbidding him or her to cross the line.

✔ **Circumspect:** Cautious; think of an imaginary circle around yourself that you venture beyond only with extreme care.

✔ **Circumvent:** To go around, as in "Bruckner circumvented the door alarm by breaking through the wall."

A distant cousin of the *circum* family is **circuitous,** an adjective that may describe the sort of route taxi drivers take with tourists in the back seat (round and round, just to drive up the fare).

5. **C.** The area of a parallelogram uses the same formula as a rectangle: *base × height*. Because the base, *AE,* is 9, and the area is 36, the height, *AB,* must be 4. (Don't be fooled into thinking that *AC* is the height. The height is always perpendicular to the base, never slanted.) Meanwhile, *BC* = 12 − 9 = 3. This is yet another right triangle, so you can use the Pythagorean theorem to get *AC* = 5. Even better, if you remember the 3-4-5 right triangle, you just know that the answer is 5 without having to do all the work. Choice (C) is the correct answer.

6. **C.** The volume of a 3-D figure equals the area of its base times its height. Because the base is a circle, its area is $\pi r^2 = \pi (2)^2 = 4\pi \approx 12.56$ m². Multiplying by 3, the height, gives you a volume of 37.68 m³. Dividing 37.68 m³ by 10 m³ per hour gives you 3.768 hours to fill the tank. This answer is a little bit closer to four hours than to 3.5 hours (3.75 would be exactly halfway), so you can round up to 4 hours. Four hours after 11 a.m. is 3 p.m. Choice (C) is correct.

7. **B.** The expression $\frac{3\pi}{2} < \theta < 2\pi$ places the angle in the fourth quadrant, and $\sin\theta = -\frac{4}{5}$ means that the ratio of the *y*-value to the hypotenuse is $-\frac{4}{5}$, or −4 to 5, because the hypotenuse is always positive. This means that drawn on the unit circle, and completing the 3-4-5 triangle, angle θ looks like this:

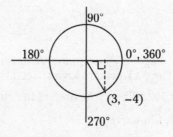

To find $\cos\theta$, place the adjacent (*x*-value) over the hypotenuse: $\frac{3}{5}$.

Chapter 16

Playing the Odds: Statistics and Probability

• •

In This Chapter

▶ Understanding probability and answering multiple-probability questions

▶ Solving problems that deal with geometric probability

▶ Using mean, median, and mode

▶ Interpreting scatter plots and other graphs

▶ Thinking logically to solve logic-based SAT questions

• •

If you take the SAT 25 times, what are the odds that you'll die of boredom before entering college? Your SAT proctor, even more bored than the 25 test-takers in front of him, launches an ink-filled balloon into the 30-square-foot classroom. What is the probability that it will miss you and land on the mouth-breather in the next row?

Questions like these — similar but humorless — confront you on the SAT. To increase the odds that you'll ace the topic of statistics and probability, read on. Also peruse this chapter to get the lowdown on the three *m*'s (mean, median, and mode) and scatter plots and other graphs as well as logic questions.

Working with the Odds: Probability

The *probability* of an event (or the odds that it will occur) is almost always defined as a fraction. So in many probability situations, you have to compute two separate numbers, one for the numerator and one for the denominator of the fraction. What do these numbers stand for? Well, here's the formula:

$$\text{the probability of an event} = \frac{\text{the number of ways for the event to happen}}{\text{the total number of possible outcomes}}$$

Say that you have a jar containing 6 red, 4 yellow, and 8 blue marbles. The probability of randomly picking a blue marble is $\frac{8 \text{ blue marbles}}{6 + 4 + 8 = 18 \text{ total marbles}}$, which can be reduced to $\frac{4}{9}$.

Probability can also be written as a percentage. The easiest way to compute the percentage is with your calculator. Suppose that the probability that a major label will sign your garage band is $\frac{2}{5}$. (In your dreams, by the way. The real probability is $\frac{1}{10,000,000}$.) Enter $2 \div 5$ on your calculator to get 0.4. Now move the decimal two places to the right. Bingo. The probability that you and your bandmates will ride to the MTV studio in a limo is 40%.

An event that is certain to happen has a probability of 1, or 100%. An event that is impossible has a probability of 0. Nothing can ever have a probability greater than 1 or less than 0. Another way to say the second fact: Negative probability doesn't exist.

When you calculate probability, remember the number 1. All the possible events must have probabilities that add up to 1 (or 100%). That fact leads to a useful rule, which may be stated in three ways:

- The probability that an event won't happen equals 1 minus the (decimal or fractional) probability of the event.

- The probability that an event won't happen equals 100% minus the (percent) probability of the event.

- The probability that an event won't happen equals

$$\frac{\text{total number of possibilities} - \text{the number of ways for the event to happen}}{\text{the total number of possible outcomes}}$$

Imagine that you're sitting in class with 19 other students, and your teacher decides to pick one student at random to stay after school for a round of eraser cleaning. What's the chance that she picks you? There's only 1 of you, and she's choosing from 20 students. The probability is $\frac{1}{20}$, or 5%.

So what's the chance that she *doesn't* pick you? Because there are 20 total possibilities (20 students), $\frac{20-1}{20} = \frac{19}{20} = 95\%$ or $100\% - 5\% = 95\%$.

The following sections discuss two variations of the typical SAT probability problem.

Psyching out multiple-probability questions

Not surprisingly, the SAT-writers have found plenty of ways to make probability problems harder. One of their favorite torture devices is to ask you about a probability involving multiple events. When a problem involves multiple events, the total number of possibilities is the product of the number of possibilities for each event. If, for example, you open your closet on laundry day and find two clean shirts and three pairs of pants, the total number of outfits you can make is $2 \times 3 = 6$ (assuming that you're not a fashionista and don't care about little things like complementary colors). This rule is known as the *counting principle,* although the "multiplication principle" may be a better name for it. This method works whether you're using whole numbers, percentages, or fractions.

Multiple-probability questions on the SAT may resemble the following example.

Jenny arranges interviews with three potential employers. If each employer has a 50% probability of offering her a job, what's the probability that she gets offered all three?

(A) 10%

(B) 12.5%

(C) 100%

(D) 150%

The answer is Choice (B). Applying the counting principle to Jenny's situation, you can say that the probability of her being offered all three jobs is $50\% \times 50\% \times 50\%$, or $\frac{1}{2} \times \frac{1}{2} \times \frac{1}{2} = \frac{1}{8}$ (12.5%).

Surviving geometric probability

Unbelievably, those SAT-writers sometimes expect you to combine your knowledge of two different areas of mathematics in a single question! In this example, the areas are *geometry* and *probability*. (Turn to Chapter 14 for a geometry review.) Check out the following example.

A dart is thrown at the dartboard below. If the radius of the circle is 5 inches, then the probability that the dart lands in the square but not in the circle is closest to

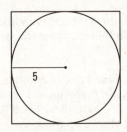

(A) 15%

(B) 21%

(C) 50%

(D) 78%

The answer is Choice (B). You may recognize this question as a variation of the shaded-area problem. (Check out Chapter 14 for more info on shaded areas.) Because the problem asks about the four corner regions of the diagram, first you have to figure out the area of these regions. The area of the circle is $\pi r^2 = \pi (5)^2 = 25\pi$ square inches. Because a side of the square equals the circle's diameter, which is 10, the square's area is $10^2 = 100$ square inches. That makes the total area of the corner regions equal to $100 - 25\pi \approx 100 - 78.54 = 21.46$ $100 - 25\pi \approx 100 - 78.54 = 21.46$. The probability of the dart hitting somewhere in one of the corner areas is found by dividing the area of the corners by the total area of the square. Because the square's area is 100, the probability that the dart lands in one of the corners is $\frac{21.46}{100} = 21.46\%$.

Finding the Three Ms: Mean, Median, and Mode

Sometimes the SAT gives you a group of numbers and asks you to find the *average* (officially called the *mean* or *arithmetic mean*). This sort of problem is probably familiar to you, especially if you're into computing your grade-point average or your favorite baseball player's batting average. To find the average, just add up the numbers and divide the total by the number of numbers you just added. For example, to find the average of 2, 4, and 9, add those three numbers (total = 15) and divide by 3. The average is 5.

If a group of numbers is evenly spaced, the mean is the middle number or the average of the two middle numbers. Suppose that you're asked to find the arithmetic mean of the numbers from 1 to 19. Even with a calculator, adding all the numbers and then dividing is time-consuming, not to mention easy to mess up. But the 19 numbers are evenly spaced (all 1 apart), and 10 is the middle number. No matter which way you start, from 1 or from 19, you find nine numbers evenly spaced on either side of 10. Therefore, 10 is the average.

Remember that this trick works only when the numbers are evenly spaced, such as 5, 10, 15, 20, and 25 having an average of 15. If you're told to find the average of 3, 5, 7, 12, and 18, you have to do the math: Add them up and divide by the number of numbers.

Moving beyond *mean*, the SAT also asks about *median*. The *median*, as those of you with drivers' licenses already know, is the strip down the middle of a road. In math, the *median* is defined as the middle number in a list, when the list is in numerical order. If you have a list such as 5, 3, 8, 7, 2, and need to find the median, put the numbers in order: 2, 3, 5, 7, 8. The middle number, or median, is 5.

If you have an even number of numbers (say, 3, 5, 6, 7, 8, 10), the list has no middle number, so take the mean of the two numbers closest to the middle. In this example, the two numbers in question are 6 and 7, so the median is 6.5.

The last of the three *m*'s is the *mode*, the easiest to find. In a mixed bag of numbers, the *mode* is the number or numbers that pop up most frequently. So if you have a set with two 4s and two 8s, plus a bunch of other single numbers, you have two modes, 4 and 8, in that set. You can also have a set with no mode at all if everything shows up the same number of times.

Which of the following is true for the set of numbers 3, 4, 4, 5, 6, 8?

(A) mean > mode

(B) median > mean

(C) median = mode

(D) median = mean

The answer is Choice (A). If you average the terms, you get $30 \div 6 = 5$, which is the mean. The median is 4.5 (halfway between the third and fourth terms), and the mode is 4. So Choice (A) is the only one that fits.

Reading Graphs

Some of the math questions on the SAT are called *data interpretation*. Sounds important, huh? Actually, it's just a pompous name for "reading a graph," something you've been doing for years. Don't let graph problems intimidate you. Here are the three most common types of graphs you're likely to see on the SAT:

✔ Bar graph

✔ Circle or pie graph

✔ Two-axes line graph

We explain these graphs in more detail in the following sections. Because the SAT-writers sometimes try to trip you up by asking you to compare statistics in two different graphs, we cover that topic here as well.

Bar graphs

A *bar graph* has vertical or horizontal bars. The bars may represent actual numbers or percentages. If a bar goes all the way from one side of the graph to the other, it usually represents 100 percent.

Circle or pie graphs

The *circle* or *pie graph* represents 100 percent. The key to this graph is determining the total that the percentages are part of. Below the graph you may be told that in 1994, 5,000 students graduated with PhDs. If a 25 percent segment on the circle graph is labeled "PhDs in history," you know that the number of history PhDs is 25 percent of 5,000, or 1,250.

Two-axes line graphs and scatter plots

A typical *line graph* has a bottom and a side axis. You plot a point or read a point from the two axes. A special kind of two-axes graph is the *scatter plot*. A scatter plot contains a bunch of dots scattered around a two-line graph. Here's an example:

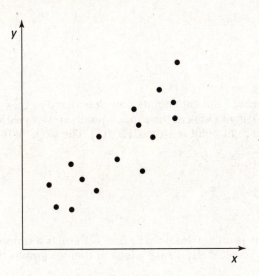

Notice how the points seem to follow a certain trend, going higher as they go to the right. When a trend is present, you can draw a line that estimates the behavior of the points. This line is known as a *trend line*. On the test, you may be given a scatter plot and have to estimate where the points are going based on the trend line.

For the following data set, the trend line has a slope closest to

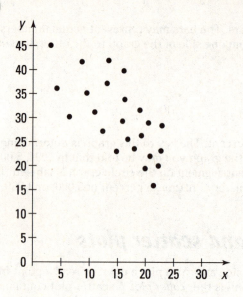

(A) –2

(B) –1

(C) 1

(D) 2

The correct answer is Choice (A). Because the data points flow downward as they go to the right, it must be Choice (A) or (B). If you look at the top left point, you can estimate its coordinates as $(5, 45)$. The bottom right point is around $(20, 15)$. The slope of the line connecting these points is $\frac{15-45}{20-5} = \frac{-30}{15} = -2$.

Multiple graphs

Some questions use two graphs in one problem. No need to fret — there is a simple art to answering multiple-graph questions. To get started, take a look at the two graphs that follow.

You must read these graphs together. The second graph is a bar graph going from 0 to 100 percent. Read the graph by subtracting to find the appropriate percentage. For example, in 1990, "Grandparents won't donate a building" begins at 20 percent and goes to 50 percent, a difference of 30 percent. You've fallen into a trap if you say that "Grandparents won't donate a building" was 50 percent. In 1993, "Just felt like it" goes from 80 percent to 100 percent, which means it was actually 20 percent.

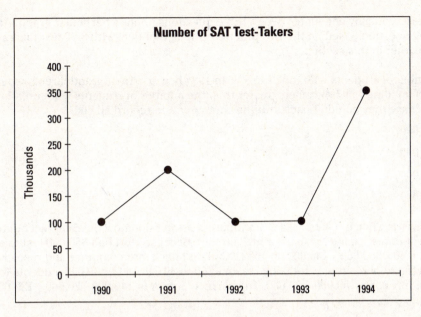

Number of SAT Test-Takers

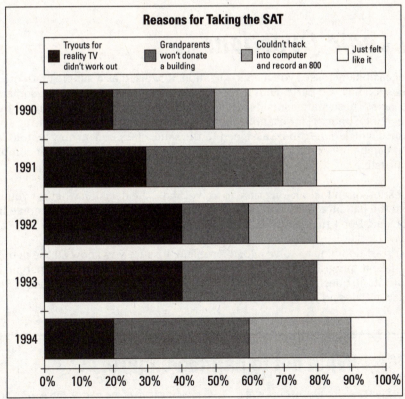

Reasons for Taking the SAT

Legend:
- Tryouts for reality TV didn't work out
- Grandparents won't donate a building
- Couldn't hack into computer and record an 800
- Just felt like it

The first graph gives you the number of SAT test-takers in thousands. (By the way, these aren't real numbers.) Be sure to look at the labels of the axes. For example, _Thousands_ along the side axis tells you that in 1990, there weren't 100 test-takers but 100,000. Using the two graphs together, you can find out the number of test-takers who took the SAT for a particular reason. For example, in 1991, 200,000 students took the test. Also in 1991, "Couldn't hack into computer and record an 800" (from 70 to 80, or 10 percent) made up 10 percent of the reasons for taking the SAT. Multiply 10 percent or $0.10 \times 200,000 = 20,000$ test-takers.

On the test, you may encounter two to three questions about a particular graph. Answer the following question based on the two practice graphs that deal with SAT test-takers and appear earlier in this section.

The number of students who took the SAT in 1994 because their grandparents wouldn't donate a building was how much greater than the number of students who took the SAT in 1992 because they couldn't hack into the computer and record an 800?

(A) 250,000

(B) 140,000

(C) 120,000

(D) 100,000

The answer is Choice (C). In 1994, "Grandparents won't donate a building" accounted for 40 percent of test-taking reasons (from 20 to 60). Because 1994 had 350,000 test-takers, multiply $0.40 \times 350,000 = 140,000$. In 1992, "Couldn't hack into computer and record an 800" counted for 20 percent of test-taking reasons (60 to 80). In 1992, 100,000 students took the test. Multiply $0.20 \times 100,000 = 20,000$. The correct answer is $140,000 - 20,000 = 120,000$, or Choice (C).

Analyzing Logic Questions

The SAT occasionally tosses you a logic question, disguised as a simple math question. This type of question has two parts. First is the set of statements or conditions, sometimes called the facts. These statements describe the relationship between or among people, items, or events. You may, for example, be given statements about students at a school and then be asked which ones can be assigned to the same classes. You may be told facts about events that can happen on certain days of the week or about what different combinations of items are possible.

A logic question often takes a long time to solve. Make the decision whether you have the time — and the patience! — to do it properly. If not, skip the question and come back to it later, if you can. Don't rush yourself.

Before you start doodling to solve a logic problem, be sure you know all the people or items involved. Make a "program" of all the players by writing down the pool of people or events. For example, if the question talks about five teachers, Mahaffey, Negy, O'Leary, Plotnitz, and Quivera, use initials and jot down M, N, O, P, and Q on the test booklet.

What not to call the umpire

Mathematicians love baseball — or at least baseball stats. So take a moment to rest from your math labors and watch your favorite team. You can call the ump *disinterested* (fair) but not *uninterested* (bored out of his skull). Unless you want to go down on strikes, also avoid calling him *pusillanimous* (cowardly) and *mendacious* (lying). Whatever you think of the pay scale, stay away from *mercenary* (in it only for the money, as opposed to in it for the love of the game) and *partial* or *partisan* (biased). Nor would an umpire appreciate being labeled *iniquitous* (evil) or *intemperate* (excessive, extreme).

To gain the ump's favor, try calling him *judicious* (showing good judgment) and *discerning* (sharp, perceptive). You may also call him *equanimous* (level headed or even tempered) to stay on his good side.

Next, use a diagram to show the relationship between people or events. Here are a few of the most common diagrams.

> ✔ **Calendar:** Draw a simple calendar and fill in the events that happen on particular days.
>
> ✔ **Ordering or sequencing:** You may have a relationship problem in which some people are taller or heavier than others. Write a line of people, with A above B if A is taller than B, C at the bottom if she is the shortest, and so on.
>
> ✔ **Grouping or membership:** This problem asks you which items or people could belong to which group. For example, membership in a club may require four out of five characteristics. Often this type of question doesn't require a graph, but it does require a lot of *if . . . then* statements, such as "If A is in the group, then B isn't."

Try your hand at this logic-based example:

Five spices — lemon pepper, marjoram, nutmeg, oregano, and paprika — are aligned next to one another between the left and right sides of a kitchen cabinet. Their arrangement must conform to the following conditions:

The marjoram is immediately to the right of the paprika.

The oregano is either all the way to the left or second from the left.

The lemon pepper is farther left than the nutmeg.

Which of the following could *not* be true?

(A) The paprika is second from the left.

(B) The marjoram is to the right of the lemon pepper.

(C) The nutmeg is exactly in the middle.

(D) The lemon pepper is exactly in the middle.

The answer is Choice (D). To help keep track of the information, write out initials for the roster of spices — L, M, N, O, and P — and make five simple dashes to represent the five positions of the spices:

___ ___ ___ ___ ___

The easiest condition to accommodate is the one that indicates that the oregano must be first or second from the left. Draw these two possibilities:

O ___ ___ ___ ___

___ O ___ ___ ___

The next thing to note is that the paprika and marjoram must always move together. So test out the answer choices, making sure to also fulfill the third condition. Choice (A) is fine, because you can write O, P, M, L, N and meet all conditions. Choice (B) also works, because you can write O, L, P, M, N. And for Choice (C), you can write either O, L, N, P, M or L, O, N, P, M.

Choice (D) is no good, though. If L is in the middle, you have to put P and M to its right, because they always travel together. But that doesn't leave room to put N to the right of L, so you can't fulfill the third condition. Choice (D) is the only option that doesn't work, so that's your answer.

Chapter 17

Practicing Problems in Probability, Statistics, and Logic

....

In This Chapter

▶ Practicing some guided questions about probability, statistics, and logic
▶ Poring over some sample questions on your own

....

Y ou can count on at least a couple of probability, statistics, and logic problems showing up on your particular version of the SAT. Don't freak out! Now's the time to practice with the help of the two sets in this chapter. After you complete each question in the first set, check your answers and read the explanations of any problem you answered incorrectly. (The answers immediately follow each question.) Don't cheat, though! Use a piece of paper to cover the answers as you work through the problems. Then hit set two, which is set up more like the real test, with the answers coming in a section separate from the questions themselves. Turn to Chapter 16 for a refresher course in any topic that stumps you in either set.

Set One: Trying Your Hand at Some Guided Questions

> *Note:* Questions 1 and 7 are grid-ins, which means you don't get answers to choose from. See Chapter 9 for tips on answering grid-ins.

1. A school cafeteria offers two soups, three main dishes, and four desserts. Find the total number of possible meals consisting of one soup, one main dish, and one dessert.

The correct answer is 24. Using the counting principle, $2 \times 3 \times 4 = 24$.

2. The chance of rain tomorrow is 25%. What is the probability that it will *not* rain tomorrow?

   (A) 4%

   (B) 25%

   (C) 40%

   (D) 75%

   The probability of an event not happening equals 100% minus the probability of it happening: $100\% - 25\% = 75\%$. Choice (D) is correct.

3. In a special deck of 20 cards, 8 cards are red on both sides, 7 cards are blue on both sides, and the other 5 cards are red on one side and blue on the other side. If a student picks a card and places it on his desk, what is the probability that the side facing up is blue?

   (A) $\dfrac{19}{40}$

   (B) $\dfrac{6}{10}$

   (C) $\dfrac{7}{40}$

   (D) $\dfrac{7}{20}$

   This one's a little tricky. Even though there are 20 cards, the question asks only about the side of the card facing up, and there are $20 \times 2 = 40$ possible sides. The 7 cards that are blue on both sides represent $7 \times 2 = 14$ blue sides, and there are 5 cards with one blue side. Add those together and you get $14 + 5 = 19$, so the probability is $\dfrac{19}{40}$. Choice (A) is correct.

   Problems 4, 5, and 6 use the following graphs.

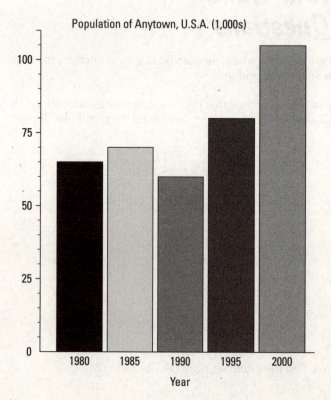

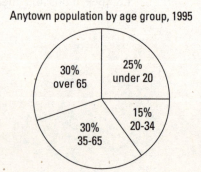

4. In 1990, what was the approximate number of Anytown residents over the age of 65?

   (A) 55,000

   (B) 25,000

   (C) 14,000

   (D) It cannot be determined from the graphs.

   Don't trip over this one. You can tell from the bar graph that in 1990 Anytown had approximately 60,000 total residents, but the pie graph tells you only about the ages of the residents in 1995. You have no way to determine anything about the ages of Anytown residents in 1990, so Choice (D) is correct.

5. During which five-year period did Anytown have the greatest percent increase in population?

   (A) 1980–1985

   (B) 1985–1990

   (C) 1990–1995

   (D) It cannot be determined from the graphs.

   You can throw out Choice (B) right away, because the population decreased. You can also throw out Choice (D), because you can use the graphs to determine the answer. That leaves Choices (A) and (C). Take a quick look at the bar graph, and the gap between 1980 and 1985, Choice (A), is far less than the gap between 1990 and 1995, Choice (C). Thus, Choice (C) is correct.

6. In 1995, roughly how many Anytown residents were between the ages of 20 and 65?

   (A) 45

   (B) 15,000

   (C) 36,000

   (D) 45,000

   A look at the pie chart tells you that $30 + 15$, or 45%, of the residents were between 20 and 65 in 1995. Because there were 80,000 residents, change 45% into 0.45, and multiply: $0.45 \times 80,000 = 36,000$. The correct answer is Choice (C).

7. A bag contains red, blue, and green marbles. The probability of picking a red marble is $\frac{1}{2}$ and the probability of picking a blue marble is $\frac{1}{3}$. If the bag holds seven green marbles, find the total number of marbles in the bag.

Your answer here is 42. To do this one, you need a little algebra. Because the probability of picking a red marble is $\frac{1}{2}$, half of the marbles are red. Similarly, one-third of the marbles are blue. So one-half of the marbles, plus one-third of the marbles, plus the seven green marbles, is the number you're looking for. If you let x represent the total number of marbles, you can write $\frac{1}{2}x + \frac{1}{3}x + 7 = x$.

Because fractions are annoying, multiply everything by 6 to get $3x + 2x + 42 = 6x$. This equation gives you $5x + 42 = 6x$, so $x = 42$.

8. If a student picks a square at random on the following grid, what is the probability that he picks a square that is not shaded?

(A) $\frac{3}{5}$

(B) $\frac{3}{8}$

(C) $\frac{2}{5}$

(D) $\frac{5}{8}$

Fifteen of the 40 squares are not shaded. Put the 15 over 40, $\frac{15}{40}$, which reduces to $\frac{3}{8}$. Choice (B) is correct.

9. Which graph could represent the trend line for this scatter plot?

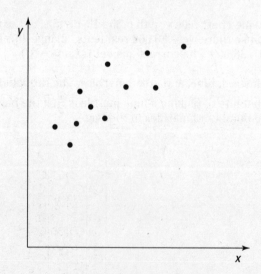

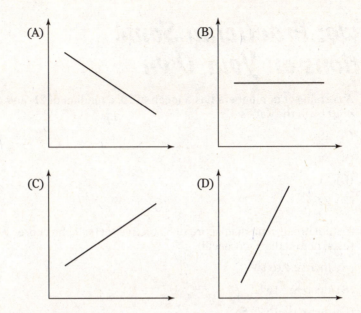

As long as you remember what the trend line is, this one is easy (see Chapter 16 if you don't). Choice (C) is correct.

10. Alison, Bob, Chris, and Darrell all arrive at school between 7:30 and 8:00.

    Chris was late to school, but Bob was not.

    Darrell arrived ten minutes after Alison.

    Bob didn't see Alison when he came into school.

Based on this information, which student(s) could have arrived at exactly 7:30?

(A) only Alison

(B) only Bob

(C) either Alison or Bob

(D) only Chris

You don't know what time the school day starts, but the first clue tells you that Chris must have arrived later than Bob, so Chris couldn't have arrived at 7:30, but (from this clue) Bob could have. The same logic applies to the second clue: Darrell arrived after Alison, so Darrell couldn't have been there at 7:30, but Alison could have. The third clue is just the SAT-makers (okay, us) messing with you; Alison might have already been in the building, or she might not have been, but you just can't tell. So Choice (C) is correct, because either of them might have arrived at 7:30; in fact, they might have both arrived then, if the school has more than one door.

Set Two: Practicing Some Questions on Your Own

1. A certain set of numbers has a mean of 20, a median of 21, and a mode of 22. Which number *must* be in the data set?

   (A) 19

   (B) 20

   (C) 21

   (D) 22

2. A student has a median score of 83 on five tests. If she scores 97 and 62 on her next two tests, her median score will

   (A) increase to 90

   (B) decrease to 82

   (C) decrease to 79.5

   (D) remain the same

3. Alicia picks a number from the set $\{1, 2, 3, 4, 5, 6\}$. Michelle picks a number from the set $\{3, 4, 5, 6, 7, 8\}$. What is the probability that they select the same number?

   (A) $\frac{1}{6}$

   (B) $\frac{1}{9}$

   (C) $\frac{2}{7}$

   (D) $\frac{3}{8}$

4. If a two-digit number is picked at random, what is the probability that the number chosen is a perfect square?

   (A) $\frac{1}{16}$

   (B) $\frac{1}{15}$

   (C) $\frac{1}{9}$

   (D) $\frac{1}{4}$

5. A class contains five boys and seven girls. In how many ways can a teacher line up two boys and two girls, in that order?

   (A) 35

   (B) 140

   (C) 210

   (D) 840

6. A magazine did a study of ten cars, comparing the number of miles each car could go on a full tank of gas. Their results are shown below. Of the labeled points, which one represents the car that goes the farthest per gallon of gas?

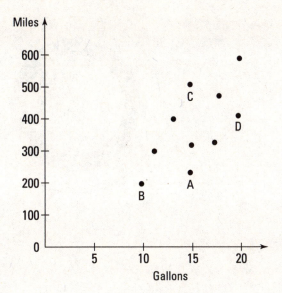

(A) A

(B) B

(C) C

(D) D

7. A junior is choosing her classes for senior year. If she takes calculus, she can also take either history or English, but not both. If she takes psychology in the first semester, she cannot take sociology or creative writing. If she takes psychology in the second semester, she cannot take calculus but can take any elective she wants during the first semester. Based only on this information, which of the following is *not* a possible choice of courses for her?

(A) English, calculus, psychology, statistics

(B) History, sociology, psychology, English

(C) Creative writing, psychology, history, English

(D) Calculus, psychology, creative writing, history

8. A student has taken three tests, with an average (arithmetic mean) of 82. What grade must he receive on his next test in order to have an overall average of 85?

(A) 85

(B) 88

(C) 90

(D) 94

9. The following dartboard consists of three circles with the same center and radii of 6, 8, and 10 inches. If someone throws a dart at the board without aiming for a particular part of the board, what is the probability that the dart lands in the shaded ring?

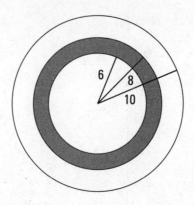

(A) $\frac{7}{25}$

(B) $\frac{4}{5}$

(C) $\frac{3}{4}$

(D) $\frac{9}{16}$

Answers to Set Two

1. **D.** If you remember how to compute the three *m*'s, you'll realize that the mean and median don't have to be in the data set. (Look in Chapter 16 for more on mean, median, and mode.) But because the mode is the most common measurement, it must be in the set. Thus, Choice (D) is correct.

2. **D.** The median is the score in the middle. If 83 is in the middle, adding a 97 on one side and a 62 on the other side doesn't change where the middle is. The correct answer is Choice (D).

3. **B.** First determine the total number of possibilities. Using the counting principle, you know you have $6 \times 6 = 36$ possibilities. Because the two sets overlap at 3, 4, 5, and 6, the girls may pick the same number in only four ways. Hence, the answer is $4/36 = 1/9$. Choice (B) is correct.

4. **B.** As usual in a probability question, you need to start by determining the total number of two-digit numbers. The two-digit numbers run from 10 to 99. The formula you can use for the number of these is as follows: The total is one more than the difference of the two numbers, or $99 - 10 + 1 = 90$. Of these, only six are perfect squares: 16, 25, 36, 49, 64, and 81. So that gives you a probability of $6/90 = 1/15$, Choice (B).

5. **D.** The teacher can't pick the same person twice, so he has five choices for the first boy but only four left for the second. Similarly, he has seven choices for the first girl and six for the second. Using the counting principle, you know the answer is $5 \times 4 \times 7 \times 6 = 840$. Choice (D) is correct.

6. **C.** Car C travels approximately 500 miles on 15 gallons, for approximately 500/15 or 33 miles per gallon. The other cars all travel fewer than 30 miles per gallon. Choice (C) is correct.

7. **D.** Start by making a list of combinations that are impossible:

   Calculus, English, history

   First-semester psychology, sociology

   First-semester psychology, creative writing

   Second-semester psychology, calculus

   Now consider the choices: Choice (A) is fine, if she takes psychology in the first semester. Choice (B) is okay if she takes psychology in the second semester. Choice (C) is fine, if she takes psychology in the second semester. Choice (D) is a problem. If she takes psychology in the first semester, then creative writing is out. But if she takes it in the second semester, then calculus is out. Choice (D) is the correct answer.

8. **D.** The formula average score × number of scores = total score helps you answer this problem. The student wants to end up with an average score of 85 on four tests, for a total score of $85 \times 4 = 340$. The student's total number of points on the first three tests is $82 \times 3 = 246$. So to make up the difference, he needs $340 - 246 = 94$ points on his next test to get (1) the car keys, and (2) permission to stay out past 7 p.m. Choice (D) is correct.

9. **A.** The shaded ring has an outer radius of 8 and an inner radius of 6. So the area of the shaded ring is the area of the radius-8 circle minus the area of the radius-6 circle, or $\pi(8)^2 - \pi(6)^2 = 64\pi - 36\pi = 28\pi$. The entire dartboard has a radius of 10, so its area is $\pi(10)^2 = 100\pi$, and the probability equals $28\pi/100\pi = 28/100 = 7/25$. Choice (A) is correct.

Part V
Where the Rubber Meets the Road: Practice Tests

Five Ways to Duplicate the Test Environment

You can take this SAT practice test little by little — a section at a time, perhaps. You get the most by mimicking real test conditions, though, and following these guidelines:

- **Set aside an entire morning for the test.** Turn off your phone, computer, siblings, and pets. (How do you turn off a dog and a brother? Barricade your room and send them outside!)

- **Use the answer sheet and bubble your answers with a #2 pencil, just as you would on the real SAT.** If you choose to write the essay, have a couple of sheets of lined paper ready. Write with a pencil, unless you're sure that a computer-based testing center is nearby and available to you. (Not many exist right now.)

- **Watch the clock, or better yet, set a timer.** Don't go over time on any section, and don't return to a section once you've started a new one.

- **Don't turn to a new section before the official time is up.** If you finish early, recheck your work or just relax in your chair.

- **Take breaks.** Take one ten-minute break after the Writing and Language section. If you're writing the essay, take another ten-minute break before you start that task.

 Head to www.dummies.com/extras/SAT for a free article that tells you how to build your test-taking stamina to make it through test day.

In this part . . .

✔ Find out how prepared you are for the SAT by taking full-length practice tests.

✔ Discover how to improve your performance by reviewing the answer explanations for all the practice questions.

✔ Score your tests quickly with the answer key.

Chapter 18

Practice Exam 1

• •

*W*elcome to SAT Land. If you read — or even glanced at — other chapters in this book, you already have a map of the territory. But as every traveler knows, reading *about* a place and actually *being* there are very different experiences. This chapter is an opportunity to visit. You won't send smiling photos to your friends from SAT Land. You aren't going on vacation! However, when you take this practice exam and check your answers in Chapter 19, you will end up with a few great souvenirs — a better understanding of your strengths and weaknesses.

You may decide to break this test into pieces, working on one section each day for a week, perhaps. Or you may block off an entire morning and do the whole thing at once, as you will at the testing center. Either way, keep to the time limit for each section. Also, be sure to read the explanations for every incorrect answer, and, if you can spare the time, for correct answers as well. The explanations in Chapter 19 are filled with tips and tricks to improve your score.

Ready? Tear out the bubble answer sheet, grab a pencil and four sheets of loose-leaf paper (if you're writing the optional essay), and place a timer where you can see it. Sit back, relax, and enjoy your trip through Practice Exam I.

Answer Sheets

For Sections 1 through 4, use the ovals and grid-ins provided with this practice exam to record your answers. Begin with Number 1 for each new section. For the essay, write on four sheets of loose-leaf or notebook paper. Or you can use the following blank pages.

Section 1: Reading

1. Ⓐ Ⓑ Ⓒ Ⓓ   12. Ⓐ Ⓑ Ⓒ Ⓓ   23. Ⓐ Ⓑ Ⓒ Ⓓ   34. Ⓐ Ⓑ Ⓒ Ⓓ   45. Ⓐ Ⓑ Ⓒ Ⓓ
2. Ⓐ Ⓑ Ⓒ Ⓓ   13. Ⓐ Ⓑ Ⓒ Ⓓ   24. Ⓐ Ⓑ Ⓒ Ⓓ   35. Ⓐ Ⓑ Ⓒ Ⓓ   46. Ⓐ Ⓑ Ⓒ Ⓓ
3. Ⓐ Ⓑ Ⓒ Ⓓ   14. Ⓐ Ⓑ Ⓒ Ⓓ   25. Ⓐ Ⓑ Ⓒ Ⓓ   36. Ⓐ Ⓑ Ⓒ Ⓓ   47. Ⓐ Ⓑ Ⓒ Ⓓ
4. Ⓐ Ⓑ Ⓒ Ⓓ   15. Ⓐ Ⓑ Ⓒ Ⓓ   26. Ⓐ Ⓑ Ⓒ Ⓓ   37. Ⓐ Ⓑ Ⓒ Ⓓ   48. Ⓐ Ⓑ Ⓒ Ⓓ
5. Ⓐ Ⓑ Ⓒ Ⓓ   16. Ⓐ Ⓑ Ⓒ Ⓓ   27. Ⓐ Ⓑ Ⓒ Ⓓ   38. Ⓐ Ⓑ Ⓒ Ⓓ   49. Ⓐ Ⓑ Ⓒ Ⓓ
6. Ⓐ Ⓑ Ⓒ Ⓓ   17. Ⓐ Ⓑ Ⓒ Ⓓ   28. Ⓐ Ⓑ Ⓒ Ⓓ   39. Ⓐ Ⓑ Ⓒ Ⓓ   50. Ⓐ Ⓑ Ⓒ Ⓓ
7. Ⓐ Ⓑ Ⓒ Ⓓ   18. Ⓐ Ⓑ Ⓒ Ⓓ   29. Ⓐ Ⓑ Ⓒ Ⓓ   40. Ⓐ Ⓑ Ⓒ Ⓓ   51. Ⓐ Ⓑ Ⓒ Ⓓ
8. Ⓐ Ⓑ Ⓒ Ⓓ   19. Ⓐ Ⓑ Ⓒ Ⓓ   30. Ⓐ Ⓑ Ⓒ Ⓓ   41. Ⓐ Ⓑ Ⓒ Ⓓ   52. Ⓐ Ⓑ Ⓒ Ⓓ
9. Ⓐ Ⓑ Ⓒ Ⓓ   20. Ⓐ Ⓑ Ⓒ Ⓓ   31. Ⓐ Ⓑ Ⓒ Ⓓ   42. Ⓐ Ⓑ Ⓒ Ⓓ
10. Ⓐ Ⓑ Ⓒ Ⓓ   21. Ⓐ Ⓑ Ⓒ Ⓓ   32. Ⓐ Ⓑ Ⓒ Ⓓ   43. Ⓐ Ⓑ Ⓒ Ⓓ
11. Ⓐ Ⓑ Ⓒ Ⓓ   22. Ⓐ Ⓑ Ⓒ Ⓓ   33. Ⓐ Ⓑ Ⓒ Ⓓ   44. Ⓐ Ⓑ Ⓒ Ⓓ

Section 2: Mathematics — Calculator Section

1. Ⓐ Ⓑ Ⓒ Ⓓ   7. Ⓐ Ⓑ Ⓒ Ⓓ   13. Ⓐ Ⓑ Ⓒ Ⓓ   19. Ⓐ Ⓑ Ⓒ Ⓓ   25. Ⓐ Ⓑ Ⓒ Ⓓ
2. Ⓐ Ⓑ Ⓒ Ⓓ   8. Ⓐ Ⓑ Ⓒ Ⓓ   14. Ⓐ Ⓑ Ⓒ Ⓓ   20. Ⓐ Ⓑ Ⓒ Ⓓ   26. Ⓐ Ⓑ Ⓒ Ⓓ
3. Ⓐ Ⓑ Ⓒ Ⓓ   9. Ⓐ Ⓑ Ⓒ Ⓓ   15. Ⓐ Ⓑ Ⓒ Ⓓ   21. Ⓐ Ⓑ Ⓒ Ⓓ   27. Ⓐ Ⓑ Ⓒ Ⓓ
4. Ⓐ Ⓑ Ⓒ Ⓓ   10. Ⓐ Ⓑ Ⓒ Ⓓ   16. Ⓐ Ⓑ Ⓒ Ⓓ   22. Ⓐ Ⓑ Ⓒ Ⓓ   28. Ⓐ Ⓑ Ⓒ Ⓓ
5. Ⓐ Ⓑ Ⓒ Ⓓ   11. Ⓐ Ⓑ Ⓒ Ⓓ   17. Ⓐ Ⓑ Ⓒ Ⓓ   23. Ⓐ Ⓑ Ⓒ Ⓓ   29. Ⓐ Ⓑ Ⓒ Ⓓ
6. Ⓐ Ⓑ Ⓒ Ⓓ   12. Ⓐ Ⓑ Ⓒ Ⓓ   18. Ⓐ Ⓑ Ⓒ Ⓓ   24. Ⓐ Ⓑ Ⓒ Ⓓ   30. Ⓐ Ⓑ Ⓒ Ⓓ

31.   32.   33.   34.   35.

36.   37.   38.

Section 3: Writing and Language

1. Ⓐ Ⓑ Ⓒ Ⓓ	10. Ⓐ Ⓑ Ⓒ Ⓓ	19. Ⓐ Ⓑ Ⓒ Ⓓ	28. Ⓐ Ⓑ Ⓒ Ⓓ	37. Ⓐ Ⓑ Ⓒ Ⓓ
2. Ⓐ Ⓑ Ⓒ Ⓓ	11. Ⓐ Ⓑ Ⓒ Ⓓ	20. Ⓐ Ⓑ Ⓒ Ⓓ	29. Ⓐ Ⓑ Ⓒ Ⓓ	38. Ⓐ Ⓑ Ⓒ Ⓓ
3. Ⓐ Ⓑ Ⓒ Ⓓ	12. Ⓐ Ⓑ Ⓒ Ⓓ	21. Ⓐ Ⓑ Ⓒ Ⓓ	30. Ⓐ Ⓑ Ⓒ Ⓓ	39. Ⓐ Ⓑ Ⓒ Ⓓ
4. Ⓐ Ⓑ Ⓒ Ⓓ	13. Ⓐ Ⓑ Ⓒ Ⓓ	22. Ⓐ Ⓑ Ⓒ Ⓓ	31. Ⓐ Ⓑ Ⓒ Ⓓ	40. Ⓐ Ⓑ Ⓒ Ⓓ
5. Ⓐ Ⓑ Ⓒ Ⓓ	14. Ⓐ Ⓑ Ⓒ Ⓓ	23. Ⓐ Ⓑ Ⓒ Ⓓ	32. Ⓐ Ⓑ Ⓒ Ⓓ	41. Ⓐ Ⓑ Ⓒ Ⓓ
6. Ⓐ Ⓑ Ⓒ Ⓓ	15. Ⓐ Ⓑ Ⓒ Ⓓ	24. Ⓐ Ⓑ Ⓒ Ⓓ	33. Ⓐ Ⓑ Ⓒ Ⓓ	42. Ⓐ Ⓑ Ⓒ Ⓓ
7. Ⓐ Ⓑ Ⓒ Ⓓ	16. Ⓐ Ⓑ Ⓒ Ⓓ	25. Ⓐ Ⓑ Ⓒ Ⓓ	34. Ⓐ Ⓑ Ⓒ Ⓓ	43. Ⓐ Ⓑ Ⓒ Ⓓ
8. Ⓐ Ⓑ Ⓒ Ⓓ	17. Ⓐ Ⓑ Ⓒ Ⓓ	26. Ⓐ Ⓑ Ⓒ Ⓓ	35. Ⓐ Ⓑ Ⓒ Ⓓ	44. Ⓐ Ⓑ Ⓒ Ⓓ
9. Ⓐ Ⓑ Ⓒ Ⓓ	18. Ⓐ Ⓑ Ⓒ Ⓓ	27. Ⓐ Ⓑ Ⓒ Ⓓ	36. Ⓐ Ⓑ Ⓒ Ⓓ	

Section 4: Mathematics — No-Calculator Section

1. Ⓐ Ⓑ Ⓒ Ⓓ	4. Ⓐ Ⓑ Ⓒ Ⓓ	7. Ⓐ Ⓑ Ⓒ Ⓓ	10. Ⓐ Ⓑ Ⓒ Ⓓ	13. Ⓐ Ⓑ Ⓒ Ⓓ
2. Ⓐ Ⓑ Ⓒ Ⓓ	5. Ⓐ Ⓑ Ⓒ Ⓓ	8. Ⓐ Ⓑ Ⓒ Ⓓ	11. Ⓐ Ⓑ Ⓒ Ⓓ	14. Ⓐ Ⓑ Ⓒ Ⓓ
3. Ⓐ Ⓑ Ⓒ Ⓓ	6. Ⓐ Ⓑ Ⓒ Ⓓ	9. Ⓐ Ⓑ Ⓒ Ⓓ	12. Ⓐ Ⓑ Ⓒ Ⓓ	15. Ⓐ Ⓑ Ⓒ Ⓓ

16. | 17. | 18. | 19. | 20. (grid-in answer boxes)

Section 1: Reading

Time: 65 minutes for 52 questions

Directions: Read these passages and answer the questions that follow based on what is stated or implied in the passages and accompanying diagrams, charts, or graphs.

Questions 1–10 refer to the following excerpt from O Pioneers *by Willa Cather.*

Line   The Bergson homestead was easier to find than many another, because it overlooked a shallow, muddy stream. This creek gave a sort of identity to the farms that bordered upon it. Of all the bewildering things about a new country, the absence of human landmarks is one of the most depressing and disheartening. The houses were small and were usually tucked away in

(05)   low places; you did not see them until you came directly upon them. Most of them were built of the sod itself, and were only the inescapable ground in another form. The roads were but faint tracks in the grass, and the fields were scarcely noticeable. The record of the plow was insignificant, like the feeble scratches on stone left by prehistoric races, so indeterminate that they may, after all, be only the markings of glaciers, and not a record of human strivings.

(10)   In eleven long years John Bergson had made but little impression upon the wild land he had come to tame. It was still a wild thing that had its ugly moods; and no one knew when they were likely to come, or why. Mischance hung over it. Its Genius was unfriendly to man. The sick man was feeling this as he lay looking out of the window, after the doctor had left him, on the day following his daughter Alexandra's trip to town. There it lay outside his door, the

(15)   same land, the same lead-colored miles. He knew every ridge and draw and gully between him and the horizon. To the south, his plowed fields; to the east, the sod stables, the cattle corral, the pond — and then the grass.

Bergson went over in his mind the things that had held him back. One winter his cattle had perished in a blizzard. The next summer one of his plow horses broke its leg in a prairie dog

(20)   hole and had to be shot. Another summer he lost his hogs from disease, and a valuable stallion died from a rattlesnake bite. Time and again his crops had failed. He had lost two children, boys, that came between Lou and Emil, and there had been the cost of sickness and death. Now, when he had at last struggled out of debt, he was going to die himself. He was only forty-six, and had, of course, counted on more time.

(25)   Bergson had spent his first five years getting into debt, and the last six getting out. He had paid off his mortgages and had ended pretty much where he began, with the land. He owned exactly six hundred and forty acres of what stretched outside his door; his own original homestead and timber claim, making three hundred and twenty acres, and the half-section adjoining, the homestead of a younger brother who had given up the fight, gone back to

(30)   Chicago to work in a fancy bakery and distinguish himself in a Swedish athletic club. So far John had not attempted to cultivate the second half-section, but used it for pasture land, and one of his sons rode herd there in open weather.

John Bergson had the Old-World belief that land, in itself, is desirable. But this land was an enigma. It was like a horse that no one knows how to break to the harness, that runs wild and

(35)   kicks things to pieces. He had an idea that no one understood how to farm it properly, and this he often discussed with Alexandra. Their neighbors, certainly, knew even less about farming

Go on to next page

than he did. Many of them had never worked on a farm until they took up their homesteads. They had been handworkers at home; tailors, locksmiths, joiners, cigar-makers, etc. Bergson himself had worked in a shipyard.

1. Which of the following statements best describes John Bergson's attitude toward nature?

   (A) Natural features are beautiful.

   (B) Human beings should not interfere with nature.

   (C) Nature is inferior to human construction.

   (D) Wilderness areas are preferable to cities and towns.

2. Which lines provide the best evidence for the answer to Question 1?

   (A) Lines 2–4 ("Of all . . . disheartening.")

   (B) Lines 10–11 ("In eleven . . . tame.")

   (C) Lines 12–14 ("The sick man . . . town.")

   (D) Lines 33–34 ("But this land . . . enigma.")

3. What best fits the definition of "human strivings" in the context of Line 9?

   (A) "shallow, muddy stream" (Line 1)

   (B) "bewildering things" (Line 3)

   (C) "new country" (Line 3)

   (D) "faint tracks in the grass" (Line 7)

4. The comparison between the plowed fields and "the feeble scratches on stone left by prehistoric races" (Line 8) serves to

   (A) introduce the idea of human weakness

   (B) show that this settlement has a long history

   (C) emphasize the primitive quality of the farming

   (D) describe the effects of glaciers

5. The "Genius" mentioned in Line 12 may best be defined as

   (A) intelligence

   (B) spirit

   (C) brain

   (D) type

6. Which of the following best explains the meaning of the pronoun "this" in Line 13?

   (A) the amount of work Bergson had invested in his land

   (B) the symptoms of Bergson's illness

   (C) Bergson's bad mood

   (D) the wild nature of Bergson's land

7. The list of events in the third paragraph (Lines 18–24) serve to

   (A) illustrate Bergson's bad luck

   (B) show that Bergson was unprepared for farming

   (C) emphasize some hope for the future of Bergson's farm

   (D) provide information about Bergson's character

8. In the context of Lines 33–34, the land is "an enigma" because

   (A) it differs from the land of the Old World

   (B) the settlers don't know how to farm it

   (C) it is too dry

   (D) John Bergson planned poorly

9. John Bergson would most likely agree with which statement?

   (A) No matter how prepared you are, you will not survive on the frontier.

   (B) Life in the Old World is superior to life on the frontier.

   (C) Survival on the frontier is dependent upon animals.

   (D) Life on the frontier is not always easy.

10. Which lines are the best evidence supporting the answer to Question 9?

   (A) Lines 4–5 ("The houses were small . . . them.")

   (B) Lines 10–11 ("In eleven long . . . tame.")

   (C) Lines 18–23 ("One winter . . . sickness and death.")

   (D) Lines 35–37 ("He had an idea . . . than he did.")

Go on to next page

Questions 11–20 refer to the following passage and diagram from A Brief History of the Olympics by David C. Young (Wiley).

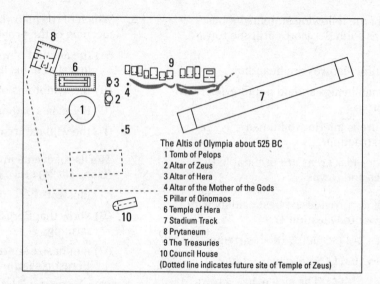

The Altis of Olympia about 525 BC
1 Tomb of Pelops
2 Altar of Zeus
3 Altar of Hera
4 Altar of the Mother of the Gods
5 Pillar of Oinomaos
6 Temple of Hera
7 Stadium Track
8 Prytaneum
9 The Treasuries
10 Council House
(Dotted line indicates future site of Temple of Zeus)

Line "Victory by speed of foot is honored above all." Those are the words of Xenophanes, a sixth century BCE philosopher who objected to athletes and their popularity. The phrase "speed of foot" may recall the words expressed in Homer's *Odyssey* stressing the glory which an athlete may win "with his hands or with his feet." The shortest foot race, the *stade,* was one

(05) length of the stadium track, the practical equivalent of our 200 meter dash (actually, only 192.27 meters at Olympia, the site of the original Olympic games). Greek tradition held that this 200 meter race was the first and only event held at the first Olympiad in 776 BCE.

The name of the winner of the 200 appears first in all lists of victors in any Olympiad. Some people think that the *stade* winner had the year named after him. This is not really true.

(10) Most Greek states had other means of dating any given year, usually by the name of one or more political leaders. But when Hippias of Elis compiled his catalogue of victors, the *stade* victor obviously headed his list for each individual Olympiad. Perhaps because the Olympic festival was one of the few truly international institutions in Greece, later Greeks found it convenient to use the sequence of Olympiads as a chronological reference. Thus an entry in

(15) Julius Africanus' text will read, for example, "Olympiad 77, Dandis of Argos [won] the stade." Subsequent years within the Olympiad are simply viewed as Olympiad 77, years two, three, and four.

As one would expect, methods of running seem to be no different then from now. Several vase paintings show a group of runners rather close to one another, their bodies pitched for-

(20) ward, their arms making large swings up and down. These are clearly runners in the 200, for modern sprinters look much the same. So also distance runners can be easily identified. Like their modern counterparts, they can run upright, with less arc in their leg movements, and their arms dangle comfortably at their sides. Some of these ancient athletes developed the effective strategy of hanging back with the rest of the pack, reserving some strength until

(25) near the end. Then they would suddenly break away from the rest and close with a strong spurt of speed, as if barely tired, passing the leaders who became weak and faded. Ancient sources never specify the exact number of laps in the distance race, and modern opinions vary greatly. The most widely accepted number is 20 laps, a distance of a little over 3845 meters (2.36 miles), more than double our classic distance race of 1500 meters.

Go on to next page

(30) The ancient stadium was shaped very differently from the modern one. It was almost twice as long as ours, and about half as wide. There was no course around an infield, no infield at all, just adjacent lanes for the runners. The athletes had therefore no gradual turns around a curve at each end, as in a modern stadium. Stephen Miller, excavator at Nemea, found a posthole not far from the north end of the stadium. He conjectures that it held a turning

(35) post. It is highly likely that, in the distance race, such a single turning post for all athletes was probably used. But in the 400, down and back, the runner would need to turn sharply around the post. Most scholars think that each 400 runner would have had his own turning post. Otherwise there would have been too much congestion at that only turn. A few vases show athletes not patently sprinters or distance runners going around a turning post. In

(40) one, a judge stands watch. But if each 400 meter runner had his own turning post, the scene probably shows a distance race.

11. The quotations in this passage primarily serve to

    (A) offer conflicting opinions

    (B) establish an authoritative voice

    (C) invite the reader to conduct further research

    (D) give a sense of Greek literary style

12. According to information presented in the passage and accompanying figure, the area where the Olympiad took place

    (A) devoted less space to athletic contests than to other activities

    (B) was consecrated to the gods

    (C) was rectangular in shape

    (D) fulfilled athletes' needs

13. In the context of Line 5, what is the best definition of "practical"?

    (A) hands-on

    (B) likely to succeed

    (C) realistic

    (D) pragmatic

14. According to the passage, which of the following statements is correct?

    (A) Winners earned glory for the state they represented, not for themselves.

    (B) The Greek stadium was similar to modern arenas.

    (C) The Olympiads served as a common reference point for time.

    (D) Running styles differed in ancient times.

15. Which lines provide supporting evidence for the answer to Question 14?

    (A) Line 2 ("philosopher who objected . . . popularity")

    (B) Lines 4–6 ("one length of the stadium . . . games")

    (C) Line 18 ("As one would expect . . . now.")

    (D) Lines 13–14 ("later Greeks . . . reference")

16. The author's comment "as one would expect" (Line 18) is probably based on

    (A) his own experience as a runner

    (B) the fact that human anatomy does not change

    (C) recent archeological discoveries

    (D) information from contemporary literature

17. In the context of Line 28, what is the best definition of "accepted"?

    (A) generally believed

    (B) taken from what is offered

    (C) approved

    (D) admitted

18. With which statement would the author of this passage most likely agree?

    (A) History is an accurate record of events.

    (B) The best historical evidence comes from literature.

    (C) Historians should tap many sources of information.

    (D) Unless written records exist, history must remain unknown.

Go on to next page

19. Which lines support the answer to Question 18?

   (A) Lines 26–28 ("Ancient sources . . . vary greatly.") and Lines 37–38 ("Most scholars think . . . post.")

   (B) Line 1 ("Victory by speed . . . above all.") and Lines 3–4 ("words expressed . . . with his feet")

   (C) Lines 11–12 ("Hippias of Elis . . . Olympiad") and Lines 15–16 ("Julius Africanus . . . stade")

   (D) Line 8 ("The name of the winner . . . Olympiad.") and Lines 19–20 ("vase paintings . . . up and down")

20. The discussion of turning posts in Lines 38–41 ("A few vases show . . . distance race.")

   (A) illustrates the difference between modern and ancient Olympic events

   (B) shows how historians misinterpret evidence

   (C) reveals a question that can be solved only by more research

   (D) explains the limits of ancient athletes

Questions 21–31 refer to the following passages. Passage I is an excerpt from Novel Plant Bioresources *by Gurib Fakim (Wiley). Passage II is an excerpt from* Biology For Dummies, *2nd Edition, by Rene Kratz and Donna Siegfried (also published by Wiley).*

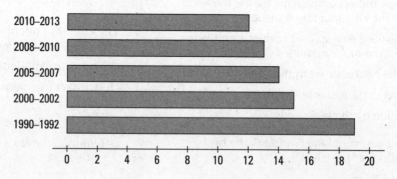

Percentage of Undernourished Persons in the World, 1990–2013

United Nations Food and Agricultural Organization

Passage I

Line The world still faces tremendous challenges in securing adequate food that is healthy, safe, and of high nutritional quality for all and doing so in an environmentally sustainable manner. With the growing demand of an expected 9 billion people by 2050, it remains unclear how our current global food system will cope. Currently, 868 million people suffer
(05) from hunger, while micronutrient deficiencies, known as hidden hunger, undermine the development, health, and productivity of over 2 billion people. The estimation of plant species that exist in the world is between 250,000 and 400,000. As many as 80% of the world's people depend on traditional medicines, which involve the use of plant extracts or their active principles for their primary health care needs. Plant diversity has a critical role
(10) to play in addressing the food and nutrition security and medicinal needs of the people of this world. Plant diversity is not evenly distributed across the world and tends to be concentrated in specific, diversity-rich areas. It is generally known that most diversity of species occurs within the warm regions of the tropics and less diversity exists in temperate regions of the world.

Go on to next page

(15) Plants are an intricate part of all our ecosystems. Besides the obvious provisioning of food in ensuring that people are food and nutritionally secured, many plants contribute directly to our agriculture by providing valuable traits and genes used by modern-day breeders for crop improvement, in particular those plants which are closely related to crop plants, the so-called "crop wild relatives," and restore health in an important human adaptation, as fun-
(20) damental a feature of human culture as is use of fire, tools, and speech. Having evolved over millennia, the knowledge, cultural traditions, and medicinal resources of many human societies may be rapidly disappearing with the loss of cultural and biological diversity.

In spite of this great diversity of plants on Earth and the fundamental role they play, the story of crops and humanity has shown an increasing reliance on a small proportion of
(25) plant species used by humans. The beginnings of exploitation of plant diversity for food and nutrition are as old as humankind, and early hunter gatherers in pre-agricultural times would have exploited their local environment for readily available fruits, berries, seeds, flowers, shoots, storage organs, and fleshy roots to complement meat obtained from hunting.

(30) Furthermore, crop plants have resulted in an even greater reliance by humans on much reduced plant diversity than was previously used for food by pre-agricultural human societies. More than 70,000 plants are known to have edible parts. The world's food comes from about 100 plant species, based on calories, protein, and fat supply. However, only four crop species (maize, wheat, rice, and sugar) supply almost 60% of the calories and protein
(35) in the human diet. There are thousands of plant species with neglected potential utility.

Many studies show that plant diversity is globally threatened. Recently a group of international experts called for the development of a global program for the conservation of useful plants and associated knowledge.

Passage II

The loss in biodiversity could have effects beyond just the loss of individual species. Living
(40) things are connected to each other and their environment in how they obtain food and other resources necessary for survival. If one species depends on another for food, for example, then the loss of a prey species can cause a decline in the predator species.

Some species, called keystone species, are so connected with other organisms in their environment that their extinction changes the entire composition of species in the area. As bio-
(45) diversity decreases, keystone species may die out, causing a ripple effect that leads to the loss of many more species. If biodiversity gets too low, then the future of life itself becomes threatened. An example of a keystone species is the purple seastar, which lives on the northwest Pacific coast of the United States. Purple seastars prey on mussels in the intertidal zone. When the seastars are present, they keep the mussel population in check, allow-
(50) ing a great diversity of other marine animals to live in the intertidal zone. If the seastars are removed from the intertidal zone, however, the mussels take over, and many species of marine animals disappear from the environment.

Biodiversity increases the chance that at least some living things will survive in the face of large changes in the environment, which is why protecting it is crucial. The combined effect
(55) of various human actions in Earth's ecosystems is reducing the planet's biodiversity. In fact, the rate of extinctions is increasing along with the size of the human population. No one knows for certain how extensive the loss of species due to human impacts will ultimately be, but there's no question that human practices such as hunting and farming have already caused numerous species to become extinct.

21. In the context of Line 3, what is the best definition of "demand"?

    (A) command

    (B) insistence

    (C) popularity

    (D) need

22. Taken as a whole, these passages may best be characterized as

    (A) an argument in favor of biodiversity

    (B) a comparison of current and prehistoric food supplies

    (C) a description of how ecosystems work

    (D) an inventory of popular crops and endangered species

23. Of the lines listed here, which represents the best evidence for the answer to Question 22?

    (A) Lines 3–4 ("With the growing . . . cope.") and Lines 41–42 ("If one species depends . . . predator species.")

    (B) Lines 6–7 ("The estimation . . . 400,000.") and Line 47 ("An example . . . purple seastar")

    (C) Lines 20–22 ("Having evolved . . . diversity.") and Lines 48–49 ("Purple seastars . . . intertidal zone.")

    (D) Lines 46–47 ("If biodiversity . . . threatened.") and Lines 53–54 ("Biodiversity increases the chance . . . environment")

24. With which statement would the authors of both passages most likely agree?

    (A) Human beings should not exploit plant and animal resources.

    (B) Slowing the rate of extinctions is no longer possible.

    (C) Reliance on a small number of food sources causes problems.

    (D) Keystone species should be protected at all costs.

25. The "9 billion people" mentioned in Line 3

    (A) rely on our current food system

    (B) are those experiencing hunger when the passage was written

    (C) represent the estimated population of Earth in 2050

    (D) is the most likely number of undernourished people in 2050

26. In the context of Line 11, which of the following best expresses the meaning of "concentrated"?

    (A) distributed

    (B) thought about

    (C) given attention

    (D) grouped

27. Passage II implies that large populations of mussels

    (A) become keystone species in their environment

    (B) displace other species

    (C) do not compete for food with purple seastars

    (D) are a major cause of extinctions

28. According to the passages and accompanying graph, which of these statements is true?

    I. The percentage of the population with an adequate amount of food rose from 1990 to 2013.

    II. The number of people who lack important nutrients is greater than the number of people who are considered "undernourished" in official surveys.

    III. The number of animal species providing food for human beings is decreasing.

    (A) I only

    (B) II only

    (C) I and II

    (D) II and III

29. The author of Passage I presents statistics about the types of crops humans cultivate for food in order to

    (A) illustrate overreliance on a small number of species

    (B) explain why food resources are scarce

    (C) show that food is harvested inefficiently

    (D) reveal the shortcomings of the average person's diet

Go on to next page

30. Which of the following would the author of Passage II most likely support?

(A) a drive to clean seashore areas

(B) a petition to ban the cultivation of mussels

(C) a program to preserve keystone species in forested areas

(D) a required course in marine biology

31. In comparison with Passage I, Passage II is

(A) more focused on food supplies

(B) less concerned with plant diversity

(C) more focused on plants

(D) more focused on ecosystems

Questions 32–42 refer to the following passage from President Abraham Lincoln's Second Inaugural Address, the speech he gave in 1865 when he took the oath of office for his second term as President. The Civil War between the North and the South was nearing its end as Lincoln spoke.

Line   Fellow Countrymen:

At this second appearing to take the oath of the presidential office, there is less occasion for an extended address than there was at the first. Then a statement, somewhat in detail, of a course to be pursued, seemed fitting and proper. Now, at the expiration of four years, during (05) which public declarations have been constantly called forth on every point and phase of the great contest which still absorbs the attention, and engrosses the energies of the nation, little that is new could be presented. The progress of our arms, upon which all else chiefly depends, is as well known to the public as to myself; and it is, I trust, reasonably satisfactory and encouraging to all. With high hope for the future, no prediction in regard to it is ventured.

(10) On the occasion corresponding to this four years ago, all thoughts were anxiously directed to an impending civil-war. All dreaded it — all sought to avert it. While the inaugural address was being delivered from this place, devoted altogether to saving the Union without war, insurgent agents were in the city seeking to destroy it without war — seeking to dissolve the Union, and divide effects, by negotiation. Both parties deprecated war; but one (15) of them would make war rather than let the nation survive; and the other would accept war rather than let it perish. And the war came.

One eighth of the whole population were colored slaves, not distributed generally over the Union, but localized in the Southern part of it. These slaves constituted a peculiar and powerful interest. All knew that this interest was, somehow, the cause of the war. To strengthen, (20) perpetuate, and extend this interest was the object for which the insurgents would rend the Union, even by war; while the government claimed no right to do more than to restrict the territorial enlargement of it.

Neither party expected for the war, the magnitude, or the duration, which it has already attained. Neither anticipated that the cause of the conflict might cease with, or even before, (25) the conflict itself should cease. Each looked for an easier triumph, and a result less fundamental and astounding. Both read the same Bible, and pray to the same God; and each invokes His aid against the other. It may seem strange that any men should dare to ask a just God's assistance in wringing their bread from the sweat of other men's faces; but let us judge not that we be not judged. The prayers of both could not be answered; that of neither has been (30) answered fully.

The Almighty has His own purposes. "Woe unto the world because of offences! for it must needs be that offences come; but woe to that man by whom the offence cometh!" If we shall

Go on to next page

suppose that American Slavery is one of those offences which, in the providence of God, must needs come, but which, having continued through His appointed time, He now wills to
(35) remove, and that He gives to both North and South, this terrible war, as the woe due to those by whom the offence came, shall we discern therein any departure from those divine attributes which the believers in a Living God always ascribe to Him? Fondly do we hope — fervently do we pray — that this mighty scourge of war may speedily pass away. Yet, if God wills that it continue, until all the wealth piled by the bond-man's two hundred and fifty years
(40) of unrequited toil shall be sunk, and until every drop of blood drawn with the lash, shall be paid by another drawn with the sword, as was said three thousand years ago, so still it must be said "the judgments of the Lord, are true and righteous altogether."

With malice toward none; with charity for all; with firmness in the right, as God gives us to see the right, let us strive on to finish the work we are in; to bind up the nation's wounds; to care
(45) for him who shall have borne the battle, and for his widow, and his orphan — to do all which may achieve and cherish a just, and a lasting peace, among ourselves, and with all nations.

32. In the context of Line 4, what is the best definition of "course"?

(A) study

(B) plan

(C) field

(D) lessons

33. In paragraph one (Lines 1–9), what does Lincoln imply about the war?

(A) Too much has been said about the war.

(B) Politicians have paid too little attention to it.

(C) His side is winning.

(D) No one will be satisfied with the result.

34. Which of the following is the best evidence supporting the answer to Question 33?

(A) Lines 2–3 ("less occasion . . . first")

(B) Line 4 ("course . . . proper")

(C) Lines 6–7 ("absorbs . . . presented")

(D) Lines 8–9 ("reasonably . . . all")

35. Lincoln most likely states that "little that is new could be presented" (Line 7) because

(A) the war monopolizes the attention and resources of the nation

(B) he has no vision of a peaceful future

(C) the public's views are unknown

(D) his listeners are not ready for the future

36. According to Lincoln, during his first inauguration

(A) citizens generally agreed on a plan for his administration

(B) the movement to disband the nation had already begun

(C) there was unconditional support for war

(D) negotiations to avoid war had already ended

37. In the context of Line 19, what is the best definition of "interest"?

(A) attention

(B) issue

(C) benefit

(D) problem

38. In the fourth paragraph of Lincoln's speech (Lines 23–30) he

(A) pleads for an end to war

(B) emphasizes what both sides have in common

(C) dismisses the concerns of his opponents

(D) argues that the war was unavoidable

39. What is the best evidence for the answer to Question 38?

(A) Lines 23–24 ("the magnitude . . . attained")

(B) Line 25 ("the conflict itself . . . cease")

(C) Line 26 ("Both read . . . same God")

(D) Lines 29–30 ("neither has . . . fully")

Go on to next page

40. Throughout the speech, Lincoln uses the pronouns *we, us,* and *our* to refer to

    (A) Northerners

    (B) Southerners

    (C) those present during the speech

    (D) both Northerners and Southerners

41. Lincoln's purpose in giving this speech was most likely to

    (A) proclaim victory

    (B) condemn slavery

    (C) emphasize the idea of a united country

    (D) encourage his troops

42. The dominant strategy in this speech is

    (A) an appeal to logic

    (B) a reliance on religious principles

    (C) an appeal for personal support

    (D) a condemnation of opponents

> *Questions 43–52 refer to the following information, excerpted and adapted from* The Story of Eclipses, *by George F. Chambers (London: George Newnes, Ltd.).*

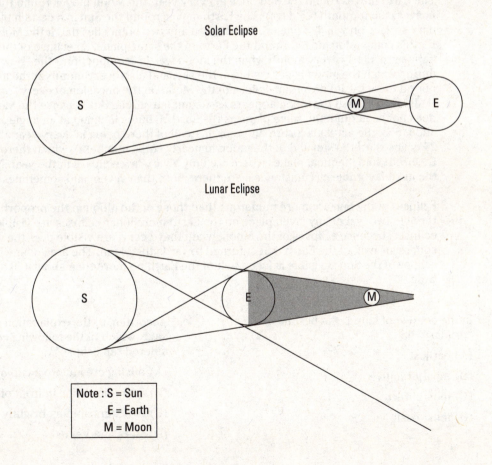

Solar Eclipse

Lunar Eclipse

Note : S = Sun
E = Earth
M = Moon

Go on to next page

Line   The primary meaning of the word "eclipse" is a disappearance, the covering over of something by something else. This apparently crude definition will be found, on investigation, to represent precisely the facts of the case.

(05)   As the Earth and the Moon are solid bodies, each must cast a shadow into space as the result of being illuminated by the Sun, a source of light. The various bodies which together make up the Solar System, the planets and their moons, are constantly in motion. Consequently, if we imagine a line to be drawn between any two bodies at any given time, such a line will point in a different direction at another time, and so it may occasionally

(10)   happen that three of these ever-moving bodies will sometimes come into one and the same straight line. When one of the extremes of the series of three bodies in a common direction is the Sun, the intermediate body deprives the other extreme body, either wholly or partially, of illumination. When one of the extremes is the Earth, the intermediate body intercepts, wholly or partially, the other extreme body from the view of observers situated at

(15)   places on the Earth which are in the common line of direction, and the intermediate body is seen to pass over the other extreme body as it enters upon or leaves the common line of direction. The phenomena resulting from such contingencies of position and direction are variously called *eclipses*, *transits*, and *occcultations*, according to the relative apparent magnitudes of the interposing and obscured bodies, and according to the circumstances that

(20)   attend them.

The Earth moves round the Sun once in every year; the Moon moves round the Earth once in every lunar month (27 days). The Earth moves round the Sun in a certain plane, an imaginary surface on which a line drawn between any two points lies flat. If the Moon as the Earth's companion moved round the Earth in the same plane, an eclipse of the Sun would

(25)   happen regularly every month when the Moon was in "conjunction," the "New Moon," during which the Moon is not visible in the sky, and also every month at the intermediate period there would be a total eclipse of the Moon on the occasion of every "opposition," or "Full Moon," when the Moon appears as a complete circle. But because the Moon's orbit does not lie in quite the same plane as the Earth's, but is inclined at an angle averaging

(30)   about 5⅛°, the actual facts are different. Instead of there being in every year about 25 eclipses (of the sun and of the moon in nearly equal numbers), which there would be if the orbits had identical planes, there are only a very few eclipses in the year. Never, under the most favorable circumstances, are there more than seven, and sometimes as few as two.

Eclipses of the Sun are more numerous than those of the Moon in the proportion of about

(35)   three to two, yet at any given place on the Earth more lunar eclipses are visible than solar eclipses, because eclipses of the Moon, when they occur, are visible over the whole hemisphere, or half, of the Earth that is turned towards the Moon. The area over which a total eclipse of the Sun is visible is just a belt of the Earth no more than about 150 to 170 miles wide.

43. In the context of Line 1, the best meaning of "primary" is

(A) earliest

(B) most primitive

(C) most direct

(D) most basic

44. According to the explanation in this passage, which of the following could be considered "an eclipse"?

(A) mixing cream into a cup of coffee

(B) an apple sitting in front of a grape

(C) two stars shining brightly in the sky

(D) Mars and Venus

Go on to next page

45. What is the best evidence for the answer to Question 44?

    (A) Lines 1–2 ("disappearance . . . else")

    (B) Lines 6–7 ("various bodies . . . motion")

    (C) Lines 17–20 ("The phenomena resulting . . . attend them")

    (D) Line 28–30 ("the Moon's orbit . . . different")

46. The most common stylistic devices in this passage are

    (A) definition and example

    (B) narration and characterization

    (C) description and figurative language

    (D) analogies and implied comparison

47. In the context of Line 11, what is the best definition of "extreme"?

    (A) exaggerated

    (B) highest degree

    (C) outer

    (D) most advanced

48. Why does any line "drawn between any two bodies at any given time" (Line 8) "point in a different direction at another time" (Line 9)?

    (A) The line is not real.

    (B) The paths of the Sun, Moon, and Earth are unknown.

    (C) The Moon and Earth are in constant motion.

    (D) The Earth is larger than the Moon.

49. Which of the following supports the answer to Question 48?

    (A) Lines 5–6 ("each must cast . . . source of light")

    (B) Lines 9–11 ("occasionally happen . . . the same straight line")

    (C) Lines 21–22 ("The Earth moves . . . 27 days.")

    (D) Lines 36–37 ("when they occur . . . towards the Moon")

50. According to the diagram, if a person stands on the unilluminated portion of the Earth during a lunar eclipse, what does he see?

    (A) a portion of the Moon

    (B) the Moon's shadow

    (C) the Sun's shadow

    (D) the Earth's shadow

51. Information about the Moon's orbit being "inclined at an angle averaging about 5⅛°" (Lines 29–30) relative to the Earth

    (A) illustrates the unimportance of the Moon

    (B) emphasizes that eclipses of the Sun are more widely seen than eclipses of the Moon

    (C) explains why the Earth, Moon, and Sun do not align more frequently

    (D) shows that eclipses of the Sun and Moon occur in equal numbers

52. According to the passage, which statement is true?

    (A) The Sun casts shadows on the Moon and on the Earth.

    (B) More people see eclipses of the Moon than eclipses of the Sun.

    (C) Our Solar System includes the Sun, stars, planets, and moons.

    (D) Eclipses of the Sun cover a larger area than eclipses of the Moon.

Section 2: Math — Calculator Section

Time: 55 minutes for 38 questions

Directions: This section contains two different types of questions. For Questions 1–30, choose the best answer to each question and darken the corresponding oval on the answer sheet. For Questions 31–38, follow the separate directions provided before those questions.

Notes:

✔ You may use a calculator.

✔ All numbers used in this exam are real numbers.

✔ All figures lie in a plane.

✔ All figures may be assumed to be to scale unless the problem specifically indicates otherwise.

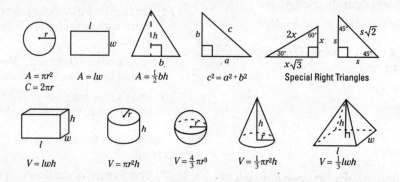

$A = \pi r^2$
$C = 2\pi r$

$A = lw$

$A = \frac{1}{2}bh$

$c^2 = a^2 + b^2$

Special Right Triangles

$V = lwh$

$V = \pi r^2 h$

$V = \frac{4}{3}\pi r^3$

$V = \frac{1}{3}\pi r^2 h$

$V = \frac{1}{3}lwh$

---

1. A box has exactly 11 marbles in it. Three of the marbles are green, six are yellow, and the rest are red. If one marble is drawn at random from the box, what is the probability that the marble is red?

    (A) $\frac{1}{11}$

    (B) $\frac{1}{9}$

    (C) $\frac{2}{11}$

    (D) $\frac{2}{9}$

2. Three cars drove past a speed-limit sign on a highway. Car A was traveling twice as fast as Car B, and Car C was traveling 20 miles per hour faster than Car B. If Car C was traveling at 60 miles per hour, how fast was Car A going?

    (A) 20 miles per hour

    (B) 30 miles per hour

    (C) 40 miles per hour

    (D) 80 miles per hour

Go on to next page

3. *No two points on the graph have the same y-coordinate.*
    Which of the following graphs has this property?

(A)

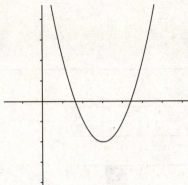

(B)

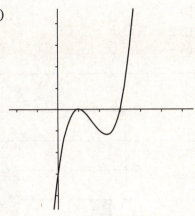

(C)

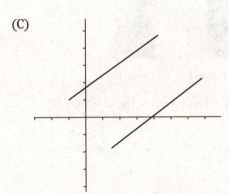

(D)

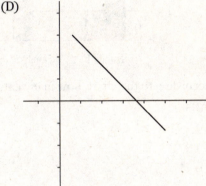

4. For integers *a, b,* and *c,* let $a \# b \# c$ be
    defined by $a \# b \# c = a^2 - bc + b$. What is
    the value of $6 \# 3 \# 4$?

    (A) 3

    (B) 12

    (C) 27

    (D) 30

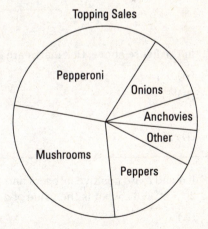

Topping Sales

5. If 3 less than twice a number is 13, what is
    5 times the number?

    (A) 8

    (B) 30

    (C) 40

    (D) 50

6. According to the circle graph, how many of
    the pizza toppings individually represent
    more than 25 percent of total sales?

    (A) one

    (B) two

    (C) three

    (D) four

Go on to next page

7. If $|10 - 3y| < 3$, which of the following is a possible value of y?

    (A) 0

    (B) 1

    (C) 2

    (D) 3

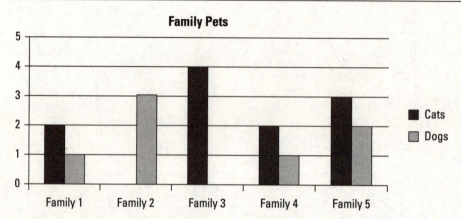

Family Pets

8. According to the chart, how many cats are kept as pets among the five families polled?

    (A) 4

    (B) 7

    (C) 9

    (D) 11

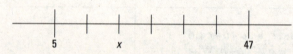

9. In the figure above, tick marks are equally spaced on the number line. What is the value of x?

    (A) 6

    (B) 17

    (C) 19

    (D) 25

10. If a and b are positive integers and $2^{3a} \times 2^{3b} = 64$, what is the value of $a + b$?

    (A) 1

    (B) $\frac{3}{2}$

    (C) 2

    (D) 4

11. If $(x - 4)^2 = 49$ and $x < 0$, what is the value of x?

    (A) −11

    (B) −5

    (C) −3

    (D) −1

Go on to next page

12. If $2a^2 = 56$, what is the value of $8a^2$?

    (A) 144

    (B) 156

    (C) 212

    (D) 224

13. In the rectangular coordinate system, the line with equation $y = 2x + 4$ crosses the x-axis at the point with coordinates (f, g). What is the value of f?

    (A) –4

    (B) –2

    (C) 0

    (D) 2

14. Which of the following represents all values of x that satisfy this inequality: $7 \geq -2x + 3$?

    (A)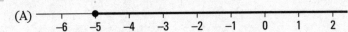

    (B)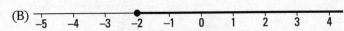

    (C)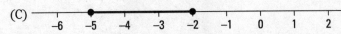

    (D)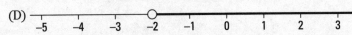

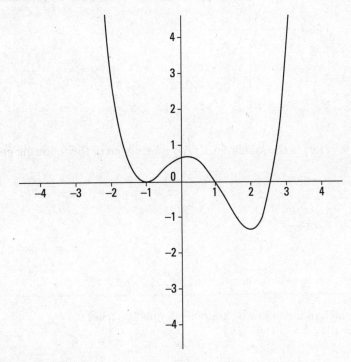

15. The figure above shows the graph of $y = f(x)$ from $x = -3$ to $x = 4$. For what value of x in this interval does the function f attain its minimum value?

    (A) 2

    (B) 1

    (C) 0

    (D) –2

Go on to next page

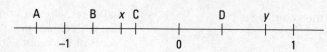

16. Above, which point on the number line best represents the product xy?

    (A) A

    (B) B

    (C) C

    (D) D

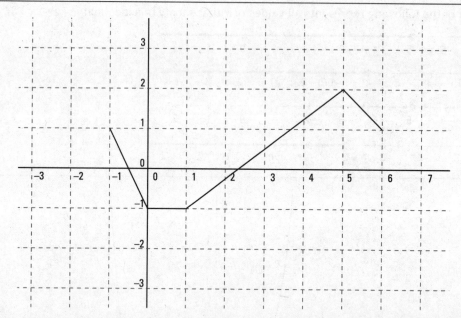

17. The graph of $y = f(x)$ is shown above. If $f(3) = ka$, which of the following could be the value of $f(k)$?

    (A) –1

    (B) $-\dfrac{1}{2}$

    (C) 0

    (D) $\dfrac{1}{2}$

18. If $-1 < x < 0$, which of the following statements must be true?

    I. $x > \dfrac{x}{2}$

    II. $x^2 > x$

    III. $x^3 > x^2$

    (A) I only

    (B) II only

    (C) I and II only

    (D) I, II, and III

Go on to next page

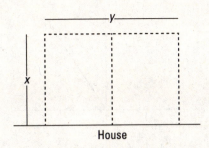

House

19. A gardener is building a fence to enclose her garden and divide it in half, as shown above. The fourth side of the garden is adjacent to her house, so it does not require fencing. The total area of the garden is 2,400 square feet. In terms of x, how many feet of fencing does the gardener require?

    (A) $2,400 - 3x$

    (B) $x + \dfrac{2,400}{x}$

    (C) $3x + \dfrac{2,400}{x}$

    (D) $3x + \dfrac{1,200}{x}$

20. An equilateral triangle has vertices at $(-1, 1)$ and $(5, 1)$. Which of the following might be the coordinates of the third vertex?

    (A) $(2, -5)$

    (B) $(2, 1 - 3\sqrt{3})$

    (C) $(2, 3\sqrt{3})$

    (D) $(3\sqrt{3}, 1)$

21. In the following sequence, the first term is 2, and each term after the first term is 3 less than 3 times the previous term. What is the value of k?

    2, 3, 6, k, 42

    (A) 10

    (B) 12

    (C) 14

    (D) 15

22. Which of the following is the graph of a linear function with a positive slope and a negative y-intercept?

(A)

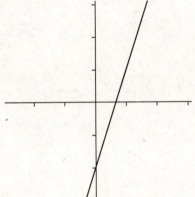

(B)

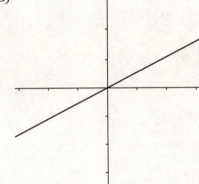

(C)

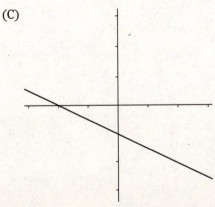

(D)

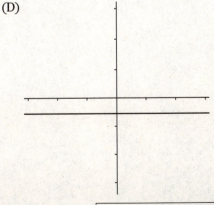

Go on to next page

23. A baker can bake three dozen cookies in 45 minutes. How many cookies can the baker make in one hour?

    (A) 4

    (B) 36

    (C) 40

    (D) 48

k	1	2	3	4	5	6
$f(k)$	15	11	7	n	−1	−5

24. The table above defines a linear function. What is the value of n?

    (A) 1

    (B) 2

    (C) 3

    (D) 4

25. When the number m is multiplied by 5, the result is the same as when 6 is subtracted from m. What is the value of $8m$?

    (A) −12

    (B) −6

    (C) $-\dfrac{3}{2}$

    (D) 3

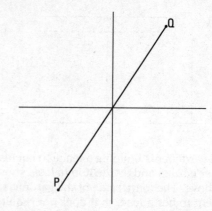

26. The coordinates of point P in the figure above are (a, b), where $|b| > |a|$. Which of the following could be the slope of PQ?

    (A) −3

    (B) $-\dfrac{1}{2}$

    (C) $\dfrac{1}{2}$

    (D) $\dfrac{3}{2}$

Go on to next page

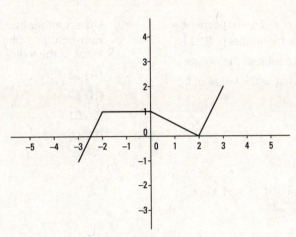

27. The graph of $y = g(x)$ is shown above. Which of the following could be the graph of $y = g(x-1)$?

(A)

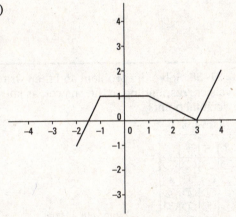

(B)

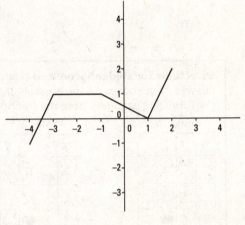

(C)

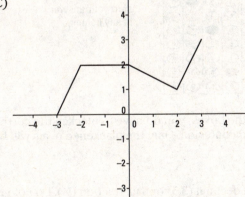

(D)

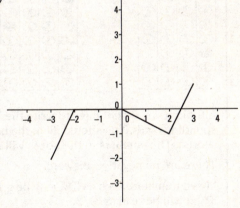

Go on to next page

28. In the xy-plane, lines p and q are perpendicular. If line p contains the points $(-2, 2)$ and $(2, 1)$, and line q contains the points $(-2, 4)$ and $(k, 0)$, what is the value of k?

    (A) –3

    (B) –2

    (C) –1

    (D) 0

29. If the arithmetic mean of 4, p, and q is 6, what is the value of $\dfrac{p+q}{2}$?

    (A) 2

    (B) 3

    (C) 6

    (D) 7

30. On a number line, 27 is exactly halfway between the point at 15 and another point. What is the value of the other point?

    (A) 12

    (B) 39

    (C) 51

    (D) 60

Directions for student-produced response Questions 31–38: Solve the problem and then write your answer in the boxes on the answer sheet. Mark the ovals corresponding to the answer, as shown in the following example. Note the fraction line and the decimal points.

Answer: 7/2   Answer: 3.25   Answer: 853

Write your answer in the box. You may start your answer in any column.

Although you do not have to write the solutions in the boxes, you do have to blacken the corresponding ovals. You should fill in the boxes to avoid confusion. Only the blackened ovals will be scored. The numbers in the boxes will not be read.

There are no negative answers.

Mixed numbers, such as $3\frac{1}{2}$, may be gridded in as a decimal (3.5) or as a fraction (7/2). Do not grid in $3\frac{1}{2}$; it will be read as 31/2.

Grid in a decimal as far as possible. Do not round your answer and leave some boxes empty.

A question may have more than one answer. Grid in one answer only.

Go on to next page

31. If $x^2 - y^2 = 39$ and $x - y = 3$, what is the value of y?

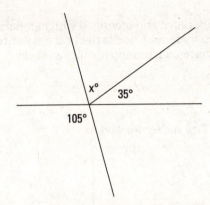

32. What is the value of x in the figure above?

33. Six times a number is the same as the number added to 6. What is the number?

34. $a, a+5$

    The first term of the sequence above is a, and each term after the first is 5 greater than the preceding term. If the sum of the first six terms is 177, what is the value of a?

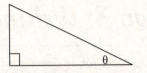

35. In the right triangle shown above, if angle $\theta = 30°$, what is $\sin\theta$?

36. A circle lies in the xy-coordinate plane. The circle is centered at $(-3, 17)$ and touches the y-axis at one point only. What is the diameter of the circle?

Questions 37 and 38 are based on the following information. $1,000 invested at i percent simple annual interest yields $200 over a 2-year period.

37. How much interest would the $1,000 investment yield if the i percent interest were compounded annually over the 2-year period? Ignore the dollar sign when gridding your answer.

38. What dollar amount invested at i percent simple annual interest will yield $1,000 interest over a 5-year period? Ignore the dollar sign when gridding your answer.

STOP DO NOT TURN THE PAGE UNTIL TOLD TO DO SO.
DO NOT RETURN TO A PREVIOUS TEST.

Section 3: Writing and Language

Time: 35 minutes for 44 questions

Directions: Some sentences or portions of sentences are underlined and identified with numbers. In the questions, you see differing versions of the underlined material. Choose the best answer to each question based on what is stated or implied in the passage and accompanying visual elements. Mark the corresponding oval on the answer sheet.

Passage 1

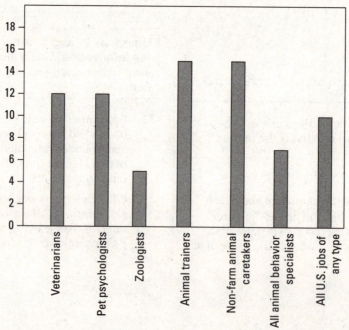

Percentage of Projected Job Growth : Animal Care and Service Workers

Illustration by John Wiley & Sons, Inc.

Dr. Vint Virga stares at Molly, a [1] Barbary sheep. Molly has been behaving strangely since her tail was amputated after an accident. Molly spends almost all of her time nervously checking for flies that she used to bat away easily with her tail. Dr. Virga decides that Molly has a phobia, an irrational fear. He prescribes medication and works to ease her fears by distracting her with food and [2] subtracting her anxiety level so that she can stand quietly when insects do approach. Virga travels from zoo to zoo, where he solves the problems of animals like Molly. [3]

Animal behaviorists may be veterinarians, as Dr. Virga is, or animal trainers, zoologists, college professors, zookeepers, and many other types of workers who specialize in animals. Animal behaviorists interpret how individuals or whole populations of animals eat, move, rest, play, and [4] relating to their environment. Identifying problems, [5] the animals may be treated by the behaviorist with medicine or behavior modification techniques.

The field is new. In earlier times, what was going on inside an animal's mind was not a concern. The Greek philosopher Aristotle (384 to 322 BCE) said that animals couldn't think. French philosopher Rene Descartes (1596 to 1650 CE) compared the cry of an animal to the squeak of a clock spring, a mechanical reaction. Even in the modern era, behaviorists are

Go on to next page

[6] <u>now sometimes accused</u> of anthropomorphism, ascribing human traits to nonhuman beings. The danger of this approach is that animals won't be seen for who they are and their behavior may be misinterpreted. Scientist Philip Low says, "If you ask my colleagues whether animals have emotions and thoughts, many will drop their voices or change the subject."

Almost [7] <u>anyone, who has pets, sees</u> evidence of animals' inner life. Recent studies show that elephants recognize themselves [8] <u>when they see themselves</u> in a mirror, and many species, such as fruit flies, ants, and chimpanzees cooperate. Zookeepers frequently report that animals grieve when others housed in the same enclosure die. In 2012, a number of scientists in Cambridge University signed a declaration asserting that animals probably have emotions and consciousness, [9] <u>but they are self-aware.</u>

Animals behaviorism is a growing field, with a projected increase in jobs in its various subspecialties of [10] <u>at least 11%</u>, according to the United States Bureau of Labor Statistics. Pay for nonfarm animal caretakers, who do not need a college degree, averages around $20,000 per year, though veterinarians make about $85,000 a year. In general, higher paid careers [11] <u>return</u> better education and training.

1. (A) NO CHANGE
   (B) Barbary sheep, and Molly has been behaving
   (C) Barbary sheep that has been behaving
   (D) Barbary sheep. Molly behaved

2. (A) NO CHANGE
   (B) lowering
   (C) increasing
   (D) subordinating

3. Which of the following is the best improvement for the first paragraph?
   (A) Add this sentence to the end of the paragraph: "He is an animal behaviorist."
   (B) Delete this sentence: "Dr. Virga decides that Molly has a phobia, an irrational fear."
   (C) Add this sentence to the beginning of the paragraph: "Barbary sheep are also known as aoudads."
   (D) Delete "since her tail was amputated after an accident."

4. (A) NO CHANGE
   (B) environmental relation of animals
   (C) the way in which they relate to their environment
   (D) relate to their environment

5. (A) NO CHANGE
   (B) the animals, treat by the behaviorist,
   (C) the behaviorist treats the animals
   (D) the behaviorists, they treat the animals

6. (A) NO CHANGE
   (B) sometimes are now accused
   (C) sometimes accused
   (D) now sometimes accusing

7. (A) NO CHANGE
   (B) anyone who has pets sees
   (C) anyone, who has pets, see
   (D) anyone who have pets see

8. (A) NO CHANGE
   (B) when one sees itself
   (C) seeing itself
   (D) when it sees itself

9. (A) NO CHANGE
   (B) being self-aware
   (C) though they are self-aware
   (D) and they are self-aware

10. (A) NO CHANGE
    (B) about 7%
    (C) perhaps 11%
    (D) 15% less

11. (A) NO CHANGE
    (B) mirror
    (C) result
    (D) reflect

Go on to next page

Passage II

Trenches in World War I

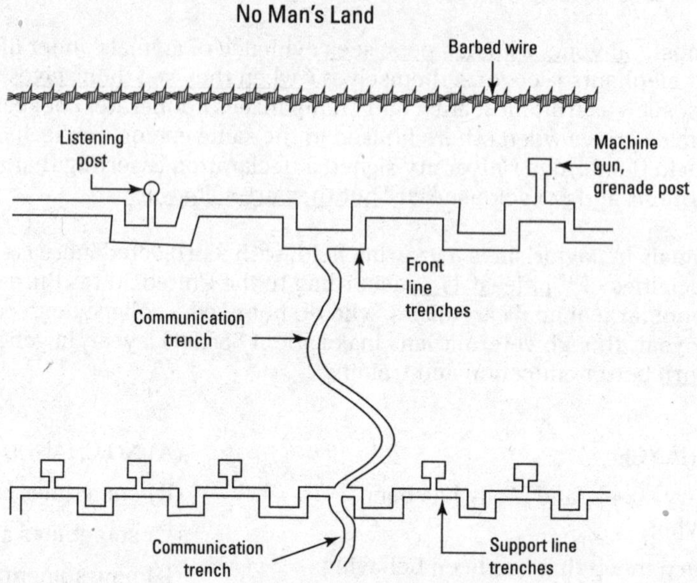

No Man's Land

About a century ago, in August, 1914, what participants called "The Great War" and, ironically, "The War to End All Wars," [12] had begun. We know this conflict as World War I, one of the bloodiest periods in human history. When it ended in 1918, about 9 million soldiers were dead and the health of 7 million more was permanently [13] disabled. They were never again healthy enough to return to their former way of life.

[1] About 25,000 miles of trenches — enough to circle the globe at the Equator — were dug to protect and shelter soldiers from enemy fire. [2] Trenches on both sides — the Allies and their foes, the Central Powers — were only a few hundred yards apart. [14] [3] A unique feature of World War I was the trench system. [4] A typical trench, diagrammed in the Figure 1, were about 6 to 8 feet deep and topped on the enemy side by sandbags.

[15] The frontline trench had short protrusions designed for shooting machine guns or launching grenades. Listening to the enemy was also done there. The frontline trenches were [16] backed by support trenches a few hundred yards away, where medical officers tended the wounded and where other, non-combat activities took place. [17] Both were connected by a communication trench, which was parallel to the others. Because fire could spread quickly in a straight line, the trenches, [18] laid out in a zigzag pattern, with fire breaks every few yards.

[1] The trenches were not pleasant places. [19] [2] Sandbags, thin iron sheets, or sticks supported the walls. [3] The frontline trench was protected by a line of barbed wire, and the area in between was called "No Man's Land" because to be caught there was to risk instant death. [4] Soldiers were stationed in the frontline trenches for 3 to 7 days and then rotated to support trenches for [20] they're rest period, eventually returning to the front line. [5] Despite four years of war and huge numbers of deaths, neither side succeeded in moving its trenches more than a short distance into enemy territory. [21] [6] The soldiers spent the day in a mixture of boredom and terror. [7] They felt boredom waiting for an attack and terror when one occurred.

[22] [1] Few civilians understood the conditions the soldiers faced. [2] A sample trench in a London park appeared comfortable. [3] Soldiers who had seen the real trenches were often bitter when they saw the luxury of the sample trench, which did not resemble those on the front.

Go on to next page

12. (A) NO CHANGE
    (B) began
    (C) will have begun
    (D) begun

13. (A) NO CHANGE
    (B) impaired
    (C) unfit
    (D) wounded

14. (A) NO CHANGE
    (B) Delete the sentence.
    (C) Place the sentence at the beginning of the paragraph.
    (D) Place the sentence after Sentence 4.

15. How may the underlined sentences best be combined?
    (A) The frontline trench had short protrusions designed for shooting machine guns or launching grenades, listening to the enemy was also done there.
    (B) Listening to the enemy, the frontline trench had short protrusions designed for shooting machine guns or launching grenades.
    (C) The frontline trench had short protrusions designed for shooting machine guns or launching grenades, and they could listen to the enemy there.
    (D) The frontline trench had short protrusions designed for shooting machine guns, launching grenades, and listening to the enemy.

16. (A) NO CHANGE
    (B) supported by
    (C) beyond
    (D) backed to

17. (A) NO CHANGE
    (B) Both were connected by a communication trench, which cut across the others.
    (C) Both were connected by a communication trench, which was near the other two trenches.
    (D) The communication trench connected the other trenches by being parallel.

18. (A) NO CHANGE
    (B) were laid
    (C) lain
    (D) were lying

19. What should be added, if anything, after Sentence 1 in paragraph four?
    (A) (A) NO CHANGE
    (B) There were many trenches, and many soldiers.
    (C) Fire was a danger.
    (D) Wooden floor boards covered a drainage area, but the narrow trenches were never quite dry.

20. (A) NO CHANGE
    (B) there
    (C) their
    (D) soldier's

21. How may the underlined sentences best be combined?
    (A) The soldiers spent the day in a mixture of boredom, waiting for an attack, and terror, when one occurred.
    (B) Bored and terrified, the soldiers spent the day.
    (C) The soldiers spent the day in a mixture of boredom and terror, feeling boredom waiting for an attack and terror when one occurred.
    (D) The soldiers spent the day in a mixture of boredom and terror, boredom waiting for an attack and terror in an attack.

22. What would be the best change, if any, to the last paragraph?
    (A) NO CHANGE
    (B) Add this sentence before Sentence 2: "Soldiers saw that the trench in the park was different."
    (C) Add this sentence after Sentence 3: "It was all too easy for civilians to see this conflict as "The Great War," but the war was not always great in the eyes of those who fought it."
    (D) Add this sentence after Sentence 3: "The war ended in 1918."

Go on to next page

Passage III

Ten years old, hair in pigtails, [23] sitting in the back seat of our pink-and-white car, which is on the way to Vermont. The elderly next door neighbors in our quiet suburb, the Hamiltons, have been pressing my parents about a vacation rental near their house on the shore of Lake Saint Catherine, and [24] they've finally given in. Mommy and Daddy don't like the Hamiltons, restricting contact with the couple to one dinner when we first [25] moved in, which Alfred Hammond served food for each of us at the head of the table. When our family ate dinner, platters circled the table, unless they were in reach of long arms and serving spoons. In that case everyone simply grabbed what [26] they wanted and ate it.

[27] We greet the Hamiltons. The two-room cabin is made of fragrant wood (pine, I think), and the air is blessedly cool. (Even at that age I couldn't take heat.) [4] Jimmy and I sleep in the bedroom in bunks attached to the wall near our parents' air mattress.

[28] [1] The water of Lake Saint Catherine is pretty deep. [2] There's no beach, just a dock, but we can both swim, so Jimmy and I jump off the dock, paddle around until we reach the little wooden ladder and then climb up to start all over again. [3] My father works in an office, and he has only three weeks' vacation time each year. [4] Once or twice Daddy rows across the lake in a little wooden boat, but he clearly doesn't [29] dote on the effort. [5] We also fish from the dock. [6] I remember holding a dead, wriggling, two-inch something that I throw back in the water as soon as Daddy takes a picture of it.

On some days we go sightseeing. I remember a marble quarry at Barre. Mostly (typical of my mother's priorities) we stay in the gift shop, where [30] shards of marble are on sale, as well as some finished items. In my view the big slabs look like tombstones, [31] and the tombstones make me nervous and they make me glad when we leave.

[32] [1] We take another trip, at night, to a drive-in movie. [2] All I remember of that evening is a white-knuckle trip back to the cabin. [3] I can tell from my parents' voices that they're scared, too. [4] At each junction they confer rapidly, and we do find the cottage, but I spend the time worrying that we'll drive off the road and into a ditch, or worse, [33] keep driving forever.

23. (A) NO CHANGE
    (B) sitting, I
    (C) I'm sitting
    (D) having sat

24. (A) NO CHANGE
    (B) the Hamiltons have
    (C) my parents have
    (D) they have

25. (A) NO CHANGE
    (B) moved in which
    (C) moved,
    (D) moved in, at which

26. (A) NO CHANGE
    (B) he or she wanted and ate
    (C) they wanted, and ate
    (D) was wanting and eating

27. (A) NO CHANGE
    (B) We greeted the Hamiltons.
    (C) In Vermont, we greet the Hamiltons.
    (D) Greeting the Hamiltons

28. What change, if any, should be made to the third paragraph?
    (A) NO CHANGE
    (B) Delete Sentence 1.
    (C) Delete Sentence 3.
    (D) Change Sentence 5 to "We also fish from the dock, which is made of wood."

Go on to next page

29. (A) NO CHANGE
    (B) be fond of
    (C) evaluate
    (D) relish

30. (A) NO CHANGE
    (B) columns
    (C) vestiges
    (D) rubbles

31. (A) NO CHANGE
    (B) which make me nervous and glad to
    (C) and the tombstones make me nervous and glad when we
    (D) nervous and glad when we

32. Which of the following would improve the last paragraph?
    (A) Before Sentence 1, add: "We take many trips throughout my childhood."
    (B) Delete Sentence 1.
    (C) Add after Sentence 2: "Without street lights, the country roads appear dark and dangerous to me, a city girl."
    (D) Add after Sentence 4: "I enjoyed the movie, though."

33. (A) NO CHANGE
    (B) that will just drive forever
    (C) just driving forever
    (D) that we'll just drive forever

Passage IV

In 1859, **34** Thomas Austin an Australian who enjoyed hunting, released 24 rabbits on his land. The hunter stated that "introduction of a few rabbits could do little harm" and "might provide a touch of home." **35** He liked to hunt. Before this time, **36** there was some domestic rabbits in Australia, mostly in cages or other enclosures. With a moderate climate, the wild rabbits bred all year round. **37** Soon Australia had a rabbit problem. More than 200 million rabbits were living there. Farms and wooded areas were overrun with rabbits; millions of dollars worth of crops were destroyed, and many young trees died when the rabbits chewed rings around the bark. **38** Less trees led to increased erosion and loss of topsoil. The hunter never thought that 24 rabbits would become a national problem. His action is an example of human **39** intervention in a natural ecosystem that is too complicated to understand completely.

40 [1] The same kind of action has been taking place in Arizona. [2] Water is precious in Arizona's desert environment. [3] Tamarisk trees, a non-native species that was imported about a century ago and planted to fight soil erosion, have very deep roots. [4] They soak up a lot of water — up to 200 gallons a day for a mature tree. [5] Chopping down tamarisks or burning them didn't solve the problem, as the trees quickly grew back. [6] So tamarisk beetles, small insects about a centimeter long, were **41** initiated into the environment.

The number of tamarisk trees **42** have decreased because of the beetles. The policy seems to be a success. However, not all factors are known. What about the birds that live in tamarisk trees? Will they die as their habitat changes? When the tamarisk trees are gone, will the beetles attack other trees? If too many trees disappear, will the soil erode, harming the habitat of still more organisms?

No one knows the answer to these questions, because nature is too complex for limited human intelligence to understand completely. **43** One answer that is known to humans is that interfering with the environment cannot be stopped, and some unforeseen consequences will occur. It is what human beings do when they plant crops, construct cities, dam rivers, and tap into energy and water supplies. The human effect on nature is everywhere.

Go on to next page

[44] [1] The solution is not to stay away from nature, but instead to be more careful in how we interact with nature. [2] Studying how organisms interact is important. [3] You should also check consumption. [4] Scientists must provide information on the environment and the potential consequences of changes to the environment. [5] Citizens must tailor their behavior according to that information.

34. (A) NO CHANGE

    (B) Thomas Austin an Australian, that enjoyed hunting, released

    (C) an Australian who enjoyed hunting and was named Thomas Austin released

    (D) Thomas Austin, an Australian who enjoyed hunting, released

35. (A) NO CHANGE

    (B) Delete the underlined words.

    (C) Thomas Austin liked to hunt.

    (D) Thomas Austin, he liked to hunt.

36. (A) NO CHANGE

    (B) their was

    (C) there were

    (D) their were

37. How may the underlined sentences best be combined?

    (A) Soon Australia had a rabbit problem, but more than 200 million rabbits were living there.

    (B) More than 200 million rabbits were living there soon, and Australia had a rabbit problem.

    (C) More than 200 million rabbits soon lived in Australia, and they caused a problem.

    (D) Soon, with more than 200 million rabbits, Australia had a problem.

38. (A) NO CHANGE

    (B) Fewer trees led

    (C) Less trees lead

    (D) Fewer trees lead

39. (A) NO CHANGE

    (B) intercession

    (C) interruption

    (D) affectation

40. Which of the following changes, if any, should be made to paragraph two?

    (A) NO CHANGE

    (B) Add this sentence after Sentence 5: "The trees wither and die when the beetles feed on them."

    (C) Delete Sentence 4.

    (D) Delete Sentence 5.

41. (A) NO CHANGE

    (B) started

    (C) commenced

    (D) introduced

42. (A) NO CHANGE

    (B) have been decreasing

    (C) has decreased

    (D) decreasing

43. (A) NO CHANGE

    (B) What we do know

    (C) One answer known to humans

    (D) Known

44. Which of the following would be the best change to the last paragraph?

    (A) Add this sentence before Sentence 1: "Everything changes."

    (B) Add this sentence after Sentence 2: "Interacting with nature should always be considered before acting."

    (C) Delete Sentence 3 and insert this sentence instead: "Monitoring consumption of water, energy, and other resources is also crucial."

    (D) Add this sentence at the end of the paragraph: "Nature is our most important resource."

Section 4: Math — No-Calculator Section

Time: 25 minutes for 20 questions

Directions: This section contains two different types of questions. For Questions 1–15, choose the best answer to each question and darken the corresponding oval on the answer sheet. For Questions 16–20, follow the separate directions provided before those questions.

Notes:

✔ You may **not** use a calculator.

✔ All numbers used in this exam are real numbers.

✔ All figures lie in a plane.

✔ All figures may be assumed to be to scale unless the problem specifically indicates otherwise.

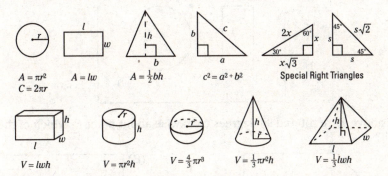

$A = \pi r^2$ $A = lw$ $A = \frac{1}{2}bh$ $c^2 = a^2 + b^2$ Special Right Triangles
$C = 2\pi r$

$V = lwh$ $V = \pi r^2 h$ $V = \frac{4}{3}\pi r^3$ $V = \frac{1}{3}\pi r^2 h$ $V = \frac{1}{3}lwh$

1. In the *xy*-coordinate plane, what is the area of the rectangle with opposite vertices at $(-3, -1)$ and $(3, 1)$?

   (A) 3

   (B) 6

   (C) 9

   (D) 12

2. The following Venn diagram shows the ice-cream flavor choice of 36 children at an ice-cream party. Each child could choose vanilla ice cream, chocolate ice cream, both, or neither. What percent of the children had chocolate ice cream only?

   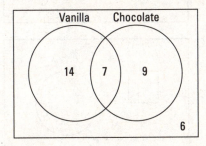

   (A) 10%

   (B) 25%

   (C) 50%

   (D) 75%

Go on to next page ➡

3. If $\frac{4}{5}$ of a number is 24, what is $\frac{1}{5}$ of the number?

    (A) 5

    (B) 6

    (C) 8

    (D) 18

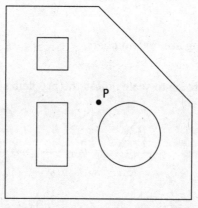

4. If the figure above were rotated 90 degrees clockwise about point *P*, which of the following would be the result?

    (A)

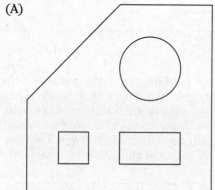

    (B)

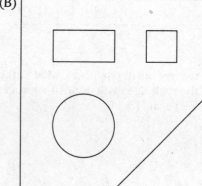

    (C)

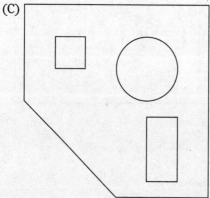

    (D)

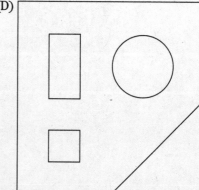

Go on to next page

5. Kate has been snowboarding for three fewer years than Chandler. If Chandler has been snowboarding for *n* years, which of the following expressions represents the number of years that Kate has been snowboarding?

   (A) $n-3$

   (B) $n+3$

   (C) $3-n$

   (D) $2n+3$

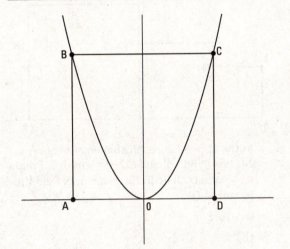

6. In the figure above, *ABCD* is a square and points *B, C,* and *O* lie on the graph of $y = \dfrac{x^2}{k}$, where *k* is a constant. If the area of the square is 36, what is the value of *k*?

   (A) 1.5

   (B) 3

   (C) 4.5

   (D) 6

7. How much greater than $t-5$ is $t+2$?

   (A) 2

   (B) 4

   (C) 5

   (D) 7

8. For all integers *n*, let $*(n)$ be defined by $*(n) = (n-1)(n+1)$. What is the value of $*(-3)$?

   (A) −9

   (B) −8

   (C) 3

   (D) 8

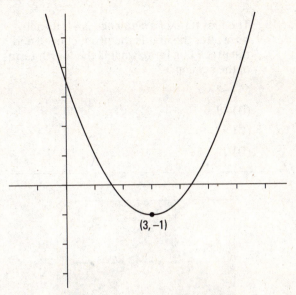

(3, −1)

9. In the parabola above, the vertex is at $(3, -1)$. Which of the following are *x*-coordinates of two points on this parabola whose *y*-coordinates are equal?

   (A) 1 and 5

   (B) 1 and 6

   (C) 2 and 5

   (D) 2 and 6

10. The price of a television was first decreased by 10 percent and then increased by 20 percent. The final price was what percent of the initial price?

   (A) 88%

   (B) 90%

   (C) 98%

   (D) 108%

11. In the *xy*-plane, the center of a circle has coordinates $(-2, 4)$. If one endpoint of a diameter of the circle is $(-2, 1)$, what are the coordinates of the other endpoint of this diameter?

   (A) $(-5, 4)$

   (B) $(-2, 6)$

   (C) $(-2, 7)$

   (D) $(1, 4)$

Go on to next page

12. The first term of a sequence is –1. If each term after the first is the product of –3 and the preceding term, what is the fourth term of the sequence?

    (A) –27

    (B) –9

    (C) 9

    (D) 27

14. In the xy-plane, line l passes through $(-1, 3)$ and is parallel to the line $4x + 2y = k$. If line l passes through the point $(p, -p)$, what is the value of p?

    (A) –2

    (B) –1

    (C) 1

    (D) 2

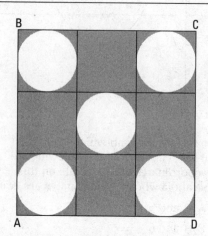

13. Square $ABCD$ is divided into nine equal squares, five of which have circles inscribed in them. If $AB = 6$, what is the total shaded area?

    (A) $24 - 10\pi$

    (B) $24 - 5\pi$

    (C) $36 - 10\pi$

    (D) $36 - 5\pi$

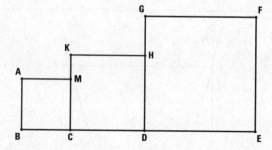

15. In the above figure, all shapes are squares, BC has length 4, and CD has length 7. Points A, K, and G all lie in the same line. Find the length of DE.

    (A) 10

    (B) 11

    (C) 11.5

    (D) 12.25

Go on to next page

Directions for student-produced response Questions 16–20: Solve the problem and then write your answer in the boxes on the answer sheet. Mark the ovals corresponding to the answer, as shown in the following example. Note the fraction line and the decimal points.

Answer: $^7/_2$

Answer: 3.25

Answer: 853

Write your answer in the box. You may start your answer in any column.

Although you do not have to write the solutions in the boxes, you do have to blacken the corresponding ovals. You should fill in the boxes to avoid confusion. Only the blackened ovals will be scored. The numbers in the boxes will not be read.

There are no negative answers.

Mixed numbers, such as $3\frac{1}{2}$, may be gridded in as a decimal (3.5) or as a fraction ($^7/_2$). Do not grid in $3\frac{1}{2}$; it will be read as 31/2.

Grid in a decimal as far as possible. Do not round your answer and leave some boxes empty.

A question may have more than one answer. Grid in one answer only.

16. Find the smallest even number that is divisible by 3, 5, and 7.

17. A certain fraction is equivalent to $\frac{2}{3}$. If the fraction's denominator is 12 less than twice its numerator, find the denominator of the fraction.

18. If $p > 0$ and $p^2 = 3p + 40$, what is the value of p?

19. A sequence of numbers begins 1, 5, 4, 8, 7, 11, 10. What is the 21st term of this sequence?

20. If $xy = 120$, and $\frac{1}{x} + \frac{1}{y} = \frac{1}{4}$, find $x + y$.

STOP DO NOT TURN THE PAGE UNTIL TOLD TO DO SO. DO NOT RETURN TO A PREVIOUS TEST.

Section 5: The Essay

> **Time:** 50 minutes
>
> As you read this passage, consider how the author uses the following:
>
> • Facts, examples, and other types of evidence to support his assertions
>
> • Logical structure to link ideas and evidence
>
> • Elements of style, such as appeals to reason, word choice, and so forth, to make his case

The following is excerpted from The NOW Habit at Work *by Neil Fiore (Wiley).*

In *Emotions Revealed: Recognizing Faces and Feelings to Improve Communication and Emotional Life,* Paul Ekman describes how to determine if people are lying by observing the universal microfacial expressions of anger, disgust, fear, joy, sadness, surprise, and contempt. Even if a person doesn't consciously know that you're lying or trying to cover up your true feelings, she will have a gut reaction that something isn't right. The hidden and often subconscious message embedded in your words, actions, facial expressions, and body movements reflects your true attitude and affects your energy level. Others may subconsciously notice the disconnection between your words and your nonverbal message and sense that you're not telling the whole truth.

We all know how leaders often preach one thing and do the opposite, causing their actions to contradict their words and professed beliefs. Colleagues have said of Viktor Frankl, a Holocaust survivor and founder of logotherapy [a form of psychotherapy], that when he advocated that every life has meaning, there was a unity between his words, his actions, and the way he lived.

Are your messages and actions integrated around your higher brain and executive self? You may want to examine how your actions and stated values are aligned with what you consciously and rationally believe. Then ask yourself, "Is my walk congruent with my talk? What underlying and overarching beliefs are revealed in the way I talk to myself and others? Is it all struggle and sacrifice?" Are you saying, "Life is tough and then you die" or "You have to work harder, but it will never be good enough"?

Even more powerful than your actual words is the impact of what you think and expect from yourself and others. Research has repeatedly shown that teachers who are led to believe that certain children have high intelligence scores paid more attention to those children and encouraged them to do their best. As a result, the test scores and behaviors of those children improved significantly, even though these children actually had the lowest intelligence scores in their class. The teachers' beliefs and expectations influenced their behavior and had real, positive effects on the children they taught. The same is true of your beliefs about yourself and your employees.

Beliefs and expectations influence much more than just your attitude. What you believe affects your brain and body the way a placebo pill — an inert substance presented as effective medicine — improves depression and physical symptoms in as many as 30% of patients. You might want to consider, therefore, telling yourself, your children, and your employees that you believe in them and their willingness to learn and do good work and that you are a firm supporter of their worth and truer, higher self. You may find it more effective to communicate to yourself and others that life is an interesting puzzle, a mystery

Go on to next page

that you were meant to solve and that you have the innate ability to do so. Your words and actions might communicate that you enjoy your life and are optimistic about your future. Pessimists tend to be more accurate about the odds of success but give up sooner, while optimists keep trying until they come up with a creative solution and are happier. You may want to communicate the message "You're going to make it, even though you don't know how. Something will come to you, and you will pick yourself up and stand on your own two feet."

Being optimistic is one way to motivate yourself to keep taking another shot at success and face the inevitable challenges of life while hoping to turn lemons into lemonade. An optimistic view of life — and of yourself, your co-workers, and employees — will turn your mind toward what's going well and has the effect of lowering depression. Research by Martin Seligman of the University of Pennsylvania's Positive Psychology Center found that those who wrote down three things that went well each day and their causes every night for one week had a significant increase in happiness and a decrease in depressive symptoms. Remarkably, the participants got so much value out of the exercise that they continued on their own for more than six months, and when tested again, they were found to be even happier. Other research points to the importance of meaning in life — interest in exploring a sense of purpose or mission for one's life — as contributing to happiness, healthy self-esteem, and effectiveness.

Directions: Write an essay in which you analyze how Fiore makes an argument that one's true beliefs influence both self and others. In your essay, discuss how Fiore uses the elements of style listed before the passage, as well as other stylistic choices, to strengthen his argument. Focus your response on the most important aspects of the passage.

Do not explain whether you agree or disagree with Fiore. Instead, focus on how the author builds his argument.

STOP DO NOT TURN THE PAGE UNTIL TOLD TO DO SO.
DO NOT RETURN TO A PREVIOUS TEST.

Chapter 19

Practice Exam 1: Answers and Explanations

•••

After you finish the practice test sections in Chapter 18, take some time to go through the answers and explanations in this chapter to find out which questions you missed and why. Even if you answered the question correctly, the explanation might offer a useful strategy that speeds up your performance on the next round. We also include additional information that'll be useful on the real SAT. If you're short on time, turn to the end of this chapter to find an abbreviated answer key.

Answers for Section 1: Reading

1. **C.** Lines 3 through 4 state that "the absence of human landmarks is one of the most depressing and disheartening." Line 6 refers to "sod," or dirt, as "inescapable." "Inescapable," "depressing," and "disheartening" — all negative descriptions that apply to nature, in John Bergson's view. (Those words also apply to the SAT, by the way.) Did you select Choice (D) based on Line 33, which mentions Bergson's "Old-World belief that land, in itself, is desirable"? That statement comes in a paragraph that laments the pioneers' inability to farm the land "properly" (Line 35). In the same paragraph, Bergson compares the land to a "horse . . . that runs wild and kicks things to pieces" (Lines 34 through 35), clearly implying that land tamed by human efforts would be better. Choice (C) is the correct answer.

2. **A.** Check out the explanation to Question 1. The land is "depressing and disheartening" because it lacks "human landmarks" (Line 3). Choice (A) is the best evidence for the correct answer to Question 1.

3. **D.** Choices (A), (B), and (C) refer to natural features. Only Choice (D) describes something made by human beings. Though the roads are primitive — "faint tracks in the grass" (Lines 6 through 7) — they are the result of human effort, or "strivings" (Line 9).

4. **C.** The first paragraph (Lines 1 through 9) shows a land that has been settled only on the most basic level. Because the "record of the plow was insignificant" (Line 7), the reader imagines shallow marks in the soil, which are similar to scratches made ages ago by primitive, or "prehistoric" people. Thus, Choice (C) is correct.

5. **B.** The usual meaning of *genius* is "supersmart." In this passage, though, a less common definition fits "the spirit or character" of a place or person or time period.

6. **D.** The first four sentences of paragraph two (Lines 10 through 13) discuss the land in negative terms. Though Bergson had "come to tame" (Line 11) the land, he had not succeeded, because it was "still a wild thing" (Line 11) and cursed by bad luck ("mischance" [Line 12]). True, Bergson is ill, but the paragraph isn't about his symptoms; it's about the land, making Choice (D) the best answer.

7. **A.** The third paragraph lists what went wrong on Bergson's farm: weather, a broken leg, snakebite, disease, and death. True, Bergson was unprepared for farming this land, as the last paragraph (Lines 33 through 39) reveals. However, simple bad luck dominates this paragraph, making Choice (A) the correct answer.

8. **B.** John Bergson had worked in a shipyard, and his neighbors were "tailors, locksmiths, joiners, cigar-makers" (Line 38). None of them were farmers. The land isn't the problem; the farmers are, because, to them, the land is an "enigma" (Line 34), or puzzle.

9. **D.** John Bergson has much to regret. The first paragraph (Lines 1 through 9) describes "depressing and disheartening" scenes. Lines 18 through 24 list the hardships Bergson endured, including the death of his animals, failure of his crops, and loss of two children to illness. After years on the homestead, John Bergson "had ended up pretty much where he began" (Line 26). Choice (D) fits nicely here, because the life you see in this passage is definitely not easy. A close second — but still incorrect answer — is Choice (A). Yes, Bergson was unprepared for the conditions in the New World (the logical term for his surroundings, as he left the "Old World" to go there). But he also faced bad luck (see the explanation to Questions 8). Therefore, Choice (A) is too extreme.

10. **C.** Reread the explanation to Question 9, and you see one bit of evidence — the hardships that Bergson endured — matches Choice (C). That's your answer!

11. **B.** The author quotes several ancient sources for information about the early Olympic games, the Olympiad. The quotations from Xenophanes (Line 1), Homer (Line 4), and Julius Africanus (Line 15) support the author's statements about the ancient games, providing evidence from people who witnessed them or who lived in ancient times and therefore were likely to know what they were talking — well, writing — about. These ancient commentators (like the experts on television during the modern games) have knowledge, and therefore, authority. As Choice (B) says, they *establish an authoritative voice*.

12. **A.** The figure accompanying this passage shows one spot — the Stadium Track — that is definitely for athletes. More space was allotted to administrative and religious structures, including the "treasuries," three altars, one temple, and a council house. Therefore, Choice (A) fits nicely here. Choice (B) is tempting, given the many religious references in the figure, but nothing in either the passage or the drawing proves that the Olympic area *was consecrated to the gods*. Choice (A) is correct.

13. **C.** The author compares the length of two races: the *stade,* the shortest race in ancient times (192.27 meters) and the 200-meter race of modern times. The modern race is nearly the same — the *realistic equivalent* of the older event.

14. **C.** Lines 13 through 14 tell you that "later Greeks found it convenient to use the sequence of Olympiads as a chronological reference" probably because the Olympics were "one of the few truly international institutions in Greece" (Line 13). Choice (C) works because it refers to *a common chronological reference point* — a measure of time for all states.

15. **D.** Take a look back to the explanation to Question 14, and you see that "later Greeks found it convenient to use the sequence of Olympiads as a chronological reference," as Choice (D) states.

16. **B.** Paragraph three (Lines 18 through 29) discusses running styles as depicted on ancient vases. The runners are compared to modern sprinters and long-distance racers. However, the author never mentions anything about himself. He may be a runner, but he may also be a couch potato who spends days watching athletic events on television. Choice (A) is a dud. Choice (C) doesn't work either, because you don't know when the vases were discovered — last week or centuries ago. Choice (D) is a nonstarter because all the evidence about running methods comes from vases, not from literature. You're left with Choice (B), which is a good bet because human anatomy *doesn't change*. Plus the paragraph devotes much attention to the way arms and legs move in each type of race. Arms and legs are parts of the body — human anatomy.

17. **A.** According to Lines 26 through 27, "Ancient sources never specify the exact number of laps" and "modern opinions vary greatly" (Lines 27 through 28). What do most historians think? The "most widely accepted" — *generally believed* — number is 20 laps. Choice (A) is your answer. Did you select Choice (C)? *To approve* is not the same as *to believe*. After all, a parent can *believe* that you blew off your homework but not *approve* of your actions!

18. **C.** In this passage, the author cites evidence from many sources, including vase paintings (Lines 19 through 20) and literature (Homer's Odyssey [Line 3]). He also quotes official documents (Hippias of Elis's catalogue of victors [Line 11]) and mentions archeological discoveries (the posthole at Nemea [Line 34]). Therefore, Choice (C) is correct. Choice (A) is clearly wrong because although the author frequently refers to historians, he also discusses areas of disagreement — such as how many turning posts were available to athletes in the ancient Olympics. *An accurate record of events* implies something that is settled and definitely true.

19. **D.** Scan the explanation to Question 18, and you see that the author refers to many types of evidence. Choice (D) provides reference to at least two, so it's the best choice here.

20. **C.** The athletes pictured on the vases might be either sprinters or long-distance runners. The author explains that "most scholars think" long-distance runners had to have their own turning posts to avoid "much congestion" (Lines 37 through 38). However, the passage ends with speculation ("But if each . . . probably shows" [Lines 40 through 41]). So one turning post or many? Only *more research,* as Choice (C) says, will determine the answer.

21. **D.** As usual in a vocabulary-in-context question, all four answers are possible definitions of the word the test-makers are asking about. In context, though, only one choice fits. The 9 billion people who'll be living on Earth in 2050 will have a demand or "need" for food, making Choice (D) the best answer here.

22. **A.** Passage I argues for biodiversity in several spots. "Plant diversity has a critical role to play" in food and medicine, according to Lines 9 through 10, and the world will lose "valuable *traits* [characteristics] and genes" (Line 17) and "knowledge, cultural traditions, and medicinal resources" (Line 21) if biological diversity decreases. Passage I ends with a statement about "international experts" who want "a program for the conservation" (Lines 36 through 37) of plants.

    Passage II goes even further, stating that if "biodiversity gets too low, then the future of life itself becomes threatened" (Lines 46 through 47). Passage II also calls protecting biodiversity "crucial" (Line 54) because doing so "increases the chance that at least some living things will survive in the face of large changes in the environment" (Lines 53 through 54). Sounds like *an argument in favor of biodiversity,* as Choice (A) states. The other choices represent information in the passages, but only Choice (A) applies to the main idea of both passages.

23. **D.** Check out the explanation to Question 22. Several lines support the fact that these passages argue for biodiversity. Only two of those lines appear in the answer choices, and they're in Choice (D), which is the correct answer.

24. **C.** Both passages make a strong case for biodiversity, as you see in the explanation for Question 22. Therefore, reliance on a small number of crops isn't a good idea, as Choice (C) indicates. Passage I states that plant diversity, a subcategory of biodiversity, "has a critical role to play in addressing the food and nutrition security and medicinal needs of the people of this world" (Lines 9 through 11). Passage II explains that biodiversity "increases the chance that at least some living things will survive in the face of large changes in the environment" (Lines 53 through 54). Choice (A) doesn't work because the author of Passage I sees exploitation as a fact of life for as long as the Earth has supported human life, not a negative factor. Choice (B) doesn't make the cut because the call for "a global program of conservation" (Line 37) implies that the rate of extinction can be slowed. Choice (D) drops out because Passage I doesn't address keystone species. Choice (C) is correct.

25. **C.** The passage refers to "an expected 9 billion people by 2050" (Line 3). In other words, that's the probable population of Earth in that year, as Choice (C) says. Did you select Choice (D)? Providing food for all of them may be a problem, because it's "unclear how our current global food system will cope" (Line 4). However, the passage doesn't state that 9 billion will be undernourished, just that they will exist. Therefore, Choice (D) isn't correct.

26. **D.** Some areas have more biodiversity and some have less, according to Lines 11 through 12. The areas with more diversity tend to be in specific areas — where they are *grouped,* or concentrated, making Choice (D) the answer you seek.

27. **B.** Passage II tells you that when "mussels take over" (Line 51), other marine animals "disappear from the environment" (Line 52). In other words, the mussels *displace* or remove other species — as Choice (B) states. Choice (D) may have tempted you, but that answer is too extreme. You know only that the other species "disappear," not that they become extinct. They could be thriving in another spot! Choice (B) is the best answer here.

28. **C.** The graph tells you that the percentage of *undernourished persons* fell steadily from 1990 to 1992 (19 percent) to 2011 to 2013 (12 percent). Therefore, Statement I is true. According to Line 6, more than 2 billion people *lack important nutrients*, but 868 million "suffer from hunger" (Lines 4 through 5). Okay, Statement II works. Statement III falls apart because although the passage refers to an increasing rate of extinctions, you don't know whether the extinct species provided food for human beings. Because Statements I and II are true, the correct answer is Choice (C).

29. **A.** The statistics show that most of the world's food comes from a small number of plant species, so Choice (A) fits nicely here.

30. **C.** Passage II discusses keystone species, which are so important that their decline wrecks entire ecosystems. Though Passage II uses a marine environment to illustrate the need for healthy keystone populations, the principle can be transferred to other areas, such as forests. Choice (C) is the right one here.

31. **D.** When you compare passages, be sure that you understand the answer choices. Both passages deal with diversity in the environment, but Passage I focuses on diversity in food supplies — the opposite of the answer given in Choices (A) and (B). Passage I is about plants, again the opposite of Choice (C). Choice (D) is the winner here because Passage II discusses the relationships between species in an ecosystem.

32. **B.** During Lincoln's first inaugural speech, he set out plans for his presidency and for the nation "to be pursued" (Line 4) or followed. Now, however, he can't, because of "the great contest" — the war — that is still going on. Therefore, he can't make a *plan,* the best meaning of *course* in this context.

33. **C.** Lincoln states that "the progress of our arms" (Line 7) is "reasonably satisfactory and encouraging to all" (Lines 8 through 9) and that there is "high hope for the future" (Line 9). Because he is speaking to his supporters, the pronoun *our* refers to those who agree with Lincoln — the Northern side of the conflict. What would be *satisfactory and encouraging?* Victory. Choice (C) is correct.

34. **D.** As you see in the explanation to Question 33, Lincoln finds "the progress of our arms" (Line 7) "reasonably satisfactory and encouraging to all" (Lines 8 through 9).

35. **A.** Just before the statement that "little that is new could be presented" (Line 7), Lincoln speaks of "the great contest which still absorbs the attention, and engrosses the energies of the nation" (Line 6). In other words, *the war monopolizes the attention and resources of the nation,* as Choice (A) says. Choice (B) doesn't work because in the last paragraph Lincoln sets forth a vision of the future, where he and others will "bind up the nation's wounds" (Line 44) and achieve "lasting peace among ourselves, and with all nations" (Line 46). The passage contains no evidence for Choices (C) and (D).

36. **B.** Line 13 explains that during his first inaugural address, "insurgent agents were in the city" trying to "destroy" the Union "without war." These agents qualify as a *movement to disband the nation,* as Choice (B) states. Did you select Choice (C)? Lincoln carefully explains that neither side wanted war: "Both parties deprecated war" (Line 14). However, both sides were willing to go to war if necessary. That last phrase — *if necessary* — tells you that support for war was not *unconditional.*

37. **C.** The third paragraph (Lines 17 through 22) discusses the issue of slavery, so Choice (B) is tempting. However, Lincoln — who strongly opposed slavery — discusses it as an "interest" that is powerful enough to cause the war. In fact, he says that to "strengthen, perpetuate, and extend this interest," the South was willing to go to war. So in this context,

Lincoln is using "interest" to describe the self-interest, or benefit, flowing to those who favored slavery.

38. **B.** Over and over, Lincoln looks for common ground: "Both sides deprecated war" (Line 14), "Neither party expected" (Line 23), "Neither anticipated" (Line 24), "Each looked" (Line 25), "Both read" (Line 26) and so forth. Choice (B) works perfectly here.

39. **C.** The explanation to Question 38 lists several possible supporting points, one of which appears as Choice (C), which is your answer.

40. **D.** A quick glance at the fourth paragraph (Lines 23 through 30) shows that Lincoln sees common ideas between both Northerners and Southerners. (Check out the explanation for Question 38 for examples.) The last paragraph of the speech underlines the same point, setting out tasks that both sides must accomplish: "bind up the nation's wounds . . . care for him who shall have borne the battle, and for his widow, and his orphan" (Lines 44 through 45). Both sides have soldiers, widows, and orphans. The best proof, though, is in Line 46, where Lincoln calls for all to "achieve and cherish a just, and a lasting peace among ourselves." Peace comes when warring sides — both Northerners and Southerners — stop fighting. No doubt about it: Choice (D) is the answer.

41. **C.** From the first words — "Fellow countrymen" (Line 1) — to the last — "peace among ourselves" (Line 46) — Lincoln focuses on the union of both North and South. True, he does condemn slavery, so Choice (B) is appealing. However, the discussion of slavery occurs in the context of the war. Many portions of the speech refer to the importance of preserving the Union ("saving the Union" [Line 12], for example) and the speech emphasizes common ground between the warring sides, as in "he gives to both North and South" (Line 35). Therefore, Choice (C) is a better answer than Choice (B).

42. **B.** In several sentences, Lincoln refers to the Bible, sometimes with a direct quotation ("Woe unto the world" [Line 31]) and sometimes with an indirect allusion ("let us judge not" [Line 28]). Specific references to God also appear in the fourth, fifth, and sixth paragraphs. For these reasons, Choice (B) is best.

43. **D.** Many answer choices here, in typical SAT fashion, are definitions of *primary*. In the context of Line 1, however, only Choice (D) makes sense. Boil everything down to the essentials, and an eclipse occurs when something disappears.

44. **B.** The passage explains that if one thing is "covering over . . . something else" (Lines 1 through 2), you have an eclipse, as the "something else" disappears. If you place an apple in front of a grape, you can't see the grape from the front. The grape is *eclipsed*. Choice (B) fits the definition and is the correct answer.

45. **A.** The definition of an eclipse is "a disappearance, the covering over of something by something else" (Line 1). The apple "covers" the grape and makes it disappear from view, so this line supports the answer to Question 44.

46. **A.** The passage begins with a definition of eclipse and moves on to the examples of eclipses of the sun and moon. You also see the definition of *plane* in Line 22, not to mention definitions of *new* and *full* moons. Choice (A) is a clear winner here!

47. **C.** Line 8 asks the reader to imagine the Sun, Moon, and Earth arranged in a line. One of these is in the middle, and each of the other two is an "extreme" — the *outer* body. The diagram may help you with this one; it illustrates the position of the three bodies during an eclipse.

48. **C.** If you're a planetary scientist, this one is easy. You aren't? Never fear. Line 10 refers to "ever-moving bodies." Another clue: The sentence containing the words the question is asking about ("drawn between any two bodies at any given time" [Line 8]) begins with the word *consequently*. Right before *consequently*, you see *constantly in motion* (Line 7). Follow these clues, Sherlock, and you arrive at Choice (C).

49. **B.** In the explanation to Question 49, you see some lines that support Choice (C). One of those lines appears here, in Choice (B), which is your answer.

50. **D.** The Earth blocks the light of the Sun, casting a shadow on the Moon — the Earth's shadow, also known as Choice (D).

51. **C.** If the universe were flat — lying on a plane — there would be "in every year about 25 eclipses (of the sun and of the moon in nearly equal numbers)" — according to Line 31. However, the passage explains that the Moon's orbit isn't on the same plane, so the three bodies line up much less frequently. The correct answer is Choice (C).

52. **B.** Lines 36 through 37 tell you that "eclipses of the Moon, when they occur, are visible over the whole hemisphere, or half, of the Earth." Eclipses of the Sun, however, are visible in "just a belt of the Earth no more than about 150 to 170 miles wide" (Lines 38 through 39). Therefore, more people see eclipses of the Moon than of the Sun, as Choice (B) states. Did you fall for Choice (C)? The Sun, planets, and moons are in the solar system, but not other stars. You may know this fact from your science classes, but you don't need outside knowledge to rule out Choice (C). Just check Line 7, which defines the solar system as "the planets and their moons."

Answers for Section 2: Math — Calculator Section

1. **C.** You know that three marbles are green and six are yellow, so nine of the marbles are already accounted for. That leaves $11 - 9 = 2$ red marbles in the box. The probability of drawing a red marble is the number of red marbles divided by the number of marbles in the box, or $\frac{2}{11}$, Choice (C).

2. **D.** You know that Car C is traveling at 60 miles per hour. Because Car C is going 20 miles per hour faster than Car B, you can determine that Car B is traveling 40 miles per hour ($60 - 20 = 40$). Finally, because Car A is traveling twice as fast as Car B, Car A's speed is $2 \times 40 = 80$ miles per hour.

3. **D.** Because no two points on the correct graph have the same y-coordinate, you know that for any y-value you pick, a horizontal line drawn at that y-value will cross the graph only once. The only option where that is true is Choice (D), because all the other answers have parts where a horizontal line could cross the graph more than once.

4. **C.** For problems like this, your best bet is to follow the rule given and use substitution. You can see that 6 is in the place of a, 3 is in the place of b, and 4 is in the place of c. That means that you can change $a^2 - bc + b$ into $6^2 - (3)(4) + 3$, which you can then simplify to $36 - 12 + 3 = 27$.

5. **C.** Call the unknown number in the question x. You know that 3 less than twice x is 13. Turning that into math: $2x - 3 = 13$. You can solve that equation by adding 3 to both sides and then dividing by 2 to get $x = 8$. Make sure that you don't get fooled here and think that 8 is the answer! The question asks for what five times the number (x) is, so $5x = 5(8) = 40$, Choice (C).

6. **B.** In this problem, you need to remember that 25 percent of something is a quarter. Because you're looking for which pizza toppings represent more than a quarter of total sales, you're looking for toppings that take up more than a quarter of the circle. Keep in mind that a quarter of a circle has a central angle of 90 degrees, so any central angle that is bigger than 90 degrees is part of a sector that is more than 25 percent. Pepperoni and Mushroom seem to be the only toppings that take up more than a quarter, so your answer is *two*, Choice (B).

7. **D.** A great idea here is to simply plug in the answer choices and see which one works out. When you plug in 0, Choice (A), you quickly see that $|10 - 3(0)| = |10 - 0| = 10$, which is bigger than 3. Plugging in 1, you end up with 7, which is also bigger than 3. Plug in 2, and

the result is 4, which is still bigger than 3 (though you're getting closer!). Now try plugging in 3: $\left|10-3(3)\right|=\left|10-9\right|=1$, and $1<3$! Choice (D) must be the right answer.

8. **D.** First, read the chart and determine how many cats each family has. Cats are indicated by the darker bars on the chart, so Family 1 has two cats, Family 2 has no cats (only dogs), Family 3 has four cats, Family 4 has two cats, and Family 5 has three cats. Add all the cats together: $2+0+4+2+3=11$. There are 11 pet cats among these five families.

9. **C.** Count the spaces between the 5 and the 47. There are six spaces that are 42 apart (because $47-5=42$). Because the spaces are all the same size, you can find the length of each space by dividing 42 into 6, for a space length of 7. The unknown number is two spaces away from 5, so if each space is 7, find x by adding 2×7 to 5, $2(7)+5=19$, for an answer of Choice (C).

10. **C.** Here's a problem where you need to remember the rules of exponents. Do you recall that $x^a \cdot x^b = x^{a+b}$? That means that, in this case, you can simplify: $2^{3a} \cdot 2^{3b} = 2^{3a+3b}$. Hopefully you also saw that 64 is a power of 2 — 2^6 to be exact. Rewriting the equation gives you $2^{3a+3b} = 2^6$. Because the base is the same on each side, 2, you can set the powers equal to each other so that $3a+3b=6$. You're looking for the value of $a+b$, so divide both sides by 3 and you get that $a+b=2$, Choice (C).

11. **C.** For this problem, you could always just plug in the answer choices to find one that works, or you can see that because $(x-4)^2 = 49$, you're looking for when $x-4=7$ or -7. The problem states that $x<0$, so solve the $x-4=-7$ equation and discover that $x=-3$.

12. **D.** You know that $2a^2 = 56$, and you're looking for $8a^2$, which is $4(2a^2) = 4(56) = 224$.

13. **B.** When a line crosses the x-axis, you know that the y-value at that point has to be 0. That means you can plug 0 into the equation for y and solve for the x:

$$0 = 2x + 4$$
$$-4 = 2x$$
$$x = -2$$

The key to this problem is remembering that when you're thinking about an x-intercept, the y-value is 0. Don't forget that it's also true that when you're working with y-intercepts, the x-value is 0.

14. **B.** The key to this problem is remembering that when you multiply or divide an inequality by a negative number, the inequality switches. For example: Subtract 3 from both sides of the original expression $7 \geq -2x+3$ to get $4 \geq -2x$. Then divide both sides by -2 (remember to switch the inequality sign!), and you end up with $-2 \leq x$ or $x \geq -2$.

So you're looking for a number line that includes values that are greater than or equal to -2. Only Choices (B) and (D) have the number line shaded in for numbers greater than or equal to -2. Choice (B) has the circle at -2 filled in, meaning that -2 is included in the solution set, which is exactly what you want because you're looking for all numbers greater than or *equal to* -2.

15. **A.** The minimum value of a function is where the y-value is the lowest. So looking at the graph in this question, the y-value looks the lowest to the right of the y-axis, where the x's are positive. That already eliminates Choice (D). When you're trying to determine *where* the minimum value is, you need to find the x-value that causes the function to have the lowest y-value. Looking at the graph, the lowest y-value occurs when x is 2, Choice (A).

16. **C.** This problem is much easier if you pick numbers for x and y. For example, you could say that x is at about -0.5 and that y is at about 0.75 on the number line. When you multiply those two numbers together, you get $(-0.5)(0.75) = -0.375$. Because you're looking for a negative number, you can already disregard Choice (D); it represents a positive number.

Similarly, Choice (A) is smaller than –1, so it's outside of the range of numbers that you're interested in. You're left with Choices (B) and (C). When you multiply a number by a number between 0 and 1, the number will get smaller (closer to 0). Therefore, when you multiply x by y, the answer is going to be closer to 0 than x is. That means that Choice (C) is your best bet.

17. **A.** If you look at the graph, you can figure out what k is. The question tells you that $f(3)$ represents the y-value on the graph when the x-value is 3. If you look on the graph, when x is 3, you can see that y is $\frac{1}{2}$, so you know that $k = \frac{1}{2}$. Now, $f(k) = f\left(\frac{1}{2}\right)$, so you're looking for the y-value when x is $\frac{1}{2}$. Check out the graph again, and you'll see that when x is $\frac{1}{2}$, y is –1.

18. **B.** This problem is easiest if you pick a number for x. One number that would work is $x = -0.5 = -\frac{1}{2}$. So now you want to test each of the statements out. Is $-0.5 > \frac{-0.5}{2}$? Simplifying, is $-0.5 > -0.25$? That's clearly not true, so Statement I is false, meaning that you can eliminate Choices (A) and (C). Choices (B) and (D) both claim that Statement II is true, so you need to check Statement III to decide which answer choice is best. Statement III says that $(-0.5)^3 > (-0.5)^2$? Using a calculator, you can simplify this inequality to $-0.125 > 0.25$, which lets you see that it's clearly not true. Because Statement III is false, Choice (B) is the best choice. You can check Statement II to make sure: Is $(-0.5)^2 > (-0.5)$? Simplifying, you get $0.25 > -0.5$, which is absolutely true. Choice (B) really is the correct answer.

19. **C.** You can see that the fence the gardener will need is equal to $3x + y$, so what you really need to do is figure out a way to represent y in terms of x. The problem tells you that the area of the garden is 2,400 square feet, so you can use your knowledge of the area of a rectangle to see that $2,400 = xy$. Divide both sides by x to solve for y, which gives you $y = \frac{2,400}{x}$, and then you can substitute that back in to the original expression for the total fencing needed: $3x + y = 3x + \frac{2,400}{x}$, Choice (C).

20. **B.** To help solve this problem, sketch a picture. Keep in mind that the triangle can point upward or downward.

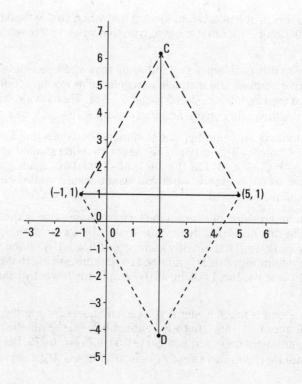

The third vertex of the triangle will lie along the line that cuts through the midpoint between the two given vertices. You can find the coordinates of that midpoint by finding the average of the x's and the average of the y's: $\left(\frac{-1+5}{2}, \frac{1+1}{2}\right) = (2,1)$. So the x-coordinate of the third vertex will be 2, which eliminates Choice (D). Because equilateral triangles have 60-degree angles in them, you can drop an altitude from the unknown vertex to make a 30-60-90 triangle. You know that the leg connecting a vertex to the midpoint is going to be 3 units long, and from there, you can use your knowledge of special triangles to see that the unknown altitude is $3\sqrt{3}$. That means that the unknown vertex is $3\sqrt{3}$ away from $3\sqrt{3}$, so it's either at $\left(2, 1 + 3\sqrt{3}\right)$ or $\left(2, 1 - 3\sqrt{3}\right)$. Choice (B) is the only choice that fits.

21. **D.** You're looking for the term that comes after 6. Because each term is three less than three times the previous term, you have to multiply 6 by 3 and then subtract 3: $6(3) - 3 = 18 - 3 = 15$. You can then check that 15 is the right answer by making sure that 42 would be the next term: $15(3) - 3 = 45 - 3 = 42$. That works, so you know that k is 15, and the answer is Choice (D).

22. **A.** For this problem, remember that a line with a positive slope looks like it's traveling uphill as you read it from left to right. Choices (A) and (B) are the only two that look like they have positive slopes; Choice (C) has a negative slope (travel downhill as you read left to right); and Choice (D) has a slope of zero. Now you're looking for the option with a negative y-intercept. The y-axis is the vertical one, so you're looking for the option where the line hits the vertical axis below the origin. Choice (A) is the only option that satisfies both the requirement for positive slope and the requirement for a negative y-intercept. In case you're wondering, Choice (C) also has a negative y-intercept, but as you saw earlier, the slope is negative.

23. **D.** If a baker bakes three dozen cookies in 45 minutes, you can deduce that the baker bakes one dozen cookies in 15 minutes. Because you want to know how many cookies are made in an hour (60 minutes), you multiply by 4 and get 4×1 dozen = 4 dozen cookies. One dozen equals 12, so in one hour, the baker can make $4 \times 12 = 48$ cookies.

24. **C.** Looking at the chart, you can see that the top row increases by one in each box. In the bottom row, each box is four fewer than the previous one. That means that n will be four fewer than 7, or n is $7 - 4 = 3$.

25. **A.** For this problem, you want to set up an equation. The problem says that when m is multiplied by 5, the result is the same as when 6 is subtracted from m. Translating that into math: $5m = m - 6$. Gather all the m terms on one side. Now you can solve for m and then determine what $8m$ equals, or you can go multiply both sides of this equation by 2 to go straight to the answer because $2(4m) = 8m$: $2(4m) = 2(-6) = -12$.

26. **D.** Looking at the picture, you can see that the line has a positive slope (as you read left to right, the line goes up). Already you can eliminate Choices (A) and (B). To find the slope of the line, use the points (a, b) and $(0, 0)$:

$$m = \frac{b - 0}{a - 0} = \frac{b}{a}$$

You know from $|b| > |a|$ that the fraction will be larger than 1, making Choice (D) the only viable choice.

27. **A.** When you change the x-value in a function, the graph changes horizontally. In this case, you're subtracting 1 from x before plugging it into the function g, so the graph shifts either left or right. Knowing this narrows your choices down to Choices (A) and (B). You can look at the original graph and see that $g(2) = 0$. To get $y = g(x - 1)$ to equal 0, you need $x - 1$ to equal 2: $x - 1 = 2$, $x = 3$. That means that $(3, 0)$ will be a point on the transformed graph. Choice (A) is the only graph with that point on it.

28. **A.** Your first step is to find the slope of line p.

$$m = \frac{2-1}{-2-2} = \frac{1}{-4} = -\frac{1}{4}$$

You know that perpendicular lines have opposite (negative) reciprocal slopes, so the slope of line q must be 4. So far, you know that line q has a slope of 4 and passes through the point $(-2,4)$. You can use the equation $y = 4x + b$ and substitute the point in to figure out what b is: $4 = 4(-2) + b$ becomes $b = 12$ when you solve it. Now you have the equation of line q: $y = 4x + 12$. Substitute in the point $(k,0)$ and solve for k: $0 = 4k + 12$, $-12 = 4k$, and $k = -3$.

29. **D.** To find the arithmetic mean (the average) of a set of numbers, you simply add the numbers together and then divide by the number of numbers. That means that if the average of 4, p, and q is 6, then $\frac{4+p+q}{3} = 6$. You can manipulate this equation by multiplying both sides by 3 ($4 + p + q = 18$) and then subtracting 4 from both sides: $p + q = 14$. You're looking for the value of $\frac{p+q}{2}$, so just divide 14 by 2 and get 7.

30. **B.** There are two good ways to solve this problem. The easy way is to figure out that 27 and 15 are 12 units away from each other, and then simply add 12 to 27 to get the other point, 39. Alternatively, you can use the idea that the average of 15 and the other point, x, is 27. Set that up like this:

$$\frac{15+x}{2} = 27$$

After you multiply both sides by 2 and then subtract 15, you get that x is 39.

31. **5.** For this problem, you need to factor a difference of perfect squares: $x^2 - y^2 = (x-y)(x+y)$. Substitute in the numbers that you know, $39 = (3)(x+y)$, and then divide both sides by 3 to get $x + y = 13$. Because you know both $x + y$ and $x - y$, you can add the two together: $(x+y) + (x-y) = 2x = 13 + 3 = 16$. Now you know that x is 8. If x is 8 and $x + y = 13$, y is 5.

32. **70.** The trick is to see that $105°$ is a vertical angle to $35° + x°$. Because vertical angles are equal, you know that $105 = 35 + x$.

33. **1.2 or 6/5.** Call the number x. Translating the words into math: "Six times x is the same as x added to 6" becomes $6x = 6 + x$. You can then gather all the x terms onto one side of the equation, $5x = 6$, and divide by 5: $x = \frac{6}{5} = 1.2$.

34. **17.** First, start by listing out each of the terms: a, $a+5$, $a+10$, $a+15$, $a+20$, and $a+25$. Now add all six terms together: $a + a + 5 + a + 10 + a + 15 + a + 20 + a + 25 = 6a + 75$. You can set that equal to 177 and then solve for a:

$$6a + 75 = 177$$
$$6a = 102$$
$$a = 17$$

35. **1/2 or .5.** If one angle is $90°$ and angle $\theta = 30°$, then the third angle is $60°$, making this a 30-60-90 triangle with a side ratio of $1 : \sqrt{3} : 2$. The sin of an angle is the angle's opposite side, which in this case the triangle's smallest side, over the triangle's hypotenuse. From the ratio, you know that the smallest side is half the length of the hypotenuse, for an answer of $\frac{1}{2}$ or 0.5. When you grid in your answer, either 1/2 or .5 is considered correct.

36. **6.** Sketch out the problem to help you solve:

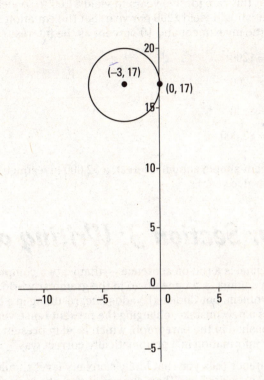

You can quickly see that for the circle to touch the *y*-axis in only one place, it must touch the *y*-axis at (0, 17). That point is three units away from the center of the circle, meaning that the radius of the circle is 3. Now just multiply that by 2 to determine the diameter of the circle is 6.

37. **210.** If $1,000 invested at *i* percent simple annual interest yields $200 over a two-year period, you can deduce that it earns $100 over one year. To find *i*, the interest rate, yielding $100 simple annual interest on $1,000, divide the amount of interest by the amount of the investment:

$$\frac{100}{1,000} = 0.1 = 10\%$$

Now you know that $i = 10$, for an interest rate of 10 percent.

To calculate compound interest, you can use the compound interest formula. However, for only two cycles, you can find the answer without the formula. Simply calculate the simple interest twice: once for the first year, and once for the second year. Start with the original $1,000 investment, and increase it 10 percent:

$$\$1,000 + \left(10\% \times \$1,000\right) = \$1,000 + \$100 = \$1,100$$

The investment is worth $1,100 at the end of the first year. To find its value at the end of the second year, increase $1,100 by ten percent:

$$\$1,100 + \left(10\% \times \$1,100\right) = \$1,100 + \$110 = \$1,210$$

The question asks for the amount of interest yielded, not the final value. To find the amount of interest, subtract the original value from the final value:

$$\$1,210 - \$1,000 = \$210$$

38. **2,000.** Knowing the interest rate is 10 percent simple annual interest, how much should be invested at this rate for five years to yield $1,000? To yield $1,000 over five years, the investment should yield $200 per year. Set the equation up for one year's worth of interest with x as the investment and 10 percent as the interest rate:

$$10\%x = \$200$$

$$\frac{10x}{100} = \$200$$

$$\frac{x}{10} = \$200$$

$$x = \$2,000$$

At 10 percent simple annual interest, a $2,000 investment will yield $200 per year and $1,000 over five years.

Answers for Section 3: Writing and Language

1. **C.** The original is a run-on sentence — that is, two complete sentences attached to each other by a comma — a huge no-no in the grammar world. Choices (B) and (D) correct the original problem, but Choice (B) adds *and,* resulting in a less mature expression. Choice (D) introduces a new mistake, changing the present-tense verb to past and breaking the pattern established in the paragraph, which is all in present tense. Choice (C) includes the necessary information in a grammatically correct way.

2. **B.** The sentence tells you that Molly's anxiety level should go down, because she is "nervously checking" and then, the vet hopes, she "can stand quietly." Okay, when you *subtract,* you do end up with a smaller number. However, anxiety isn't a number; it's a feeling. You can *lower* the intensity of a feeling, but you can't *subtract* it. Choice (B) is the word you seek here. Choice (C), by the way, is the opposite of what you want. Choice (D) establishes a level of importance — not what you need in this sentence.

3. **A.** The first paragraph focuses on one patient, Molly, and Dr. Virga's treatment of her. The second paragraph explains what an animal behaviorist does. By adding "He is an animal behaviorist," you establish a strong transition from paragraph one to paragraph two.

4. **D.** The original sentence has a list of activities that behaviorists study. Whenever you see a list, check that it's *parallel.* That's an English-teacher term for this rule: Everything doing the same job in the sentence must be in the same form. You have *eat, move, rest, play,* and, in the original, *relating.* Nope. Change *relating* to *relate* and read the list. Can you hear how everything matches? Now it's parallel and correct.

5. **C.** The sentence begins with a verb form, *identifying.* By the rules of grammar, the subject of the sentence must be doing the action expressed by an introductory verb form. The subject of the original sentence is *animals,* who are definitely not *identifying* problems. Switch the sentence around so that the behaviorist does the *identifying.* Both Choices (C) and (D) solve the problem. Choice (C) is better than Choice (D), though, because Choice (D) drags in an extra word, *they.*

6. **C.** Check the context of the underlined words. The sentence begins with *Even in this modern era.* Why include *now?* Both express the same idea, but only *now* is underlined. Delete *now,* and the sentence is fine.

7. **B.** When you place commas around a descriptive statement in a sentence, the commas act like little handles. You can lift out the words they surround and still say the same thing with just a bit less detail. In this sentence, though, removing *who has pets* changes the meaning of the sentence. Instead of talking about pet owners, you're talking about all people — *anyone.* To keep the intended meaning, dump the commas. Now you have to

choose between Choices (B) and (D). *Anyone* is a singular pronoun. It must be matched with singular verbs. Choice (D) improperly introduces plural verbs *(have, see)*. Go for Choice (B), and you're right.

8. **A.** *Elephants* is a plural word and should be matched with other plurals, as the original sentence does *(they see themselves)*. This one needs no change, so Choice (A) is your answer.

9. **D.** If elephants recognize themselves in a mirror, they are self-aware, so the original makes no sense. *But* signals some sort of change, such as an exception to the first part of the sentence. However, you don't want to reverse course here; you want to continue, and the conjunction *and* fills the role nicely, making Choice (D) your answer.

10. **B.** Take a close look at the graph. The figure 11% comes from the projected increase in *all United States jobs of any type,* not jobs solely in the field of animal behavior. Now look at the number for *all animal behavior specialists.* The number there is 7%, so Choice (B) is correct.

11. **D.** You study more, and you make more money. That's the meaning of the last sentence, but *return* isn't the appropriate word in this context. Instead, the *higher paid careers reflect,* because they *show* the worth of *better education and training.* Choice (D) is the right answer.

12. **B.** The sentence focuses on a single point in the past, so simple past tense, *began,* is best here.

13. **B.** The underlined word describes *health,* not the wounded soldiers. Health may be *impaired* (weakened or damaged), but not *disabled.* That description, along with *unfit* and *wounded* — Choices (C) and (D) — may refer to people, but not to health.

14. **C.** The sentence establishes the topic of the paragraph: the trench system. Placed at the beginning of paragraph two, the topic sentence creates a link to the first paragraph, which is a general introduction to World War I, because the sentence mentions *World War I* and *the trench system.*

15. **D.** The three activities show up in a list in Choice (D), stated concisely and correctly. Choice (A) is a run-on sentence (two complete thoughts linked only by a comma, a grammatical crime). Choice (B) creates what English teachers call a misplaced modifier, because an introductory verb form *(Listening to the enemy)* must describe the subject of the sentence. In Choice (B), the *frontline trench* is *listening to the enemy* — not the intended meaning. Choice (C) is wordy and introduces a pronoun, *they,* without telling you who *they* are.

16. **A.** The frontline trenches, as the diagram and text make clear, were closest to the enemy. Behind those were the support trenches. The original sentence uses *backed by,* which tells the reader both the location and the function, because when you *back* something, you also provide support.

17. **B.** Check out the figure. The communication trench isn't parallel to the others. How could it be when it was supposed to connect them? Parallel lines, like railroad tracks, never meet. Instead, the communication trench cuts across the other two, as you see in the figure.

18. **B.** The original sentence isn't a sentence at all. It's a fragment because it has no logical subject-verb pair. *The trenches laid* (the original wording) has the trenches placing themselves in the ground. Nope! Instead, *the trenches were laid* or *placed* by someone not named in the sentence.

19. **D.** The paragraph begins by telling the reader that the trenches *were not pleasant places,* but little else in the paragraph supports that statement except the information about the walls. Add Choice (D), and you have better evidence *(narrow, never quite dry).*

20. **C.** The underlined word, *they're,* means "they are" — not the meaning you want here. Opt for the possessive pronoun *their,* Choice (C), for a grammatically correct expression.

21. **A.** Choice (A) combines the sentence concisely, wasting no words. Choice (B) is concise, but it says too little. Choice (C) is wordy, and Choice (D) is wrong because it's a run-on sentence — two complete sentences can't be joined with just a comma.

22. **C.** The passage stops, but it has no real conclusion, so Choice (A) doesn't work. Choice (B) repeats information from the third sentence of the paragraph, and repetition is seldom a good idea. Choice (D) doesn't relate to the topic of the last paragraph and also repeats information from the first paragraph — two good reasons to reject it. The correct answer is Choice (C) because the sentence takes into account the topic of the last paragraph — the gap between civilians and soldiers — and also refers to "The Great War," an idea introduced in the first paragraph. By returning to this idea, the added sentence sums up the last paragraph and links the first and last paragraphs, giving a sense of unity to the passage.

23. **C.** The original sentence has no subject, so you have to add one. The rest of the passage is in first person — the narrator uses *I, me, my,* and so forth. It makes sense to add the subject *I.* In Choice (B), the *I* doesn't work as a subject because it doesn't pair with the verb form *sitting.* Choice (C), on the other hand, is a perfect match, because *I'm* is a contraction of *I am.* Choice (D) has no subject, so it fails. Go for Choice (C), which corrects the error.

24. **C.** The problem with the original is that *they've* (the contraction for *they have*) can have two meanings, because the pronoun *they* may refer to either *the Hamiltons* or the *parents.* The passage is clear: The parents have given in and gone to Vermont; the Hamiltons haven't given in and withdrawn their suggestion for a vacation spot.

25. **D.** The pronoun *which* refers to *dinner,* but Standard English requires the preposition *at,* because the family is *at the dinner.* Go for Choice (D).

26. **B.** The pronoun *everyone* is strange. It looks and sounds plural, but it's actually singular. (I know, grammar is dumb.) Because the next pronoun refers to *everyone,* it, too, must be singular, but *they* is plural. Change *they* to *he or she* (a singular, all-inclusive expression), and the pronouns match. Choice (B) is your answer.

27. **C.** Did you choose Choice (A)? If so, you fell for a common SAT trick. The original sentence is grammatically correct, but the SAT Writing and Language exam covers more than grammar. As written, the passage jumps from a memory of dinner with neighbors at home to greeting them in Vermont. The reader, with a little work, can figure out the meaning, but Choice (C) provides a transition to improve the flow from one idea to the next.

28. **C.** This question tests whether you can recognize or create focus in a paragraph. Most of the sentences deal with lake activities — swimming, boating, and fishing. Sentence 3 veers off course into the amount of vacation time the father has. Because it has no relation to the rest of the ideas in the paragraph, Sentence 3 has to go, and Choice (C) is your answer.

29. **D.** If the underlined words were an empty blank, what would you insert? Probably "like" or something similar. *Relish* means "enjoy." Choice (D) works in this context because the father doesn't like rowing. To *dote on,* by the way, means to act like a typical grandparent and to give way too much attention to something — not the word you need in the context of this sentence.

30. **A.** A *shard* is a small, sharp piece of something — the kind of thing that's leftover when you're cutting large chunks of marble. Even if you aren't acquainted with marble quarries, you can rule out the other choices. Choice (B) doesn't work because *columns* are finished products, and the end of the sentence indicates that the gift shop sells something *as well as* (in addition to) *finished items. Vestiges* are traces; you can't sell a trace! *Rubbles* isn't a word; the singular form, *rubble,* is the name for chunks of rock left after a building falls down. Choice (A), the original, is the only one that fits and is the correct answer.

31. **B.** The original wording is like someone who eats 4,000 calories a day and does nothing but sit on the couch and watch television. Diet time! When you slim down (in real life or in writing), you must do so carefully. Choice (B) conveys the correct meaning more concisely

than the original. Choice (C) keeps the meaning, but it has to lose a few more pounds . . . er, I mean words. Choice (D) changes the meaning, because the *tombstones* aren't *nervous and glad* — the narrator is.

32. **C.** Why is the trip home so frightening? The paragraph supplies a little evidence: The narrator is worried that they will *drive into a ditch* or fail to find the cabin. Choice (C) adds more support for the fear expressed, explaining the reaction of *a city girl* to unlighted roads.

33. **D.** The tiny word *or* joins two statements, and by the rules of grammar, those statements must be parallel. In other words, they must match grammatically. Before *or,* you have a subject-verb statement — *that we'll drive off the road and into a ditch.* You have a subject *(we)* and a verb *(will drive,* when the contraction is removed). After the *or,* you need another subject-verb statement, which only Choice (D) supplies.

34. **D.** Commas surrounding a description make the description nonessential, or extra, to the meaning of the sentence. The original sentence identifies the rabbit-releaser by name. After you know the name, everything else — in this case, the fact that *Thomas Austin* was *an Australian* and someone *who enjoyed hunting* — is extra. The original sentence gets you halfway to the goal of correct punctuation by placing a comma after *hunting.* Halfway isn't good enough! Choice (D) isolates the description properly by inserting another comma after *Austin.*

35. **B.** The passage begins by explaining that *Thomas Austin . . . enjoyed hunting.* Why repeat the information? Delete this sentence, as Choice (B) indicates, and you create a more concise paragraph without sacrificing meaning.

36. **C.** In a sentence beginning with *there was* or *there were* (as well as *here was* or *here were*), the subject follows the verb. *There* (or *here*) can never be a subject. In this sentence, *some domestic rabbits* follows the verb. The subject, *rabbits,* is plural, so you need the plural verb *were.* Why Choice (C) and not Choice (D)? *Their* is a possessive pronoun, and the meaning of the sentence has nothing to do with possession.

37. **D.** Choice (D) is the most concise, yet it conveys the same information as the original. The other choices aren't incorrect, but they are all wordy.

38. **B.** This question tests you on two word pairs: less/fewer and led/lead. *Less* applies to quantities that you can measure but not count (*sand,* for example). *Fewer* is for counting things, such as *trees.* *Led* is the past tense form of the verb *to lead.* *Lead* is the present tense form (not what you need here) or, as a noun, a metal. *Fewer trees led,* Choice (B), is correct,

39. **A.** Don't mess with Mother Nature! That's what you do in an *interference,* a word that's correct in this context. Time to build your vocabulary: An *intercession* takes place when one pleads on behalf of another. (Don't confuse this word with *intersession,* which is a period of time between school semesters.) An *interruption* stops the flow of activity, and an *affectation* is a pretense or artificial expression. None of the other choices fit, so Choice (A) is your answer.

40. **B.** The original paragraph tells you little about why the beetles were introduced into the environment. When you add the information in Choice (B), the paragraph makes more sense.

41. **D.** The usual meaning of *introduce* is to bring two strangers together (*Alice, this is George.*) In this context, the strangers are a species (the tamarisk beetle) and an ecosystem. *To initiate* (the original word), as well as *to start* and *to commence,* is to begin something new. None of these words fits the context.

42. **C.** *The number of* is a singular subject referring to a single number, no matter how big that number is. Therefore, you have to pair this singular expression with a singular verb, *has decreased.* Choice (C) is correct here.

43. **B.** The original is wordy. Choice (B) puts the original on a diet and slims it down correctly. True, Choice (D) is even shorter, but it leaves the sentence without a subject and isn't Standard English.

44. **C.** Choice (C) adds specific examples to the more general original *(You should also check consumption),* which also inappropriately shifts from third person (talking about the subject) to second person (talking to the reader). The examples strengthen the writer's recommendation — that human interaction with nature should be accomplished carefully. Choices (A) and (D) are too general, and Choice (B) is repetitive. No doubt about it, Choice (C) is best.

Answers for Section 4: Math — No-Calculator Section

1. **D.** Sketch out this problem to help you solve it:

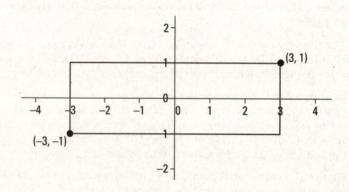

   The length of the rectangle is 6, and the height is 2. The area of a rectangle is *length* times *width,* so the area of this rectangle is $(6)(2) = 12$.

2. **B.** Because you're interested in the children who had only chocolate ice cream, you want to look in the chocolate circle where it doesn't overlap with the vanilla circle; the number in that section is 9. That means 9 kids had only chocolate ice cream, out of the 36 kids at the party. To find the percent of children who had chocolate ice cream, simply divide the part that you're interested in (9) by the whole (36):

$$\frac{9}{36} = \frac{1}{4} = 25\%$$

3. **B.** Set up the equation with x as the number and solve for x.

$$\frac{4}{5}x = 24$$
$$4x = 120$$
$$x = 30$$

Now find $\frac{1}{5}$ of 30, which is 6.

4. **B.** The best way to do this problem is to simply turn the test booklet. Look at the original image after turning the booklet 90 degrees clockwise (to the right), and then find the answer that looks most like the original did when it was turned. Choice (B) turns out to be the right one.

5. **A.** A good method for solving this one is to pick numbers for the variable. You could say, for example, that Chandler has been snowboarding for ten years — now you're using $n = 10$. If Kate has been snowboarding for three fewer years than Chandler, she has been snowboarding for 7 years. So you're looking for an answer choice where if you plug in $n = 10$, you get 7 as the result. Choice (A) works perfectly.

6. **A.** The key to this problem is paying attention to the fact that the figure is a square. Knowing that the area is 36, you can immediately deduce that the length of a side of the square is 6 because $6^2 = 36$. You also know that the length of half the side of the square is 3. That means that the (x, y) coordinates of point C will be $(3,6)$. You can then plug those coordinates into the equation $y = \dfrac{x^2}{k}$ and solve for k:

$$6 = \frac{3^2}{k}$$
$$6 = \frac{9}{k}$$
$$6k = 9$$
$$k = \frac{3}{2} \text{ or } 1.5$$

7. **D.** Get rid of the t, and the question becomes, "How much greater than –5 is 2?" Well, that would be 7, so Choice (D) is the right answer.

8. **D.** You want to use substitution to solve this problem. Wherever you see n in the original definition, substitute in -3: $(n-1)(n+1) = (-3-1)(-3+1) = (-4)(-2) = 8$. Choice (D) is the best answer.

9. **A.** The key to this problem is remembering that parabolas are symmetrical along the line that passes vertically through the vertex (known as the *axis of symmetry*). That means that if you were to fold the parabola along that line, both sides would line up. For the purpose of this problem, it means that x-values with the same y-coordinates must be the same distance from the axis of symmetry, which is at $x = 3$ in this case. Both values in Choice (A) are two away from 3, so that looks like a great option. In Choice (B), 1 is two away from 3, but 6 is three away, so that option doesn't work. For Choice (C), 2 is one away from 3, but 5 is two away; again they're not the same distance from the axis of symmetry. Choice (D) keeps 2, which is still one away from 3, and moves the other point further away, to 6. Choice (A) it is!

10. **D.** Whenever you're working on percentage problems, it's a great idea to assume that the starting price is $100. So if the TV cost $100 to start, and then the price was decreased by 10 percent ($10), the reduced price is $90. You add 20 percent on to 90 by finding 20 percent of 90 and adding it to $90: $0.20(90) = 18$; $\$90 + \$18 = \$108$. It's easy to see that $108 is 108 percent of $100: $\dfrac{\$108}{\$100} = 1.08 = 108\%$.

11. **C.** It's always a great idea to sketch problems where you're told the coordinates but not given a picture.

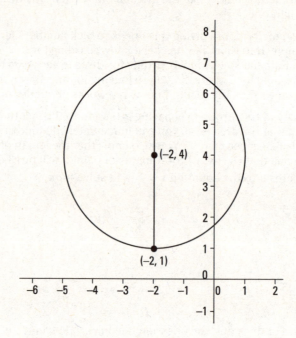

Looking at your picture, it's easy to see that the other endpoint of the diameter is also going to have –2 as its x-coordinate. Now all you need to do is determine the radius of the circle so you can figure out the y-coordinate. Looking at the two points that were given in the problem, you can see that the radius is 3 $(4-1=3)$. That means that the y-coordinate of the other endpoint will be 3 away from the center: $(-2, 4+3) = (-2, 7)$.

12. **D.** For this problem, it's a good idea to just calculate each of the terms. You know that the first term is –1. To get the second term, multiply –1 by –3: $(-1)(-3) = 3$. To get the third term, multiply the second term by –3: $(-1)(-3) = 3$. For the fourth term, multiply the third term by –3: $(-9)(-3) = 27$. Therefore the fourth term is 27, Choice (D).

13. **D.** The first step is to find the area of square ABCD. You know the length of one of the sides, so you know that the area is that length squared: $6^2 = 36$. Now you just need to subtract off the area of the five circles. You can see that each of the nine smaller squares has a side length equal to one-third of the length of the big square: $\frac{1}{3}(6) = 2$. That means that the diameter of each of the circles is 2, so the radius is 1. The area of a circle is $A = \pi r^2$, so the area of each of these circles is $A = \pi(1)^2 = \pi$. Now you can find the area of the shaded part of the diagram. The area will be the total square area minus the area of five circles: $36 - 5\pi$, or Choice (D).

14. **C.** The first step is to find the slope of the given line by solving for y:

$$2y = -4x + k$$

$$y = -2x + \frac{k}{2}$$

The slope of this line is –2 Because you know that line l is parallel to this line, you now know that line l has a slope of –2. Now you can use the point $(1, 3)$ and $y = mx + b$ to determine the equation of l. Substitute –2 for m, –1 in for x, and 3 in for y, and then solve for b: $3 = -2(-1) + b$, so $b = 1$. Now you know the equation for l is $y = -2x + 1$. You can substitute p and –p in for x and y, respectively, to solve the problem: $-p = -2(p) + 1$. Simplifying, $-p = -2p + 1$, or $p = 1$.

15. **D.** This is a tricky question! It's a good idea to sketch some axes in on the diagram so you can play with coordinates. You might choose to sketch them in so that the origin is at the lower left corner of the smallest square, like so:

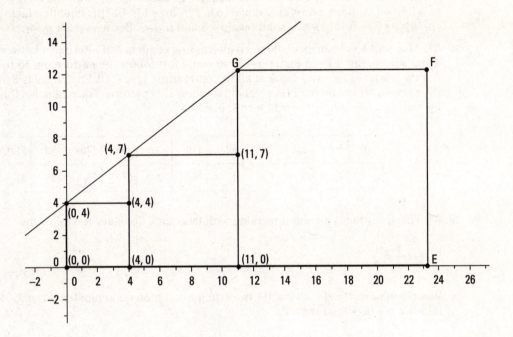

Now you can call point $A\left(0, 4\right)$ and point $K\left(4, 7\right)$. Because you have two points, you can determine the equation of the line passing through them (and through point G). The slope is $m = \dfrac{7-4}{4-0} = \dfrac{3}{4}$. You already know the y-intercept is 4, so the equation of the line is $y = \dfrac{3}{4}x + 4$. To figure out the coordinates of point G, you just need to plug the known x-value $(4+7=11)$ into the equation of the line:

$$y = \frac{3}{4}(11) + 4 = \frac{33}{4} + \frac{16}{4} = \frac{49}{4} = 12\frac{1}{4} = 12.25$$

Therefore, the coordinates of point G are $\left(11, 12.25\right)$. Because you set the axes up so that the square was sitting on the x-axis, the y-coordinate of point G is equal to the length of a side of the largest square. DE is just another side of the same square, so the length of DE is also 12.25, Choice (D).

16. **210.** Every even number must be divisible by 2, so $2 \times 3 \times 5 \times 7 = 210$.

17. **36.** If you let the numerator equal n, then the denominator is $2n - 12$; thus,

$$\frac{2}{3} = \frac{n}{2n-12}$$

So $2(2n-12) = 3n$, or $4n-24 = 3n$. Subtracting $4n$ from both sides gives you $-24 = -n$, and dividing by -1 gives you $n = 24$. But wait! That's not the answer: n is the numerator, but the problem asks for the denominator. So plug 24 into $2n-12 : 2\left(24\right)-12 = 36$. And, of course,

$$\frac{2}{3} = \frac{24}{36}$$

18. **8.** Although you may be able to get the answer by trial and error, this problem is really begging to be factored. To factor a *quadratic equation* (that is, an equation with something "squared" in it), you must first set the equation equal to 0. Making the squared term negative is never a good idea, so you should solve as follows. Start with the equation: $p^2 = 3p + 40$. And set everything equal to 0: $p^2 - 3p - 40 = 0$. This equation factors out to $(p - 8)(p + 5) = 0$. It has two solutions: $p = 8$ and $p = -5$. Because $p > 0, p = 8$.

19. **31.** This problem is an example of an alternating sequence; it alternates between adding 4 and subtracting 1 from each term. You could just follow the pattern out to the 21st term, but there's an easier way. Look at all the odd terms: 1, 4, 7, 10. Each term is 3 more than the previous term. So the 21st term must follow this pattern. You can solve this problem by making a list of only the odd terms, like this:

1st	3rd	5th	7th	9th	11th	13th	15th	17th	19th	21st
1	4	7	10	13	16	19	22	25	28	31

20. **30.** This question is all about working with fractions. Consider the following:

$$\frac{1}{x} + \frac{1}{y} = \frac{1}{4}$$

When you're working with fractions, getting a common denominator on each side is a good idea. Here's how it works out:

$$\left(\frac{y}{y}\right)\frac{1}{x} + \left(\frac{x}{x}\right)\frac{1}{y} = \frac{1}{4}$$

$$\frac{y}{xy} + \frac{x}{xy} = \frac{1}{4}$$

$$\frac{x + y}{xy} = \frac{1}{4}$$

Notice how letters are put in alphabetical order; that's standard practice in algebra. Does anything about the fraction on the left side look familiar? It should: The numerator is $x + y$, which is what you're looking for; the denominator is xy, which equals 120. Now you can write $\frac{x + y}{120} = \frac{1}{4}$, so $4(x + y) = 120$, and $x + y = 30$.

Answer Guidelines for Section 5: The Essay

Here are some possible points to make in your essay in response to the prompt.

Reading

Note how many of these ideas you mentioned:

- ✔ The main argument is that everyone gives "messages" to others, either through words or body language and facial expression.

- ✔ Positive messages create positive results, and negative messages do the opposite.

- ✔ Immediately after the reference to Ekman, the author elaborates on the main point by explaining that even unconscious lies have an effect on the listener.

- The passage explains some steps that the reader can take to nurture a positive attitude.

- The conclusion also reinforces the main idea, that one can achieve greater "happiness, self-esteem, and effectiveness."

How did you do? If you covered all these points in your essay, give yourself a 4. If you discussed three or four, award yourself 3 points. Only two? Take 2 points. If you mentioned the main idea and nothing else, give yourself 1 point.

Analysis

The most important part of your essay is analysis of the writer's technique. Here are some possible points:

- The passage begins with a reference to the views of an expert witness, Paul Ekman. Although Ekman's credentials don't appear in the passage, the implication is that the book is an authoritative source.

- At the end of paragraph one, the author appeals to fear by warning: "Others may subconsciously notice the disconnection between your words and your nonverbal message" and sense the lie.

- The example of Viktor Frankl in paragraph two contrasts Frankl's honesty ("unity between his words, his actions, and the way he lived") with the warning about lying at the end of paragraph one.

- Also countering the fear are the recommendations in paragraphs six and seven, which suggest positive messages the reader can give to him- or herself and to others. The passage ends with a practical method — a journal exercise — for nurturing a positive attitude.

- Personal pronouns — *we* and *you* (as in *We all know* and *What are you communicating to yourself*) create a bond between the author and reader.

- In the third and fourth paragraphs, a series of rhetorical questions (asked for effect, with no answer from the author) draw the reader into the discussion and provoke reflection on the topic.

- Sophisticated vocabulary choices, such as *executive, aligned,* and *congruent,* create a serious, businesslike tone. These words imply that the reader (even one who has to look up the definitions!) is serious and businesslike. That impression, flattery or not, may make the reader more open to the writer's argument.

- The research experiment on teachers' attitudes and the information about placebos discussed in paragraphs five and six provide scientific backing for the author's ideas.

- The conclusion refers to "meaning in life" and unifies the passage by taking the reader back to the example of Viktor Frankl.

How were your analytical skills? If you mentioned seven or more of the ideas, you earned 4 points. If you discussed four, five, or six of the techniques, take 3 points. Only two or three? You earned 2 points. Just one? Take 1 point.

Writing

Your final category is writing and applies to your own essay. Evaluating your own writing may be difficult. If you can find a friendly teacher or a helpful adult, ask for assistance in checking your grammar and style. Pay attention to these factors:

- ✔ **Structure:** Does your essay have a solid, logical structure? One possibility is to work in order from the first paragraph of the passage, where the author states the *thesis* (idea to be proved), and then move through paragraph after paragraph until you reach the end of the passage. Another possibility is to examine writing techniques in separate paragraphs. For example, you may have one paragraph on Eckman and Frankl, one on word choice (including personal pronouns), and one on rhetorical questions.

- ✔ **Evidence:** Do you back up every statement you make with quotations or specific references to the passage? Count how many times you zeroed in on details. You should have at least two in every paragraph you write and maybe more.

- ✔ **Language:** Does your essay sound formal, as if a teacher were explaining the passage? If you lapsed into slang or informal word choice, your essay is weaker.

- ✔ **Mechanics:** English teachers group grammar, spelling, and punctuation in this category. As you reread, underline any sentence fragments or run-ons, misspelled words, and faulty commas or quotation marks.

Adding up points to evaluate your writing is tricky. In general, give yourself 1 point (up to a total of 4) for every category in the bulleted list in which you excelled. If you stumbled slightly in a category (say, three or four grammar or spelling mistakes), give yourself 3/4 of a point. If you feel your performance in one of these categories was poor (perhaps you drifted off topic or made seven or eight grammar errors), take only a half point.

Scoring your essay

To get a fair idea of how your essay measures up to College Board standards, fill in this grid.

Category	Reading	Analysis	Writing
Number of Points			

Double the number in each box. The results are your essay scores in Reading, Analysis, and Writing. For more guidance on scoring your essay, check Chapters 7 and 8.

Answer Key

Section 1: Reading

1. C	2. A
3. D	4. C
5. B	6. D
7. A	8. B
9. D	10. C
11. B	12. A
13. C	14. C
15. D	16. B
17. A	18. C
19. D	20. C
21. D	22. A
23. D	24. C
25. C	26. D
27. B	28. C
29. A	30. C
31. D	32. B
33. C	34. D
35. A	36. B
37. C	38. B
39. C	40. D
41. C	42. B
43. D	44. B
45. A	46. A
47. C	48. C
49. B	50. D
51. C	52. B

Section 2: Math – Calculator Section

1. C	2. D
3. D	4. C
5. C	6. B
7. D	8. D
9. C	10. C
11. C	12. D
13. B	14. B
15. A	16. C
17. A	18. B
19. C	20. B
21. D	22. A
23. D	24. C
25. A	26. D
27. A	28. A
29. D	30. B
31. **5**	32. **70**
33. **1.2 or 6/5**	34. **17**
35. **1/2 or .5**	36. **6**
37. **210**	38. **2,000**

Section 3: Writing and Language

1. C	2. B
3. A	4. D
5. C	6. C
7. B	8. A
9. D	10. B
11. D	12. B
13. B	14. C
15. D	16. A
17. B	18. B
19. D	20. C
21. A	22. C
23. C	24. C
25. D	26. B
27. C	28. C
29. D	30. A
31. B	32. C
33. D	34. D
35. B	36. C
37. D	38. B
39. A	40. B
41. D	42. C
43. B	44. C

Section 4: Math — No-Calculator Section

1. D	2. B
3. B	4. B
5. A	6. A
7. D	8. D
9. A	10. D
11. C	12. D
13. D	14. C
15. D	16. **210**
17. **36**	18. **8**
19. **31**	20. **30**

Chapter 20

Practice Exam 2

● ●

If you survived Practice Exam 1 in Chapter 18, you may be on your way to the movies right now to see the latest Hollywood vampire movie. Still here? Okay, that means you want to try again. Follow the procedures described at the beginning of Chapter 18 (the first practice exam): Sit in a quiet room, turn off the phone, and place a timer (an ordinary watch or clock works fine) right in front of your face. Spend no more than the allotted time on each part (check the number of minutes at the beginning of each section) and resist the temptation to (a) fold the answer sheet into a paper airplane and fly it out the window, (b) peek at Chapter 21, which contains the answers and explanations, or (c) call a friend to set up your weekend party schedule.

Answer Sheets

For Sections 1 through 4, use the ovals and grid-ins provided with this practice exam to record your answers. Begin with Number 1 for each new section. For the essay, write on four sheets of loose-leaf or notebook paper. Or you can use the following blank pages.

Section 1: Reading

1. Ⓐ Ⓑ Ⓒ Ⓓ   12. Ⓐ Ⓑ Ⓒ Ⓓ   23. Ⓐ Ⓑ Ⓒ Ⓓ   34. Ⓐ Ⓑ Ⓒ Ⓓ   45. Ⓐ Ⓑ Ⓒ Ⓓ
2. Ⓐ Ⓑ Ⓒ Ⓓ   13. Ⓐ Ⓑ Ⓒ Ⓓ   24. Ⓐ Ⓑ Ⓒ Ⓓ   35. Ⓐ Ⓑ Ⓒ Ⓓ   46. Ⓐ Ⓑ Ⓒ Ⓓ
3. Ⓐ Ⓑ Ⓒ Ⓓ   14. Ⓐ Ⓑ Ⓒ Ⓓ   25. Ⓐ Ⓑ Ⓒ Ⓓ   36. Ⓐ Ⓑ Ⓒ Ⓓ   47. Ⓐ Ⓑ Ⓒ Ⓓ
4. Ⓐ Ⓑ Ⓒ Ⓓ   15. Ⓐ Ⓑ Ⓒ Ⓓ   26. Ⓐ Ⓑ Ⓒ Ⓓ   37. Ⓐ Ⓑ Ⓒ Ⓓ   48. Ⓐ Ⓑ Ⓒ Ⓓ
5. Ⓐ Ⓑ Ⓒ Ⓓ   16. Ⓐ Ⓑ Ⓒ Ⓓ   27. Ⓐ Ⓑ Ⓒ Ⓓ   38. Ⓐ Ⓑ Ⓒ Ⓓ   49. Ⓐ Ⓑ Ⓒ Ⓓ
6. Ⓐ Ⓑ Ⓒ Ⓓ   17. Ⓐ Ⓑ Ⓒ Ⓓ   28. Ⓐ Ⓑ Ⓒ Ⓓ   39. Ⓐ Ⓑ Ⓒ Ⓓ   50. Ⓐ Ⓑ Ⓒ Ⓓ
7. Ⓐ Ⓑ Ⓒ Ⓓ   18. Ⓐ Ⓑ Ⓒ Ⓓ   29. Ⓐ Ⓑ Ⓒ Ⓓ   40. Ⓐ Ⓑ Ⓒ Ⓓ   51. Ⓐ Ⓑ Ⓒ Ⓓ
8. Ⓐ Ⓑ Ⓒ Ⓓ   19. Ⓐ Ⓑ Ⓒ Ⓓ   30. Ⓐ Ⓑ Ⓒ Ⓓ   41. Ⓐ Ⓑ Ⓒ Ⓓ   52. Ⓐ Ⓑ Ⓒ Ⓓ
9. Ⓐ Ⓑ Ⓒ Ⓓ   20. Ⓐ Ⓑ Ⓒ Ⓓ   31. Ⓐ Ⓑ Ⓒ Ⓓ   42. Ⓐ Ⓑ Ⓒ Ⓓ
10. Ⓐ Ⓑ Ⓒ Ⓓ   21. Ⓐ Ⓑ Ⓒ Ⓓ   32. Ⓐ Ⓑ Ⓒ Ⓓ   43. Ⓐ Ⓑ Ⓒ Ⓓ
11. Ⓐ Ⓑ Ⓒ Ⓓ   22. Ⓐ Ⓑ Ⓒ Ⓓ   33. Ⓐ Ⓑ Ⓒ Ⓓ   44. Ⓐ Ⓑ Ⓒ Ⓓ

Section 2: Mathematics — Calculator Section

1. Ⓐ Ⓑ Ⓒ Ⓓ   7. Ⓐ Ⓑ Ⓒ Ⓓ   13. Ⓐ Ⓑ Ⓒ Ⓓ   19. Ⓐ Ⓑ Ⓒ Ⓓ   25. Ⓐ Ⓑ Ⓒ Ⓓ
2. Ⓐ Ⓑ Ⓒ Ⓓ   8. Ⓐ Ⓑ Ⓒ Ⓓ   14. Ⓐ Ⓑ Ⓒ Ⓓ   20. Ⓐ Ⓑ Ⓒ Ⓓ   26. Ⓐ Ⓑ Ⓒ Ⓓ
3. Ⓐ Ⓑ Ⓒ Ⓓ   9. Ⓐ Ⓑ Ⓒ Ⓓ   15. Ⓐ Ⓑ Ⓒ Ⓓ   21. Ⓐ Ⓑ Ⓒ Ⓓ   27. Ⓐ Ⓑ Ⓒ Ⓓ
4. Ⓐ Ⓑ Ⓒ Ⓓ   10. Ⓐ Ⓑ Ⓒ Ⓓ   16. Ⓐ Ⓑ Ⓒ Ⓓ   22. Ⓐ Ⓑ Ⓒ Ⓓ   28. Ⓐ Ⓑ Ⓒ Ⓓ
5. Ⓐ Ⓑ Ⓒ Ⓓ   11. Ⓐ Ⓑ Ⓒ Ⓓ   17. Ⓐ Ⓑ Ⓒ Ⓓ   23. Ⓐ Ⓑ Ⓒ Ⓓ   29. Ⓐ Ⓑ Ⓒ Ⓓ
6. Ⓐ Ⓑ Ⓒ Ⓓ   12. Ⓐ Ⓑ Ⓒ Ⓓ   18. Ⓐ Ⓑ Ⓒ Ⓓ   24. Ⓐ Ⓑ Ⓒ Ⓓ   30. Ⓐ Ⓑ Ⓒ Ⓓ

31.   32.   33.   34.   35.

36.   37.   38.

Section 3: Writing and Language

1. Ⓐ Ⓑ Ⓒ Ⓓ   10. Ⓐ Ⓑ Ⓒ Ⓓ   19. Ⓐ Ⓑ Ⓒ Ⓓ   28. Ⓐ Ⓑ Ⓒ Ⓓ   37. Ⓐ Ⓑ Ⓒ Ⓓ
2. Ⓐ Ⓑ Ⓒ Ⓓ   11. Ⓐ Ⓑ Ⓒ Ⓓ   20. Ⓐ Ⓑ Ⓒ Ⓓ   29. Ⓐ Ⓑ Ⓒ Ⓓ   38. Ⓐ Ⓑ Ⓒ Ⓓ
3. Ⓐ Ⓑ Ⓒ Ⓓ   12. Ⓐ Ⓑ Ⓒ Ⓓ   21. Ⓐ Ⓑ Ⓒ Ⓓ   30. Ⓐ Ⓑ Ⓒ Ⓓ   39. Ⓐ Ⓑ Ⓒ Ⓓ
4. Ⓐ Ⓑ Ⓒ Ⓓ   13. Ⓐ Ⓑ Ⓒ Ⓓ   22. Ⓐ Ⓑ Ⓒ Ⓓ   31. Ⓐ Ⓑ Ⓒ Ⓓ   40. Ⓐ Ⓑ Ⓒ Ⓓ
5. Ⓐ Ⓑ Ⓒ Ⓓ   14. Ⓐ Ⓑ Ⓒ Ⓓ   23. Ⓐ Ⓑ Ⓒ Ⓓ   32. Ⓐ Ⓑ Ⓒ Ⓓ   41. Ⓐ Ⓑ Ⓒ Ⓓ
6. Ⓐ Ⓑ Ⓒ Ⓓ   15. Ⓐ Ⓑ Ⓒ Ⓓ   24. Ⓐ Ⓑ Ⓒ Ⓓ   33. Ⓐ Ⓑ Ⓒ Ⓓ   42. Ⓐ Ⓑ Ⓒ Ⓓ
7. Ⓐ Ⓑ Ⓒ Ⓓ   16. Ⓐ Ⓑ Ⓒ Ⓓ   25. Ⓐ Ⓑ Ⓒ Ⓓ   34. Ⓐ Ⓑ Ⓒ Ⓓ   43. Ⓐ Ⓑ Ⓒ Ⓓ
8. Ⓐ Ⓑ Ⓒ Ⓓ   17. Ⓐ Ⓑ Ⓒ Ⓓ   26. Ⓐ Ⓑ Ⓒ Ⓓ   35. Ⓐ Ⓑ Ⓒ Ⓓ   44. Ⓐ Ⓑ Ⓒ Ⓓ
9. Ⓐ Ⓑ Ⓒ Ⓓ   18. Ⓐ Ⓑ Ⓒ Ⓓ   27. Ⓐ Ⓑ Ⓒ Ⓓ   36. Ⓐ Ⓑ Ⓒ Ⓓ

Section 4: Mathematics — No-Calculator Section

1. Ⓐ Ⓑ Ⓒ Ⓓ   4. Ⓐ Ⓑ Ⓒ Ⓓ   7. Ⓐ Ⓑ Ⓒ Ⓓ   10. Ⓐ Ⓑ Ⓒ Ⓓ   13. Ⓐ Ⓑ Ⓒ Ⓓ
2. Ⓐ Ⓑ Ⓒ Ⓓ   5. Ⓐ Ⓑ Ⓒ Ⓓ   8. Ⓐ Ⓑ Ⓒ Ⓓ   11. Ⓐ Ⓑ Ⓒ Ⓓ   14. Ⓐ Ⓑ Ⓒ Ⓓ
3. Ⓐ Ⓑ Ⓒ Ⓓ   6. Ⓐ Ⓑ Ⓒ Ⓓ   9. Ⓐ Ⓑ Ⓒ Ⓓ   12. Ⓐ Ⓑ Ⓒ Ⓓ   15. Ⓐ Ⓑ Ⓒ Ⓓ

16.   17.   18.   19.   20.

(grid-in answer bubbles for questions 16–20)

Section 1: Reading

Time: 65 minutes for 52 questions

Directions: Choose the best answer to each question based on what is stated or implied in the passage. Mark the corresponding oval on the answer sheet.

Questions 1–10 refer to the following excerpt from David Copperfield, *by Charles Dickens.*

Line It was Miss Murdstone who was arrived, and a gloomy-looking lady she was; dark, like her
brother, whom she greatly resembled in face and voice; and with very heavy eyebrows,
nearly meeting over her large nose, as if, being disabled by the wrongs of her sex from wear-
ing whiskers, she had carried them to that account. She brought with her two uncompromis-
(05) ing hard black boxes, with her initials on the lids in hard brass nails. When she paid the
coachman she took her money out of a hard steel purse, and she kept the purse in a very jail
of a bag which hung upon her arm by a heavy chain, and shut up like a bite. I had never, at
that time, seen such a metallic lady altogether as Miss Murdstone was.

She was brought into the parlour with many tokens of welcome, and there formally recog-
(10) nized my mother as a new and near relation. Then she looked at me, and said, "Is that your
boy, sister-in-law?" My mother acknowledged me. "Generally speaking," said Miss
Murdstone, "I don't like boys. How d'ye do[1],boy?" Under these encouraging circumstances, I
replied that I was very well, and that I hoped she was the same; with such an indifferent
grace, that Miss Murdstone disposed of me in two words: "Wants manners!"

(15) Having uttered which, with great distinctness, she begged the favour of being shown to her
room, which became to me from that time forth a place of awe and dread, wherein the two
black boxes were never seen open or known to be left unlocked, and where (for I peeped in
once or twice when she was out) numerous little steel fetters and rivets, with which Miss
Murdstone embellished herself when she was dressed, generally hung upon the looking-
(20) glass in formidable array.

As well as I could make out, she had come for good, and had no intention of ever going
again. She began to "help" my mother next morning, and was in and out of the store-closet
all day, putting things to rights, and making havoc in the old arrangements. Almost the first
remarkable thing I observed in Miss Murdstone was, her being constantly haunted by a sus-
(25) picion that the servants had a man secreted somewhere on the premises. Under the influence of this delusion, she dived into the coal-cellar at the most untimely hours, and scarcely
ever opened the door of a dark cupboard without clapping it to again, in the belief that she
had got him. Though there was nothing very airy about Miss Murdstone, she was a perfect
Lark in point of getting up. She was up (and, as I believe to this hour, looking for that man)
(30) before anybody in the house was stirring. Peggotty gave it as her opinion that she even
slept with one eye open; but I could not concur in this idea; for I tried it myself after hearing
the suggestion thrown out, and found it couldn't be done.

1. A shortened form of "How do you do?"

Go on to next page

1. The narrator compares Miss Murdstone's eyebrows to

   (A) her brother

   (B) overweight people

   (C) boxes

   (D) men's whiskers

2. In Lines 4–8, Miss Murdstone is "a metallic lady" in the narrator's view for all the following reasons except

   (A) her nasty disposition

   (B) her boxes

   (C) her purse

   (D) her handbag

3. In the context of Line 4, "account" may best be defined as

   (A) story

   (B) version

   (C) reason

   (D) sum

4. In the context of Lines 13–14, "indifferent" may best be defined as

   (A) uncaring

   (B) mediocre

   (C) exceptional

   (D) unconventional

5. The narrator implies that in the future his relationship with Miss Murdstone

   (A) becomes more loving

   (B) pleases his mother

   (C) revolves around her search for a hidden man

   (D) is characterized by fear

6. Which lines provide the best evidence for the answer to Question 5?

   (A) Lines 9–10 ("She was brought . . . new and near relation.")

   (B) Lines 12–14 ("Under these encouraging . . . indifferent grace")

   (C) Line 16 ("which became to me . . . dread")

   (D) Lines 22–23 ("She began to 'help' . . . old arrangements.")

7. The word "help" is in quotation marks in Line 22 because

   (A) the author wants to add emphasis to the word

   (B) the word is a direct quotation from the narrator

   (C) the word is a direct quotation from Miss Murdstone

   (D) Miss Murdstone's actions aren't helpful

8. The interaction between the narrator and Peggotty

   (A) shows the ignorance of the narrator

   (B) characterizes Peggotty as ignorant

   (C) reveals antagonism between the narrator and Peggotty

   (D) exemplifies the narrator's inquisitive nature

9. Which lines provide the best evidence for the answer to Question 8?

   (A) Lines 21–22 ("As well as I could make out . . . going again.")

   (B) Lines 24–28 ("a suspicion that the servants . . . had got him")

   (C) Lines 28–29 ("Though there was nothing airy. . . getting up.")

   (D) Lines 31–32 ("I tried it myself . . . couldn't be done")

10. The tone of this passage may best be described as

    (A) nostalgic

    (B) authoritative

    (C) critical

    (D) regretful

Questions 11–21 refer to the following excerpt from a 1910 article entitled "Negro 'Suffrage' in a Democracy," by Ray Stannard Baker. **Note:** *"Suffrage" is the right to vote.*

Upon this question, we, as free citizens, have the absolute right to agree or disagree with the present laws regulating suffrage; and if we want more people brought in as partakers in government, or some people who are already in, barred (05)

Go on to next page ➡

out, we have a right to organize, to agitate, to do our best to change the laws. Powerful organizations of women are now agitating for the right to vote; there is an organization which
(10) demands suffrage for Chinese and Japanese who wish to become citizens. It is even conceivable that a society might be founded to lower the suffrage age-limit from twenty-one to nineteen years, thereby endowing a large number of young
(15) men with the privileges, and therefore the educational responsibilities, of political power. On the other hand, a large number of people, chiefly in our Southern States, earnestly believe that the right of the Negro to vote should be cur-
(20) tailed, or even abolished.

Thus we disagree, and government is the resultant of all these diverse views and forces. No one can say dogmatically how far democracy should go in distributing the enormously impor-
(25) tant powers of active government. Democracy is not a dogma[1]; it is not even a dogma of free suffrage. Democracy is a life, a spirit, a growth. The primal necessity of any sort of government, democracy or otherwise, whether it be more
(30) unjust or less unjust toward special groups of its citizens, is to exist, to be a going concern, to maintain upon the whole a stable and peaceful administration of affairs. If a democracy cannot provide such stability, then the people go back
(35) to some form of oligarchy[2]. Having secured a fair measure of stability, a democracy proceeds with caution toward the extension of the suffrage to more and more people — trying foreigners, trying women, trying Negroes.
(40) And no one can prophesy how far a democracy will ultimately go in the matter of suffrage. We know only the tendency. We know that in the beginning, even in America, the right to vote was a very limited matter. In the early years, in New
(45) England, only church-members voted; then the franchise[3] was extended to include property-owners; then it was enlarged to include all white adults; then to include Negroes; then, in several Western States, to include women.
(50) Thus the line has been constantly advancing, but with many fluctuations, eddies, and back-currents — like any other stream of progress. At the present time the fundamental principles which underlie popular government, and especially the
(55) whole matter of popular suffrage, are much in the public mind. The tendency of government throughout the entire civilized world is strongly in the direction of placing more and more power in the hands of the people. In our own country we
(60) are enacting a remarkable group of laws providing for direct primaries in the nomination of public officials, for direct election of United States Senators, and for direct legislation by means of the initiative and referendum; and we are even
(65) going to the point, in many cities, of permitting the

people to recall an elected official who is unsatisfactory. The principle of local option, which is nothing but that of direct government by the people, is being everywhere accepted.

1. System of belief not open to discussion. 2. Rule by a small group. 3. Right to vote.

11. What is the purpose of the first paragraph (Lines 1–20)?

    (A) to demand the right to vote for non-white citizens

    (B) to explain the constitution

    (C) to assert the right to criticize laws

    (D) to condemn organized protests

12. When the passage was written, all the following were barred from voting except

    (A) non-citizens

    (B) 20-year-old men

    (C) citizens of Chinese background

    (D) African American men

13. Which of the following lines support the answer to Question 12?

    (A) Lines 1–7 ("we, as free citizens . . . change the laws")

    (B) Lines 7–9 ("Powerful organizations . . . right to vote")

    (C) Lines 9–20 ("demands suffrage . . . abolished")

    (D) Lines 35–39 ("Having secured . . . Negroes.")

14. According to the author of this passage, which expression describes democracy?

    (A) a system in which all voices are equal

    (B) a process that allows disagreement

    (C) a peaceful government

    (D) the right to vote

15. With which of these statements would the author probably agree?

    (A) Power brings responsibility.

    (B) Laws should rarely be changed.

    (C) Voting restrictions are always wrong.

    (D) State officials are more important than ordinary citizens.

Go on to next page

16. Which lines provide the best evidence for the answer to Question 15?

    (A) Lines 3–6 ("if we want more people brought in . . . barred out")

    (B) Lines 12–16 ("lower the suffrage age-limit . . . political power")

    (C) Lines 21–25 ("Thus we disagree . . . active government.")

    (D) Lines 56–59 ("The tendency of government . . . power in the hands of the people.")

17. In the context of Lines 38–39, which is the best definition of "trying"?

    (A) experimenting with

    (B) attempting to reach

    (C) placing on trial

    (D) striving for

18. In the context of Line 42, which of the following best defines "tendency"?

    (A) way

    (B) goal

    (C) ability

    (D) trend

19. The extended metaphor of a "stream" in Lines 50–52 serves to

    (A) show that setbacks are a natural part of the process

    (B) criticize opposition to voting rights

    (C) praise those who work for voting rights

    (D) reveal the boundaries of voting rights

20. The author of this passage would most likely support which of the following?

    (A) required permits for protests against the government

    (B) strict rules for absentee ballots

    (C) petitions directed at elected officials

    (D) campaign finance laws

21. What is most likely the intended audience for this passage?

    (A) those who want to expand voting rights

    (B) those who question the suffrage movement

    (C) women

    (D) noncitizens

Questions 22–32 refer to the following passages and the accompanying chart. Passage I is excerpted from Bacteria: The Benign, the Bad, and the Beautiful *by Trudy M. Wassenaar (Wiley). Passage II is excerpted from an interview with Colleen Cavanaugh, a scientist who researches the partnerships between animals and bacteria on the ocean floor (from* Talking Science, *edited by Adam Hart-Davis and published by Wiley).*

Passage I

Every surface around us is covered with bacteria. One drop of seawater contains a minimum of one million bacterial cells, at least up to a depth of 200 meters; the number decreases by a factor of ten as one dives deeper. Bacteria live in (05) all depths of the water column, all the way down to the bottom of the ocean. One gram of soil also contains roughly 10 million bacterial cells, of types different from those found in seawater. Deeper soil will hold fewer bacteria, but no sur- (10) face on earth is naturally sterile, apart from places where temperatures soar, such as volcanoes. Add to the marine and soil bacteria those living in submerged sediments, another major habitat full of life, and one can estimate the total number of all (15) bacteria on earth at a given time. It results in a number written with 30 digits, give or take a digit.

If only we could see them without the necessity of a microscope! How practical it would be to be able to see the bacteria growing in a freshly (20) made dessert that had raw egg whites and sugar as the key ingredients and is now standing on the kitchen counter to set. One egg contained *Salmonella* bacteria, which feed on the sugar and start multiplying at the ambient temperature to (25) reach critical numbers in only a few hours, and which will make half of the dinner party guests ill. If only we could learn to recognize the dangerous ones, to avoid or kill them, and to leave the others alone. No longer would we need the (30) soaps, cleansers, toothbrushes, dishwashing or laundry detergents, hand lotions, and all the other products that the advertisements make us believe would be unsafe to use without the addition of antibacterial agents. Imagine we were (35) able to check the bacteria added to a health drink and they were all dead, and possibly useless, by the time the product was bought. Being able to see and recognize bacteria would tell us that, in most cases, such additions are com- (40) pletely unnecessary, even ineffective, or useless.

Go on to next page

Passage II

Some giant worms living near deep-sea vents in the ocean floor can grow up to two meters (about six feet) long. They look like long, very
(45) white tubes with red tips. They're made of material similar to your fingernails. The scientists had already established that the food chain was supported by bacteria living on pure chemicals. But these tube-worms were bizarre. Not only were
(50) they huge, but they also completely lacked mouths and guts. They had cousins the size of a piece of hair that had been shown to take up organic molecules as food through their skin. So that's what the scientists assumed the tube-
(55) worms were doing.

I saw a slide of a trophosome, brown spongy tissue, from a tube-worm. . . . When a scientist was dissecting the tissue, he discovered a lot of white crystals, which turned out to be pure, ele-
(60) mental sulphur. This is where I jumped up and said, "Whoa! It's perfectly clear. There must be sulphur-oxidizing bacteria that can use the hydrogen sulphide that's in the water from the vents, and react it with oxygen, and get energy
(65) from that reaction." In other words, there must be symbiotic[1] bacteria within the tissue that are feeding the animals." They would be similar to algae — the photosynthetic organisms[2] that live in coral and feed the coral internally. But the

scientist said, "No, no. Sit down, kid. We think
(70) it's a detoxifying organ. Hydrogen sulphide is a potent toxin. It binds to your hemoglobin.[3] Hydrogen sulphide is as toxic as cyanide[4]."

He continued, "We think it's a detoxifying organ, and it's oxidizing sulphide to elemental
(75) sulphur, which is nontoxic." And I said, "Well, that's fine. But if you have bacteria doing the sulphide oxidation, they can detoxify the sulphide, make energy, and fix carbon dioxide, and feed this mouthless, gutless animal." Eventually I was
(80) able to convince him, and he sent me a small piece of tissue to examine for the presence of bacteria.

[Another scientist] found a substance that is only known to occur in organisms that are auto-
(85) trophic — that is, self-feeding. They can take carbon dioxide out of water or the air and fix it into organic molecules to be used as food. So to me, finding it in the animal tissue was a clincher. And together we wrote a series of papers
(90) establishing that there was this symbiosis — interdependence — between bacteria and these giant tube-worms.

1. Organisms in interdependent relationships.
2. Organisms that combine water, carbon dioxide, and sunlight and convert them into oxygen and food.
3. A substance in red blood cells that transports oxygen.
4. A deadly poison.

United States: Bacterial Infections from Food Sources, rate per 100,000 population

Bacteria	2011	2012	2013	Goal for 2020
Salmonella	16.47	16.42	15.9	11.4
E-coli	0.98	1.12	1.15	0.6
Campylobacter	14.31	14.30	13.82	8.5

Source: US Centers for Disease Control (http://www.cdc.gov)

22. According to Passage I, which statement is true?

(A) Bacteria are present in nearly every part of the earth.

(B) The number of bacteria present under the earth increases as the distance from the surface increases.

(C) Bacteria exist everywhere on earth.

(D) The number of bacteria on earth can be counted accurately.

23. Which lines support the answer to Question 22?

(A) Lines 1–2 ("Every surface . . . with bacteria.")

(B) Line 10 ("Deeper soil will hold fewer bacteria")

(C) Lines 10–12 ("no surface . . . such as volcanoes")

(D) Lines 16–17 ("It results in a number . . . take a digit.")

Go on to next page

24. In the context of Line 14, what is "another major habitat"?

    (A) the ocean

    (B) dirt

    (C) all underwater areas

    (D) soil that is underwater

25. According to the information in Passage I and the graph, which statement is not true?

    (A) Salmonella may be present in raw eggs.

    (B) Salmonella-related infections have been increasing.

    (C) Anti-bacterial cleaners may kill Salmonella.

    (D) Salmonella bacteria grow at room temperature.

26. With which statement would the author of Passage I most likely agree?

    (A) Antibacterial household products are not really necessary.

    (B) Harmful bacteria cannot be identified.

    (C) Homeowners should buy microscopes.

    (D) Eggs are not safe.

27. According to Passage II, tube-worms are "bizarre" (Line 49) because they

    (A) live on pure chemicals

    (B) are found in extreme conditions

    (C) have no digestive organs

    (D) take in food through their skin

28. According to Passage II, living beings receive nourishment in all these ways except

    (A) through the skin

    (B) by mouth

    (C) from chemicals

    (D) directly from oxygen

29. In the context of Line 64, what is the best definition of "react"?

    (A) mix

    (B) behave as

    (C) process

    (D) answer

30. According to Passage II, bacteria in tube-worms are similar to the algae mentioned in Line 68 because both

    (A) create nourishment within other organisms

    (B) need sunlight to survive

    (C) nourish coral

    (D) detoxify oxygen

31. With which statement would the authors of both passages probably agree?

    (A) Bacteria should be destroyed whenever possible.

    (B) Bacteria can be easily managed.

    (C) Bacteria are sometimes beneficial.

    (D) No one understands much about bacteria.

32. The best evidence for the answer to Question 31 is

    (A) Lines 10–11 ("no surface on earth is naturally sterile") and Lines 50–51 ("also completely lacked mouths and guts")

    (B) Lines 19–22 ("How practical . . . key ingredients") and Line 73 ("Hydrogen sulphide is as toxic as cyanide")

    (C) Lines 35–37 ("Imagine we were . . . to a health drink") and Lines 91–93 ("this symbiosis . . . giant tube-worms")

    (D) Lines 40–41 ("such additions . . . or useless") and Lines 86–88 ("They can take carbon dioxide out of the air . . . used as food.")

Go on to next page

Questions 33–42 refer to the following excerpt and chart from Small Loans, Big Dreams by Alex Counts (Wiley). This passage focuses on the work of Mohammed Yunus, an economist and banker from Bangladesh who created the Grameen Bank to give small loans to those too poor to qualify for traditional loans.

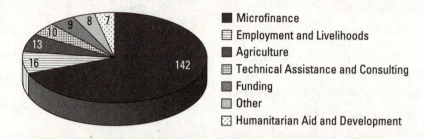

- ■ Microfinance
- ▤ Employment and Livelihoods
- ■ Agriculture
- ▦ Technical Assistance and Consulting
- ■ Funding
- ▨ Other
- ⠇ Humanitarian Aid and Development

This chart shows types of organizations that use a statistical tool created by the Grameen Foundation called the "Progress out of Poverty Index" to measure the effectiveness of antipoverty initiatives.

Line

The genius of Muhammed Yunus's work is not that he figured out how to empower poor people with loans, but that he was able to develop a model that he could replicate more
(05) than a thousand times while maintaining control over the quality of the enterprise. The difference is critical to understanding the implications of what he has accomplished. One branch can serve 2,000 people, whereas a thousand
(10) branches can serve 2 million. It takes an entirely different set of skills to start a pilot project than it does to successfully franchise it. Pilot projects reach hundreds of poor people; franchises can touch millions.

(15) In circles where poverty and environmental issues are discussed, one often hears the comment "Small is beautiful." Tiny programs tailored to local needs are romanticized, while anything big — governments, corporations, even large
(20) nonprofit organizations — is distrusted. Rarely is it considered that while small may often be beautiful, small is, after all, still small. A world in which thousands of successful pilot projects reach a tiny percentage of the world's poor, and
(25) leave the vast majority untouched, is a world where mass poverty is destined to persist and deepen.

It is hardly an exaggeration to say that nearly every major problem facing the world has
(30) several solutions that have been proven effective on a small scale. But only if the best of those projects can be replicated or franchised, and expanded while maintaining reasonably high quality, will there be hope for resolving the inter-
(35) connected mesh of social, environmental, and economic injustices that are tearing at the insides of humanity.

Muhammed Yunus has demonstrated that large-scale replication of an effective antipoverty strategy can be both successful and profitable. (40) He resisted the temptation to keep Grameen small (and easily controlled by him), and in the process reached 2 million borrowers, created a decentralized management structure, and trained a workforce of 11,000 people. Doing so (45) has not always been easy. Striking the right balance between keeping all Grameen branches similar while allowing for innovation and experimentation came after years of trial and error. The conditions that gave rise to wide- (50) spread employee discontent in 1991 were a result of bigness, and so was the gradual decline in the zealousness with which some employees carried out their duties.

Fueling the aggressive expansion program (55) was the managing director's faith in the ability of people to use credit well even when they were not directly supervised by him. Many Grameen critics predicted disaster when Yunus was not there to monitor everything, but their fears have (60) proven largely unfounded. Bangladeshis, long portrayed as lacking the skills for middle management and business ownership, have demonstrated those abilities as Grameen staff and borrowers. (65)

Other poverty-focused credit programs in Bangladesh, many of them Grameen imitators, now reach 2.5 million *additional* families. Furthermore, Grameen replication programs in other Third World countries now reach tens of (70)

Go on to next page ➡

thousands of people, and many projects are grow-ing rapidly. Each month, dozens of people from other developing countries come to Bangladesh to learn how Grameen works so that they can
(75) start similar projects after returning home.

For many years, one of the most serious crit-icisms of Grameen was that credit was not the magic bullet that some accused Yunus as touting it to be. The problem of poverty, critics argued,
(80) was complex, and needed a solution that took into account not only its financial dimensions, but also things like ignorance, political power-lessness, and ill health. Other programs that pro-vided credit, for example, required that
(85) borrowers undergo a six-month course on liter-acy and political organizing before they were allowed to take a loan. Experts scoffed at Grameen's requiring as little as seven hours of training before releasing loans to borrowers. The
(90) conventional wisdom questioned whether poor, uneducated people knew what to do with small loans without more guidance from above.

Yunus rejected these ideas. He admitted that poverty was a multifaceted problem, but he did
(95) not believe it necessarily needed a multifaceted solution. The poor, he argued, already had skills, were already politically conscious, and were already aware of the need for schooling and taking care of their health. It was first and fore-
(100) most their lack of income that made using their skills impossible. Providing investment capital for additional income generation, he asserted, would unlock the capacity of poor people to solve many, if not all, of the manifestations of
(105) poverty that affected their lives.

33. As used in Line 11, "pilot project" is best defined by which other phrase from the passage?

    (A) "a model that he could replicate more than a thousand times" (Lines 4–5)

    (B) "Tiny programs tailored to local needs" (Lines 17–18)

    (C) "a tiny percentage of the world's poor" (Line 24)

    (D) "solutions that have been proven effec-tive on a small scale" (Lines 30–31)

34. The author's objections to pilot projects include all the following except that they

    (A) involve too few people

    (B) often apply only to a specific situation

    (C) can't be reproduced

    (D) are too expensive

35. The comment that "Tiny programs . . . are romanticized" implies that such programs

    (A) aren't evaluated fairly

    (B) bring people together

    (C) are seen as impractical

    (D) can accomplish more than programs with more limited goals

36. With which statement would the author of the passage most likely agree?

    (A) Poverty causes environmental problems.

    (B) Poor people are unjustly deprived in several different ways.

    (C) Wealthy people look down upon the poor.

    (D) Economic troubles should be solved through the justice system.

37. Which lines provide support for the answer to Question 36?

    (A) Lines 12–14 ("Pilot projects reach hundreds . . . touch millions")

    (B) Lines 34–36 ("the interconnected mesh . . . injustices")

    (C) Lines 46–50 ("Striking the right balance . . . trial and error")

    (D) Lines 101–105 ("Providing investment capital for . . . affected their lives")

38. The author of this passage would most likely agree that

    (A) Progress in antipoverty programs is nearly impossible.

    (B) Only microfinance data is relevant to antipoverty work.

    (C) Antipoverty work is too complex to be measured.

    (D) Successful interventions to reduce poverty can be measured.

Go on to next page

39. Lines 50–54 ("the conditions that gave rise to . . . their duties")

    (A) indicate that Yunus's critics were correct when they "predicted disaster" (Line 59)

    (B) are an example of the "trial and error" mentioned in Lines 49–50

    (C) show that the "managing director's faith in the ability of people to use credit well" (Lines 56–57) was misplaced

    (D) reveal the need for Yunus "to monitor everything" (Line 60)

40. The critics of the Grameen Bank most likely favor programs that focus on which of the following?

    I. Better education

    II. Universal healthcare

    III. Political power for the poor

    (A) I only

    (B) II only

    (C) III only

    (D) all of the above

41. Which lines support the answer to Question 40?

    (A) Lines 28–30 ("It is hardly an exaggeration . . . have been proven effective")

    (B) Lines 50–54 ("The conditions that gave rise . . . carried out their duties")

    (C) Lines 79–83 ("The problem of poverty . . . and ill health")

    (D) Lines 96–99 ("The poor, he argued . . . health")

42. In the context of Line 97, what is the best definition of "conscious"?

    (A) aware

    (B) alert

    (C) awake

    (D) deliberate

Questions 43–52 refer to the following passage from a recent book, Freud: Darkness in the Midst of Vision *by Louis Breger (Wiley). It discusses the work of Jean-Marie Charcot, a psychologist, and the condition of hysteria.*

By the late 1880s, Charcot had turned his attention to hysteria, and it was here that his need for power and control most interfered with his scientific aims. Hysteria — from the Greek word for "womb" — was a little understood condition, sometimes believed to be no more than malingering. It was stigmatized by the medical establishment and associated with witchcraft and medieval states of possession. Hysterical patients displayed a variety of symptoms including amnesias, paralyses, spasms, involuntary movements, and anesthesias. Closely related were cases of so-called neurasthenia, characterized by weakness and lassitude. Unlike the neurological conditions that Charcot had previously studied, no anatomical basis could be found for these syndromes. Looking back from today's vantage point, it is doubtful if there ever was a single entity that could be described as hysteria. The diagnosis was, rather, a grab bag for a variety of conditions whose common feature was that they were "psychological," that no discernable physical causes could be found for them. From a modern standpoint, the so-called hysterics comprised a diverse group: some probably had medical conditions that were undiagnosable at the time, others psychotic and borderline disorders, and many — it seems clear from the descriptions — suffered from severe anxiety, depression, the effects of a variety of traumas, and dissociated states.

Charcot made crucial contributions to the understanding of hysteria, clarifying the psychological-traumatic nature of symptoms and conducting convincing hypnotic demonstrations. In addition to the so-called hysterical women on the wards of the [hospital], there were a number of persons of both sexes who had been involved in accidents — for example, train wrecks — who displayed symptoms such as paralyses after the accident. Some of them were classified as cases of "railway spine" and "railway brain" because their symptoms mimicked those found after spinal cord or brain injuries. Physicians debated, with much fervor, whether these conditions had a physical basis. Charcot studied several such patients and was able to demonstrate the absence of damage to the nervous system, hence

Line

(05)

(10)

(15)

(20)

(25)

(30)

(35)

(40)

(45)

Go on to next page ⇨

proving the psychological nature of the symp-
(50) toms. His most convincing demonstration relied
on the use of hypnosis, a procedure which he
had rehabilitated and made scientifically respectable. He was able to hypnotize subjects and suggest that when they awoke from their trances
(55) their limbs would be paralyzed. These hypnoti-
cally induced symptoms were exactly the same
as those of both hysterical patients and the victims of accidents. He was also able to remove
such symptoms with hypnotic suggestion. In a
(60) related demonstration, he was able to distinguish
between hysterical and organic amnesia, using
hypnosis to help patients recover lost memories,
which was not possible, of course, when the
amnesia was based on the destruction of brain
(65) tissue. While these demonstrations established
the psychological nature of hysterical symptoms,
it was a psychology without awareness. The
patients were not conscious, either of the origin
and nature of their symptoms — they were not
(70) malingering or deliberately faking — or of their
reactions to the hypnotic suggestions. Charcot
spoke of a post-traumatic "hypnoid state" —
what today would be called dissociation — the
blotting out of consciousness of events and emo-
(75) tions associated with traumatic events.

　　Charcot's genuine contributions were
several. He made hysteria a respectable subject
of scientific study, described and classified syndromes on the basis of symptoms, and
(80) differentiated the condition from known neurological diseases. By documenting a number of
cases of male hysteria, he disproved the old link
between the condition and the organs of female
sexuality. He reestablished hypnotism as a
(85) research tool and showed how it could be
employed to induce and remove hysterical and
post-traumatic symptoms. Finally, and perhaps
most significant in terms of its long-range importance for Freud, all these findings and demon-
(90) strations gave evidence of an unconscious mind.

43. The author cites all the following conditions as hysterical except

(A) amnesia

(B) inability to move

(C) uncontrolled bodily activity

(D) wild laughter

44. The meaning of "psychological" (Line 49) in
this context may best be described as

(A) mentally ill

(B) requiring psychotherapy

(C) not arising from a physical condition

(D) the result of childhood events

45. According to the passage, Charcot

(A) linked hysteria to disturbing events in
the patient's life

(B) cured hysteria

(C) understood that hysteria was actually a
group of illnesses, not one condition

(D) relied primarily on drug therapy for his
patients

46. Which lines best support the answer to
Question 45?

(A) Lines 4–7 ("Hysteria — from the Greek
word . . . malingering.")

(B) Lines 20–23 ("The diagnosis was,
rather, a grab bag . . . found for them.")

(C) Lines 37–50 ("a number of persons of
both sexes . . . psychological nature of
the symptoms")

(D) Lines 77–81 ("He made hysteria a
respectable subject . . . diseases.")

47. The author probably mentions patients "of
both sexes" (Line 38)

(A) to counter the idea that only females
become hysterical

(B) to be fair to both male and female
patients

(C) to indicate that Charcot treated only
women

(D) to show that Charcot treated everyone
who asked

48. "Railway spine" and "railway brain"
(Line 42) are

(A) injuries resulting from train accidents

(B) terms once used for conditions resembling paralysis and head injuries

(C) physical injuries that take a psychological toll

(D) states displayed only under hypnosis

Go on to next page

49. Charcot used hypnosis for all the following except

    (A) to distinguish between physical and psychological symptoms

    (B) to enable a patient to move body parts that were previously immobile

    (C) to restore memories to some patients

    (D) to retrieve memories from brain-damaged patients

50. In the context of Line 61, what is the best definition of "organic"?

    (A) physical

    (B) natural

    (C) mental

    (D) psychological

51. Based on information in the passage, the author of this passage would probably agree with which of the following statements?

    (A) Hysteria is best treated with hypnosis.

    (B) Hysterics should not be treated medically.

    (C) Hysteria is always linked to severe physical danger, such as a train wreck.

    (D) To scientists today, hysteria is a meaningless term.

52. Which lines best support the answer to Question 51?

    (A) Lines 1–4 ("By the late 1880s . . . his scientific aims.")

    (B) Lines 24–31 ("From a modern standpoint . . . dissociated states.")

    (C) Lines 55–58 ("These hypnotically induced symptoms . . . accidents.")

    (D) Lines 81–84 ("By documenting a number of cases . . . female sexuality.")

STOP DO NOT TURN THE PAGE UNTIL TOLD TO DO SO. DO NOT RETURN TO A PREVIOUS TEST.

Section 2: Mathematics — Calculator Section

Time: 55 minutes for 38 questions

Directions: This section contains two different types of questions. For Questions 1–30, choose the best answer to each question and darken the corresponding oval on the answer sheet. For Questions 31–38, follow the separate directions provided before those questions.

Notes:

✔ You may use a calculator.

✔ All numbers used in this exam are real numbers.

✔ All figures lie in a plane.

✔ All figures may be assumed to be to scale unless the problem specifically indicates otherwise.

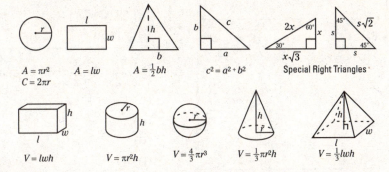

$A = \pi r^2$
$C = 2\pi r$ $A = lw$ $A = \frac{1}{2}bh$ $c^2 = a^2 + b^2$ Special Right Triangles

$V = lwh$ $V = \pi r^2 h$ $V = \frac{4}{3}\pi r^3$ $V = \frac{1}{3}\pi r^2 h$ $V = \frac{1}{3}lwh$

1. In a 28-student class, the ratio of boys to girls is 3:4. How many girls are there in the class?

   (A) 4

   (B) 9

   (C) 12

   (D) 16

2. If $f(x) = 2x^4$, then $f(-2) =$

   (A) −256

   (B) −32

   (C) 32

   (D) 256

3. In a drawer are seven pairs of white socks, nine pairs of black socks, and six pairs of brown socks. Getting dressed in a hurry, Josh pulls out a pair at a time and tosses them on the floor if they are not the color he wants. Looking for a brown pair, Josh pulls out and discards a white pair, a black pair, another black pair, and another white pair. What is the probability that on his next reach into the drawer he will pull out a brown pair of socks?

   (A) $\frac{1}{3}$

   (B) $\frac{3}{11}$

   (C) $\frac{6}{17}$

   (D) $\frac{7}{18}$

Go on to next page

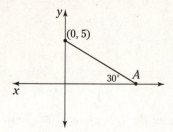

4. What are the coordinates of point A in the diagram above?

    (A) $(0,10)$

    (B) $(5,0)$

    (C) $(5\sqrt{3},0)$

    (D) $(10\sqrt{3},0)$

5. Evaluate $\left(4^0 + 64^{1/2}\right)^{-2}$

    (A) –81

    (B) $\dfrac{1}{81}$

    (C) $\dfrac{1}{6}$

    (D) 3

6. The ratio of Dora's money to Lisa's money is 7:5. If Dora has $24 more than Lisa, how much does Dora have?

    (A) $10

    (B) $14

    (C) $60

    (D) $84

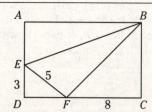

7. Given that $ABCD$ is a rectangle, and triangle BCF is isosceles, find the length of the line segment BE in this diagram.

    (A) 10

    (B) 11

    (C) 12

    (D) 13

8. On a number line, point A is at –4, and point B is at 8. Where would a point be placed $\dfrac{1}{4}$ of the distance from A to B?

    (A) –2

    (B) –1

    (C) 1

    (D) 2

9. A batch of mixed nuts was created by adding 5 pounds of peanuts, costing $5.50 per pound, to 2 pounds of cashews, costing $12.50 per pound. What would be the cost, per pound, of the resulting mixture?

    (A) $7.35

    (B) $7.50

    (C) $9.00

    (D) $10.50

10. If $\dfrac{x-1}{x-2} = \dfrac{x+7}{x+2}$, then x equals:

    (A) 1

    (B) 2

    (C) 3

    (D) 4

11. Let $*x$ be defined as $x+3$ if x is prime and $2x$ if x is composite. Which of the following would produce a result of 18?

    I. $*15$

    II. $*9$

    III. $*36$

    (A) I only

    (B) II only

    (C) both I and II

    (D) both II and III

12. The volume of a gas, V, in cubic centimeters (cc), is directly proportional to its temperature, T, in Kelvins (K). If a gas has a volume of 31.5 cc at 210 K, then its volume at 300 K would be

    (A) 121.5 cc

    (B) 49 cc

    (C) 45 cc

    (D) 22.05 cc

Go on to next page

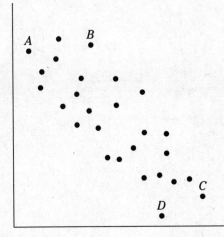

13. If the data in the scatter plot above were approximated by a linear function, the line would come closest to which pair of points?

    (A) *A* and *B*

    (B) *A* and *C*

    (C) *B* and *C*

    (D) *C* and *D*

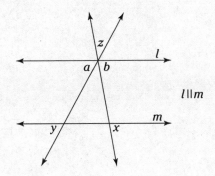

$l \| m$

14. In the above diagram, $x = 70°$ and $y = 30°$. The sum $a + b + z$ equals

    (A) 90°

    (B) 100°

    (C) 120°

    (D) 180°

15. In a sequence of evenly spaced numbers, the first term is 7, and the 20th term is 159. The fourth term of the sequence would be

    (A) 32

    (B) 31

    (C) 30

    (D) 29

Go on to next page

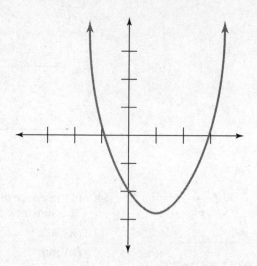

16. This graph represents a function, $f(x)$. Which of the following graphs could represent $f(x+4)$?

(A)

(B)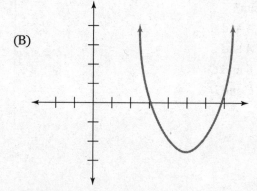

(C)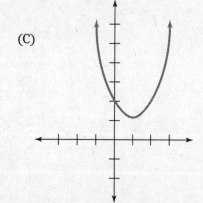

(D)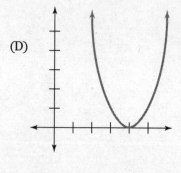

Go on to next page

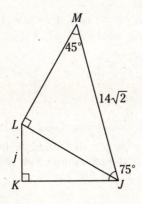

17. In this diagram, the measure of side j is

(A) 7

(B) $7\sqrt{2}$

(C) $7\sqrt{3}$

(D) 14

18. In a class of 100 students, 65 take Spanish, 32 take art, and 14 take both Spanish and art. How many students do not take either Spanish or art?

(A) 3

(B) 11

(C) 17

(D) 35

19. Max has three hours to study for his tests the next day. He decides to spend k percent of this time studying for math. Which of the following represents the number of minutes he will spend studying for math?

(A) $\dfrac{k}{300}$

(B) $\dfrac{3k}{100}$

(C) $\dfrac{100k}{180}$

(D) $\dfrac{180k}{100}$

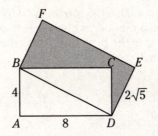

20. Given that $ABCD$ and $BDEF$ are rectangles, find the shaded area in this diagram.

(A) 24

(B) $16\sqrt{5}$

(C) 20

(D) $8\sqrt{5}$

21. A 26-inch-diameter bicycle wheel rotates a half turn. What is the exact distance traveled, in inches, of the logo printed on the edge of the wheel?

(A) 26π

(B) 13π

(C) 6.5π

(D) 3.25π

22. Find x if $2(x+4)=6$.

(A) –1

(B) 0

(C) 1

(D) 2

23. A certain radioactive element has a half-life of 20 years. Thus, a sample of 100 grams deposited in 1980 would have decayed to 50 grams by 2000 and to 25 grams by 2020. How much of this sample would remain in 2100?

(A) $\dfrac{25}{16}$ grams

(B) $\dfrac{25}{8}$ grams

(C) $\dfrac{25}{4}$ grams

(D) $\dfrac{25}{2}$ grams

Go on to next page

24. Set S contains the numbers 20 to 40, inclusive. If a number is chosen at random from S, what is the probability that the number is even?

    (A) $\dfrac{1}{2}$

    (B) $\dfrac{10}{21}$

    (C) $\dfrac{11}{21}$

    (D) $\dfrac{11}{20}$

25. The number n satisfies the following properties:

    It has three digits.

    Its units digit is the sum of its tens digit and its hundreds digit.

    It is a perfect square.

    Which number could be n?

    (A) 156

    (B) 400

    (C) 484

    (D) 729

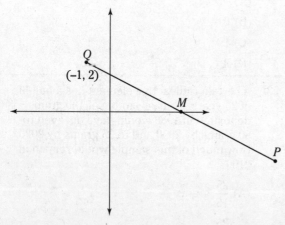

26. In this figure, the slope of line m is $-\dfrac{1}{3}$, and M is the midpoint of the line PQ. What are the coordinates of point P?

    (A) $(8, -1)$

    (B) $(9, -1)$

    (C) $(10, -2)$

    (D) $(11, -2)$

27. If $ab = n$, $b + c = x$, and $n \neq 0$, which of the following must equal n?

    (A) $ax + c$

    (B) $ax - c$

    (C) $ax + ac$

    (D) $ax - cx$

28. The number g is divisible by 3 but not by 9. Which of the following could be the remainder when $7g$ is divided by 9?

    (A) 0

    (B) 2

    (C) 4

    (D) 6

29. If $a > 0$, which of the following statements must be true?

    (A) $a^2 > a$

    (B) $a > \dfrac{1}{a}$

    (C) $2a > a$

    (D) $\dfrac{1}{a} < 1$

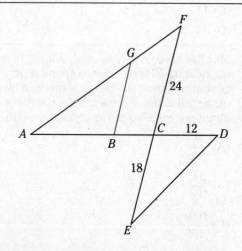

30. In this diagram, $AF \parallel ED$, $GB \parallel EF$, and $AG = GF$. What is the length of AB?

    (**Note:** Figure not drawn to scale.)

    (A) 18

    (B) 16

    (C) 12

    (D) 8

Go on to next page

Directions for Questions 31–38. Solve the problem and then write your answer in the box provided on the answer sheet. Mark the ovals corresponding to the answer, as shown in the following example. Note the fraction line and the decimal points.

Answer: 7/2   Answer: 3.25   Answer: 853

Write your answer in the box. You may start your answer in any column.

Although you do not have to write the solutions in the boxes, you do have to blacken the corresponding ovals. You should fill in the boxes to avoid confusion. Only the blackened ovals will be scored. The numbers in the boxes will not be read.

There are no negative answers.

Mixed numbers, such as $3\frac{1}{2}$, may be gridded in as a decimal (3.5) or as a fraction (7/2). Do not grid in $3\frac{1}{2}$; it will be read as 31/2.

Grid in a decimal as far as possible. Do not round it.

A question may have more than one answer. Grid in only one answer.

31. Darren receives $9 an hour for his after-school job, but gets paid $1\frac{1}{2}$ times this rate for each hour he works on a weekend. If he worked 18 hours one week and received $189, how many of these hours did he work during the weekends?

32. In a school survey, 40% of all students chose history as their favorite subject; 25% chose English; and 14 students chose some other subject as their favorite. How many students were surveyed?

33. Find the value of x that satisfies $\sqrt{4x-8}+1=7$.

34. For all numbers p and q, where $p \ne 4$, let $p \therefore q$ be defined as $\dfrac{pq}{p-4}$. For what value of p does $p \therefore 7 = 21$?

35. The ratio of a rectangle's width to its length is 2:5. If its perimeter is 84 feet, find its width, in feet.

36. To rent a private party room in a restaurant, there is a fixed cost plus an additional fee per person. If the cost of a party of 8 is $270 and the cost of a party of 10 is $320, find the cost, in dollars, of a party of 18.

Questions 37 and 38 are based on the following information. Tom invested $1,200 into two accounts. One account yields 5 percent simple annual interest, and the other yields 7 percent simple annual interest.

37. If after exactly one year, the two investments yielded a total of $74 in interest, how much, in dollars, was invested into the account earning 5 percent interest? Ignore the dollar sign when gridding your answer.

38. If Tom wants his investment to yield a total of $160 in interest over a period of exactly two years, how much, in dollars, must he transfer from the account yielding 5 percent to the account yielding 7 percent? Ignore the dollar sign when gridding your answer.

STOP DO NOT TURN THE PAGE UNTIL TOLD TO DO SO. DO NOT RETURN TO A PREVIOUS TEST.

Section 3: Writing and Language

Time: 35 minutes for 44 questions

Directions: Some sentences or portions of sentences are underlined and identified with numbers. In the questions, you see differing versions of the underlined material. Choose the best answer to each question based on what is stated or implied in the passage and accompanying visual elements. Mark the corresponding oval on the answer sheet.

Passage 1

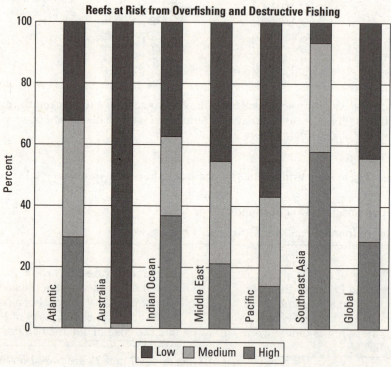

Source: World Resources Institute, Reefs at Risk Revisited, 2011

Coral reefs are large underwater structures, usually in shallow water near [1] coastlines, they are made up of thousands upon thousands of tiny marine animals. A single coral, which is known as a polyp, ingests still smaller marine creatures. A coral has no internal bones but rather an exoskeleton, [2] which is a hard structure outside its body. When you see a coral reef, [3] your looking at a colony that may be centuries old.

More than 10% of the coral reefs on earth [4] had died in the last few decades. About 30% more are so damaged that they may also [5] conclude within ten or twenty years. [6] Doing nothing to slow the destruction of coral, by 2050 about 60% of the earth's coral will be dead. Who should care about the death of a coral reef? Just scientists, environmental activists, or scuba divers? Actually, all of us should care. Coral reefs cover less than 0.2% of the oceans, but [7] they contain fish species. Reefs protect the coastline from storms. Worldwide, about 450 million people live near coral reefs, and most make their living or are supplied with food directly or indirectly [8] stemming from coral reefs.

Go on to next page

Dr. David Vaughan, a scientist at the Mote Tropical Research Laboratory in Key West, Florida. Dr. Vaughan discovered a technique called microfragmenting. By "seeding" small stone or ceramic disks with 1.5 inch fragments of coral cut from a healthy reef and [9] then he was adding nutrients, Dr. Vaughan has been able to coax the fragments to grow about 25 times faster than they would in the wild. [10] Massive coral that usually makes up the bulk of a reef usually grows about two inches a year. With microfragmentation, some species of coral have grown at 50 times their normal rate! Returned to the ocean, these bits of coral spread across a dead or dying reef and continue to grow there, reviving the reef.

Of course, the destruction of coral must be addressed in other ways, mainly by changing conditions that kill coral in the first place. Global warming has raised the average temperature of the ocean and helped to increase the water's acidity; furthermore, seawater is increasingly polluted by run-off from coastal settlements. Species of fish that are beneficial to a reef's ecosystem have been overfished. Dr. Vaughan's discovery is part of the answer. [11] Every nation must also address overfishing, because damage to coral is spread evenly around the globe.

1. (A) NO CHANGE
   (B) coastlines,
   (C) coastlines. They are
   (D) coastlines which are

2. (A) NO CHANGE
   (B) which an exoskeleton is
   (C) being that is a
   (D) defined as being a

3. (A) NO CHANGE
   (B) you're
   (C) you
   (D) your'

4. (A) NO CHANGE
   (B) were dying
   (C) has died
   (D) have died

5. (A) NO CHANGE
   (B) terminate
   (C) expire
   (D) become void

6. (A) NO CHANGE
   (B) If we do nothing to slow the destruction of coral,
   (C) If no one does nothing to slow the destruction of coral,
   (D) The destruction of coral having done nothing to slow,

7. (A) NO CHANGE
   (B) Delete the underlined material.
   (C) Insert the number of species.
   (D) Define species.

8. (A) NO CHANGE
   (B) coming out of
   (C) originating by way of
   (D) from

9. (A) NO CHANGE
   (B) then adding
   (C) having added then
   (D) he, then adding,

10. (A) NO CHANGE
    (B) Place the sentence at the end of the paragraph.
    (C) Place the sentence at the beginning of the paragraph.
    (D) Delete the sentence.

11. (A) NO CHANGE
    (B) Because damage to coral is spread evenly around the globe, every nation must also address overfishing.
    (C) Although damage to coral from improper fishing is not spread evenly around the globe, every nation must also address this destructive practice.
    (D) With the fact that damage to coral is worldwide, every nation must also address overfishing.

Go on to next page

Passage II

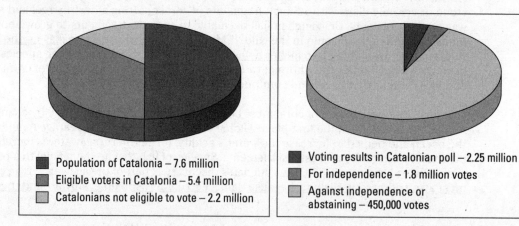

Population of Catalonia – 7.6 million
Eligible voters in Catalonia – 5.4 million
Catalonians not eligible to vote – 2.2 million

Voting results in Catalonian poll – 2.25 million
For independence – 1.8 million votes
Against independence or abstaining – 450,000 votes

[12] To separate and to join, these two things are the impulses that drive human behavior on an individual level and on a national level. On a personal level, people are drawn to form groups and partnerships as well as to create a unique identity and personality. On a global stage, throughout history, countries and empires have formed, broken apart, and then sometimes reconsolidated. Recently, separatism seems to be on the rise. The former Soviet Union [13] fell apart in 1991, what had been one country changed into fifteen independent nations. In the same time period in Eastern Europe, some nations, such as Czechoslovakia and Yugoslavia, divided into smaller units. The Czech Republic and Slovakia were created from the former Czechoslovakia, and Yugoslavia dissolved into Croatia, Slovenia, Montenegro, and other countries.

[14] In 2014, residents of two different countries voted on the question of staying as part of a larger entity or [15] to form an independent nation. In September, Scottish citizens voted to [16] retain themselves as part of Great Britain. [17]

[18] Two months later, citizens of Catalonia, an autonomous region of Spain, overwhelmingly favored independence. Catalonia, which has a population of 7.6 million, has a strong economy based on industry, tourism, and agriculture. From 1939 to 1975, Catalonia's language and culture [19] was suppressed by the dictatorship then in power. The central Spanish government banned Catalan, Catalonia's language, in government and public institutions. In 1978, though, the new Spanish constitution returned some independence to the region. These changes did not completely quiet the call for a separate identity and sovereign political power in Catalonia. The region has had many elections in which independence for Catalonia was a major issue.

However, the 2014 vote was merely [20] symbolic; days earlier the Spanish Constitutional Court had ruled that the vote was not binding. About 2.25 million votes were cast, out of 5.4 million eligible voters. More than 80% of the votes were for independence. [21] The poll accomplished little practical change. It was a huge victory for Catalonians. It was very emotional. Because it was not a legal vote, no government officials [22] had been involved. About 40,000 volunteers worked at the polls and counted the ballots. During the last regional elections in 2012, the secessionist party received about 1.8 million votes of the 3.7 million cast. There is no doubt that independence for Catalonia and other areas will continue to be an issue.

12. (A) NO CHANGE
   (B) Separating and to join, these are
   (C) To separate and to join are
   (D) To separate and to join;

13. (A) NO CHANGE
   (B) fell apart in 1991. What had been
   (C) falling apart in 1991, and what was
   (D) fell apart in 1991 because what had been

Go on to next page

14. (A) NO CHANGE

    (B) Add to the beginning of the paragraph: "Separatism is still in the news."

    (C) Add to the beginning of the paragraph: "Currently, separatism is now in the news."

    (D) Add to the beginning of the paragraph: "Now in the news."

15. (A) NO CHANGE

    (B) to be formed

    (C) to have formed

    (D) forming

16. (A) NO CHANGE

    (B) guard

    (C) keep

    (D) remain

17. What change, if any, should be made to paragraph two?

    (A) NO CHANGE

    (B) Add information on the history of Scotland.

    (C) Add information on the economy of Scotland.

    (D) Add information on the movement for Scottish independence.

18. (A) NO CHANGE

    (B) Voting in

    (C) Two months later, those who voted in

    (D) Two months later, those who live in

19. (A) NO CHANGE

    (B) were suppressed

    (C) was censored

    (D) were censoring

20. (A) NO CHANGE

    (B) figurative

    (C) imaginary

    (D) illusory

21. (A) NO CHANGE

    (B) The poll accomplished little practical change. It was a huge victory for Catalonians, but it was very emotional.

    (C) The poll accomplished little practical change. And it was a huge victory for Catalonians. It was very emotional.

    (D) The poll accomplished little practical change, but it was a huge, emotional victory for Catalonians.

22. (A) NO CHANGE

    (B) was involved

    (C) were involved

    (D) had been themselves involved

Passage III

Author Virginia Woolf wrote that [23] wannabe writers need financial independence and "a room of one's own" in order to create art. [24] This statement is seen as a truth, believed to be true by many who struggle to become writers, painters, and musicians. Phyllis Dorothy James White had reason to disagree with Woolf. Under the name "P. D. James," she wrote [25] more than 20 highly acclaimed novels, most featuring a character, Adam Dalgleish, who was simultaneously a poet and a detective for Scotland Yard. [26] James brooding hero, as well as her clear sense of the psychology and effects of violent behavior, gave unusual depth to her work.

James was born in 1920 in Oxford, England. Her father, Sidney James, believed that education was not necessary for women, and Phyllis left school at 16. She was always interested in writing mysteries. She claimed that when she first heard about Humpty Dumpty, she wanted to know whether he fell or was pushed! [27] James always wanted to be a mystery writer; she was [28] hampered by World War II. She was a nurse during the war, and afterwards, when her

Go on to next page ➡

husband returned from combat with a mental illness, she had to work to support her family. She studied hospital administration and labored for Britain's National Health Service. For years, she arose very early in the morning and wrote for several hours before heading off to her job. With this schedule, James needed three years to complete her first book, *Cover Her Face,* which was published in 1962. That novel was successful, [29] even though James continued to work while writing in her off hours. She served as an administrator in the forensic science and criminal law departments of the Department of Home [30] Affairs, that experience gave realistic details to her novels. She was famous for her thorough research. [31] She said that ideas for her work nearly always came from "a particular place." She added that she liked to "create in books some kind of opposition between places and characters."

James did not retire from her job until 1979, whereupon she was able to write full time. Instead of money and a private room, she accomplished much while raising two children, caring for an ill husband, and holding a job. When she [32] had died in late 2014, James was praised as a unique and talented author who made a lasting contribution not just to the mystery genre but to literature itself.

[33] James's work has been translated into dozens of languages and often appeared on the bestseller list. Her last novel, *Death Comes to Pemberley,* was a sequel to Jane Austen's famous novel *Pride and Prejudice,* with Austen's characters acting as suspects and detectives.

23. (A) NO CHANGE
(B) possible
(C) aspiring
(D) hopeful

24. (A) NO CHANGE
(B) Many who struggle to become writers, painters, and musicians believe this statement is true.
(C) Struggling to become writers, painters, and musicians, this statement is seen as true.
(D) A truth, believed by many who struggle to become writers, painters, and musicians, is this statement.

25. (A) NO CHANGE
(B) more than 20 novels
(C) novels
(D) highly acclaimed novels

26. (A) NO CHANGE
(B) Ms. James
(C) James's
(D) Jame's

27. (A) NO CHANGE
(B) omit the underlined words
(C) Always wanting to be a mystery writer,
(D) James had always wanted to be a mystery writer,

28. (A) NO CHANGE
(B) disadvantaged
(C) banned
(D) barred

29. (A) NO CHANGE
(B) so
(C) however
(D) but

30. (A) NO CHANGE
(B) Affairs; that experience gave
(C) Affairs, gave
(D) Affairs, that experience had given

31. (A) NO CHANGE
(B) Add examples of her research.
(C) Describe the plot of one of the novels.
(D) Change to "She was famous for her thorough research before writing."

Go on to next page

32. (A) NO CHANGE
     (B) was dead
     (C) dies
     (D) died

33. (A) NO CHANGE
     (B) Delete this paragraph.
     (C) Place this paragraph before the preceding paragraph.
     (D) Eliminate the paragraph break, so that this paragraph completes the preceding paragraph.

Passage IV

Field	Ten-Year Job Outlook (2012–2022)
fashion designers	– 3%
graphic designers	+ 7%
art directors	+ 3%
crafts and fine artists	+ 3%
architects	+ 17%
multimedia artists and designers	+ 6%
writers (literary)	+ 3%
technical writers	+ 17%
all US jobs, in any field	+ 10.8%

Source: US Bureau of Labor Statistics

Those with creative spirits too often think in limited terms when it comes to careers. Writers consider novels or film scripts, and visual artists envision their paintings or drawings in museum shows. However, creativity is a job requirement in many [34] fields being lesser known. Sometimes those fields give applicants a greater chance at success in job-finding than [35] highly-profile positions.

Someone interested in fashion, for example, may think about television reality shows that focus on careers designing clothing or modeling it. Besides those jobs are many other fashion-related positions. Magazine editors, pattern-makers, and photographers are only a few of the many posts that maintain a connection with fashion. A multimedia artist, who creates websites or advertisements for fashion lines using sound and visuals, has a much better chance of [36] hiring than a fashion designer. A graphic designer — someone who concentrates on visuals for magazines, television, websites, and [37] media — can have as fulfilling a career as a clothing designer. A novelist may be struck by the lightning of fame and achieve a spot on the bestseller list, but technical writers are more likely to find steadier work writing instruction manuals for computers and communicating advanced technical information in journals and reports. [38] Those who work in creative fields have a better outlook for employment than the projected average increase in all jobs. Architects, who design homes and commercial structures, have an especially [39] robust job outlook.

To explore these jobs and [40] finding out about many others, the United States government publishes the *Occupational Outlook Handbook,* online and in print. In this handbook, thousands upon thousands of occupations [41] are being described. The [42] medium salary is listed; furthermore, they give you the entry-level education requirement. Each occupations is cross-referenced to "similar occupations," so a person can find [43] their other potential careers. The handbook also discusses duties associated with the job, the working conditions, and training.

Go on to next page

Even in high school, students should begin to consider how to enter the workforce and in what capacity. Of course, the future always presents some unknown factors, and people change as they experience life. It's possible for someone interested in, for example, chemistry, to decide that law is more appealing after taking courses in political science or criminal justice. Still, planning can pay off. It's not impossible to change majors in college or to jump from one field to another after graduating, but sometimes catching up is harder than starting out with a goal in mind. The key is to maintain an open mind when thinking about careers [44] and balancing it with solid preparation. This preparation may be classes in an area of interest, summer or after-school employment, or internships.

34. (A) NO CHANGE
    (B) fields that are known to a lesser extent
    (C) lesser known fields
    (D) fields known lesser

35. (A) NO CHANGE
    (B) high-profile
    (C) large-profile
    (D) high-profiled

36. (A) NO CHANGE
    (B) hiring than a fashion designer does
    (C) having been hired than a fashion designer
    (D) being hired than a fashion designer

37. (A) NO CHANGE
    (B) other media
    (C) other medias
    (D) medias

38. (A) NO CHANGE
    (B) The projected outlook for creative fields is slightly better than the outlook for employment in all United States jobs.
    (C) The projected outlook for creative fields is not as good as the outlook for employment in all United States jobs.
    (D) Those who work in creative fields have good outlook for employment than the projected average increase in all jobs.

39. (A) NO CHANGE
    (B) full
    (C) complete
    (D) hearty

40. (A) NO CHANGE
    (B) to find out about
    (C) to find out on
    (D) finding out for

41. (A) NO CHANGE
    (B) have been described
    (C) describe
    (D) are described

42. (A) NO CHANGE
    (B) median
    (C) media
    (D) medial

43. (A) NO CHANGE
    (B) their
    (C) other
    (D) the other

44. (A) NO CHANGE
    (B) balancing by
    (C) and balanced
    (D) balanced

STOP DO NOT TURN THE PAGE UNTIL TOLD TO DO SO.
DO NOT RETURN TO A PREVIOUS TEST.

Section 4: Mathematics — No-Calculator Section

Time: 25 minutes for 20 questions

Directions: This section contains two different types of questions. For Questions 1–15, choose the best answer to each question and darken the corresponding oval on the answer sheet. For Questions 16–20, follow the separate directions provided before those questions.

Notes:

✔ You may **not** use a calculator.

✔ All numbers used in this exam are real numbers.

✔ All figures lie in a plane.

✔ All figures may be assumed to be to scale unless the problem specifically indicates otherwise.

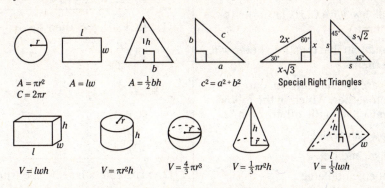

1. If $2a + 3b = 17$ and $2a + b = 3$, then $a + b =$

   (A) 1

   (B) 5

   (C) 7

   (D) 10

2. A bicycle has a front wheel radius of 15 inches. If the bicycle wheel travels 10 revolutions, how far has a point on the outside of the wheel traveled, in inches?

   (A) 10π

   (B) 30π

   (C) 300π

   (D) 450π

3. If p and q are positive integers, then $\left(5^{-p}\right)\left(5^{q+1}\right)^{p}$ is equivalent to

   (A) 5^{pq+p}

   (B) 5^{pq}

   (C) 5^{pq-p}

   (D) 5^{q+1}

4. In a set of five positive whole numbers, the mode is 90 and the average (arithmetic mean) is 80. Which of the following statements is false?

   (A) The number 90 appears two, three, or four times in the set.

   (B) The number 240 cannot appear in the set.

   (C) The number 80 must appear exactly once in the set.

   (D) The five numbers must have a sum of 400.

Go on to next page

5. In a triangle, the second side is 3 centimeters longer than the first side. The length of the third side is 5 centimeters less than twice the length of the first side. If the perimeter is 34 centimeters, find the length, in centimeters, of the longest side.

   (A) 3

   (B) 9

   (C) 12

   (D) 13

6. Melvin, Chris, Enoch, Dave, Carey, Mike, Dan, and Peter are choosing dorm rooms for college. Each room holds four people. They have the following requirements:

   (i) Mike and Melvin refuse to live together.

   (ii) Enoch will live with Chris or Carey (or possibly both).

   (iii) If Dave and Dan live together, Peter will live with them.

   When rooms are chosen, Melvin, Carey, and Dan live together. Which of the following groups must live in the other room?

   (A) Chris, Dave, and Mike

   (B) Chris, Mike, and Peter

   (C) Dave, Enoch, and Peter

   (D) Dave, Mike, and Peter

7. If the distance from Springfield to Watertown is 13 miles and the distance from Watertown to Pleasantville is 24 miles, then the distance from Pleasantville to Springfield in miles could not be

   (A) 10

   (B) 11

   (C) 13

   (D) 24

8. In a certain game, there are only two ways to score points; one way is worth 3 points, and the other is worth 5 points. If Brandon's total score is 61, which of the following could be the number of 3-point scores that Brandon had?

   (A) 10

   (B) 11

   (C) 12

   (D) 13

9. A number n is defined as a "tweener" if both $n-1$ and $n+1$ are prime. Which of the following numbers is a tweener?

   (A) 2

   (B) 8

   (C) 30

   (D) 36

10. If the square of x is 12 less than the product of x and 5, which of the following expressions could be used to solve for x?

    (A) $x^2 = 5x - 12$

    (B) $x^2 = 12 - 5x$

    (C) $2x = 12 - 5x$

    (D) $2x = 5x - 12$

11. If $2y - c = 3c$, then $y =$

    (A) $\dfrac{c}{2}$

    (B) c

    (C) $\dfrac{3c}{2}$

    (D) $2c$

12. The solution set to the equation $|3x - 1| = 7$ is

    (A) $\{2\}$

    (B) $\left\{2, \dfrac{2}{3}\right\}$

    (C) $\{-2\}$

    (D) $\left\{2, 2\dfrac{2}{3}\right\}$

Go on to next page

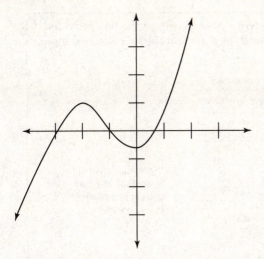

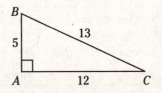

13. If this graph represents $f(x)$, then the number of solutions to the equation $f(x) = 1$ is

    (A) zero

    (B) one

    (C) two

    (D) three

14. A square with an area of 25 is changed into a rectangle with an area of 24 by increasing the width and reducing the length. If the length was reduced by 2, by how much was the width increased?

    (A) 2

    (B) 3

    (C) 4

    (D) 5

15. In the triangle ABC above, what is the value of tan C?

    (A) $\dfrac{5}{13}$

    (B) $\dfrac{12}{13}$

    (C) $\dfrac{5}{12}$

    (D) $\dfrac{12}{5}$

Go on to next page

Directions for Questions 16–20: Solve the problem and then write your answer in the box provided on the answer sheet. Mark the oval corresponding to the answer, as shown in the following example. Note the fraction line and the decimal points.

Answer: $^7/_2$

Answer: 3.25

Answer: 853

Write your answer in the box. You may start your answer in any column.

Although you do not have to write the solutions in the boxes, you do have to blacken the corresponding ovals. You should fill in the boxes to avoid confusion. Only the blackened ovals will be scored. The numbers in the boxes will not be read.

There are no negative answers.

Mixed numbers, such as $3\frac{1}{2}$, may be gridded in as a decimal (3.5) or as a fraction ($^7/_2$). Do not grid in $3\frac{1}{2}$; it will be read as $31/2$.

Grid in a decimal as far as possible. Do not round it.

A question may have more than one answer. Grid in one answer only.

16. Lauren took four exams. Her scores on the first three are 89, 85, and 90. If her average (arithmetic mean) on all four exams is 90, what did she get on the fourth exam?

17. If $p > 0$ and the distance between the points $(4, -1)$ and $(-2, p)$ is 10, find p.

18. If $a - b = 8$ and $ab = 10$, find $a^2 + b^2$.

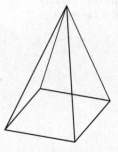

19. The pyramid above has a square base of length 10 centimeters and a height of 12 centimeters. Determine the total surface area of all five faces, in square centimeters.

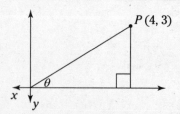

20. In the drawing above, what is $5(\sin\theta)$?

DO NOT TURN THE PAGE UNTIL TOLD TO DO SO.
DO NOT RETURN TO A PREVIOUS TEST.

Section 5: The Essay

Time: 50 minutes

As you read this passage, consider how the author uses the following:

- Facts, examples, and other types of evidence to support his assertions
- Logical structure to link ideas and evidence
- Elements of style, such as figurative language, word choice, and so forth, to make his case

This passage is excerpted from Content Nation *by John Blossom (Wiley).*

If you use technology to create information and experiences that can be shared with others, you're a publisher. Some of your personal activities may seem to be too small in scope to put under the banner of a word like "publishing." After all, not everything that we publish has a huge audience or seems to be very important, but if others find that what you've shared is valuable, then you've achieved what every publisher in the world tries to achieve.

With the advent of the Internet and other advanced communication networks, though, the scale of what one person can do with publishing tools has changed radically. Affordable computers, mobile phones, and many other types of devices connected to communications networks have enabled billions of people to share content with one another locally and globally as never before. Technology now allows any person on the planet to publish things to virtually any number of people in any place at any time at little or no cost — without their knowing in great detail how it happens. Worldwide publishing, once the pursuit of a handful of wealthy and powerful people, is now a tool in the hands of the world. Students, farmers, business professionals, teachers, researchers, politicians, homemakers, and anyone else who can access our global communications networks are now engaging with other people who have similar interests and establishing appreciation for one another through their common publishing capabilities. Much of this publishing takes place on social media.

Because of its publishing capability, social media offers us the opportunity to consider what it is to be human in ways that humankind has not been able to explore effectively for thousands of years. When the people with whom we build close bonds and upon whom we rely for success in life could be anywhere in the world from any way of life, the potential for our future as a species of life on this planet takes on a new and startling form. Instead of the organism of centralized civilization, we have been handed back the keys to create our own new civilizations as we please. Many will choose to enhance very traditional forms of human existence through social media, with many rapidly evolving and shifting points of highly valuable collaboration and production, which can scale to mass goods and services very efficiently.

In enabling major shifts in where value is produced in human society, we will not be throwing away the advantages and legacies of modern civilization. Instead, we will be leveraging them to support new forms of value, allowing mass production and mass culture to benefit us when and where it pleases us, but being able to produce more value independent of the highly centralized distribution and control mechanisms of traditional civilization. The culture of artificial scarcity, encouraged by highly centralized publishing and marketing

Go on to next page

mechanisms, will give way through social media to a culture more focused on identifying and exploiting the natural abundance of human insight and innovation rapidly and efficiently, enabling more people to collaborate on projects large and small that respond to the threats and opportunities in a changing world more effectively.

In the process of becoming a society focused on exploiting the abundance found in human abilities, we are likely to see political changes as well. It will become ever harder to communicate political themes and objectives that don't have authentic support from everyday people. If the era of television ushered in mass communications that enabled the selling of politicians like tubes of toothpaste, social media ushers in the era of politics in which most facts impacting politics and policies are known instantly and openly. Political victories go to politicians who know how to influence grass-roots political conversations most effectively. Like many things in social media, the transformation that can come in political circles is less about technologies than it is about the ability of those technologies to scale rapidly and effectively to any level of human organization to build effective bonds between people.

The impact of social media's influence can be deceptively simple depending on the scale you use to apply it, just like the changes that a piece of ice can make may be deceptively simple based on scale. Let a small cube of ice melt on a table, and something simple has changed. Put a mile of ice over a continent and life is changed forever. So it will be with the scale and depth of Content Nation's influential impact as it begins to reach into the lives of every person on the planet.

Directions: Write an essay in which you explain how Blossom builds an argument to persuade his audience that social media has created a fundamental change in the way human beings relate to one another. In your essay, analyze how Blossom uses elements of style to persuade readers to agree with his argument. Concentrate your analysis on the most important features of the passage.

Do not state whether you agree with Blossom's claims. Instead, show how Blossom argues his point.

STOP DO NOT TURN THE PAGE UNTIL TOLD TO DO SO.
DO NOT RETURN TO A PREVIOUS TEST.

Chapter 21

Practice Exam 2: Answers and Explanations

●●●

After you finish taking Practice Exam 2 in Chapter 20, spend some time going through the answers and explanations in this chapter to find out which questions you missed and why. Even if you answered every question correctly, read the explanations in this chapter because you'll find some tips and warnings in the explanations that will help you be ready-set-go for the actual SAT. If you're short on time, you can quickly check your answers with the abbreviated answer key at the end of the chapter.

Note: To determine your score on this practice test, turn to the appendix.

Answers for Section 1: Reading

1. **D.** This passage displays Dickens's famous ability to create a character with just a few words. Miss Murdstone's "very heavy eyebrows" (Line 2) are described as the whiskers (facial hair) she would have on her chin and cheeks if she were a man. The wording is a little confusing, so this question is really testing whether you can decode old-fashioned and complicated expressions. Here's the translation: Miss Murdstone is "disabled by the wrongs of her sex" (women don't, in general, have whiskers!), and she "carried" (Line 4), or wore, the eyebrows "to that account," which in modern terms would be *on account of that fact* or *because of that fact.*

2. **A.** Miss Murdstone is literally covered with metal. Choice (B) is wrong because her "hard black boxes" (Line 5) have "her initials on the lids in hard brass nails" (Line 5). Choice (C) is out because her purse is made of "hard steel" (Line 6). You can eliminate Choice (D) because the purse is kept in a "jail of a bag" (Lines 6 through 7) and suspended by a "chain" (Line 7). Jails are characterized by metal bars, and chains are usually made of metal. All that's left is her *disposition*, or tendency, which is certainly nasty but not made of metal.

3. **C.** Miss Murdstone is described as having a version of men's whiskers as eyebrows, because women can't grow whiskers. She wore her eyebrows "to that account" (Line 4), or for that *reason.* Choice (C) is correct.

4. **B.** The narrator has just heard Miss Murdstone say, "Generally speaking . . . I don't like boys" (Lines 11 through 12), followed by the social formula, "How d'ye do" (Line 12), which is "How do you do?" in modern terms. It's not surprising that the narrator's response, hoping that Miss Murdstone is well, doesn't have a lot of sincerity in it. She starts the social formality of asking how you're doing, and he finishes it in a *mediocre* (so-so or unexceptional) way.

5. **D.** According to the narrator, Miss Murdstone's room is "from that time forth a place of awe and dread" (Line 16). *Dread* is another word for extreme fear, so Choice (D) wins the gold medal for this question. Did Choice (B) catch your eye? The SAT-makers like to throw in an

answer that appears in the passage but doesn't answer the question they're asking. Miss Murdstone is supposed to "help" (Line 22) the narrator's mother, but the narrator's relationship with Miss Murdstone isn't included in that statement.

6. **C.** As you see in the explanation to Question 5, the room of "awe and dread" supports the correct answer — Choice (D) — *is characterized by fear.*

7. **D.** Most of the time, quotation marks signal that you're reading the exact words of a character (or, in nonfiction, of a real person). However, quotation marks can also indicate a gap between intention and reality. Miss Murdstone is supposed to be helping, and she may even have used that word in describing her own actions. But later in the sentence, the narrator says that she made *havoc in the old arrangements* by moving things around. *Havoc* means "chaos," and creating chaos doesn't help anyone. Thus, Choice (D) is the best answer.

8. **A.** When Peggotty says that Miss Murdstone "slept with one eye open" (Line 31), Peggotty is describing Murdstone's *vigilance*, or watchfulness, in fanciful terms (with a figure of speech). The narrator says that he "tried it" (Line 31) and "found it couldn't be done" (Line 32) because he accepted Peggotty's words as the *literal*, or actual, truth. His confusion comes from his ignorance; he's just too young to separate a figure of speech from reality. The only other possibility is Choice (D) because the narrator does experiment with his own sleep. However, Choice (A) is better because the narrator isn't questioning Peggotty's comment (and *inquisitive* means "tending to ask questions"). Instead, he's trying to duplicate what he believes is Miss Murdstone's habit.

9. **D.** You probably thought you'd need a line about Peggotty here, but in fact the best evidence shows the narrator's reaction to Peggotty. As you see in the explanation to Question 8, the narrator reveals his ignorance by trying to sleep with "one eye open" (Line 31).

10. **C.** The narrator is *not* a fan of Miss Murdstone; he criticizes her harsh nature (all those references to metal in the first paragraph!) and her behavior toward him (she says that she doesn't like boys). She turns her room into a place of "awe and dread" (Line 16). Sounds *critical,* don't you think? Choice (C) is correct.

11. **C.** The passage begins with the statement that citizens "have the absolute right to agree or disagree with the present laws" (Lines 1 through 3). Later, the author says that people have the right "to organize, to agitate, to do our best to change the laws" (Lines 6 through 7). Although the passage as a whole discusses who has the right to vote, the more *fundamental* (basic) message is that citizens can protest and work to change laws that they believe are unjust. Choice (C) fits perfectly here.

12. **D.** The passage refers to an age limit of 21, so Choice (B) doesn't work. Because an organization "demands suffrage for Chinese and Japanese who wish to become citizens" (Lines 9 through 11), you can deduce that Choices (A) and (C) are out. The passage refers to "a large number of people . . . [who] earnestly believe that the right of the Negro to vote should be curtailed, or even abolished" (Lines 17 through 20). *Curtail* is "to restrict," and *abolish* is "to do away with." You can't curtail something unless it exists. Furthermore, the third paragraph describes the gradual extension of the right to vote from the original small group of church members to "all white adults, then to include Negroes" (Lines 47 through 48). No doubt about it, Choice (D) is your answer.

13. **C.** The explanation to Question 12 includes the lines cited in Choice (C), which is your answer.

14. **B.** The author favors the expansion of voting rights and equality, but those are only part of what the author discusses. In Lines 25 through 26, he states that democracy is not "a dogma." The footnote explains that a *dogma* is "system of belief not open to discussion." Therefore, democracy *is* open to discussion, or, as Choice (B) puts it, *a process that allows disagreement.* This question illustrates a typical SAT trap — answer choices that refer only to parts of the passage and that miss the big picture. Because the passage is about voting rights, Choices (A) and (D) are appealing. Appealing but wrong!

15. **A.** Decades before the first Spider-Man film, in which the superhero's uncle explains that "great power brings great responsibility," the author of this passage grasped that concept. In Lines 14 through 16, he states that lowering the voting age would give "a large number of young men with the privileges, and therefore the educational responsibilities" of exercising that right. Choice (A) rules!

16. **B.** Check out the explanation to Question 15, and you see the lines cited in Choice (B), which is your answer.

17. **A.** Lines 36 through 37 state that "democracy proceeds with caution toward the extension" of the right to vote to "more and more people." The phrase "with caution" is key here, because the extension is an experiment. If one step works, the next step seems possible. Choice (A) is the answer.

18. **D.** Lines 40 through 41 say that "no one can prophesy how far a democracy will ultimately go," so the endpoint is unclear. The paragraph describes a gradual expansion of voting rights, which is a direction of, as Choice (D) states, a *trend*.

19. **A.** The "line" referred to in Line 50 is the limit of voting rights. It's been "constantly advancing, but with many fluctuations, eddies, and back-currents" (Lines 50 through 52). *Fluctuations* are changes, which can be in any direction. Similarly, *eddies* are little swirls of water, stuck for a while in one place. The "back-currents" occur when the water in the stream moves backward. All these elements are what you expect to encounter when you look at a stream — not a constant, steady move forward, but a messy flow with setbacks. Because water is part of nature, its movement is natural. Put these ideas together and you end up with Choice (A).

20. **C.** The passage *advocates* (pushes for) activism, for "more people . . . as partakers in government" (Line 4). The passage mentions the "right to organize" (Line 6), which includes petitions. How does the author feel about absentee ballots and campaign finance? No hints appear in the passage, so Choices (B) and (D) don't work. Choice (C) is the correct answer.

21. **B.** The passage argues that democracy involves discussion and disagreement, so *those who question* are participating in democracy. Choice (A) is tempting, but you don't have to argue with someone who agrees with you. Choice (B) is the best answer.

22. **A.** This question is a bit tricky because one of the answers is *almost* correct. *Almost* isn't good enough, though, on the SAT. Line 1 states that "Every surface around us is covered with bacteria," so you may have jumped on Choice (C). The catch is *around us,* because no one lives in a volcano, which is bacteria-free, according to Lines 10 through 12. Those lines cite volcanoes as exceptions to the rule that "no surface on earth is naturally sterile." So bacteria are present nearly everywhere — as Choice (A) states. Choice (B), by the way, is the direct opposite of the what the author says, and you can rule out Choice (D) because that answer choice says that the "number of bacteria on earth can be counted accurately." If the number is accurate, it is specific. The author's statement about "30 digits, give or take a digit" is vague and implies that an accurate count cannot be made.

23. **C.** As you see in the explanation to Question 22, volcanoes are the exception to the "naturally sterile" rule, and Choice (C) is correct.

24. **D.** This question tests your ability to read carefully. The phrase "submerged sediments" comes just before "another major habitat," and defines that habitat. What are *submerged sediments?* The adjective *submerged* means "underwater," and *sediment* is "matter, mostly soil, that settles to the bottom of a body of water." Choice (D) is your answer here.

25. **B.** The chart shows that the rate of infection from Salmonella has dropped every year from 2011 to 2013. True, the target number for 2020 has not been achieved, but because 2020 is in the future, that fact says nothing about the present day.

26. **A.** Lines 31 through 34 refer to advertisements that "make us believe" we are not safe without "the soaps, cleansers, toothbrushes, dishwashing or laundry detergents, hand lotions" and other products. Because the ads have to "make us believe," the implication is that this

idea is not true. In other words, such products aren't necessary, as Choice (A) says. Choices (B) and (C) are too general. Passage I states, "If only we could see them . . ." but doesn't say that *harmful bacteria cannot be identified* or that *homeowners should buy microscopes.* Choice (D) doesn't work because the passage refers to "raw egg whites" (Line 21) sitting on a counter, not to eggs in general.

27. **C.** This question checks whether you read carefully. The author of Passage II first discusses other organisms that live on bacteria that in turn live on "pure chemicals" (Line 48). Tube-worms, then, are part of a group. Then comes the description of these worms as "bizarre" (Line 49), followed by a statement that tube-worms are "not only huge, but they also completely lacked mouth and guts." "Guts" is another word for *digestive organs,* and Choice (C) is therefore correct.

28. **D.** Lines 62 through 64 refer to "sulphur-oxidizing bacteria that can use hydrogen sulphide" to react with oxygen to "get energy." The oxygen itself isn't a direct source of nourishment; it's part of a process. Because Choice (D) is not true, it's your answer.

29. **C.** In science, *react* means "to change as a result of a chemical process" — the definition best suited to the sentence, in which bacterial "use the hydrogen sulphide that's in the water" (Lines 62 through 63) and "react it with oxygen" (Line 64). Choice (C) is a good fit here. The runner-up is Choice (A), but *mix* is too general a word for a much more complicated process.

30. **A.** Photosynthetic organisms, the footnote tells you, combine water, carbon dioxide, and sunlight into oxygen and food. Lines 68 through 69 refer to organisms of this type that "live in coral and feed the coral internally." Okay, that definition fits Choice (A), because the organisms live inside the coral and supply "feed the coral internally" (Line 69). The bacteria in tube-worms use "hydrogen sulphide that's in the water" and convert it and feed the worms. Another (somewhat gross) example of food arriving from the inside, not from the supermarket! Choice (A) is best here.

31. **C.** The author of Passage I talks about "bacteria added to a health drink (Lines 36 through 37). If the health-food crowd wants to eat some types of bacteria, at least a few types are *benign* (a word meaning "harmless," with an added hint of goodness). The word *benign,* by the way, appears in the subtitle of the book. (You read the subtitle in the introduction, right?) The author of Passage II discusses the interaction between bacteria and tube-worms — a situation that is definitely beneficial to the worms. Choice (C) is your answer.

32. **C.** Reread the explanation to Question 31, and you see that these lines support the idea that bacteria aren't always the bad guys. In this case, *c* — Choice (C), that is — is for "correct."

33. **B.** A pilot project leads the way, much as the pilot of a plane leads the passengers to their destination. (Their luggage, however, is another story entirely.) The passage tells you that not all pilot projects can be replicated, so Choice (A) can't be correct. Choice (C) doesn't apply to the term *pilot project* at all. You're left with Choices (B) and (D). Of the two, Choice (B) is better because the passage refers to *successful* pilot projects (Line 23), implying that not all succeed, and Choice (D) assumes that the projects have been *proven effective.* Choice (C) is your answer.

34. **D.** The passage concerns what the author sees as the best quality of the Grameen Bank — that its model can be replicated and adapted easily, thus reaching many more poor people. The author contrasts this success with pilot projects, which, as he explains in Line 13, reach *hundreds of people* instead of the millions affected by the Grameen Bank. Choices (A), (B), and (C) deal with this limitation. Nowhere does the passage address funding, so Choice (D) is clearly the best answer.

35. **A.** How do you feel when romance hits? Happy and optimistic, probably. Your newly beloved can do no wrong. But romance doesn't last. Either your relationship deepens into love, when you see and accept your beloved's faults, or it crashes and burns. This real-life experience helps you decode the statement that in the do-good crowd — "circles where poverty and environmental issues are discussed" (Lines 15 through 16) — small projects

are seen with a romantic eye and thus aren't evaluated fairly, as Choice (A) states. Choice (B) bets that you'll go for the hug-kiss sort of romance (which, we might add, is wrong); Choice (C) is the opposite of what the author says in the passage. Choice (D) doesn't cut it because tiny programs have limited goals, and you can't compare something to itself.

36. **B.** A *mesh* is a net, woven from threads. Lines 34 through 36 refer to "the interconnected mesh" of three types of problems — "social, environmental, and economic injustices." Thus, poverty, which is the topic discussed in the passage as a whole and in this paragraph in particular, affects its victims in several ways, as Choice (B) states.

37. **B.** As you see in the explanation to Question 36, "the interconnected mesh" is the best evidence for the idea that the poor are *deprived in several different ways.* Choice (B) is your answer.

38. **D.** The caption and the graph are your clues to the correct answer here. The passage makes clear that progress is not rare, so you can rule out Choice (A). The chart shows that the Progress out of Poverty Index (the PPI) is used by many different types of organizations, so Choice (B) doesn't work. Similarly, the fact that the PPI exists shows that progress can be measured. Goodbye, Choice (C). What's left is the correct answer, Choice (D) — because the PPI measures real progress from many types of antipoverty initiatives.

39. **B.** The lines cited in the question show that Grameen Bank had some growing pains. The right formula wasn't immediately present, though the passage as a whole makes clear that the Bank has succeeded. In 1991, some employees experienced "discontent" and some "carried out their duties" badly (Lines 51 through 54). These troubles fall into the category of *trial and error* because when you try things, you fail until you happen upon the road to success. Thus, Choice (B) is the one you seek. Choice (A) may have tempted you, but the eventual success of the Grameen Bank shows that the critics were wrong. Choice (C) flops because Bangladeshis "demonstrated those abilities as Grameen staff and borrowers" (Lines 63 through 65). The successful "decentralized management structure" (Line 44) contradicts Choice (D). Choice (B) is the correct answer.

40. **D.** Lines 79 through 83 tell you that critics see the problem of poverty as complex, one needing "a solution that [takes] into account . . . ignorance, political powerlessness, and ill health. Ignorance is cured by *better education,* ill health is alleviated by *universal healthcare,* and political powerlessness is reduced by giving *political power to the poor.* Therefore, all three options are correct, and the right answer is Choice (D).

41. **C.** Check out the answer to Question 40. As you see, Lines 96 through 99 take care of all three items (education, healthcare, and political power). Choice (C) is the correct answer.

42. **A.** All the answer choices are a possible meaning of the word *conscious,* but the poor are *aware* of politics, not *alert* or *awake* or any of the other choices.

43. **D.** Did the SAT-writers trip you up on this one? When you think of *hysteria,* you probably picture out-of-control laughter that brings forth a slap. But Lines 11 through 12 mention Choice (A), *amnesia,* Choice (B), *paralyses,* and Choice (C), *spasms* or *involuntary movements.* Only *laughter* is missing from the passage, so Choice (D) is your answer.

Real-world knowledge helps on the SAT, but the final answer must always make sense in the context of the reading material provided.

44. **C.** The passage defines *psychological* as a state with "no discernable physical causes." Choice (C) comes the closest to this definition.

45. **A.** Paragraph two says that Charcot clarified the "psychological-traumatic nature of symptoms" and mentions survivors of train wrecks, so you can choose Choice (A) with confidence.

Choice (C) is a favorite SAT trap: It contains a statement that actually appears in the passage but doesn't fit the question. Beware of such traps!

46. **C.** The answer to Question 45 clearly relates to these lines, which link hysteria to train wrecks and other trauma.

47. **A.** The term *hysteria* comes from the Greek word for "womb," and the passage implies that it was once thought to be only a female disease. Hence, "of both sexes" counters that idea. Choice (A) is the right one. Also, Line 82 mentions "the old link" between hysteria and women.

48. **B.** According to Lines 42 through 44, Charcot says the "railway spine" and "railway brain" were cases in which "symptoms mimicked those found after spinal cord or brain injuries." This question is chock-full of little traps. Choice (A) tempts you because it mentions trains, and Choice (D) may grab your attention because Charcot did use hypnosis. Choice (C) makes sense in the real world, because when you're hurt, you have to cope with stress. But Choice (B) fits the passage and the question best.

49. **D.** Lines 61 through 65 tell you that memories blotted out by physical injuries to the brain couldn't be retrieved by hypnosis, so you know Choice (D) is the right answer.

50. **A.** The cited line separates amnesia, or memory loss, resulting from "hysterical and organic" causes. Lines 60 through 65 tell you that hypnosis helped those who were suffering from hysteria recover memories, but not those whose "amnesia was based on the destruction of brain tissue" — in other words, a physical condition. Choice (A) fits perfectly here.

51. **D.** To answer this question properly, you have to distinguish between Charcot and *the author of the passage,* a phrase that appears in the question stem. If you chose Choice (A), you fell into a trap. Charcot did treat hysteria with hypnosis, but Charcot worked in the late 19th century, and the author of the passage is writing in the 21st century. (You read the introduction to the passage, we presume. If not, resolve to read every introduction, every time. Great information can pop up there!) Choice (A) contains a present-tense verb *(is)*. Medicine has certainly changed in the last hundred years or so, and for this reason, Choice (A) doesn't measure up. Choice (D), on the other hand, is supported by Line 24, which refers to "so-called hysterics."

52. **B.** Charcot contributed much to the understanding of hysteria, but he couldn't reach into the future and understand "medical conditions that were undiagnosable at the time" (Lines 26 through 27) and psychological conditions defined much later, including "severe anxiety, depression, the effects of a variety of traumas, and dissociated states" (Lines 29 through 31). Choice (B) is your best evidence here.

Answers for Section 2: Mathematics — Calculator Section

1. **D.** If you add the numbers in the ratio, you get 7. There are 28 total students, which is 7×4. Therefore, multiply the original ratio numbers by 4 to get 12 boys and 16 girls. Double-check to see that $12 + 16 = 28$.

2. **C.** Plugging in the numbers gives you $2(-2)^4$. Using PEMDAS (see Chapter 12), do the exponents first, and then multiply by 2: $(-2)^4 = (-2)(-2)(-2)(-2) = +16$, and $2(16) = 32$.

3. **A.** The drawer had 22 pairs of socks originally. However, Josh has thrown four pairs on the floor (and you can bet his mom's going to have something to say about that). So there are now 18 pairs to choose from, of which 6 are brown. His probability of success is therefore $\frac{6}{18} = \frac{1}{3}$.

4. **C.** There is no shortage of the 30-60-90 triangle on these practice exams. In these triangles, the hypotenuse is always twice the shorter leg, while the longer leg equals the shorter leg

times $\sqrt{3}$. Because you know the shorter leg equals 5, that makes the longer leg $5\sqrt{3}$, and so the coordinates are $\left(5\sqrt{3},0\right)$.

5. **B.** You did fine on this one if you remembered your exponent rules: $4^0 = 1$ by definition (because anything to the 0 power equals 1), and $64^{1/2}$ is the square root of 64, which is 8. So the expression in parentheses equals $1 + 8 = 9$. And 9^{-2} is the reciprocal of 9^2, which is 81, so the answer is $\dfrac{1}{81}$.

6. **D.** Find two numbers in the ratio 7:5 that have a difference of 24. Then set it up with algebra: Call Dora's money $7x$ and Lisa's money $5x$, so $7x = 5x + 24$. Thus, $2x = 24$, and $x = 12$. Plugging the numbers back in (always an important step) tells you that Lisa's money is $5(12) = \$60$, and Dora's is $7(12) = \$84$.

7. **D.** Because triangle *BCF* is isosceles, $BC = CF = 8$. Because angle *D* is a right angle, triangle *DEF* is the world-famous 3-4-5 right triangle, and $DF = 4$. Because $DC = 4 + 8 = 12$, *AB* is also 12. And, because $AD = BC = 8$, $AE = 8 - 3 = 5$. Now you're ready to find *EB*, the hypotenuse of the right triangle *ABE*. You can, of course, use the Pythagorean theorem, but you'll save time if you realize that you're face to face with a 5-12-13 right triangle, and $BE = 13$.

8. **B.** You can draw the line and count spaces to determine that the points are 12 units apart, or you can simply subtract: $8 - (-4) = 12$ (distance always involves a difference). Because $\dfrac{1}{4}$ of 12 is 3, you're looking for the point 3 units to the right of -4, and $-4 + 3 = -1$.

9. **B.** Five pounds of peanuts times $\$5.50$ per pound is $\$27.50$, and 2 pounds of cashews times $\$12.50$ per pound is $\$25.00$, so the total cost is $\$52.50$ for 7 pounds. Divide $\$52.50$ by 7 pounds to get $\$7.50$ per pound.

10. **C.** You could solve for x by cross-multiplying or plugging in answers. Pick your poison. Cross-multiplying is probably more straightforward and saves you the risk of having to go through the process four times.

$$\frac{x-1}{x-2} = \frac{x+7}{x+2}$$
$$(x-1)(x+2) = (x-2)(x+7)$$
$$x^2 + x - 2 = x^2 + 5x - 14$$
$$x - 2 = 5x - 14$$
$$-4x = -12$$
$$x = 3$$

11. **B.** A composite number is made from two or more primes multiplied together (see Chapter 10). Because 15 is composite (it's 3×5), $*15 = 2(15) = 30$. And 9 is also composite, so $*9 = 2(9) = 18$. Finally, 36 is composite, too, so $*36 = 2(36) = 72$. Only Statement II, $*9$, produces a result of 18.

12. **C.** Direct proportion problems require a ratio — in this case, the ratio of volume to temperature. Thus, you can write $\dfrac{cc_1}{K_1} = \dfrac{cc_2}{K_2}$ and $\dfrac{31.5}{210} = \dfrac{x}{300}$. Cross-multiply to get $210x = 9,450$, and divide by 210 to get $x = 45$.

13. **B.** This scatter plot shows a negative trend, so the line of best fit would go roughly from the top left to the bottom right. However, point *D* is significantly lower than the rest of the points. If you try drawing a line between *A* and *D*, or *B* and *D*, you'll see that it's really not that close to a lot of the points. However, the line from *A* to *C* is a good approximation of the scatter plot as a whole, as you can see in this diagram.

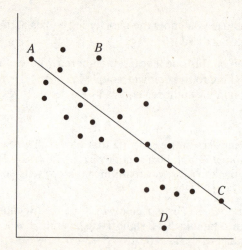

14. **D.** You don't even need to know what x and y equal in this problem. Look at the angle marked c in the following diagram. c and z are vertical angles, which means that their measures are equal. Also, a, c, and b form a straight line, so $a + c + b = 180°$. Therefore, $a + b + z = 180°$.

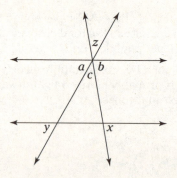

15. **B.** There are 19 terms between 7 and 159. Because $159 - 7 = 152$ and $152 \div 19 = 8$, each term must be 8 units greater than the one before it. So the sequence begins 7, 15, 23, 31, and there's your answer.

16. **A.** This question is based on the rules of graphed figures. $f(x)$ is another name for the y-value based on x. A higher x-value moves the point farther to the right. $f(x + 4)$ reads the value inside the parentheses (usually x, but in this case $x + 4$) as four spaces farther to the right than it actually is, so the graph moves four spaces to the left to compensate.

17. **A.** Do you remember your special triangle ratios? If not, it's okay: They're at the top of each Math section of the SAT. First, you have to realize that the triangles in this problem are special, by breaking up the 75° angle at the bottom right into a 45° and a 30° angle. The top right triangle is a 45-45-90 triangle, which makes both of its legs equal to 14. The bottom leg is also the hypotenuse of the 30-60-90 triangle at the bottom. In a 30-60-90 triangle, the hypotenuse must be twice the shortest leg, which is j. Therefore, j is 7.

18. **C.** This problem can be solved with simple arithmetic. If you add up the 65 Spanish students and the 32 art students, you get 97 total students. However, the 14 students who take both are counted twice, so subtract 14, leaving 83 students in either Spanish or art. If 83 students are in Spanish and/or art, you're left with $100 - 83 = 17$ who don't take either subject.

19. **D.** Because the answer is supposed to be in minutes, start by turning 3 hours into 180 minutes. You know that k percent of these 180 minutes is going to be used for math. Remember that k percent means $\dfrac{k}{100}$. Taking a percent of a number involves multiplication, so your answer is $180 \times \dfrac{k}{100}$, or $\dfrac{180k}{100}$.

20. **A.** You need the areas of rectangle *BDEF* and triangle *BCD*. For the rectangle, you need the length of segment *BD*, which is also part of triangle *ABD*. Because you have two sides of right triangle *ABD*, use the Pythagorean theorem to find the length of the third side, which is your target *BD*: $4^2 + 8^2 = (BD)^2$, so $BD = \sqrt{80}$, or $4\sqrt{5}$. The area of the rectangle is $4\sqrt{5} \times 2\sqrt{5} = 8 \times 5 = 40$. The area of triangle *BCD* is $\dfrac{8 \times 4}{2} = 16$. Subtract the two, and $40 - 16 = 24$.

21. **B.** The circumference of the wheel is πd, where d is the diameter of the wheel. Because $d = 26$ inches, the circumference is 26π inches. The logo traveled half this distance, so divide the circumference by 2, for an answer of 13π inches.

22. **A.** Just distribute the 2 and isolate x:

$$2(x+4) = 6$$
$$2x + 8 = 6$$
$$2x = -2$$
$$x = -1$$

23. **A.** Make a table for this one, dividing by 2 every 20 years:

2000	2020	2040	2060	2080	2100
50	25	$\dfrac{25}{2}$	$\dfrac{25}{4}$	$\dfrac{25}{8}$	$\dfrac{25}{16}$

The final answer is $\dfrac{25}{16}$ grams.

24. **C.** First of all, there are 21 numbers, not 20, to choose from. Remember that to find the size of a list of numbers, you subtract the first and last numbers, and then add one. (You can also count them to be sure.) Now, the even numbers are 20, 22, . . . and so on, up to 40, which makes five numbers in the 20s, five in the 30s, and 40, which is 11 numbers out of 21.

25. **D.** All the numbers have three digits. Only Choices (A) and (D) have a units (ones) digit that equals the sum of the other two digits. A calculator can tell you that the square root of 156 is a decimal, while the square root of 729 is 27.

26. **D.** A slope of $-\dfrac{1}{3}$ means that the line goes down 1 unit every time it moves 3 units to the right. Because M is on the x-axis, the line has gone down 2 units by the time it reaches M, so it must have moved 6 units to the right. That means that M is at $(5, 0)$. M is the midpoint, which means that it's halfway to P. So, to get to P, move another 2 units down and 6 units right, which puts you at $(11, -2)$.

27. **C.** Because $b + c = x$, $b = x - c$. So you can substitute $(x - c)$ for b in the first equation, and write $a(x - c) = n$. It's vital that you remember the parentheses, because now you have to use the distributive property to get $ax - ac = n$, which is Choice (C).

28. **D.** Possible numbers for g are numbers like 3, 6, 12, 15, 21, and so on. If you try multiplying these numbers by 7 and then dividing by 9, you discover that the remainder is always 3 or 6. Because 3 isn't one of the answer choices, the correct answer is 6. Note that the problem asks for which *could* be the remainder.

29. **C.** A lot of these answer choices look true. However, if you let a equal 1, or a number less than 1, you realize that most of answer choices become false. This question is an old SAT trap; numbers between 0 and 1 (such as fractions) behave in funny ways. The only statement that is true for all positive numbers is Choice (C): Twice any positive number must be bigger than the original number.

30. **D.** Because there are parallel lines in this problem, you need to look for angles that are congruent. You can find them by looking for lines that make a Z or a backward Z. Looking first at the bigger triangles, you can mark the diagram as follows:

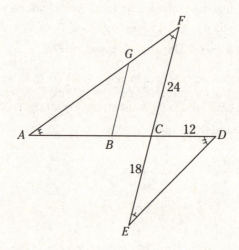

Notice that the two angles in the middle are vertical, so they're also equal. This is a picture of similar triangles: Angle F matches angle E, angle A matches angle D, and angle C is the same for both triangles. Therefore, you can use a ratio to figure out the length of AC:

$$\frac{AC}{CD} = \frac{CF}{CE} \text{ and } \frac{AC}{12} = \frac{24}{18}, \text{ which reduces to } \frac{AC}{12} = \frac{4}{3}$$

Be very careful that you match up the right parts when writing a ratio. If you matched AC with CE by accident, you'd get the wrong answer. Cross-multiplying your ratio tells you that $3(AC) = 48$, and $AC = 16$. Now, because $GB \parallel EF$, triangle ABG is similar to ACF as well. And, because $AG = GF$, the line GB cuts triangle ACF in half. That means that AB is half of AC, or 8.

31. **6.** Trial and error can work, but algebra is more reliable. Darren makes \$9 an hour on weekdays, and $1\frac{1}{2} \times \$9 = \$13.50$ an hour on weekends. If you let d equal his weekday hours and e equal his weekend hours, you know that $\$9(d) + \$13.50(e) = \$189.00$. You also know that $d + e = 18$ (his total hours), so you can solve this by substitution: $d = 18 - e$, which you can plug into the other equation. This gives you $\$9(18 - e) + \$13.50e = \$189$. Distribute to get $\$162 - \$9e + \$13.50e = \$189$. And then combine like terms: $\$162 + \$4.50e = \$189$. Now just subtract 162 from both sides and divide by 4.50, to get $e = 6$. He worked 6 hours during the weekends. Just like that.

32. **40.** Sixty-five percent chose history or English, leaving 35 percent for other subjects. This 35 percent represents 14 students, so you're basically being asked, "35 percent of what number is 14?" You can use the "is/of" method from Chapter 10:

$$\frac{is}{of} = \frac{\%}{100}, \text{ so } \frac{14}{x} = \frac{35}{100}$$

Cross-multiply to get $35x = 1,400$, and $x = 40$.

33. **11.** In a radical problem, you first need to isolate the radical. Therefore you have to subtract 1 from both sides before doing anything else, giving you $\sqrt{4x - 8} = 6$. Now, square both sides to eliminate the radical: $4x - 8 = 36$. Adding 8 and dividing by 4 gives you $x = 11$.

34. **6.** Plug in 7 for q, and set the expression equal to 21. Then use algebra to solve for p:

$$21 = \frac{p(7)}{p-4}$$
$$21(p-4) = p(7)$$
$$21p - 84 = 7p$$
$$14p = 84$$
$$p = 6$$

35. **12.** If the ratio of the width to length is 2:5, then the actual length is $2x : 5x$, because you multiply both numbers by the same amount (represented by x) to maintain the ratio. Thus, the width is $2x$ and the length is $5x$. Now it can't hurt to draw and label a rectangle:

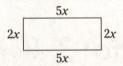

The perimeter is 84, so set up the equation to solve for x: $2x + 2x + 5x + 5x = 84$, and $x = 6$. Don't put 6, because that's not the width of the rectangle: it's the value of x. The length is $2x$, which is 12.

36. **520.** If the fee for each person is the same amount, and the difference in the total cost between eight people and ten people is $50 (because $320 - 270 = 50$), then each addition of two people adds $50 to the total price, and each person costs an extra $25. So 10 people cost $320, and 18 people is 8 more than 10, so these 8 people add $200 to the price (because $8 \times 25 = 200$). Add the new $200 to the existing $320 for 10 people, and 18 people cost $520.

37. **500.** You know that Tom's two investments total $1,200, so set x as the amount earning 5 percent and $(1,200 - x)$ as the amount earning 7 percent. Five percent of x plus 7 percent of $(1,200 - x)$ equals $74, so set the equation up like this:

$$5\%(x) + 7\%(1,200 - x) = 74$$

Remember that 5 percent is 5 "per hundred," so turn 5 percent into a decimal, 0.05. Do the same with 7 percent (0.07), and solve for x:

$$0.05(x) + 0.07(1,200 - x) = 74$$
$$0.05x + 84 - 0.07x = 74$$
$$84 - 0.02x = 74$$
$$-0.02x = -10$$
$$x = 500$$

Because x represents the number of dollars earning 5 percent, the answer is 500.

38. **300.** An investment that yields $160 simple interest over a period of two years yields $80 over a period of one year. Start by calculating the investment amounts needed to earn 5 percent and 7 percent. Just as in Part I, because Tom's two investments total $1,200, set x as the amount earning 5 percent and $(1,200 - x)$ as the amount earning 7 percent. Five percent of x plus 7 percent of $(1,200 - x)$ equals $80 (for one year), so set the equation up like this:

$$5\%(x) + 7\%(1,200 - x) = 80$$

Remember that 5 percent is 5 "per hundred," so turn 5 percent into a decimal, 0.05. Do the same with 7 percent (0.07), and solve for x:

$$0.05(x) + 0.07(1,200 - x) = 80$$
$$0.05x + 84 - 0.07x = 80$$
$$84 - 0.02x = 80$$
$$-0.02x = -4$$
$$x = 200$$

To earn $80 per year (totaling $160 over two years), Tom would need to have $200 in the account yielding 5 percent and the remaining $1,000 in the account yielding 7 percent. The question asks for the amount to be transferred from the 5 percent account to the 7 percent account. You know from Part 1 that the 5 percent account currently has $500, so Tom needs to transfer $300 to the other account, because $500 - $200 = $300.

Answers for Section 3: Writing and Language

1. **C.** A comma isn't strong enough to glue two complete sentences together, so the original has to change. Choices (B) and (D), however, trade one error for another because they imply that the *coastlines* are made of marine animals, not the coral reefs. Choice (C) takes care of the run-on sentence without losing the intended meaning.

2. **A.** If it isn't broken, don't fix it. (Yes, the proverb says that "if it ain't broke, don't fix it," but that expression breaks several grammar rules, and with anything to do with the SAT, you want correct grammar!) The definition of *exoskeleton* is nicely tucked into the original sentence, set off by a proper comma. Choice (A) is your answer.

 TIP

Set off a description with a comma (or two commas, if the sentence continues) if it adds extra information to the sentence. Think of the commas as little handles that can lift the description out of the sentence. If the meaning doesn't change, the commas are necessary. If you remove the description and the meaning is different, the commas have to go.

3. **B.** The possessive pronoun *your* implies ownership, but here you need a contraction for *you are*, which is *you're*. Choice (B) is correct. Choice (D), by the way, doesn't exist in Standard English. A possessive pronoun never includes an apostrophe.

4. **D.** The passage makes a big deal (and rightfully so!) about the past, present, and probable future death of coral reefs. To link past and present, present perfect tense is best. To match the plural subject, *reefs,* you need a plural verb form, *have died.*

5. **C.** This vocabulary-in-context question throws four synonyms for *end* or *die* at you. The only one appropriate for the end of a living being is *expire*. Choice (C) is correct.

6. **B.** When a sentence begins with a verb form not attached to a subject, the subject of the main portion of the sentence performs the action expressed by that verb form. Yet "about 60% of the earth's coral" can't attach to "doing nothing." Choice (B) inserts *we,* and the problem is solved.

7. **C.** The sentence includes the word *but,* which implies a change in direction. You know that coral reefs cover only a small portion of the earth. The most obvious need here is a statement about their relative importance as a habitat. Stating that "they contain fish species" is a start but a fairly weak one. More evidence, such as the number of species, would strengthen the writer's case for the importance of coral reefs. (In case you're interested, coral reefs are home to a full 25 percent of all marine fish species!)

8. **D.** This question tests your ear for Standard English expression and vocabulary in context. Salaries and food come *from* coral reefs, either directly or indirectly. No other verb form works in this sentence. Choice (D) is simplest and best.

9. **B.** If you "say" the original sentence in your mind, you hear the preposition *by,* followed by two things — *seeding* and *then he added*. Mismatch! Go for *seeding* and *then adding* and the sentence is parallel — and correct.

10. **C.** Two sentences praise the quick growth of coral obtained by microfragmentation. Placing information on the normal growth rate between those two sentences makes no sense. The most logical spot for this information is at the beginning of the paragraph, where it serves as an introduction to the work of Dr. Vaughan. Choice (C) is better than Choice (D) because deleting the sentence deprives the reader of informative detail — an essential technique of argument.

11. **C.** The chart shows that coral suffers more from overfishing and destructive fishing in some parts of the world (Southeast Asia, for example) than in others (such as Australia). Choice (C) correctly interprets the visual evidence.

12. **C.** The original version is wordy. Why label "to separate and to join" as "things"? Choice (C) cuts unnecessary words and expresses the meaning clearly. Did you select Choice (B)? If so, you eliminated wordiness but created another problem. *Separating* and *to join* don't match, so, in grammar terms, they aren't parallel. Choice (D) inserts a semicolon, but that punctuation mark joins two complete sentences, which you don't have here. Choice (C) is the best answer.

13. **B.** The problem with the original is the comma. Two complete sentences can't be joined with just a comma. You need a semicolon (;) or a period. Choice (B) provides the period, creating two grammatically correct sentences. Choices (C) and (D) address the comma issue, but Choice (C) creates a fragment by changing *fell* to *falling,* and Choice (D) changes the meaning by introducing *because.* Go for Choice (B), the right answer.

14. **B.** You need a transition from older separatist events (the breakup of the Soviet Union and Eastern European nations) to the discussion of Scotland and Catalonia. Choice (B) creates a good bridge from the late 90s to more recent votes. Choices (C) and (D) are also attempts at transitions, but Choice (C) is repetitive (*currently* and *now* say the same thing), and Choice (D) is not a complete sentence.

15. **D.** The sentence links two ideas — *staying* and, in the original version, *to form.* Mismatch! Change *to form* to *forming* and the ideas become parallel, and therefore, correct.

16. **D.** This question tests vocabulary in context. To *retain* is "to keep," but you can't *keep as* part of something. You can, however, *remain as,* which is the answer here.

17. **D.** The inclusion of relevant details always strengthens an essay, unless those details stray from the topic. Here, the vote on Scottish independence is mentioned but not developed. Inserting more information on the independent movement is an appropriate change.

18. **C.** The pie charts (the circle graphs accompanying this passage) show that not everyone in Catalonia was eligible to vote, and of those eligible, not all voted. The statement in the passage, therefore, is misleading because it applies to all citizens, not to *those who voted.* Choice (C) corrects the error.

19. **B.** To *suppress* is "to restrain or to prevent the expression of." This word is better than to *censor,* which is more specific to the expression of ideas and particular words, not an entire language and culture. Choice (B) is better than the original because the subject (*language and culture*) is plural and requires the plural form *were.*

20. **A.** The vote wasn't legally binding, so its value was as a symbol of discontent with the *status quo* (things as they are). The other words aren't appropriate in this context. *Figurative* refers to imaginative use of language, and *imaginary* labels something that isn't real. *Illusory* creates an illusion.

21. **D.** Mature writers eliminate short, choppy sentences by combining them. Choice (D) does so efficiently and correctly.

22. **C.** The first part of the sentence tips you off to the correct choice here. It contains the simple past-tense verb *was*. The meaning of the sentence provides no reason to switch to *had been involved* (the past perfect tense). The subject *(officials)* is plural, so you need a plural verb. Add all this together and you get the plural past tense, *were involved,* Choice (C).

23. **C.** The word *wannabe* has the right meaning, but it's too informal to match the tone of this passage. Go for *aspiring,* a formal word with the same definition, and steer clear of slang!

24. **B.** When you're faced with a choice between active and passive voice (*believe* or *believed by*), go for active voice. Also, always cut unnecessary words. The original sentence repeats *truth* and *believed to be true.* Choice (B) is active, concise, and correct.

25. **A.** When it comes to evidence, more detail is nearly always better than less. The original gives two specific facts: the number of novels James wrote and the fact that her work was "highly acclaimed." Both of these details add to the strength of the paragraph.

26. **C.** In this sentence, you need a possessive noun, which the apostrophe creates. Choice (C) correctly adds an apostrophe and the letter *s.* Choice (D) doesn't work because the author's name is *James,* not *Jame,* so the apostrophe can't appear after the letter *e.* Did you select Choice (B)? The addition of *Ms.* in just one sentence creates an imbalance, because elsewhere the author is referred to as *James.* Consistency is important!

27. **B.** Earlier in the paragraph, you find out that James "was always interested in writing mysteries." Repetition isn't necessary. Choice (B) is your answer.

28. **A.** To *hamper* is to "slow down" or to "place an obstacle in the way." This word nicely fits the context here. The war slowed James's plans for writing, but she eventually became an author.

29. **D.** The conjunction *even though* implies a limitation or a contradictory thought. You might say that *she went to the mall, even though she had no interest in shopping.* The meaning of this sentence doesn't fit the conjunction. Choices (C) and (D) do, but *however* isn't a conjunction and isn't allowed to link two complete sentences. Go for Choice (D) and you're correct.

30. **B.** The original sentence is a run-on, with two complete thoughts linked only by a comma. A semicolon is allowed to join complete thoughts, but a comma isn't. Go for Choice (B).

31. **B.** The paragraph *alludes to* (refers to) James's research, but you have no way of knowing what she actually did — check books out of the library, go to the site where her novel was set, kill someone to test a murder method — whatever! Adding information (for example, that she spent time at a power plant before writing a novel set there) makes this paragraph better.

32. **D.** The past perfect tense, *had died,* places one event before another when the sequence of events matters. Here, the timing of James's death isn't particularly relevant to the meaning of the paragraph, so the simple past, *died,* is better. Choice (D) is correct.

33. **C.** The preceding paragraph refers to the introductory paragraph by mentioning "money and a private room," a *rebuttal* (contrary arguments) to Woolf's idea of what a writer needs. The last paragraph is the best spot to bring a passage full circle. Move the original last paragraph up a bit, and the passage gains a fine conclusion. Choice (C) is your answer.

34. **C.** Choice (C) is the winner here because of its smooth, concise expression.

35. **B.** Two words, *high* and *profile,* combine with a hyphen to form one adjective that describes the noun *positions. Highly* is an adverb and doesn't work as a description of a noun. The correct answer is Choice (B).

36. **D.** The *artist* doesn't have a chance of *hiring* but of *being hired*. (The employer does the *hiring*.) You can therefore eliminate Choices (A) and (B). Choice (C) incorrectly places the action in the past *(having been hired)*. Choice (D) is just what you need here.

Comparisons with *than* often omit a word. In Question 36, the word *does* is implied. Because the implied word is obvious, the meaning isn't affected and the sentence is properly constructed.

37. **B.** Magazines, television, and websites are media. To correct the logic of this comparison, add *other*. Choice (B) is the right answer.

38. **C.** The chart tells you that the Bureau of Labor Statistics expects a 10.8 percent growth in all jobs. The creative jobs don't rise to that number, with the exception of architects. Choice (C) corrects the mistake.

39. **A.** The word *robust* can describe someone who has a strong, healthy body, but it also applies to *intangibles* (things that are abstract, not concrete). Here, the word correctly describes the *job outlook*.

40. **B.** This question tests two concepts: parallel structure (everything doing the same job in the sentence has the same grammatical identity) and prepositions (*about, on,* or *for* in this example). The original sentence isn't parallel because *to explore* can't pair up with *finding*. When *finding* becomes *to find,* the problem of parallel structure is solved. Next up, prepositions: In Standard English, you *find out about,* not *on* or *for.* Add these together and you arrive at Choice (B).

41. **D.** Simple present tense *(are described)* is best here. You don't need progressive tense, which puts you in the midst of an ongoing action. Nor should you connect to the past, as Choice (B) does. The *Occupational Outlook Handbook* is a book, and traditionally, present tense is best for explaining what a book contains. (Past tense works when you're talking about how the book was written or published.) Choice (C) is wrong because the *occupations* don't *describe;* they *are described.* No doubt about it, Choice (D) is the best answer.

42. **B.** *Median* is a type of "average," which is the meaning you want here. *Medium* is a size, *media* refers to means of communication, and *medial* is a description of something in the middle. Here a description doesn't work, but the noun *median* does.

43. **C.** The sentence refers to *a person,* a singular noun. The plural pronoun *their* is a bad match, because singular and plural don't play nicely together in the world of grammar. You can change *their* to *his or her,* but that's not an option offered. The easiest fix is to drop the pronoun entirely, as Choice (C) does.

44. **D.** The original sentence isn't parallel, because *to keep* doesn't pair well with *and balancing it.* The simplest fix is to drop the *and* so you're not creating a pair. Then the description *balanced* works nicely. Choice (D) is correct.

Answers for Section 4: Mathematics — No-Calculator Section

1. **B.** If you add the two expressions you're given, you discover that $4a + 4b = 20$, so $a + b = 5$.

2. **C.** Ah, yes, an SAT classic. (The SAT should have its own YouTube channel. Oh wait, it does.) If the wheel has a radius of 15 inches, it has a circumference of 30π (because circumference is $2\pi r$). Ten revolutions carries a point on the outside of the wheel 10 times the circumference for $10 \times 30\pi = 300\pi$.

3. **B.** Start with $\left(5^{q+1}\right)^{p}$. When you take a power of a power, such as $\left(5^{q+1}\right)^{p}$, you multiply the powers: $\left(5^{q+1}\right)^{p} = \left(5^{pq+p}\right)$. Next, multiply this by the other part of the question, $\left(5^{-p}\right)$. When you multiply the same numbers with exponents, you add the exponents, so leave the 5 and just add the exponents. In this case, the p and $-p$ cancel out, leaving the pq: $\left(5^{pq+p}\right)\left(5^{-p}\right) = 5^{pq}$.

4. **C.** Look at the statements one at a time. Choice (A) is true. The mode appears most often, so there will be two, three, or four 90s. Choice (B) requires you to remember the formula *total = number × mean*. In this case, the five numbers must add up to $5 \times 80 = 400$. Because you know there are at least two 90s, which add up to 180, the other three numbers must add up to 220. But because the numbers are all positive, and 240 is greater than 220, there is no room in the set for 240 and 2 additional values. However, for Choice (C), you can make a list that averages 80 but doesn't have 80 in it. The list *could* have 80 but doesn't *have* to have 80. Choice (D) is definitely true; you used this fact already when you checked Choice (A).

5. **D.** Quick quiz: What's the first thing you need to do when you read this problem? If you answered, "Draw the triangle," you win a prize. (The prize, of course, is improved SAT scores.) Drawing the triangle is only half the battle; you also have to label the triangle properly. Use this guideline: Let your variable stand for the second thing mentioned in the problem. In this case, the second thing mentioned is the first side, so let $x =$ the first side. The second side is then $x + 3$, and the third side is $2x - 5$. (Don't fall into the trap of thinking it's $5 - 2x$). The finished triangle looks like this:

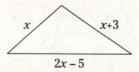

The perimeter, 34, is the sum of all the sides, so $(x) + (x + 3) + (2x - 5) = 34$. Combining the like terms on the left side gives you $4x - 2 = 34$. Adding 2 to each side leaves you with $4x = 36$ and $x = 9$. Now you need to plug in the value of x: The first side is 9 centimeters, the second is $(9) + 3 = 12$ centimeters, and the third is $2(9) - 5 = 13$ centimeters. Because this side is the longest, it's also the answer.

6. **A.** Call the room shared by Melvin, Carey, and Dan room X, and the other room Y. Because Mike and Melvin won't live together, Mike must be in room Y. Now, if Dave and Dan live together, Peter will live with them, but you can't fit two more people into room X, so Dave and Dan must live apart, which puts Dave in room Y also. Similarly, you know that Enoch will live with Chris or Carey, so Chris can't be in room X, either. That puts Chris, Dave, and Mike in room Y.

7. **A.** Make a quick drawing of the situation. (Remember, the towns don't have to be in a straight line.)

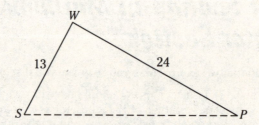

The distance you're interested in is the dotted line. Hey, wait a minute: This is a triangle! So you can use the triangle inequality, which tells you that the sum of any two sides of a triangle must be greater than the third side. The number 10 doesn't satisfy the inequality, because $10 + 13 = 23$, which is less than 24.

8. **C.** If you multiply each of the choices by 3 points, you get 30, 33, 36, and 39. Because all the other scores are worth 5 points, you must be able to add a multiple of 5 to one of these numbers to get 61. The only one that works is 36, because $36 + 25 = 61$.

9. **C.** Don't fall into the trap of thinking that 1 is prime. Therefore, 2 isn't a tweener, because $2 - 1 = 1$ isn't prime. And 8 isn't a tweener, because $8 + 1 = 9$ isn't prime. But 30 works, because $30 - 1 = 29$ is prime, and so is $30 + 1 = 31$. Just to be sure, check that 36 doesn't work, and it doesn't, because $36 - 1 = 35$ isn't prime.

10. **A.** Twelve less than something is the thing minus 12, not the other way around. So you want an expression that says "x squared is 5 times x minus 12," and that's Choice (A).

11. **D.** To solve for y, isolate y on one side of the equation:

$$2y - c = 3c$$
$$2y = 4c$$
$$y = 2c$$

12. **D.** In general, absolute-value equations have two solutions. So if you were just guessing, guess either Choice (B) or Choice (D). Solving it the long way, you get

$$|3x - 1| = 7$$

$$3x - 1 = 7 \quad \text{or} \quad 3x - 1 = -7$$
$$\underline{+1 \quad +1} \qquad\qquad \underline{+1 \quad +1}$$
$$\frac{3x}{3} = \frac{8}{3} \qquad\qquad \frac{3x}{3} = \frac{-6}{3}$$
$$x = 2\frac{2}{3} \quad \text{or} \quad x = -2$$

13. **C.** The number of solutions to the equation $f(x) = 1$ is just the number of times that the graph has a height of 1, as shown here.

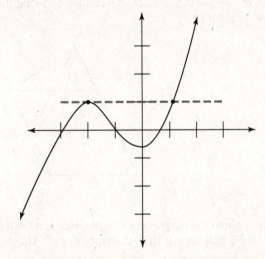

14. **C.** The length and width of the square are 5 (because $5 \times 5 = 25$), so the new length, being narrower by 2, is 3. And 3 times the new width is 24 (the area of the rectangle), so the new width is 8 (because $24 \div 3 = 8$). The width was 5 and increased by 3.

15. **C.** Using the ol' fallback SOH-CAH-TOA, focus on the TOA, which stands for "tangent opposite adjacent" but really means, tangent = $\dfrac{\text{opposite}}{\text{adjacent}}$. "Opposite" and "adjacent" refer to the sides of the triangle that are opposite and adjacent to the angle, C, which in this case are 5 and 12, respectively: $\tan C = \dfrac{5}{12}$.

16. **96.** This problem is easy if you remember an easy trick: *total = number × average*. In this case, the total must equal $4 \times 90 = 360$. Adding up Lauren's first three scores gives you 264, and $360 - 264 = 96$.

17. **7.** Remember the distance formula? It tells you that the distance between two points, (x_1, y_1) and (x_2, y_2) is $\sqrt{(x_2 - x_1)^2 + (y_2 - y_1)^2}$. Substituting your numbers, you get

$$10 = \sqrt{([-2]-[4])^2 + (p-[-1])^2} = \sqrt{(-6)^2 + (p+1)^2} = \sqrt{36 + (p+1)^2}.$$

Square both sides, and $100 = 36 + (p+1)^2$. Now solve for p:

$$64 = (p+1)^2$$
$$8 = p+1$$
$$7 = p$$

18. **84.** You could try to figure out what a and b equal, but you don't need to. The key to getting this question right is remembering the formulas discussed in Chapter 12 — specifically, the one that says that $(a-b)^2 = a^2 - 2ab + b^2$. You know that $a - b = 8$, so $(a-b)^2 = a^2 - 2ab + b^2 = 64$. You're being asked for $a^2 + b^2$, which is $(a^2 - 2ab + b^2) + 2ab$, or $64 + 2(10) = 84$.

19. **360.** The total surface area is the sum of the area of the square and the area of the four triangles. The square is easy: It's $10 \times 10 = 100$. The triangles are tougher. They don't have a height of 12. Twelve is the height of the pyramid, but the triangles are slanted. However, you can find the height of the slanted triangles by using the Pythagorean theorem, as shown in the following diagram:

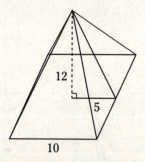

That little triangle in the diagram is a right triangle. One leg is 12, the height of the pyramid. The second leg is half the width of the square, or 5. This is actually the world's second-most famous right triangle, the 5-12-13 triangle. (If you didn't remember this one, you could have figured it out with the Pythagorean theorem.)

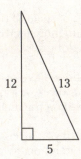

The hypotenuse, 13, is the altitude of each of the tilted triangles that make up the sides of the pyramid. Because the triangle's area is $\frac{1}{2} \times base \times height$, each triangle's area is $\frac{1}{2} \times 10 \times 13 = 65$. The four triangles together have an area of $4 \times 65 = 260$. Adding in the 100 from the base gives you 360.

20. **3.** Find the value of $\sin\theta$ and multiply it by 5. If the coordinates of point P are $(4, 3)$, the diagonal is 5 (as in, 3-4-5 right triangle). Use the SOH from SOH-CAH-TOA to get that $\text{sine } \theta = \dfrac{\text{opposite}}{\text{hypotenuse}}$, which in this case is $\dfrac{3}{5}$. Multiply this by 5 for an answer of 3.

Answer Guidelines for Section 5: The Essay

Here are some possibly points to make in your essay in response to the prompt.

Reading

John Blossom tackles the issue of "publishing" over the Internet and on social media to create what he calls a "content nation." (When you pronounce the word, the emphasis is on the first syllable, *con-,* because he refers to information.) Showing that you grasped these points contributes to your reading score:

- ✔ Blossom begins by redefining *publishing,* a term which he views broadly. The traditional meaning, printing and distributing through an established company, now means communicating ideas over the Internet and other electronic media.

- ✔ Blossom acknowledges the power of technology to spread ideas but concedes that the audience for some "published" work is very small.

- ✔ Blossom sees new media as a force that levels the playing field. Not only the elite or traditional power structures can spread ideas but also "students, farmers, business professionals, teachers, researchers, politicians, homemakers, and anyone else" with access to the Internet.

- ✔ New ways to communicate are actually redefining what it is to be human and form bonds with others.

- ✔ Marketing of goods is changing because of mass media. Again, power is spread out. Not only do stores or companies market through the Internet, but individuals may also buy and sell goods.

✔ Politics is changing, too. Blossom refers to "authentic support from everyday people." In this sense, social media and other electronic means of communication strengthens democracy.

✔ Everything is a question of scale to Blossom. One person can make a difference by speaking to a small group, but electronic media allows messages to reach millions of people throughout the globe.

How did you do? If you mentioned five or six of the seven bullet points, give yourself 4 points for reading. If you hit three or four, take 3 points for reading. Only two? Award yourself 2 points. If you stayed on the main idea, take 1 point for reading.

These guidelines are flexible. If you discussed these ideas in different terms, or if you came up with something we didn't mention, take credit — and points — for reading.

Analysis

Now consider Blossom's writing style. All these ideas (and some not listed here) may be part of your analysis score:

✔ The second-person pronoun _you_ immediately connects to the reader. The reader has probably used technology, so the connection becomes stronger because the reader has a stake in what Blossom is going to say.

✔ The first paragraph begins with a dramatic assertion: _You're a publisher._ (That's news to you, right?) The reader may begin to argue with Blossom at that point, but he's ready with an answer. He concedes that your "personal activities may be small in scope" but replies that "if others find that what you've shared is valuable," you have achieved what traditional publishers do. This technique is called "concession and reply." Blossom uses the same technique in paragraph four, when he says that "we will not be throwing away the advantages and legacies" civilization already has. You don't need to name this literary technique, but you should point out what Blossom does.

✔ In the second paragraph, Blossom gives several examples of new publishing tools: the Internet, affordable computers, mobile phones, and "other types of devices." These examples make his argument real to the reader, who probably owns or uses at least one of the listed tools.

✔ The third paragraph employs figurative language (language that moves away from reality into the world of imagination). Civilization is "an organism" — a living creature — a metaphor that gives a sense of natural growth and development as well as human interdependence. (After all, an organism can't survive without all its parts, which work together to sustain life.) Figurative language also pops up in the statement that "we have been handed back the keys" to make a new society. The _keys_ aren't literal (real); they are a metaphor for the transfer of power. The simile in the last paragraph, comparing the influence of social media to an ice cube, serves to illustrate large and small changes.

Don't obsess over technical vocabulary. Pointing out the effect of comparisons is more important than saying that one phrase is a metaphor (a comparison without _like_ or _as_) and another is a simile (a comparison made with _like_ or _as_). If you know the terms, use them, but don't omit an idea because you're unsure of the proper label.

✔ Blossom tends to pair off ideas, often to illustrate opposites. The ice cube/ice sheet example in the last paragraph is one spot where he creates a pair. In paragraph two, he contrasts the past ("once the pursuit of a handful of wealthy and powerful people") to the present ("now a tool in the hands of the world").

✔ Many contrasting pairs refer to scale. You find several references to *small*, such as in paragraph one, and large ("huge" in the same paragraph). In the third paragraph, you see "scale to mass goods and services," an implied comparison with smaller markets.

✔ Often, the pairs referred to in the preceding bullet point appear in parallel sentences or portions of sentences. Check out where the contrast between past and present appears. Can you "hear" that the ideas are presented in parallel structure? Parallel structure links the ideas grammatically, matching the link Blossom sees in meaning.

✔ The diction is formal but accessible. You don't see slang or friendly references (apart from *you* in paragraph one), but you don't have to swallow a dictionary to understand what Blossom is trying to say, either.

Evaluate your analysis. If you mentioned six or more of the eight bullet points, give yourself 4 points for analysis. If you hit four or five, take 3 points for analysis. Only two or three? Award yourself 2 points. If you discussed only one technique, take 1 point for analysis.

These guidelines are flexible. If you discussed other style points or grouped several together, adjust your analysis score.

Writing

Your final category is writing and applies to your own essay. Check these factors:

✔ **Structure:** Does your essay have a solid, logical structure? One possibility is to work in order from the first paragraph of the passage, where the author states the *thesis* (idea to be proved), and then move through paragraph after paragraph until you reach the end of the passage. Another possibility is first to examine Blossom's ideas on publishing, mass production, politics, and the shift of power to a larger mass of people. Then you might discuss Blossom's style, with a paragraph on his use of parallel pairs and second-person connection. Finally, examples of his diction and figurative language create a third paragraph.

✔ **Evidence:** Do you back up every statement you make with quotations or specific references to the passage? Count how many times you zeroed in on details. You should have at least two in every paragraph you write, and maybe more.

✔ **Language:** Does your essay sound formal, as if a teacher were explaining the passage? If you lapsed into slang or informal word choice, your essay is weaker.

✔ **Mechanics:** English teachers group grammar, spelling, and punctuation in this category. As you reread, underline any sentence fragments or run-ons, misspelled words, and faulty commas or quotation marks.

Adding up points to evaluate your writing is tricky. In general, give yourself 1 point (up to a total of 4) for every category in the bulleted list in which you excelled. If you stumbled slightly in a category (say, three or four grammar or spelling mistakes), give yourself 3/4 of a point. If you feel your performance in one of these categories was poor (perhaps you drifted off topic or made seven or eight grammar errors), take only a half point.

To help you evaluate your essay, take a look at the sample essays in Chapter 7. They give you a model of a poor, medium, and great essay. You can compare your work to those graded essays.

To get a fair idea of how your essay measures up to College Board standards, fill in the scoring grid in the appendix.

Answer Key

Section 1: Reading		*Section 2: Mathematics — Calculator Section*	
1. **D**	2. **A**	1. **D**	2. **C**
3. **C**	4. **B**	3. **A**	4. **C**
5. **D**	6. **C**	5. **B**	6. **D**
7. **D**	8. **A**	7. **D**	8. **B**
9. **D**	10. **C**	9. **B**	10. **C**
11. **C**	12. **D**	11. **B**	12. **C**
13. **C**	14. **B**	13. **B**	14. **D**
15. **A**	16. **B**	15. **B**	16. **A**
17. **A**	18. **D**	17. **A**	18. **C**
19. **A**	20. **C**	19. **D**	20. **A**
21. **B**	22. **A**	21. **B**	22. **A**
23. **C**	24. **D**	23. **A**	24. **C**
25. **B**	26. **A**	25. **D**	26. **D**
27. **C**	28. **D**	27. **C**	28. **D**
29. **C**	30. **A**	29. **C**	30. **D**
31. **C**	32. **C**	31. **6**	32. **40**
33. **B**	34. **D**	33. **11**	34. **6**
35. **A**	36. **B**	35. **12**	36. **520**
37. **B**	38. **D**	37. **500**	38. **300**
39. **B**	40. **D**		
41. **C**	42. **A**		
43. **D**	44. **C**		
45. **A**	46. **C**		
47. **A**	48. **B**		
49. **D**	50. **A**		
51. **D**	52. **B**		

Section 3: Writing and Language

1. C	2. A
3. B	4. D
5. C	6. B
7. C	8. D
9. B	10. C
11. C	12. C
13. B	14. B
15. D	16. D
17. D	18. C
19. B	20. A
21. D	22. C
23. C	24. B
25. A	26. C
27. B	28. A
29. D	30. B
31. B	32. D
33. C	34. C
35. B	36. D
37. B	38. C
39. A	40. B
41. D	42. B
43. C	44. D

Section 4: Mathematics — No-Calculator Section

1. B	2. C
3. B	4. C
5. D	6. A
7. A	8. C
9. C	10. A
11. D	12. D
13. C	14. C
15. C	16. 96
17. 7	18. 84
19. 360	20. 3

Part VI
The Part of Tens

Find a listing of ten new features of the redesigned SAT at www.dummies.com/extras/SAT.

In this part . . .

- Discover ten ways to maximize your score.
- Find out ten ways to calm down and focus on the task at hand.
- Find out how to score your practice tests in the book's appendix.

Chapter 22

Ten Ways to Maximize Your Score

In This Chapter
▶ Making SAT day go as smoothly as possible
▶ Eliminating mistakes that sink your SAT score

*W*ould you like to wake up on the morning of your SAT test day filled with confidence and joy? Okay, joy isn't likely, but here you find ten ways to make your SAT morning a little less painful so that you can arrive at the test center in the proper mood to ace the test.

Stash Your Admission Ticket in Plain Sight

Before you go to sleep the night before the SAT — at a reasonable hour, not after an all-night SAT Stinks Party — place your admission ticket, photo ID, car keys or carfare, pencils, good eraser, calculator (with fresh batteries), watch, snacks, and everything else you need for the test in plain sight. Be sure to dress in layers in order to be prepared for any room temperature. Check out Chapter 2 for the lowdown on what you should have with you as you head to the test.

Keep Your Blanks in the Right Row

As you take the SAT, you may skip a question here and there. No problem. Just be sure that the answers you do fill in end up in the correct rows. As you fill in the bubbles for your answers, consciously match each question number with the number on the answer sheet. At the end of a section, recheck your answers to make sure you've finished at the right number. When you reach the last minute of your time, go back to the empty lines and fill in a bubble — any bubble — so that you've answered every question.

Follow All Directions

When the proctor says, "Turn to Section 3," triple-check that you've actually opened the booklet to Section 3. You'd be surprised what sweaty hands can do. If you work on the wrong section, the proctor may seize your exam booklet and send you home, scoreless and unhappy. Then you have to take the test again!

Face the Grid-Ins Head-On

When you come up against a grid-in question (the math torture chamber that makes you come up with an actual answer without supplying four handy choices), remember that you can't grid in a mixed number ($2\frac{1}{2}$, for example). The computer will read your answer as "21 divided by 2," or 10.5. Instead, grid in 5/2. See Chapter 9 for more on grid-ins.

Order the Operations

In the heat of battle, you may forget to attack a math problem in the proper order. When you start a Math section, take a moment to write "PEMDAS" at the top of the page to help you remember which steps you should take, in the right order. Then recheck the order of operations as you move through the questions. Turn to Chapter 10 for more on PEMDAS.

Give Them What They Want

No matter how much you understand about a topic, if you don't give the SAT-writers what they ask for, you won't get a point for your answer. For example, a question that asks about the number of people with orange ties may be chock-full of information about people with purple, tie-dyed, spaghetti-stained, and other ties. One of the answers will undoubtedly be the number of people with tie-dyed ties. Always double-check to make sure you've answered the question being asked.

Stay in Context

Once upon a time, before you started preparing for the SAT, you may have had a real life. And that life gave you some experience and knowledge that may help you on the SAT. But be sure to answer reading-comprehension questions in the passage's context; don't ignore what's in the passage and substitute something from your life experience. Real life can help, but don't let it distract you from the material provided on the test because all the questions on the SAT are based on that material.

Scrap the Meaningless Scrap Paper

The SAT-scoring brigade (mostly a machine, with minimal human help) doesn't read anything written in the question booklet, your "scrap paper" for the exam. Be sure that all your answers actually make it to the answer sheet. Otherwise, you may be unpleasantly surprised when you receive your test score.

Erase Your Errors

You may (shocking as it may seem) make a mistake from time to time. Before you sign off on a changed answer, take care that you've fully erased the wrong answer. If the scoring machine detects two answers for one question, it marks the answer wrong, even if one of the answers is correct.

Write Legibly

Okay, your essay doesn't have to look like a work of art, but it does have to be readable. If your handwriting resembles the flight of a drunken chicken, the scorer won't be happy. And you definitely want a happy scorer. If you choose to write the optional essay, recheck it and neatly rewrite any illegible words. If you have to scratch out a few words to make them legible, do so. You don't lose points for strikethroughs, but you may lose points if the reader can't read enough of your essay to understand your ideas.

Chapter 23

Ten Ways to Calm Down

What's that grinding noise? Oh, it's your teeth. The SAT can ratchet up the anxiety level of every test-taker. A few techniques in this chapter — ten, to be exact — can help you de-stress.

Prepare Well

Well before SAT day, make sure that you go over this book carefully and shore up your weak spots. Try a practice test or two (or three or four online!) in Part V. Then rest, because you're ready for the big time.

Sleep It Off

Don't party the night before SAT day. Instead, celebrate when the whole thing's over. Fight SAT nerves with restful sleep. Also, don't study on the last night before the exam. Watch television, build an anthill, or do whatever you find relaxing. Then hit the mattress at a decent hour.

Start Early

On SAT morning, set your alarm for a little earlier than you think you need to be up and about. Don't go overboard! You don't want too much extra time to obsess about all the things you haven't mastered yet. With a safety margin of, say, arriving at the testing center a half hour before the test begins, you can ready yourself for the exam with minimal pressure. Plus you have time to find the room, get a good seat, admire the view, and run to the restroom.

Use the Tension

Research shows that some stress (notice the *some*) can actually help you perform better. Before you enter the testing room, envision a time in your life when you were nervous and had a good experience — say, just before the roller coaster hit the top of the track. Remind yourself that everything worked out fine, just as it will when you take the SAT.

Stretch Your Muscles

Before you start an SAT section, stretch your arms above your head as high as they'll go. Slide your legs straight out in front of you and wriggle your ankles. Feel better?

Roll Your Head

Not the type of rolling that occurs after a session with the **guillotine** (a device that chops heads off), but a yoga-inspired exercise that **induces** (brings about) calmness. Close your eyes whenever you feel yourself tensing up. Let your head drop all the way forward, roll it in a circle, open your eyes, and hit the test again.

Breathe Deeply

Breathing is always a good idea, and deep breathing is an even better one. When the SAT overwhelms you, pull in a slow bucketful of air and then exhale even more slowly.

Isolate the Problem

On SAT day, friends are a pain in the neck. Why? Because your friends will say things like "What's the meaning of *supercilious*?" "How do you solve for three variables?" And you'll think, "I don't know what *supercilious* means! I have no idea what a *variable* is! I'm going to fail, and no college will take me, and my life will be ruined." Make a pact with your friends to stay silent about SAT questions or SAT-related information, or sit by yourself in the corner.

Become Fatalistic

A **fatalist** (one who accepts that much of life is out of control and that whatever happens, happens) does best on the SAT. Stop obsessing. Just sit down and do the test. You can worry about how you did after you've handed in the answer sheet.

Focus on the Future

No matter how bad it is, when you're taking the SAT, you're getting ever-closer to a truly wonderful time: the moment when you realize that the SAT is over, done, history. Focus on the future — that moment — whenever you feel yourself clench.

Appendix

Scoring Tables for SAT Practice Exams

Three hours of work, and you're still not finished! After you take each practice test, if you want to calculate your scores, just follow the steps and use the handy scoring tables provided here.

The scoring of the new SAT is a work in progress, as the College Board refines the exam. Check www.dummies.com/go/sat for the latest updates.

Converting Your Score

Use the following tables to convert the number of answers you got right in each section of the SAT to your overall score.

1. **Check your responses with the answer chapters.**

   Don't skimp on time here. Read the explanations for each incorrect answer (if you had any!) and figure out what went wrong.

2. **Add up the number of correct answers for the Reading, Writing and Language, and Math sections.**

   Keep these numbers separate.

   Note that Question 37 of the Math Calculator section (the last question of that section) is worth 4 points, while every other question is worth 1 point. No partial credit is given for Question 37.

3. **Convert your scores, using the tables in this appendix.**

   The following tables give you an idea of how you did in the traditional 200 to 800 score format for the exam's three categories: (1) Reading, (2) Writing and Language, and (3) Mathematics.

4. **Add the number of correct answers in the Reading section to the number of correct answers in the Writing and Language section. Exclude the essay.**

   This number represents your work in two major verbal areas.

5. **Convert the total number of Reading and Writing and Language correct answers.**

   Now you have a number between 200 and 800 for the verbal portion of the test.

6. **Add the converted Math score to the converted Reading and Writing and Language score.**

   Your result, which will range from 400 to 1600, is your Composite Score.

7. **If you wrote the essay, score it.**

   Your essay should have three scores, each from 1 to 4: Reading (whether you understood the passage), Analysis (how well you picked apart the arguments and writing style of the passage), and Writing (your own ability to express your thoughts). Because two readers grade your essay, double each of the scores (Reading, Analysis, and Writing) to see the score you would receive on the real SAT for each of these three areas. Each essay is a little different, so a general set of instructions doesn't apply. The answer chapters provide specific guidelines for the essay question(s) you worked on. Read those guidelines carefully. To see some sample graded responses, turn to Chapter 7.

8. Fill in the Score Report at the end of this appendix.

Now you know your strengths and weaknesses. Resolve to work on any problem areas, so your next attempt at the SAT will result in a higher score.

The College Board has stated that it will keep working on the redesigned SAT and its scores, even after the new exam debuts in March 2016. Check www.dummies.com for up-to-date scoring changes as they occur.

Table A-1	Reading
Number of Right Answers	**Converted Score**
49 or above	800
48	790
47	780
46	760
45	750
44	740
43	720
42	710
41	700
40	690
39	670
38	660
37	650
36	630
35	620
34	610
33	600
32	580
31	570
30	560
29	540
28	530
27	520
26	510
25	490
24	480
23	470
22	450
21	440
20	430

Number of Right Answers	Converted Score
19	410
18	400
17	390
16	380
15	360
14	350
13	340
12	320
11	310
10	300
9	290
8	270
7	260
6	250
5	230
4	210
3 or below	200

Table A-2	Writing and Language (Multiple-Choice Questions)
Number of Right Answers	**Converted Score**
44	800
43	790
42	770
41	750
40	740
39	730
38	720
37	710
36	700
35	690
34	670
33	660
32	650
31	640
30	630
29	600
28	580
27	560
26	540

(continued)

Table A-2 *(continued)*

Number of Right Answers	Converted Score
25	520
24	500
23	480
22	470
21	450
20	430
19	410
18	390
17	370
16	360
15	350
14	340
13	320
12	300
11	290
10	270
9	260
8	250
7	240
6	230
5	220
4	210
3 or below	200

Table A-3   Combined Reading and Writing and Language Scores

Number of Right Answers on the Reading and the Writing and Language Sections	Converted Score
94 or above	800
91–93	790
88–90	780
86–87	770
84–85	760
82–83	740
80–81	730
79	720
78	710
77	700

Number of Right Answers on the Reading and the Writing and Language Sections	Converted Score
76	690
75	680
74	670
70–73	660
67–69	650
65–66	640
62–64	630
59–61	620
58	610
57	620
56	630
55	620
54	610
53	600
52	590
51	580
50	570
49	560
48	550
47	540
46	530
45	520
44	510
43	500
42	490
41	480
40	470
39	460
38	450
37	440
36	430
35	420
34	410
33	400
32	390
31	380
30	370
29	360
28	350

(continued)

Table A-3 *(continued)*

Number of Right Answers on the Reading and the Writing and Language Sections	Converted Score
27	340
26	330
25	320
24	310
23	300
21–22	290
19–20	270
17–18	260
15–16	250
12–14	240
9–11	230
7–8	220
6	210
5 or below	200

Table A-4   Essay

Reading	Analysis	Writing

Note: Follow the guidelines in the answer chapters to score your essay. Insert the numbers in each column. Essay scores should be doubled because the essay is graded by two people.

Table A-5   Mathematics

Number of Right Answers*	Converted Score
60	800
59	790
58	780
57	770
56	760
55	750
54	740
53	730
52	720
51	710
50	700
49	690
48	680
47	670

Number of Right Answers*	Converted Score
46	660
45	650
44	640
43	630
42	620
41	610
40	600
39	590
38	580
37	570
36	560
35	550
34	540
33	530
32	520
31	510
30	500
29	490
28	480
27	470
26	460
25	450
24	440
23	430
22	420
21	410
20	400
19	390
18	380
17	370
16	360
15	350
14	340
13	330
12	320
11	310
10	300
9	290
8	280
7	270

(continued)

Table A-5 (continued)

Number of Right Answers*	Converted Score
6	260
5	250
4	240
3	230
2	220
1	210
0	200

* Questions 37 and 38 of the Math Calculator section are each worth 2 points, for a total of 4 points.

Recording Your Final Scores

For each test, fill in this form.

Converted Reading Score _____ (200–800)

Converted Writing and Language Score _____ (200–800)

Converted Reading and Writing and Language Score _____ (200–800)

Converted Mathematics Score _____ (200–800)

Composite Score _____ (400–1600)

Essay:

Reading _____ (2–8)

Analysis _____ (2–8)

Writing _____ (2–8)

Total for Reading, Analysis, and Writing multiplied by 2 _____

Index

• *Y* •

• *Z* •

Notes

Notes

Notes

Notes

Notes

Notes

Notes

Notes

Notes

Notes

Notes

Notes

Notes

Notes

Notes

Notes

About the Authors

Geraldine Woods has prepared students for the SAT, both academically and emotionally, for the past four decades. She is the author of more than 50 books, including *English Grammar For Dummies, English Grammar Workbook For Dummies, 1,001 Grammar Practice Questions For Dummies,* and earlier editions of *SAT For Dummies,* all published by Wiley. She blogs on grammar at www.grammarianinthecity.com.

Ron Woldoff completed his dual master's degrees at Arizona State University and San Diego State University, where he studied the culmination of business and technology. After several years as a corporate consultant, Ron opened his own company, National Test Prep, where he helps students reach their goals on the GMAT, GRE, SAT, ACT, and PSAT. He created the programs and curricula for these tests from scratch, using his own observations of the tests and feedback from students. Ron has also taught his own GMAT and GRE programs as an adjunct instructor at both Northern Arizona University and the internationally acclaimed Thunderbird School of Global Management. Ron lives in Phoenix, Arizona, with his lovely wife, Leisah, and their three amazing boys, Zachary, Jadon, and Adam. You can find Ron on the web at testprepaz.com.

Dedication

This book is humbly dedicated to the thousands of students whom we have helped reach their goals. You have taught us as much as we have taught you.

Authors' Acknowledgments

Geraldine Woods: I'd like to thank Peter Bonfanti and Kristin Josephson, whose earlier work on SAT math has been enormously helpful. I appreciate the efforts of Carmen Krikorian, Erin Calligan Mooney, Tim Gallan, and Sophia Seidner — professionals who never let me down.

Ron Woldoff: I would like to thank my friend Elleyne Kase, who first connected me with the *For Dummies* folks and helped make this book happen. I would also like to thank my friends Ken Krueger, Lionel Hummel, and Jaime Abromovitz, who helped me get things started when I had this wild notion of helping people prepare for standardized college-admissions tests. And more than anyone else, I would like to thank my wife, Leisah, for her continuing support and for always being there for me.

Publisher's Acknowledgments

Acquisitions Editors: Erin Calligan Mooney, Lindsay Sandman Lefevere

Editorial Project Manager: Carmen Krikorian

Development Editor: Christina Guthrie

Copy Editor: Jennette ElNaggar

Technical Editors: Cindy Kaplan, Suzanne Langebartels

Production Editor: Suresh Srinivasan

Cover Photos: Casper1774 Studio/Shutterstock

le & Mac

d For Dummies, 6th Edition
-1-118-72306-7

 one For Dummies, 7th Edition
-1-118-69083-3

:s All-in-One For Dummies,
Edition
-1-118-82210-4

X Mavericks For Dummies
-1-118-69188-5

gging & Social Media

ebook For Dummies, 5th Edition
-1-118-63312-0

ial Media Engagement For Dummies
-1-118-53019-1

rdPress For Dummies, 6th Edition
-1-118-79161-5

siness

ck Investing For Dummies,
Edition
-1-118-37678-2

esting For Dummies, 6th Edition
-0-470-90545-6

sonal Finance For Dummies,
Edition
-1-118-11785-9

ickBooks 2014 For Dummies
-1-118-72005-9

all Business Marketing Kit
Dummies, 3rd Edition
-1-118-31183-7

Careers

Job Interviews For Dummies, 4th Edition
978-1-118-11290-8

Job Searching with Social Media
For Dummies, 2nd Edition
978-1-118-67856-5

Personal Branding For Dummies
978-1-118-11792-7

Resumes For Dummies, 6th Edition
978-0-470-87361-8

Starting an Etsy Business For Dummies,
2nd Edition
978-1-118-59024-9

Diet & Nutrition

Belly Fat Diet For Dummies
978-1-118-34585-6

Mediterranean Diet For Dummies
978-1-118-71525-3

Nutrition For Dummies, 5th Edition
978-0-470-93231-5

Digital Photography

Digital SLR Photography All-in-One
For Dummies, 2nd Edition
978-1-118-59082-9

Digital SLR Video & Filmmaking
For Dummies
978-1-118-36598-4

Photoshop Elements 12 For Dummies
978-1-118-72714-0

Gardening

Herb Gardening For Dummies,
2nd Edition
978-0-470-61778-6

Gardening with Free-Range Chickens
For Dummies
978-1-118-54754-0

Health

Boosting Your Immunity For Dummies
978-1-118-40200-9

Diabetes For Dummies, 4th Edition
978-1-118-29447-5

Living Paleo For Dummies
978-1-118-29405-5

Big Data

Big Data For Dummies
978-1-118-50422-2

Data Visualization For Dummies
978-1-118-50289-1

Hadoop For Dummies
978-1-118-60755-8

Language & Foreign Language

500 Spanish Verbs For Dummies
978-1-118-02382-2

English Grammar For Dummies,
2nd Edition
978-0-470-54664-2

French All-in-One For Dummies
978-1-118-22815-9

German Essentials For Dummies
978-1-118-18422-6

Italian For Dummies, 2nd Edition
978-1-118-00465-4

Math & Science

Algebra I For Dummies, 2nd Edition
978-0-470-55964-2

Available in print and e-book formats.

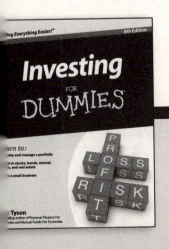

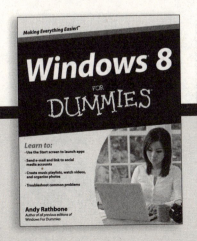

Available wherever books are sold. **For more information or to order direct visit www.dummies.com**

Anatomy and Physiology For Dummies, 2nd Edition
978-0-470-92326-9

Astronomy For Dummies, 3rd Edition
978-1-118-37697-3

Biology For Dummies, 2nd Edition
978-0-470-59875-7

Chemistry For Dummies, 2nd Edition
978-1-118-00730-3

1001 Algebra II Practice Problems For Dummies
978-1-118-44662-1

Microsoft Office

Excel 2013 For Dummies
978-1-118-51012-4

Office 2013 All-in-One For Dummies
978-1-118-51636-2

PowerPoint 2013 For Dummies
978-1-118-50253-2

Word 2013 For Dummies
978-1-118-49123-2

Music

Blues Harmonica For Dummies
978-1-118-25269-7

Guitar For Dummies, 3rd Edition
978-1-118-11554-1

iPod & iTunes For Dummies, 10th Edition
978-1-118-50864-0

Programming

Beginning Programming with C For Dummies
978-1-118-73763-7

Excel VBA Programming For Dummies, 3rd Edition
978-1-118-49037-2

Java For Dummies, 6th Edition
978-1-118-40780-6

Religion & Inspiration

The Bible For Dummies
978-0-7645-5296-0

Buddhism For Dummies, 2nd Edition
978-1-118-02379-2

Catholicism For Dummies, 2nd Edition
978-1-118-07778-8

Self-Help & Relationships

Beating Sugar Addiction For Dummies
978-1-118-54645-1

Meditation For Dummies, 3rd Edition
978-1-118-29144-3

Seniors

Laptops For Seniors For Dummies, 3rd Edition
978-1-118-71105-7

Computers For Seniors For Dummies, 3rd Edition
978-1-118-11553-4

iPad For Seniors For Dummies, 6th Edition
978-1-118-72826-0

Social Security For Dummies
978-1-118-20573-0

Smartphones & Tablets

Android Phones For Dummies, 2nd Edition
978-1-118-72030-1

Nexus Tablets For Dummies
978-1-118-77243-0

Samsung Galaxy S 4 For Dummies
978-1-118-64222-1

Samsung Galaxy Tabs For Dummies
978-1-118-77294-2

Test Prep

ACT For Dummies, 5th Edition
978-1-118-01259-8

ASVAB For Dummies, 3rd Edition
978-0-470-63760-9

GRE For Dummies, 7th Edition
978-0-470-88921-3

Officer Candidate Tests For Dummies
978-0-470-59876-4

Physician's Assistant Exam For Dumm
978-1-118-11556-5

Series 7 Exam For Dummies
978-0-470-09932-2

Windows 8

Windows 8.1 All-in-One For Dummies
978-1-118-82087-2

Windows 8.1 For Dummies
978-1-118-82121-3

Windows 8.1 For Dummies, Book + DV Bundle
978-1-118-82107-7

e **Available in print and e-book formats.**

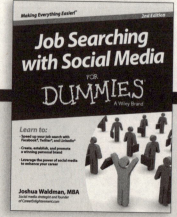

Available wherever books are sold. **For more information or to order direct visit www.dummies.com**

Take Dummies with you everywhere you go!

Whether you are excited about e-books, want more from the web, must have your mobile apps, or are swept up in social media, Dummies makes everything easier.

Leverage the Power

For Dummies is the global leader in the reference category and one of the most trusted and highly regarded brands in the world. No longer just focused on books, customers now have access to the For Dummies content they need in the format they want. Let us help you develop a solution that will fit your brand and help you connect with your customers.

Advertising & Sponsorships

Connect with an engaged audience on a powerful multimedia site, and position your message alongside expert how-to content.

Targeted ads • Video • Email marketing • Microsites • Sweepstakes sponsorship

21 Million Monthly Page Views & 13 Million Unique Visitors